Itsuwaribito 空

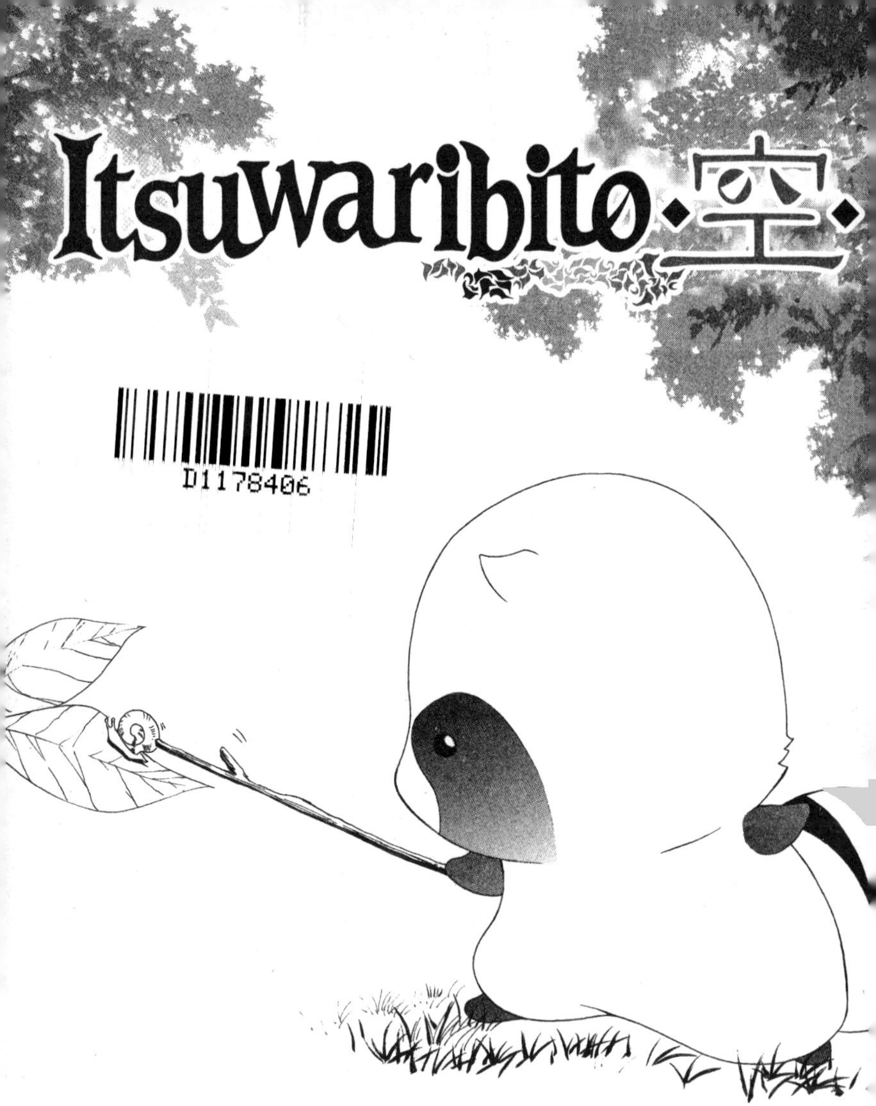

2

YUUKI IINUMA

Contents

Chapter 8
Even Though We Think Differently

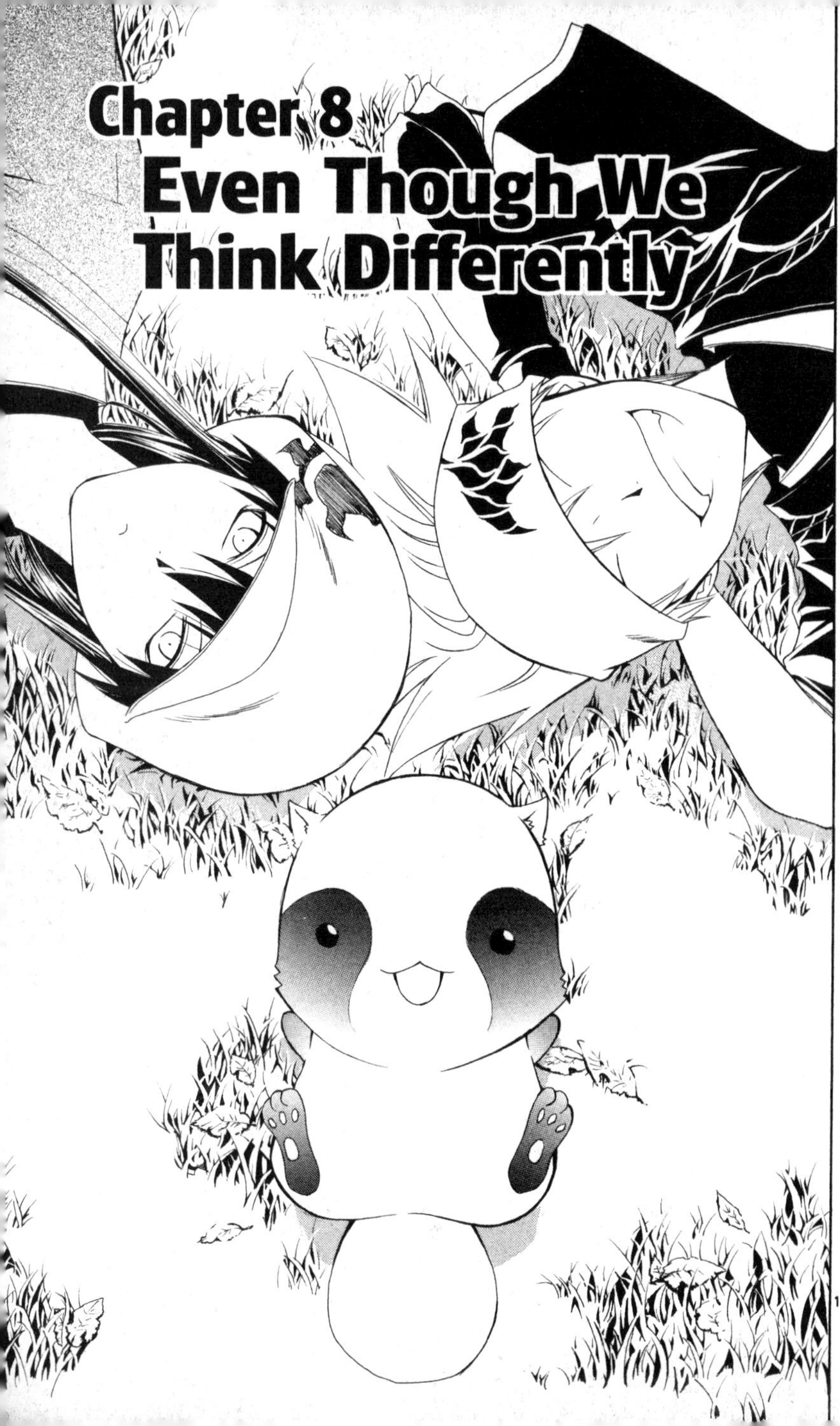

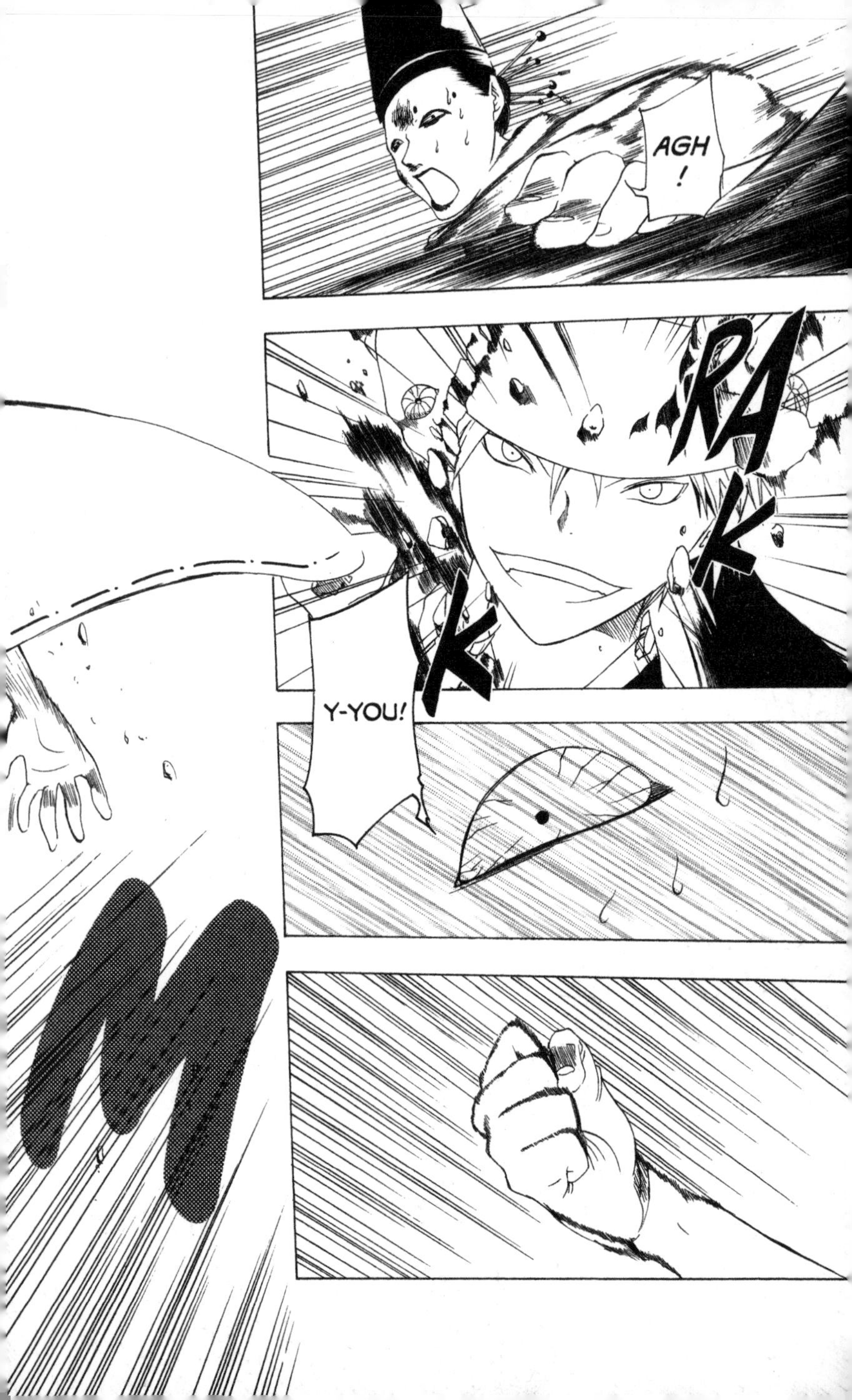
AGH!
RAKK
Y-YOU!
M

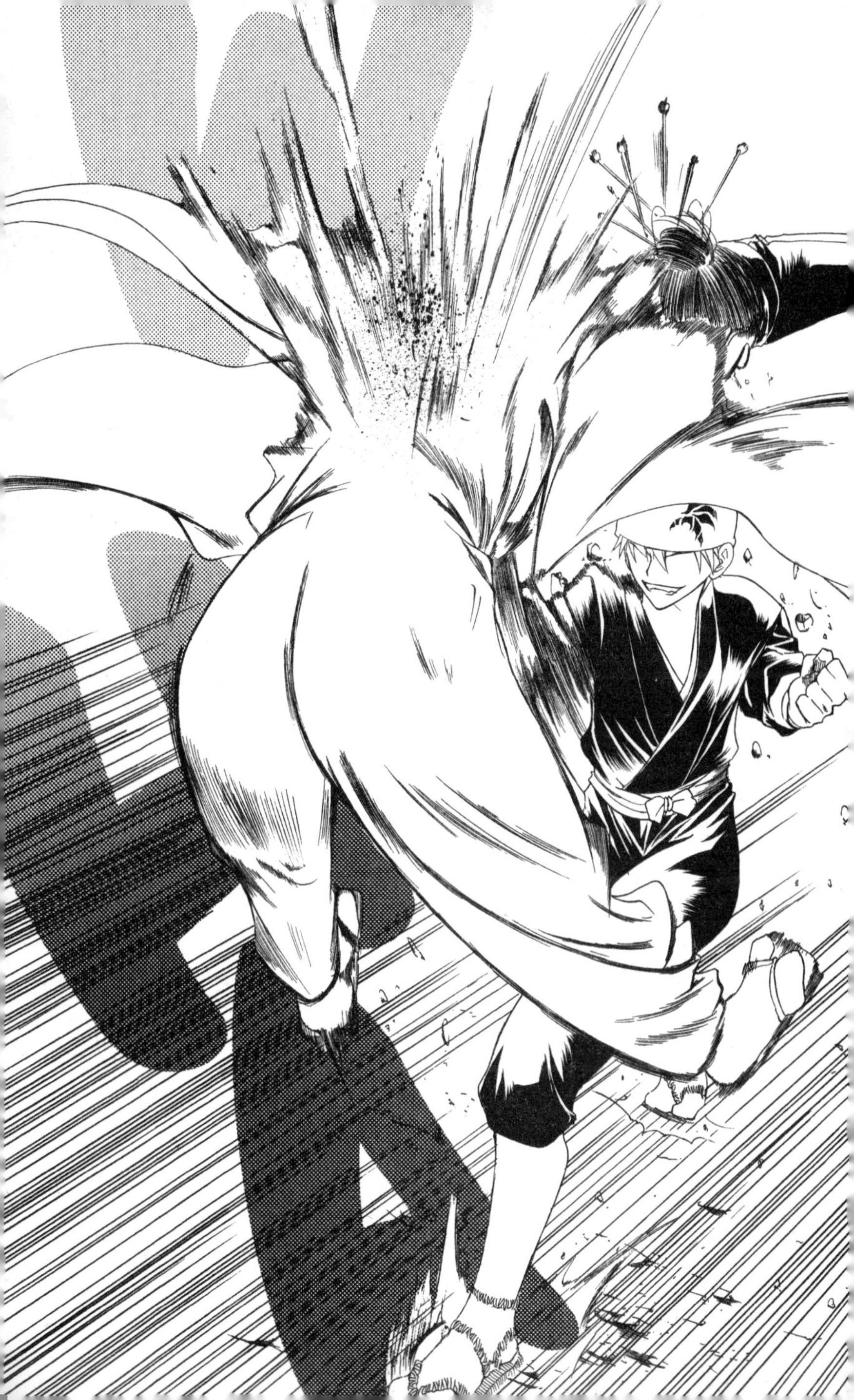

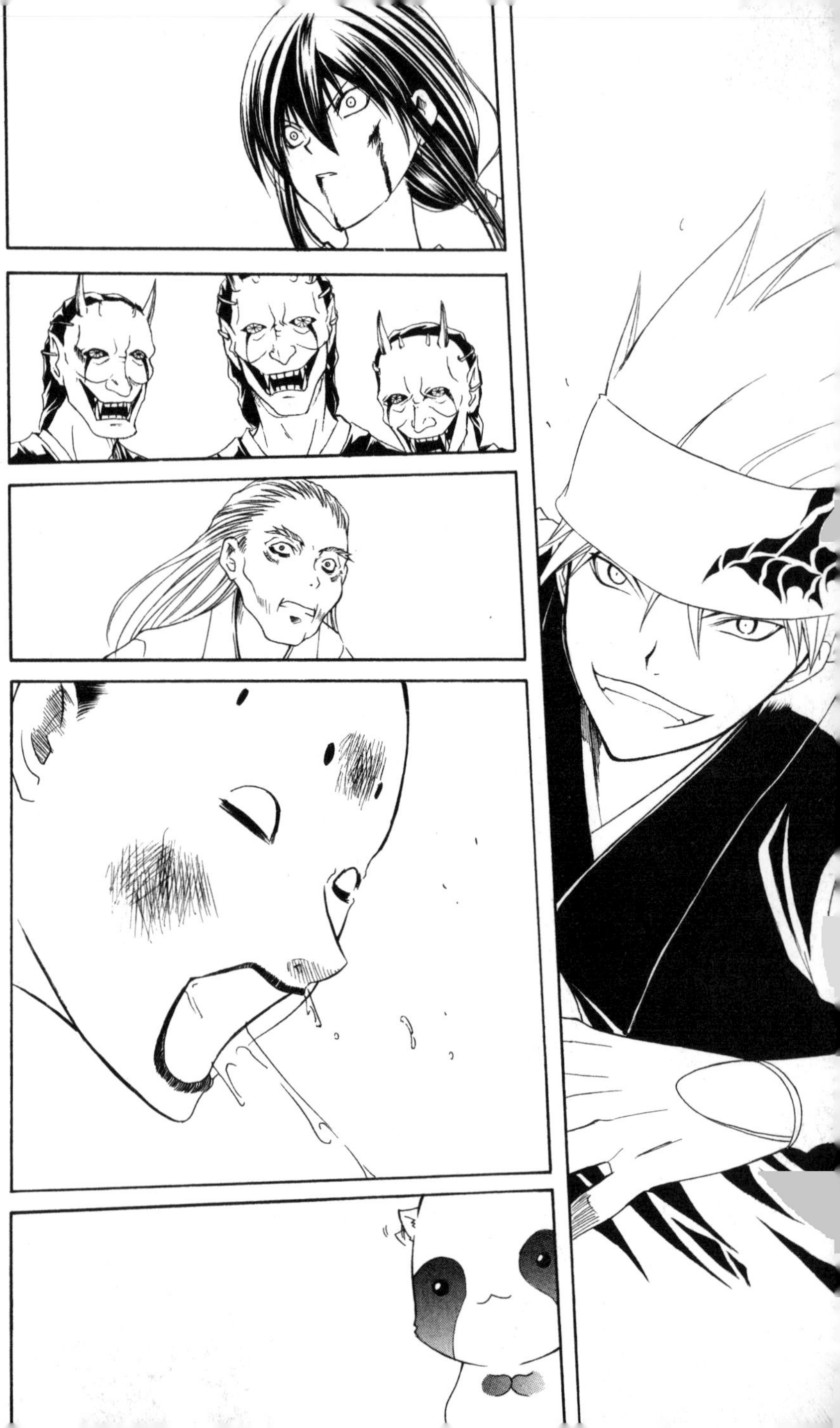

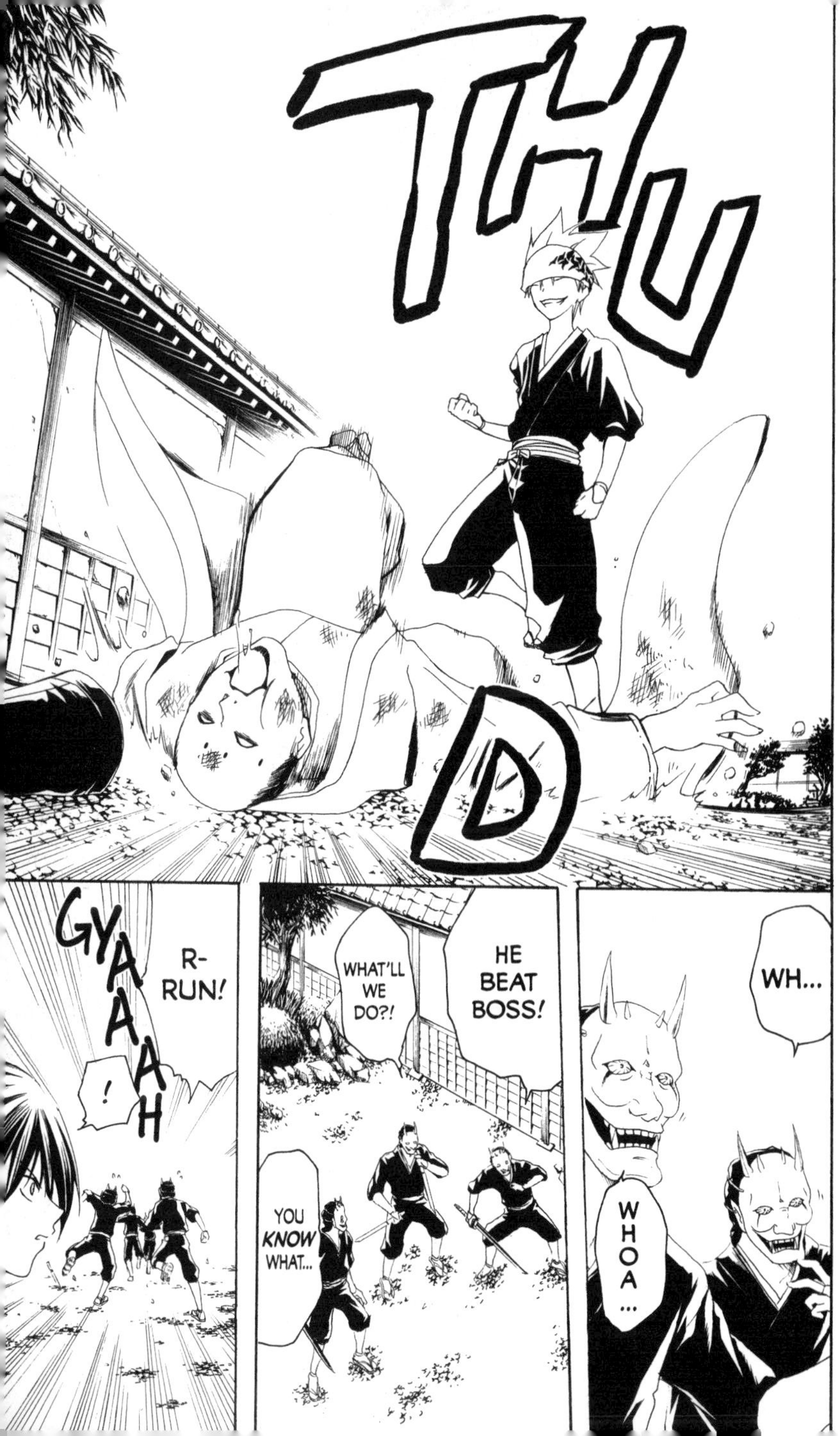
THUD
WH...
WHOA...
HE BEAT BOSS!
WHAT'LL WE DO?!
YOU *KNOW* WHAT...
R-RUN!
GYAAAAH
!

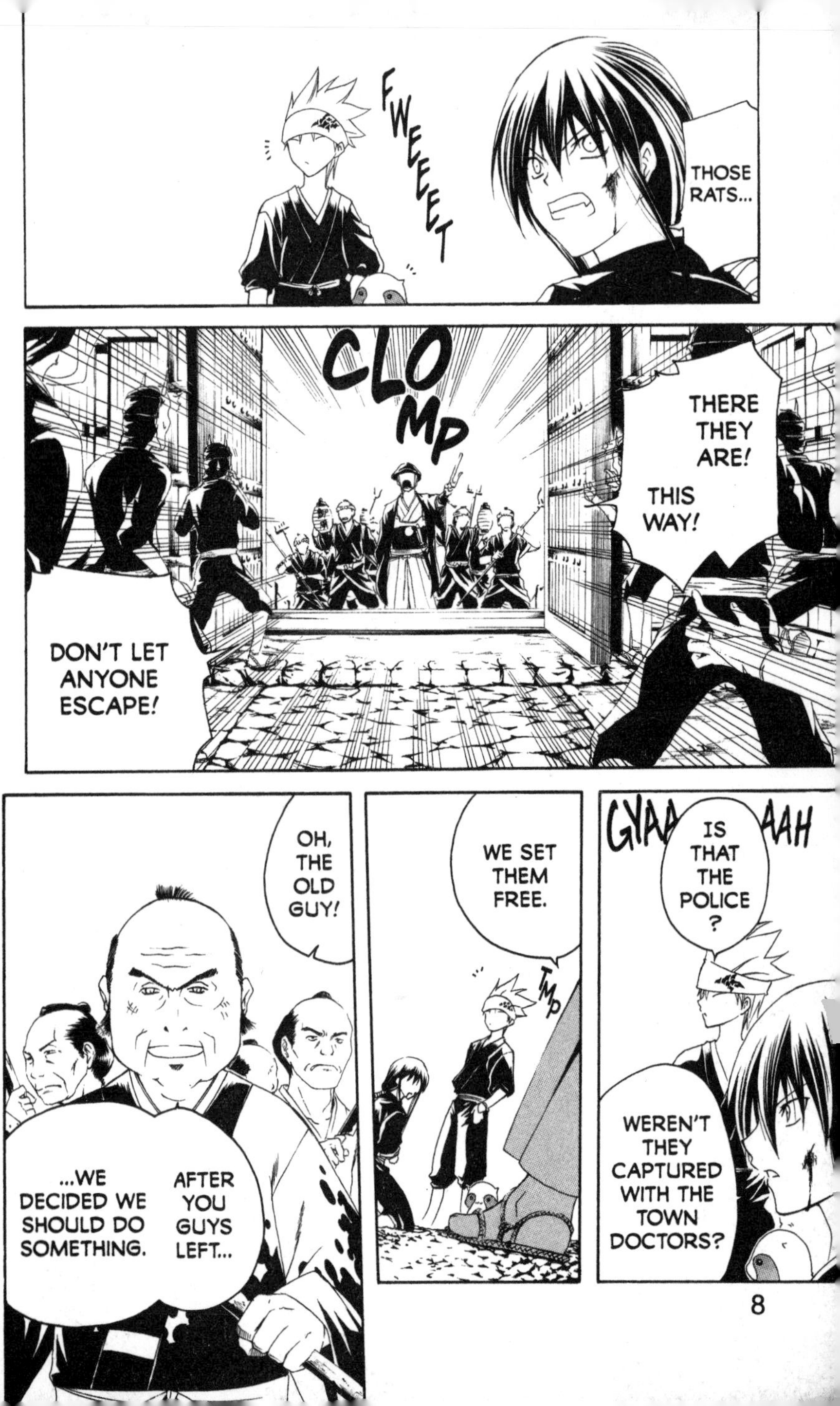
THOSE RATS...
FWEEEET
CLOMP
THERE THEY ARE!
THIS WAY!
DON'T LET ANYONE ESCAPE!
GYAAAAH
IS THAT THE POLICE?
WEREN'T THEY CAPTURED WITH THE TOWN DOCTORS?
WE SET THEM FREE.
TMP
OH, THE OLD GUY!
AFTER YOU GUYS LEFT...
...WE DECIDED WE SHOULD DO SOMETHING.

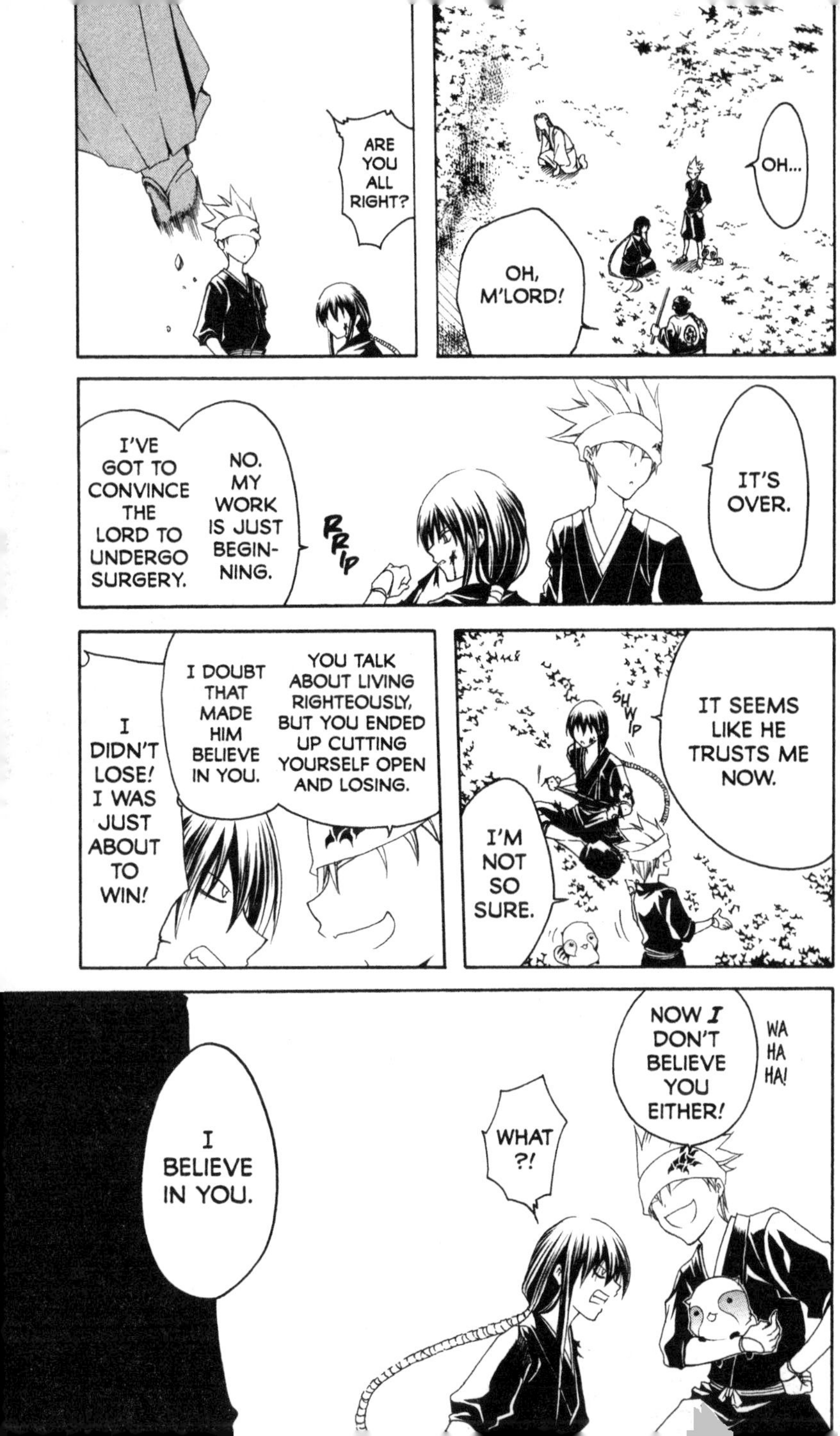
OH...
OH, M'LORD!
ARE YOU ALL RIGHT?
IT'S OVER.
RRIP
NO. MY WORK IS JUST BEGIN-NING.
I'VE GOT TO CONVINCE THE LORD TO UNDERGO SURGERY.
IT SEEMS LIKE HE TRUSTS ME NOW.
SHWIP
I'M NOT SO SURE.
YOU TALK ABOUT LIVING RIGHTEOUSLY, BUT YOU ENDED UP CUTTING YOURSELF OPEN AND LOSING.
I DOUBT THAT MADE HIM BELIEVE IN YOU.
I DIDN'T LOSE! I WAS JUST ABOUT TO WIN!
WA HA HA!
NOW I DON'T BELIEVE YOU EITHER!
WHAT?!
I BELIEVE IN YOU.

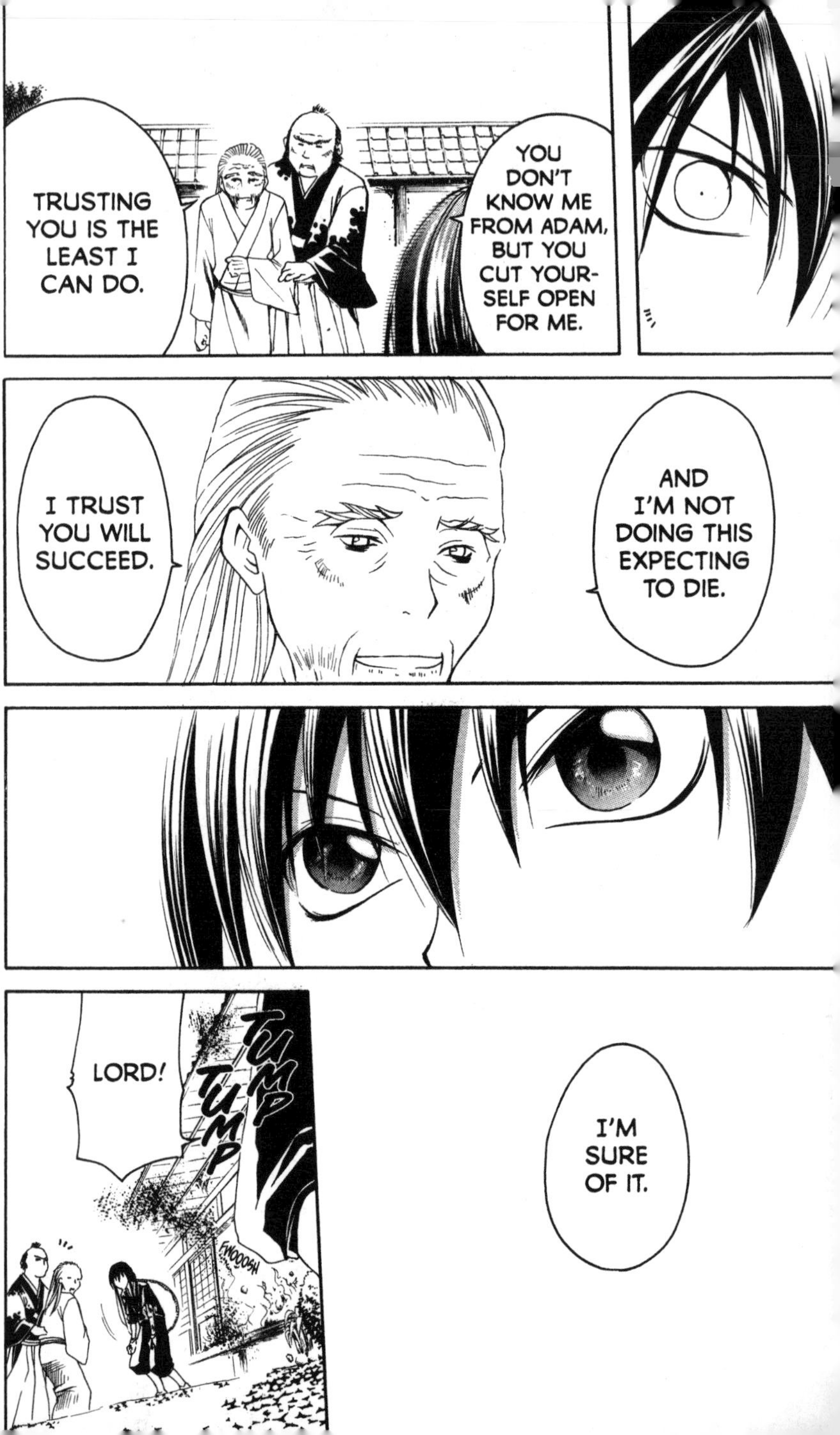
YOU DON'T KNOW ME FROM ADAM, BUT YOU CUT YOUR-SELF OPEN FOR ME.
TRUSTING YOU IS THE LEAST I CAN DO.
AND I'M NOT DOING THIS EXPECTING TO DIE.
I TRUST YOU WILL SUCCEED.
I'M SURE OF IT.
TUMP TUMP
LORD!
FWOOOSH

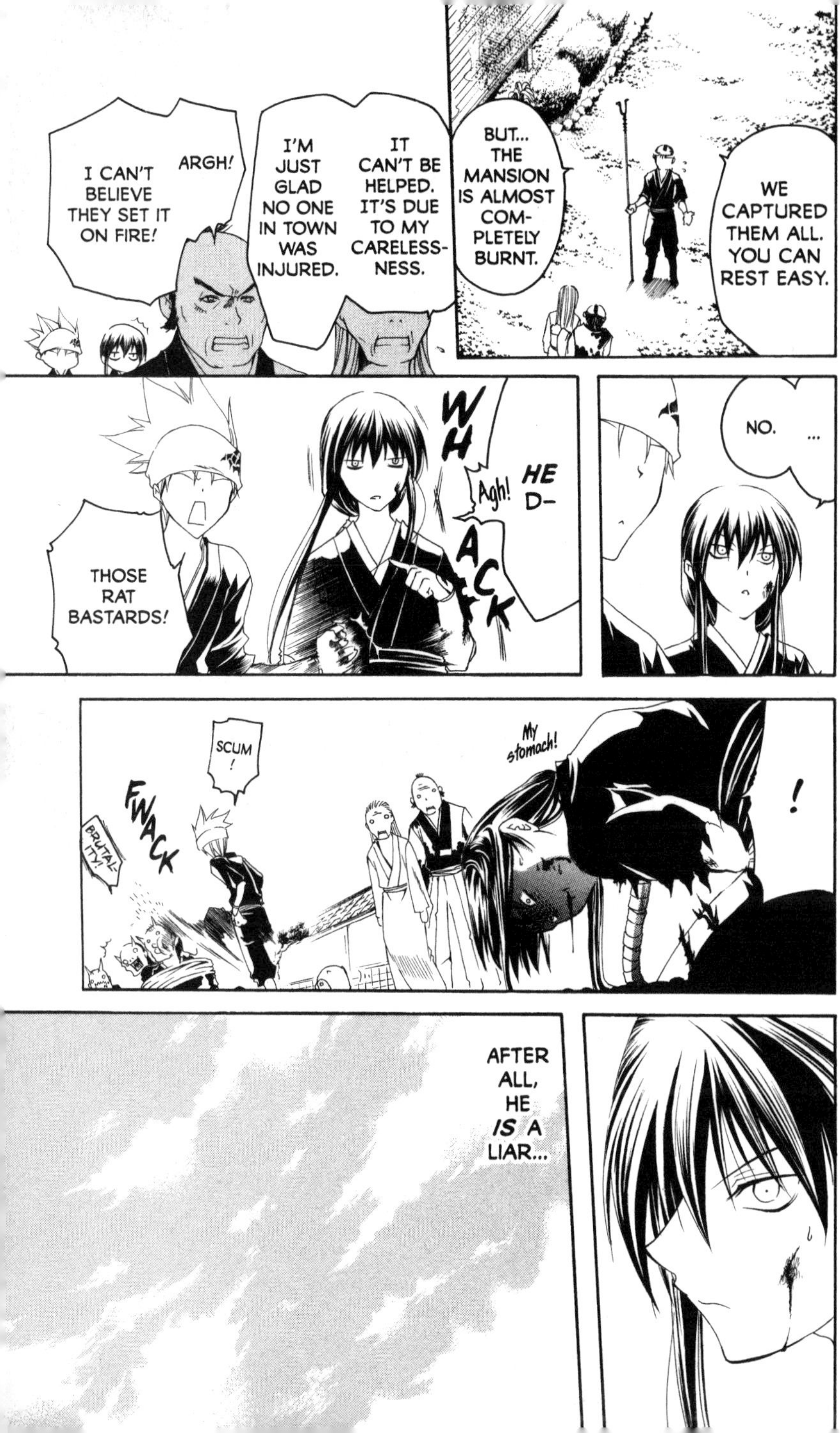
WE CAPTURED THEM ALL. YOU CAN REST EASY.
BUT... THE MANSION IS ALMOST COM-PLETELY BURNT.
IT CAN'T BE HELPED. IT'S DUE TO MY CARELESS-NESS.
I'M JUST GLAD NO ONE IN TOWN WAS INJURED.
ARGH!
I CAN'T BELIEVE THEY SET IT ON FIRE!
NO.
...
HE D-
Agh!
WHACK
THOSE RAT BASTARDS!
!
My stomach!
SCUM!
FWACK
BRUTAL-ITY!
AFTER ALL, HE *IS* A LIAR...

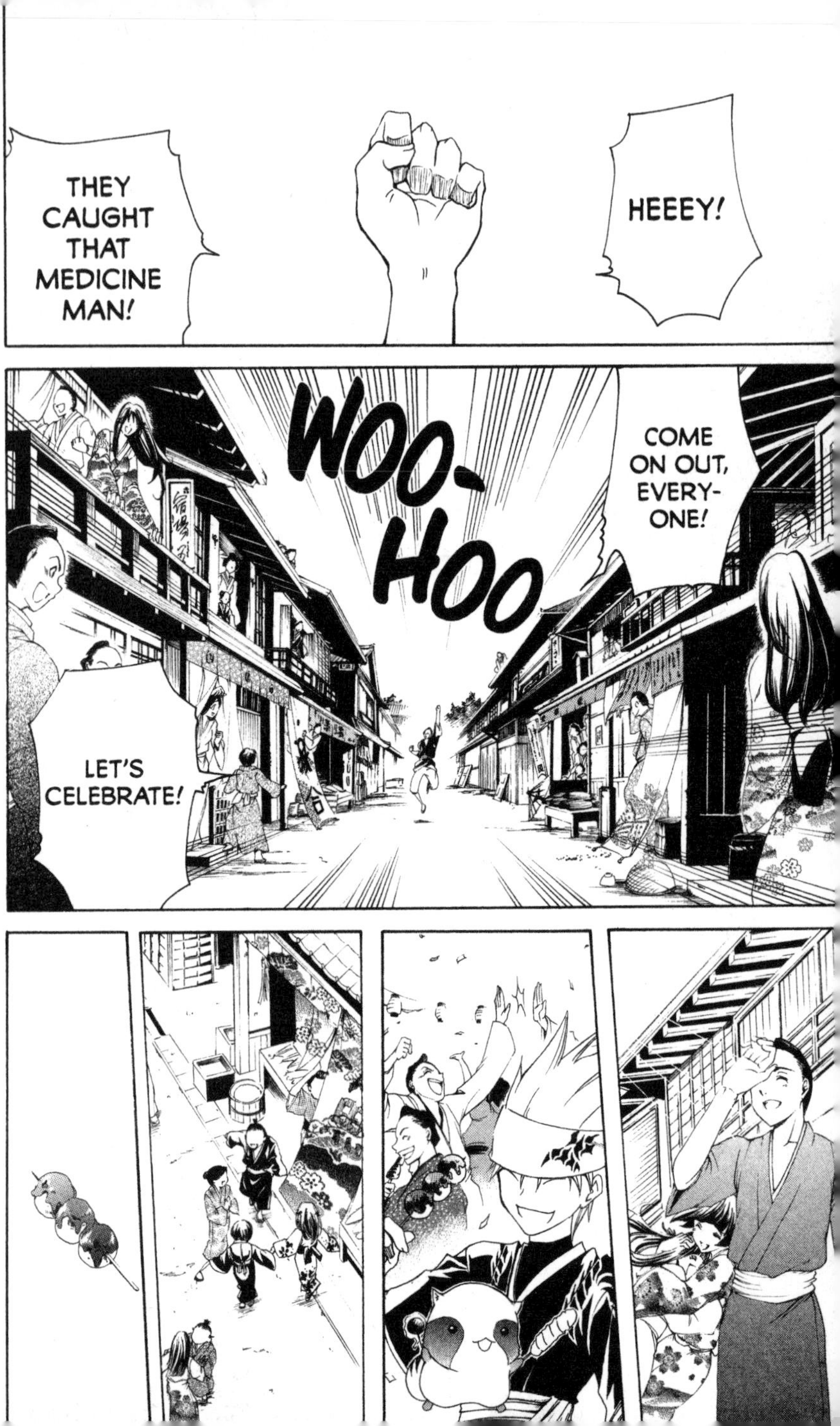
HEEEY!
THEY CAUGHT THAT MEDICINE MAN!
COME ON OUT, EVERY-ONE!
WOO-HOO
LET'S CELEBRATE!

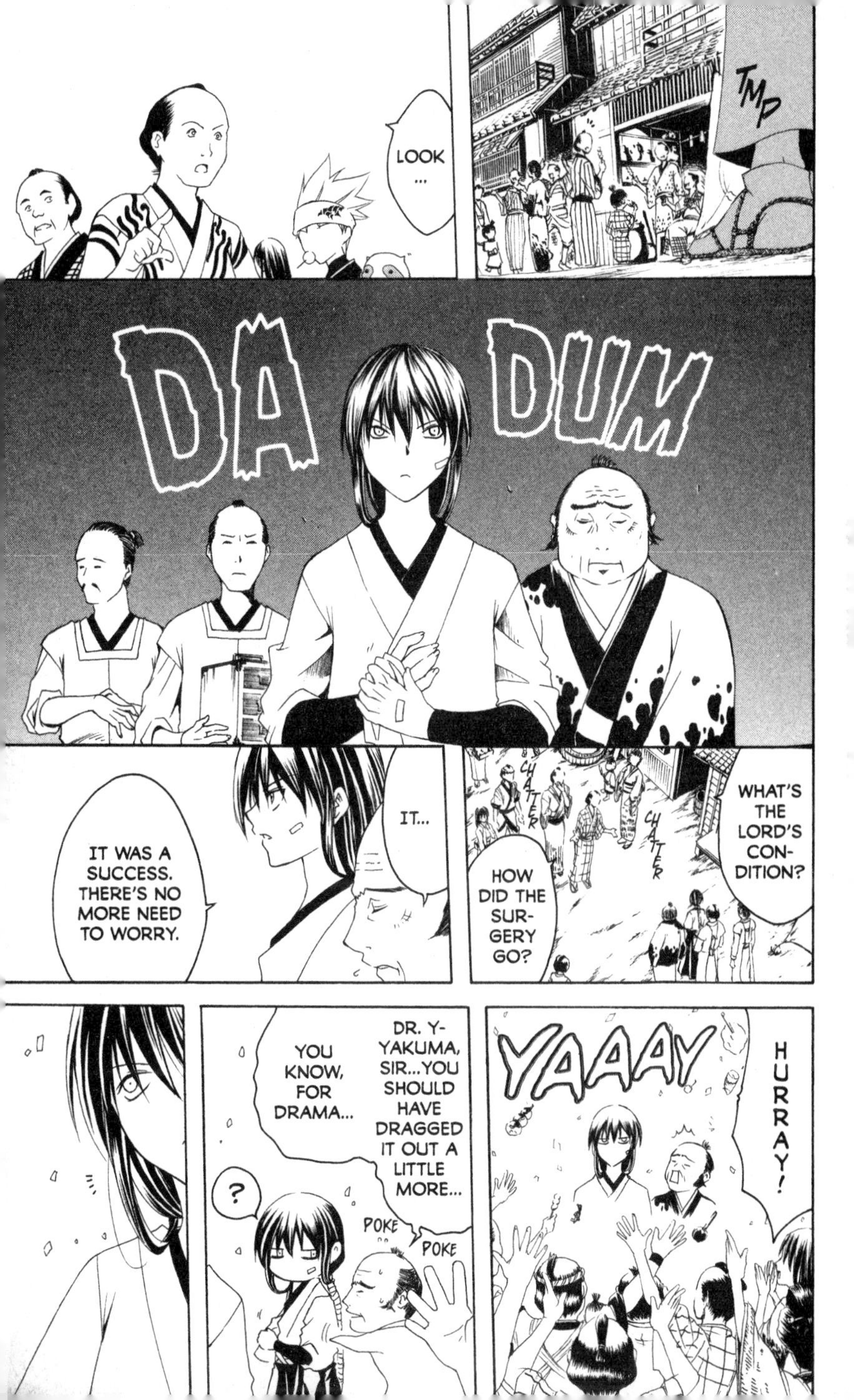
TMP
LOOK...
DA DUM
WHAT'S THE LORD'S CONDITION?
CHATTER
CHATTER
HOW DID THE SURGERY GO?
IT...
IT WAS A SUCCESS. THERE'S NO MORE NEED TO WORRY.
YAAAY
HURRAY!
DR. Y-YAKUMA, SIR...YOU SHOULD HAVE DRAGGED IT OUT A LITTLE MORE...
YOU KNOW, FOR DRAMA...
POKE
POKE
?

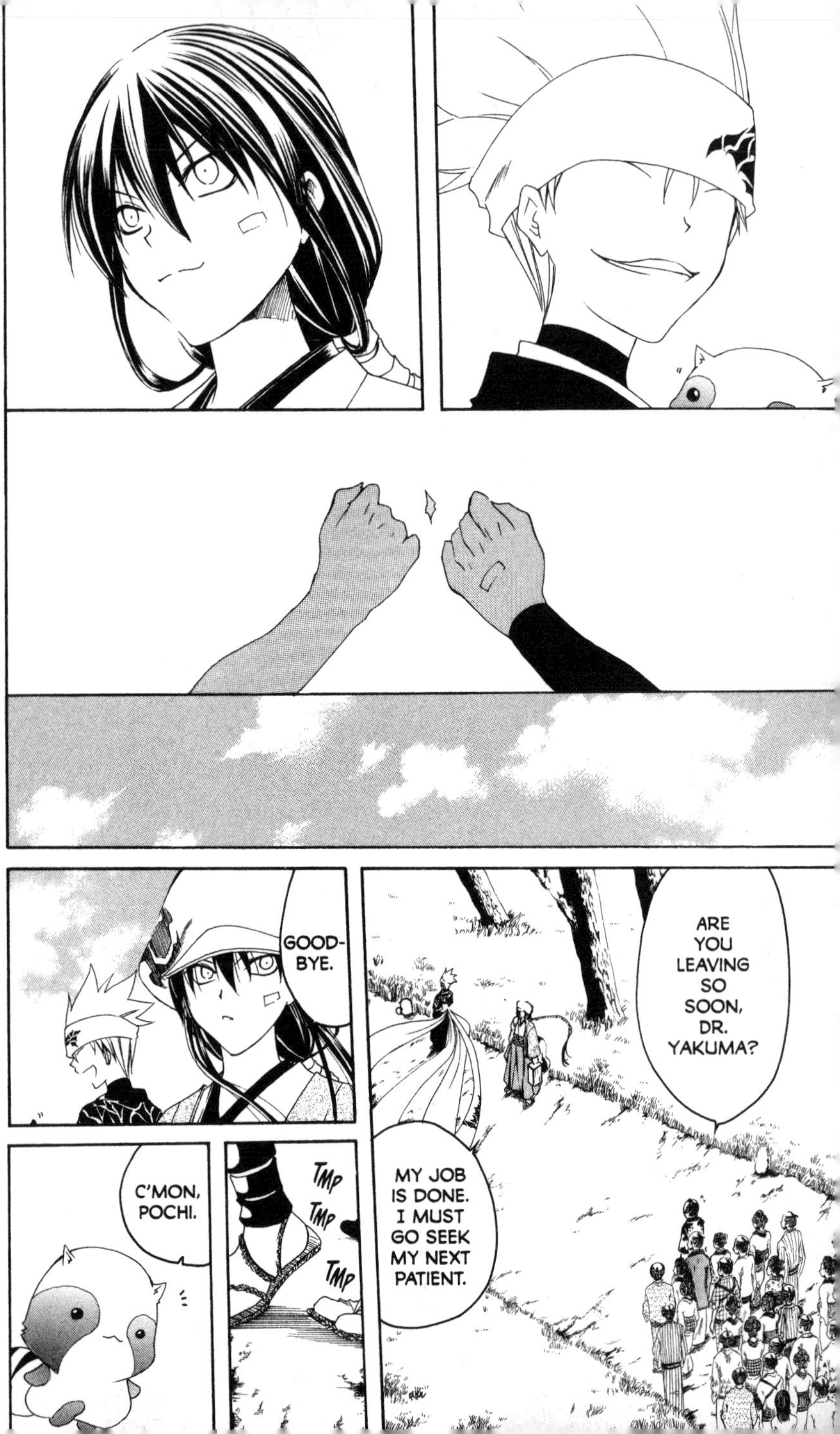
ARE YOU LEAVING SO SOON, DR. YAKUMA?
MY JOB IS DONE. I MUST GO SEEK MY NEXT PATIENT.
GOOD-BYE.
TMP
TMP
TMP
C'MON, POCHI.

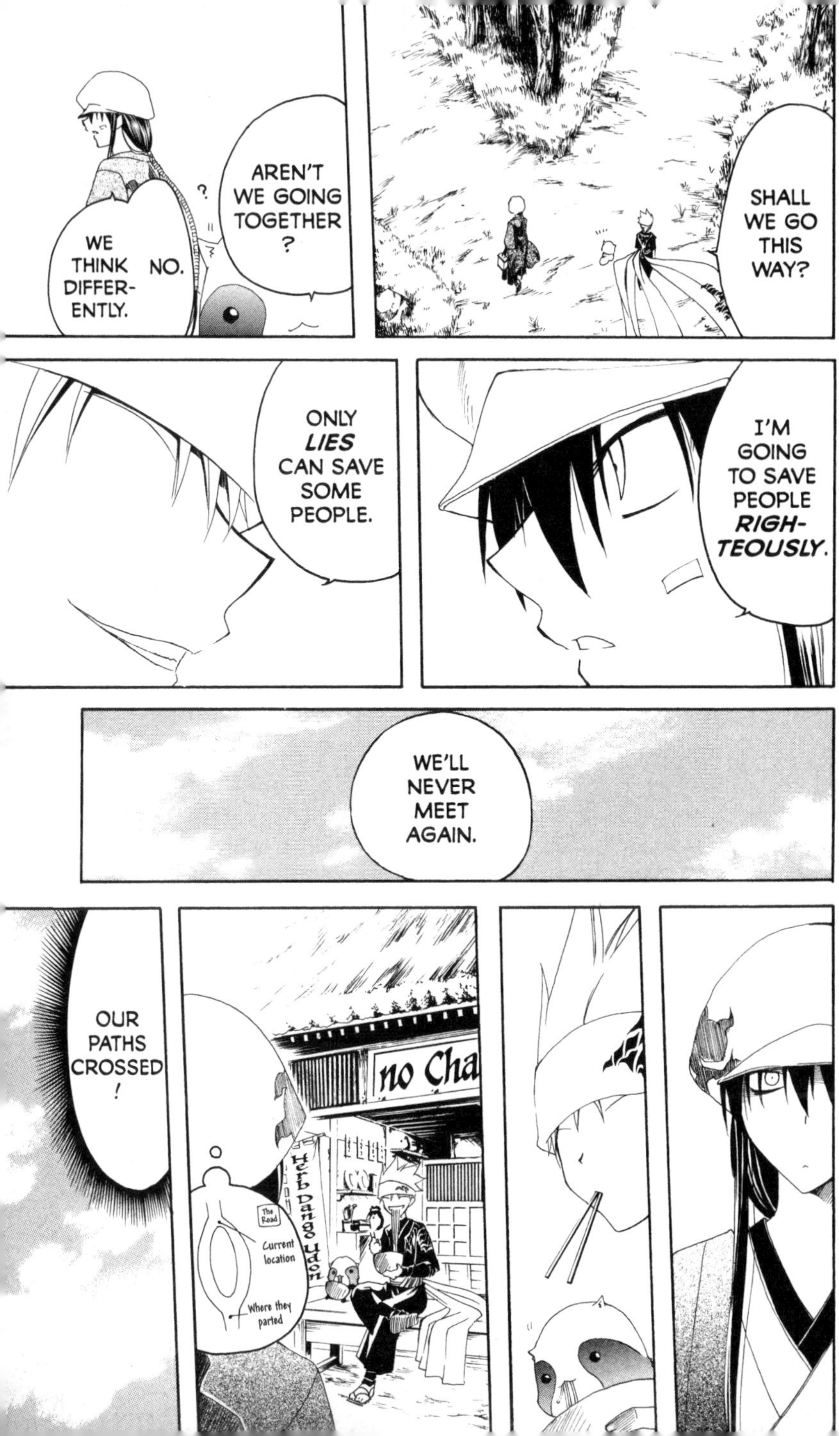
SHALL WE GO THIS WAY?
AREN'T WE GOING TOGETHER?
NO.
WE THINK DIFFERENTLY.
I'M GOING TO SAVE PEOPLE RIGHTEOUSLY.
ONLY LIES CAN SAVE SOME PEOPLE.
WE'LL NEVER MEET AGAIN.
no Cha
Herb Dango Udon
The Road
Current location
Where they parted
OUR PATHS CROSSED!

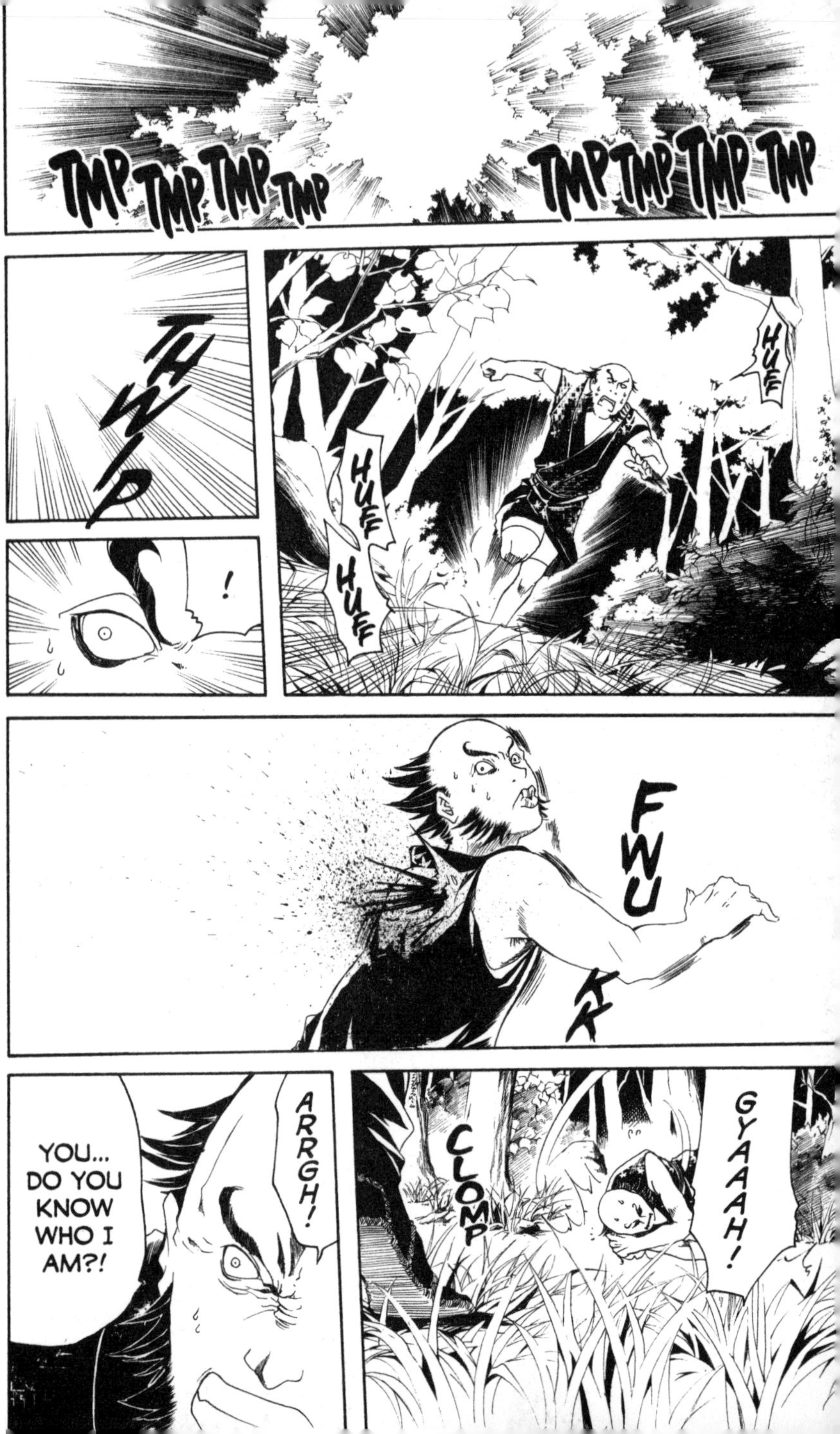
TMP TMP TMP TMP
TMP TMP TMP TMP
HUFF
HUFF HUFF
THWIP
!
FWUKK
GYAAAH!
CLOMP
ARRGH!
YOU... DO YOU KNOW WHO I AM?!

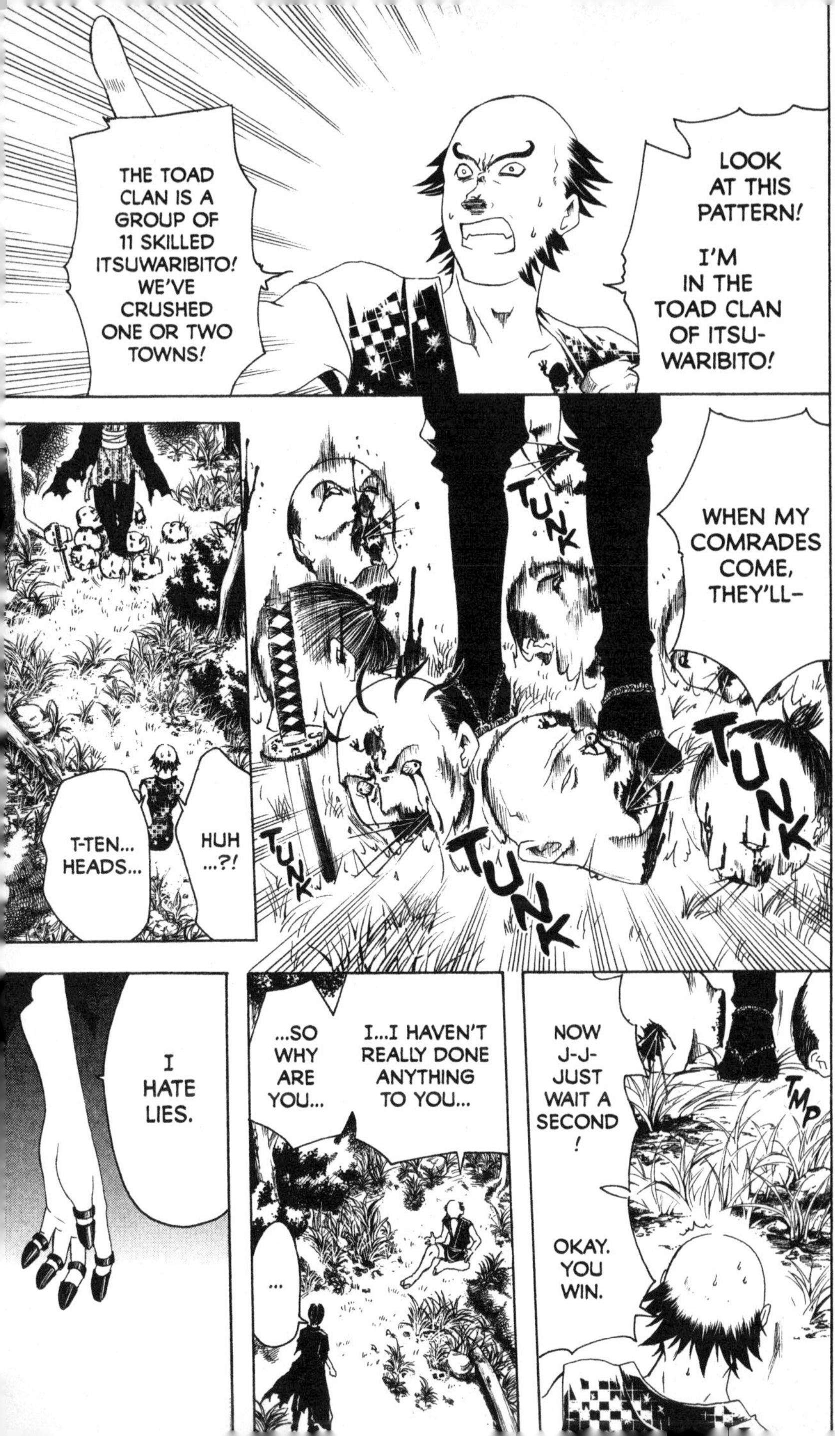
LOOK AT THIS PATTERN!
I'M IN THE TOAD CLAN OF ITSU-WARIBITO!
THE TOAD CLAN IS A GROUP OF 11 SKILLED ITSUWARIBITO! WE'VE CRUSHED ONE OR TWO TOWNS!
WHEN MY COMRADES COME, THEY'LL-
TUNK
TUNK
TUNK
TUNK
HUH ...?!
T-TEN... HEADS...
NOW J-J-JUST WAIT A SECOND!
TMP
OKAY. YOU WIN.
I...I HAVEN'T REALLY DONE ANYTHING TO YOU...
...SO WHY ARE YOU...
...
I HATE LIES.

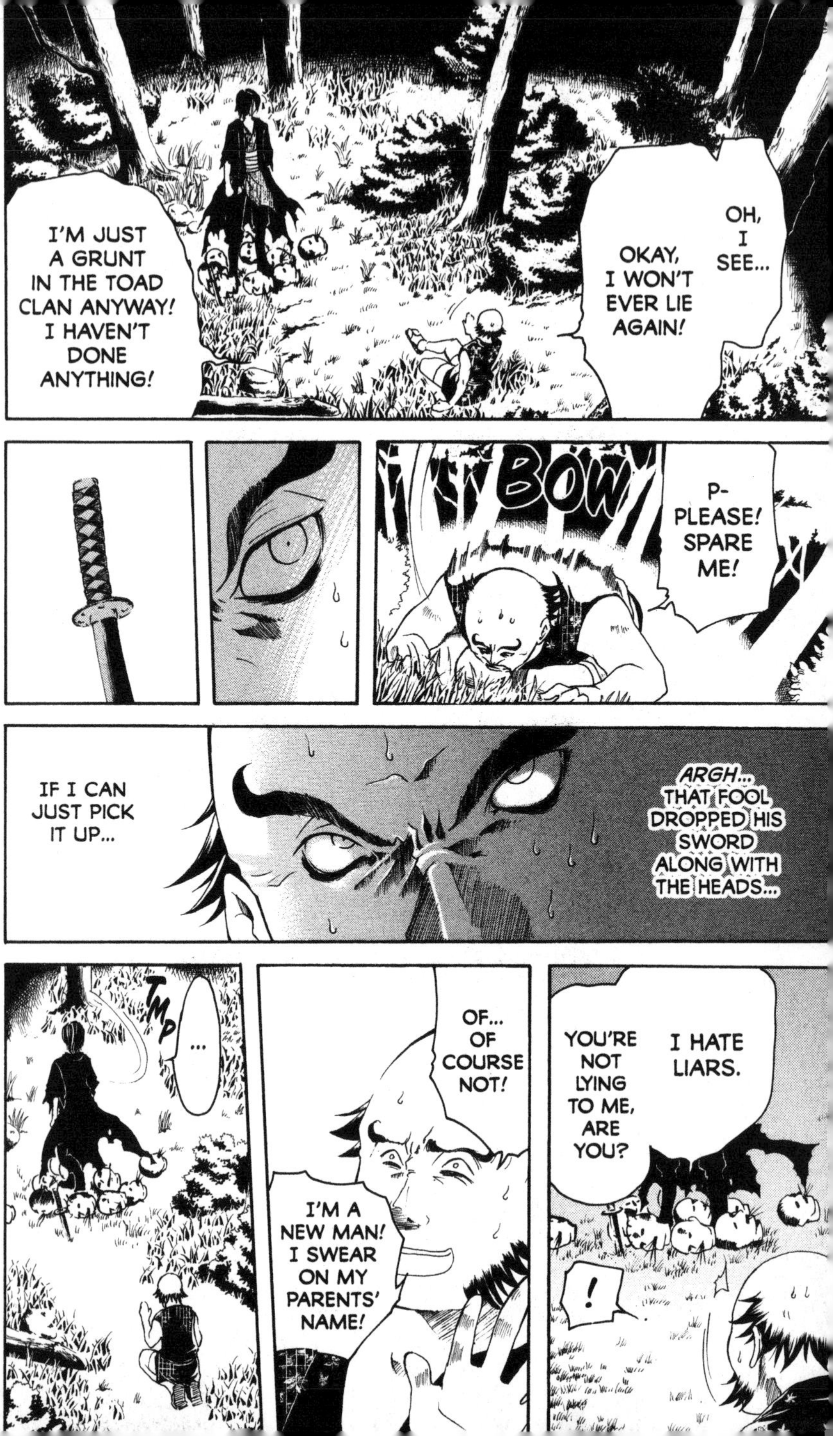
OH, I SEE...
OKAY, I WON'T EVER LIE AGAIN!
I'M JUST A GRUNT IN THE TOAD CLAN ANYWAY! I HAVEN'T DONE ANYTHING!
P-PLEASE! SPARE ME!
BOW
ARGH... THAT FOOL DROPPED HIS SWORD ALONG WITH THE HEADS...
IF I CAN JUST PICK IT UP...
I HATE LIARS.
YOU'RE NOT LYING TO ME, ARE YOU?
!
OF... OF COURSE NOT!
I'M A NEW MAN! I SWEAR ON MY PARENTS' NAME!
TMP
...

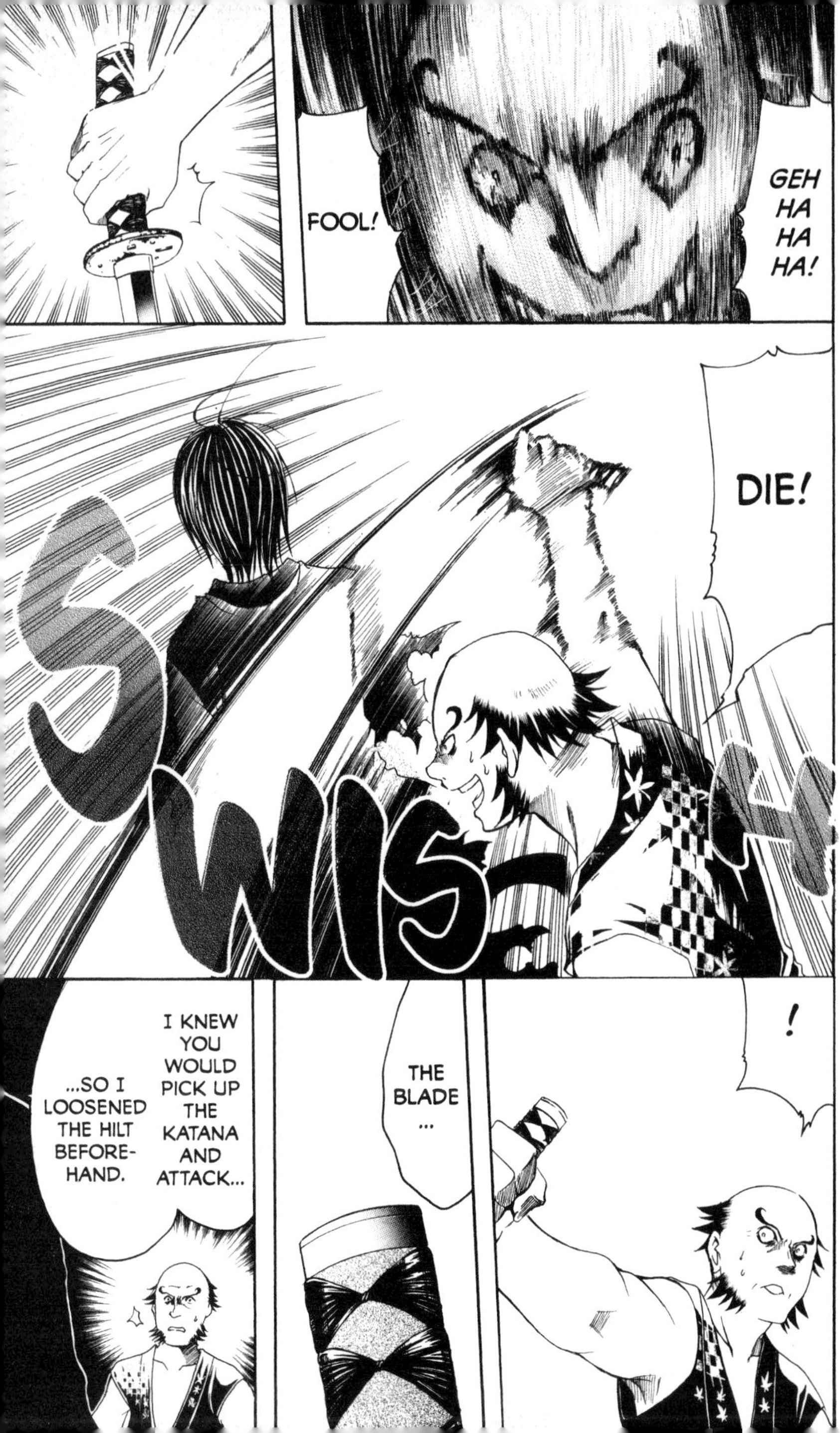
GEH HA HA HA!
FOOL!
DIE!
SWISH
!
THE BLADE ...
I KNEW YOU WOULD PICK UP THE KATANA AND ATTACK...
...SO I LOOSENED THE HILT BEFORE-HAND.

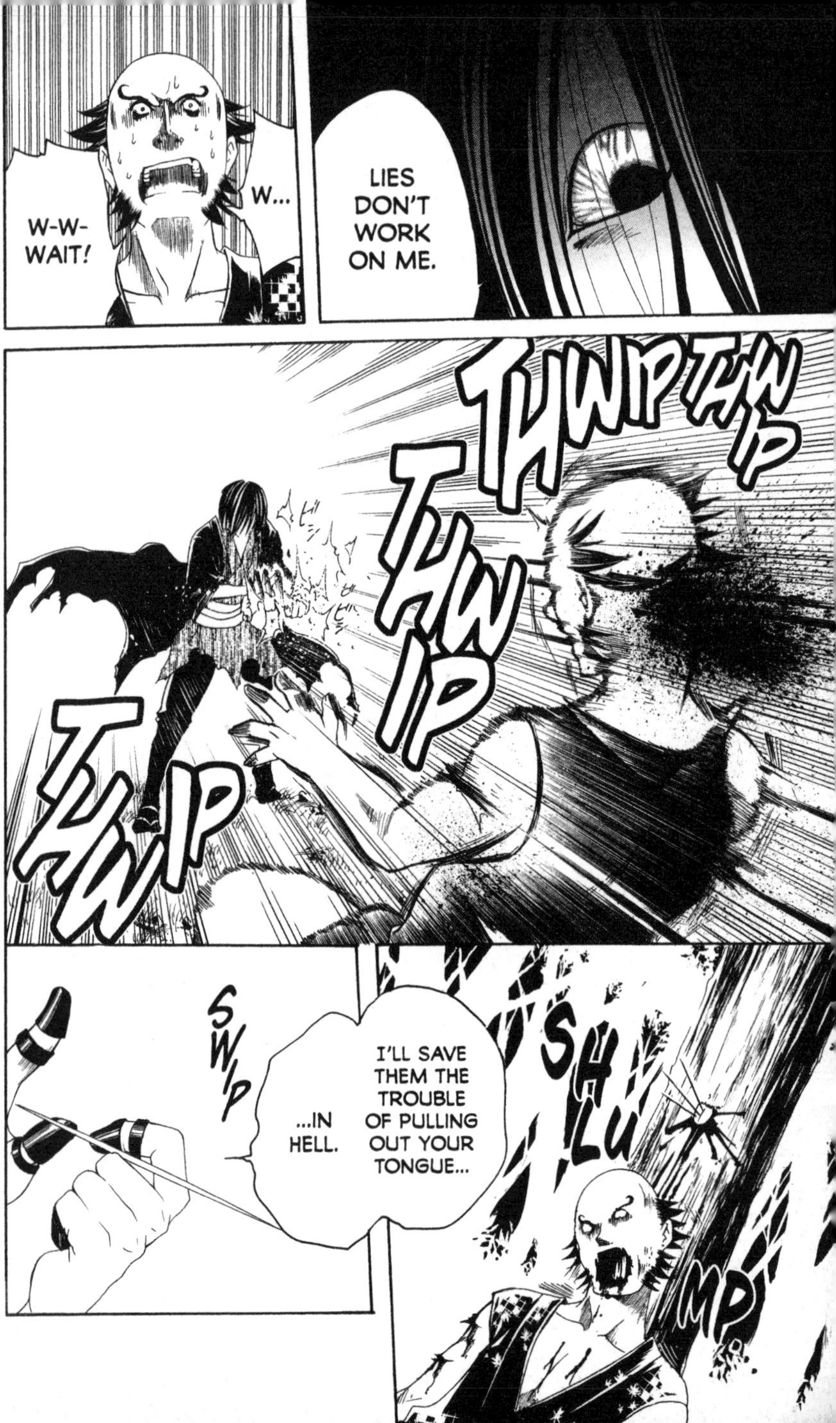
LIES DON'T WORK ON ME.
W...
W-W-WAIT!
THWIP THWIP
THWIP
THWIP
SHLUMP
I'LL SAVE THEM THE TROUBLE OF PULLING OUT YOUR TONGUE...
...IN HELL.
SWIP

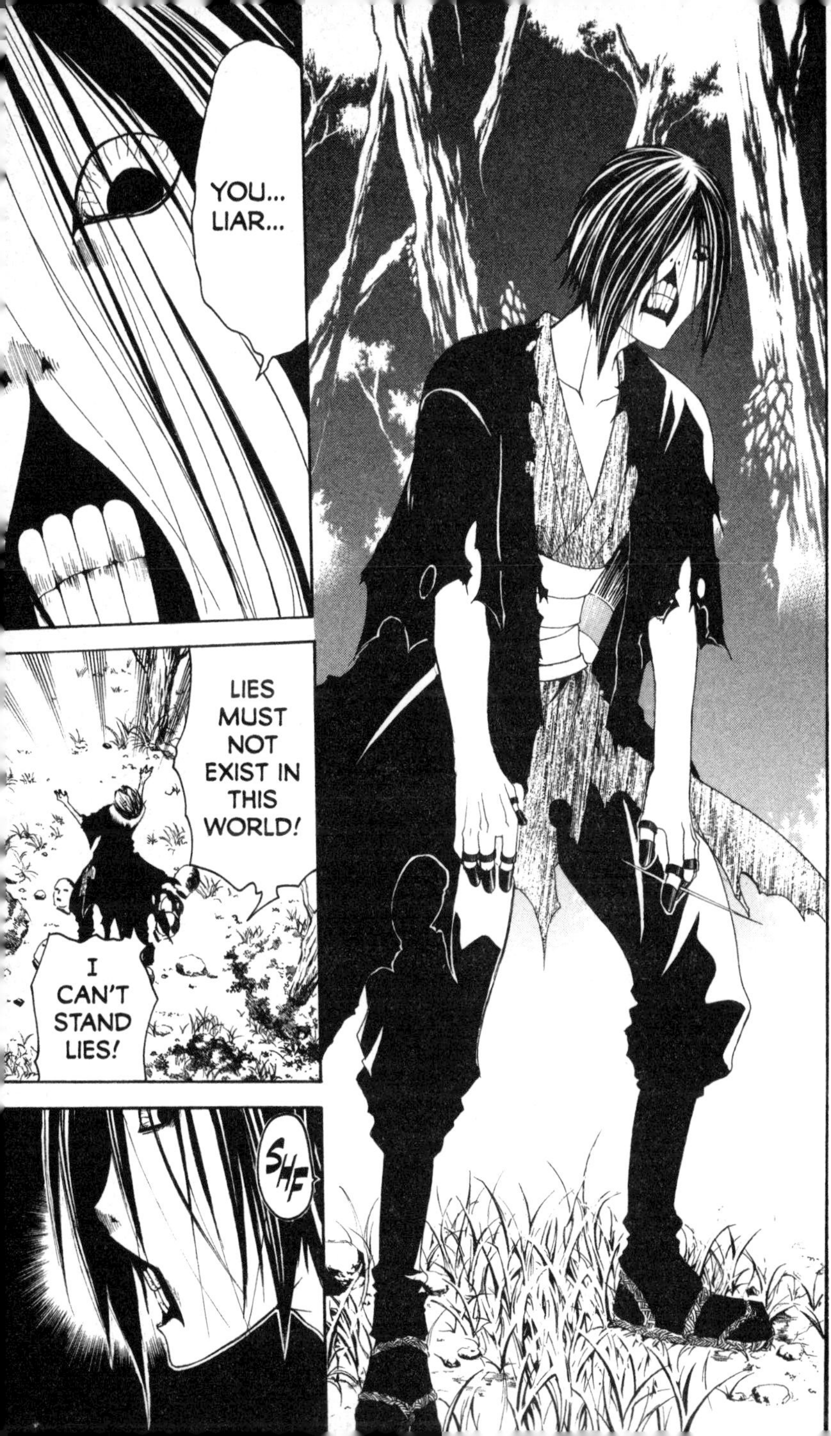
YOU... LIAR...
LIES MUST NOT EXIST IN THIS WORLD!
I CAN'T STAND LIES!
SHF

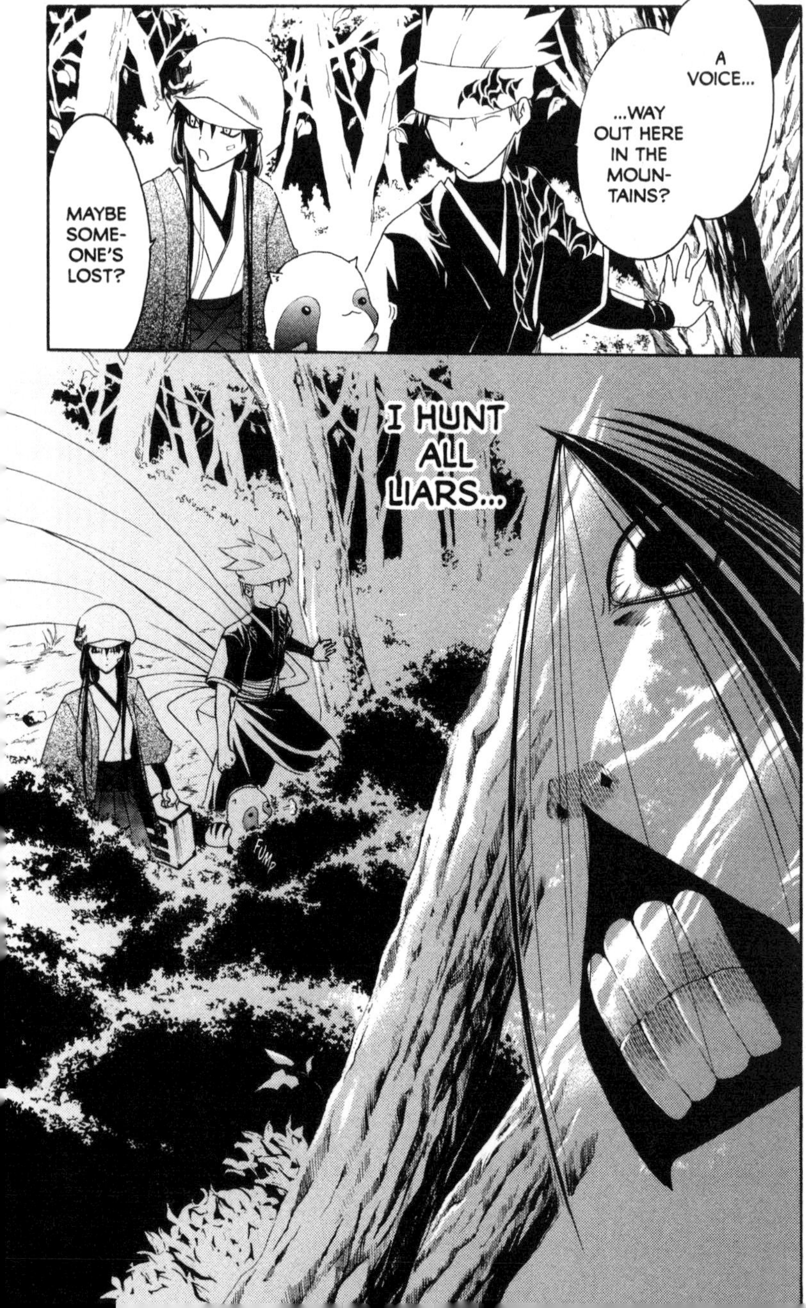
A VOICE...
...WAY OUT HERE IN THE MOUN-TAINS?
MAYBE SOME-ONE'S LOST?
I HUNT ALL LIARS...
FUMP

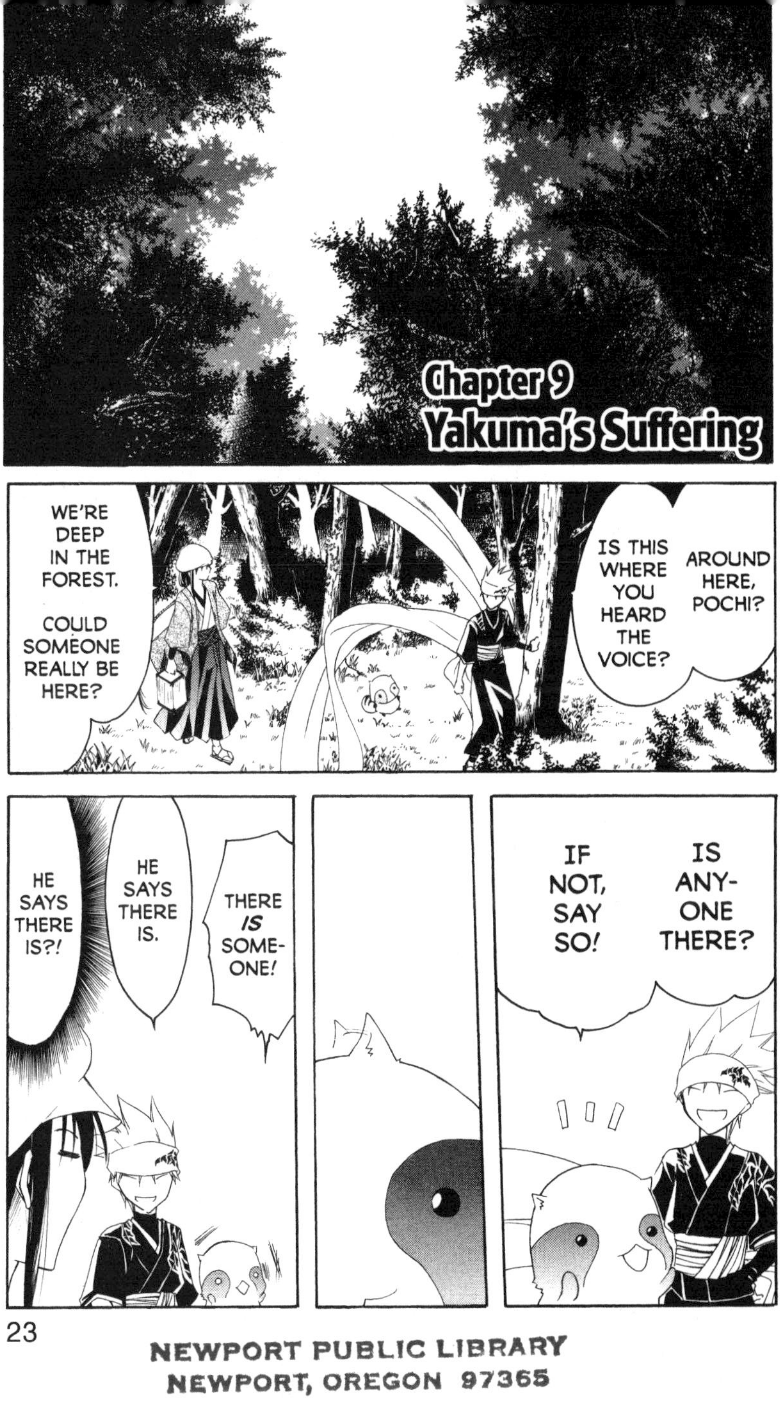
Chapter 9
Yakuma's Suffering
AROUND HERE, POCHI?
IS THIS WHERE YOU HEARD THE VOICE?
WE'RE DEEP IN THE FOREST.
COULD SOMEONE REALLY BE HERE?
IS ANY-ONE THERE?
IF NOT, SAY SO!
THERE *IS* SOME-ONE!
HE SAYS THERE IS.
HE SAYS THERE IS?!

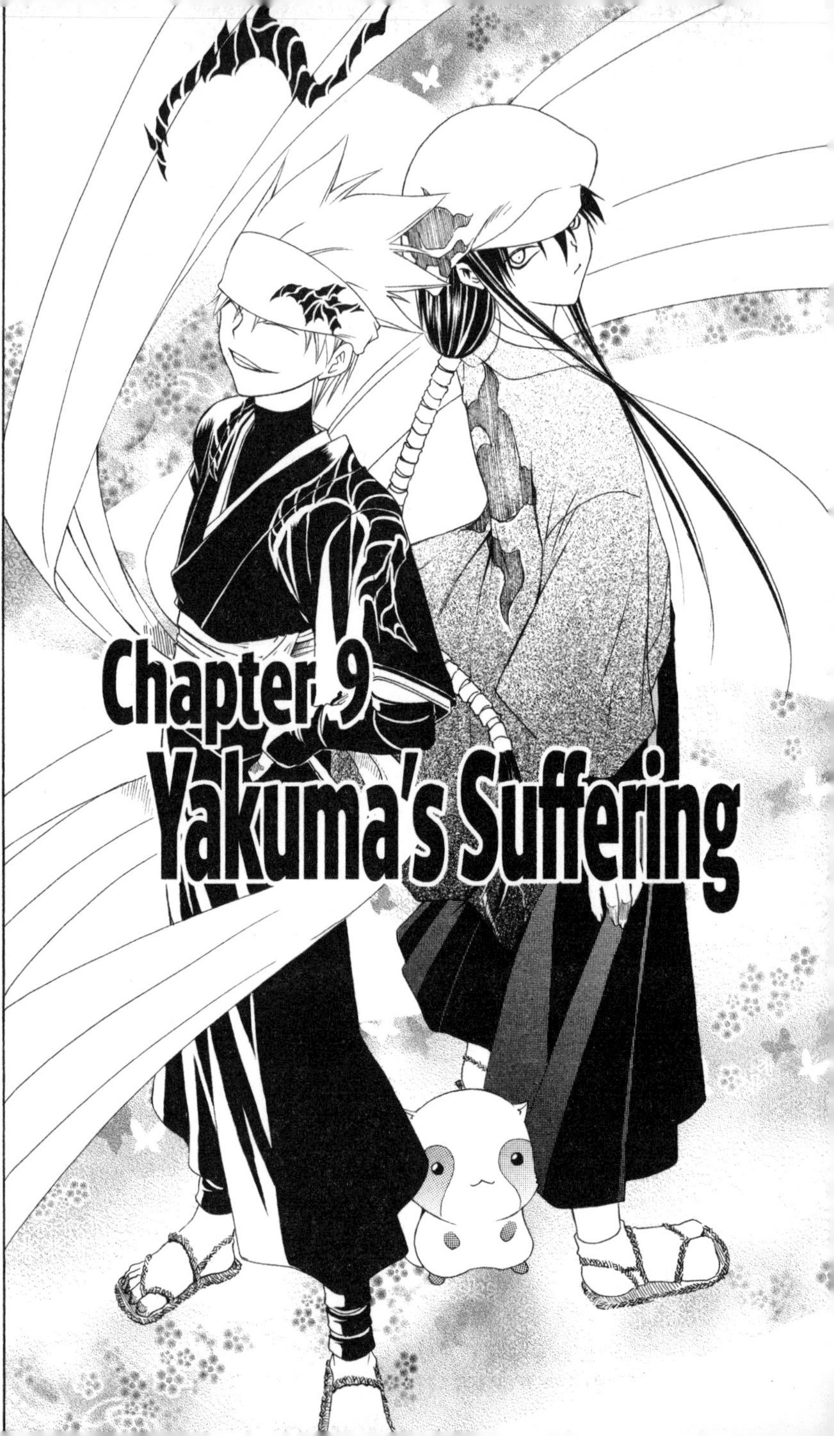
Chapter 9
Yakuma's Suffering

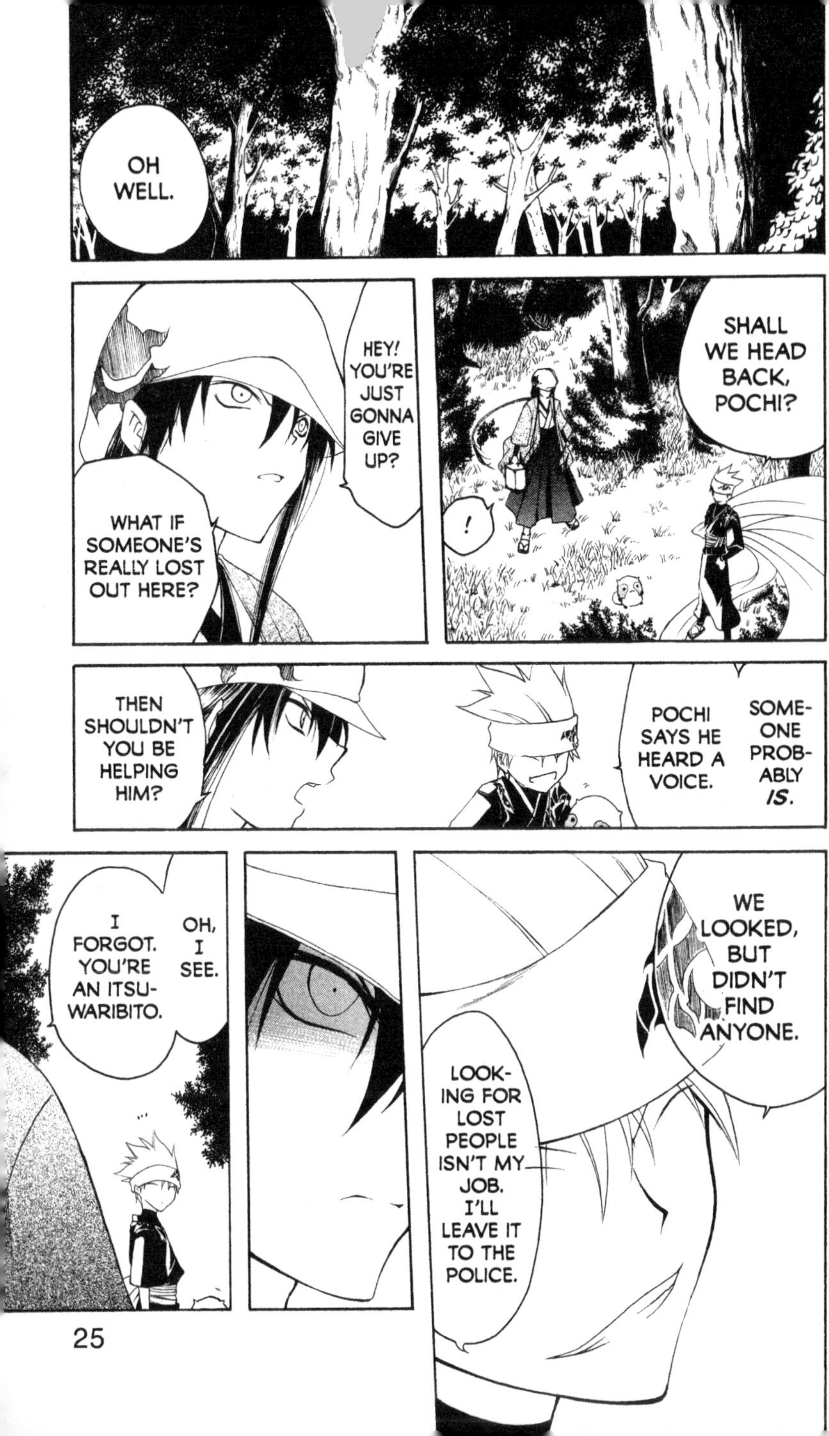
OH WELL.
SHALL WE HEAD BACK, POCHI?
!
HEY! YOU'RE JUST GONNA GIVE UP?
WHAT IF SOMEONE'S REALLY LOST OUT HERE?
SOME-ONE PROB-ABLY *IS*.
POCHI SAYS HE HEARD A VOICE.
THEN SHOULDN'T YOU BE HELPING HIM?
WE LOOKED, BUT DIDN'T FIND ANYONE.
LOOK-ING FOR LOST PEOPLE ISN'T MY JOB. I'LL LEAVE IT TO THE POLICE.
OH, I SEE.
I FORGOT. YOU'RE AN ITSU-WARIBITO.
...

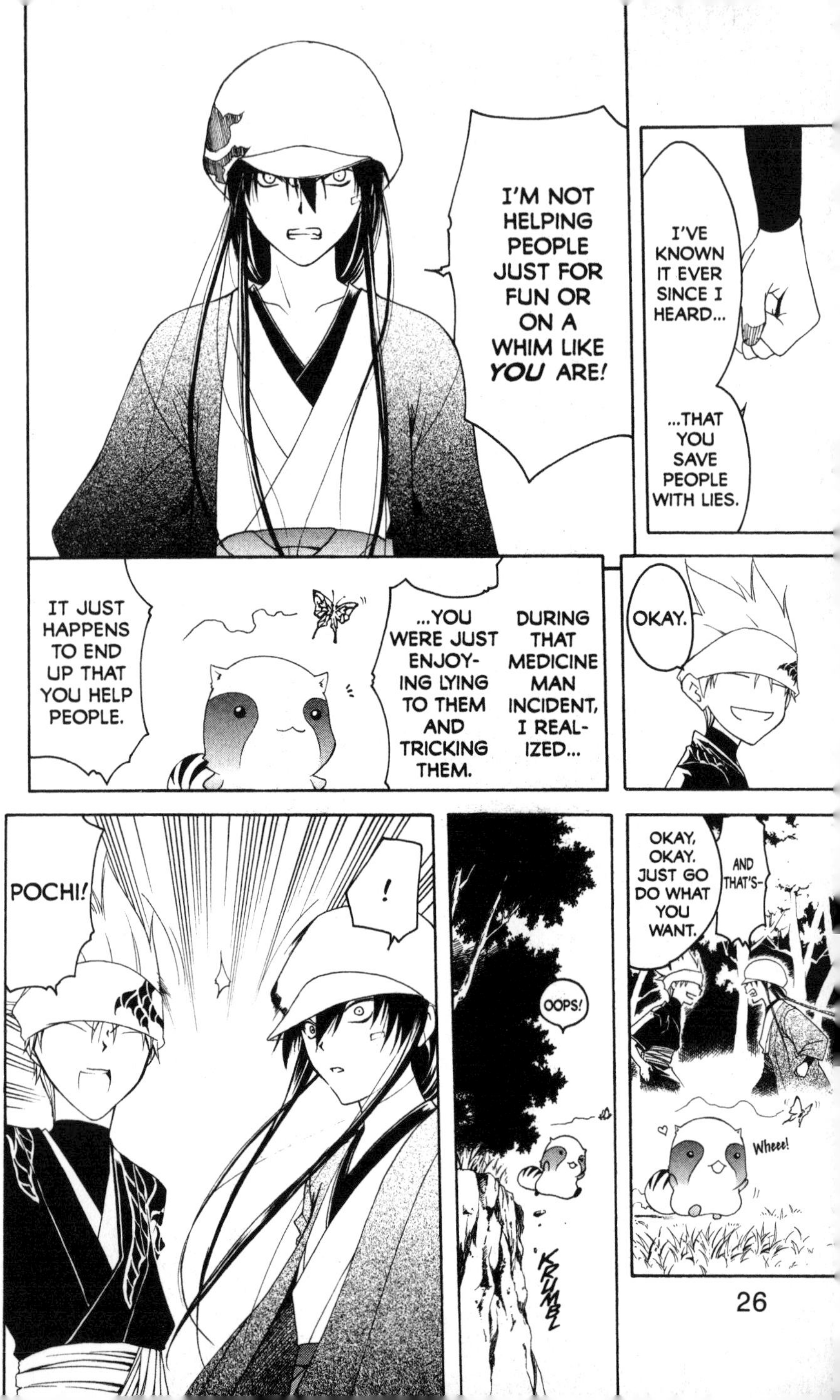
I'VE KNOWN IT EVER SINCE I HEARD...
...THAT YOU SAVE PEOPLE WITH LIES.
I'M NOT HELPING PEOPLE JUST FOR FUN OR ON A WHIM LIKE *YOU* ARE!
OKAY.
DURING THAT MEDICINE MAN INCIDENT, I REALIZED...
...YOU WERE JUST ENJOYING LYING TO THEM AND TRICKING THEM.
IT JUST HAPPENS TO END UP THAT YOU HELP PEOPLE.
OKAY, OKAY. JUST GO DO WHAT YOU WANT.
AND THAT'S-
Wheee!
OOPS!
KRUMBL
!
POCHI!

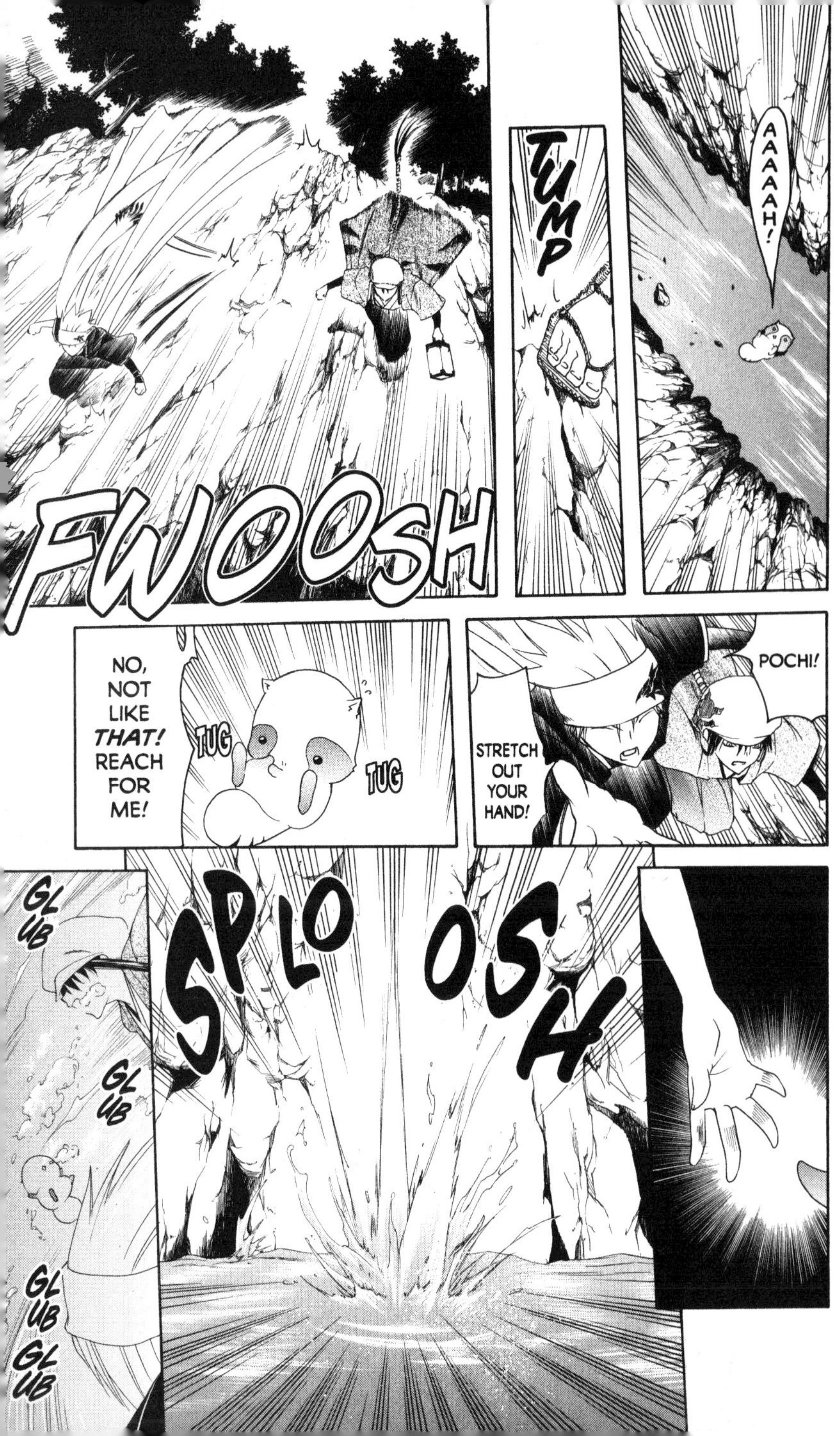
AAAAAH!
TUMP
FWOOSH
POCHI!
STRETCH OUT YOUR HAND!
NO, NOT LIKE *THAT!* REACH FOR ME!
TUG
TUG
SPLOOSH
GLUB
GLUB
GLUB GLUB
GLUB

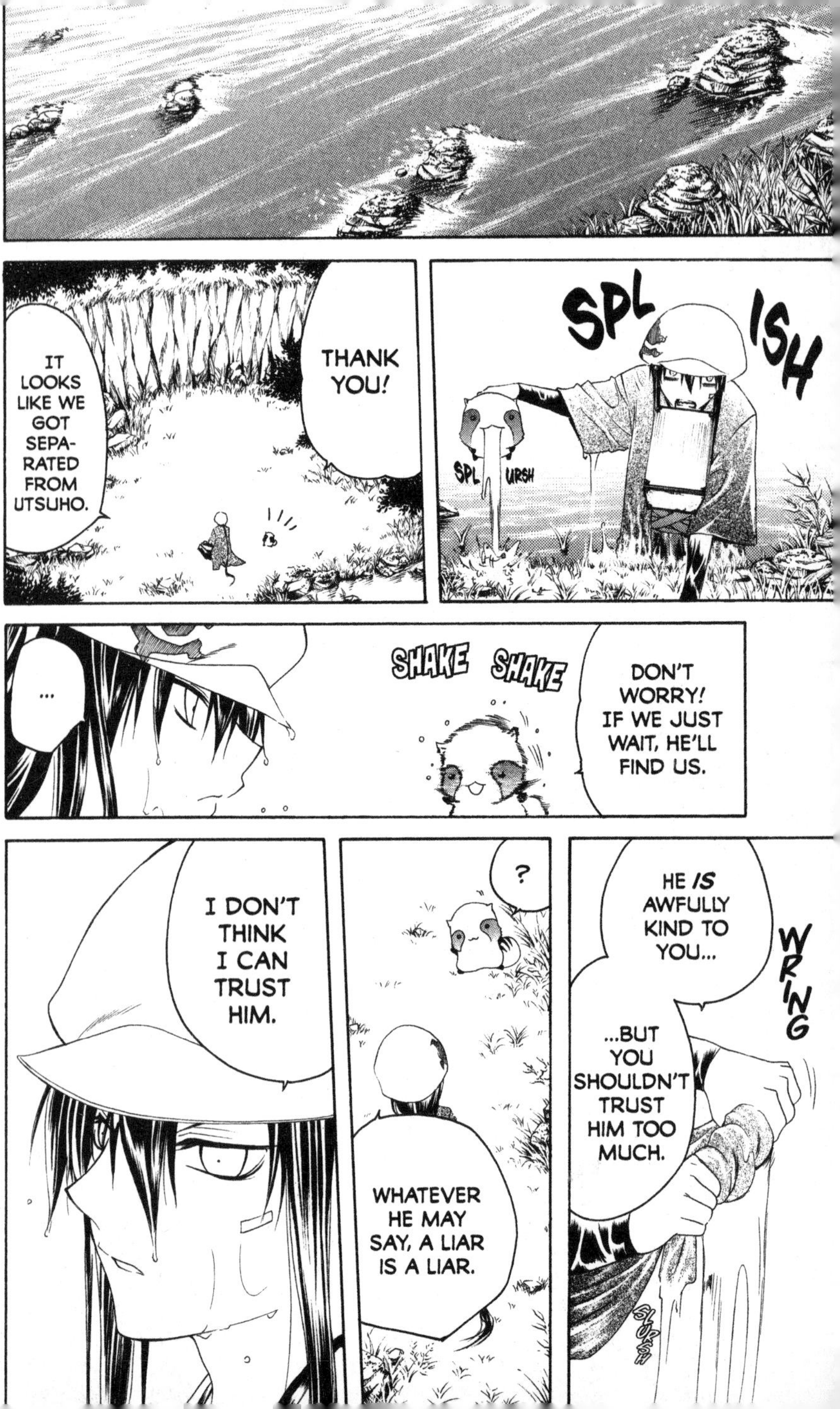
SPL ISH
SPL URSH
THANK YOU!
IT LOOKS LIKE WE GOT SEPA-RATED FROM UTSUHO.
DON'T WORRY! IF WE JUST WAIT, HE'LL FIND US.
SHAKE SHAKE
...
HE *IS* AWFULLY KIND TO YOU...
WRING
...BUT YOU SHOULDN'T TRUST HIM TOO MUCH.
?
WHATEVER HE MAY SAY, A LIAR IS A LIAR.
I DON'T THINK I CAN TRUST HIM.

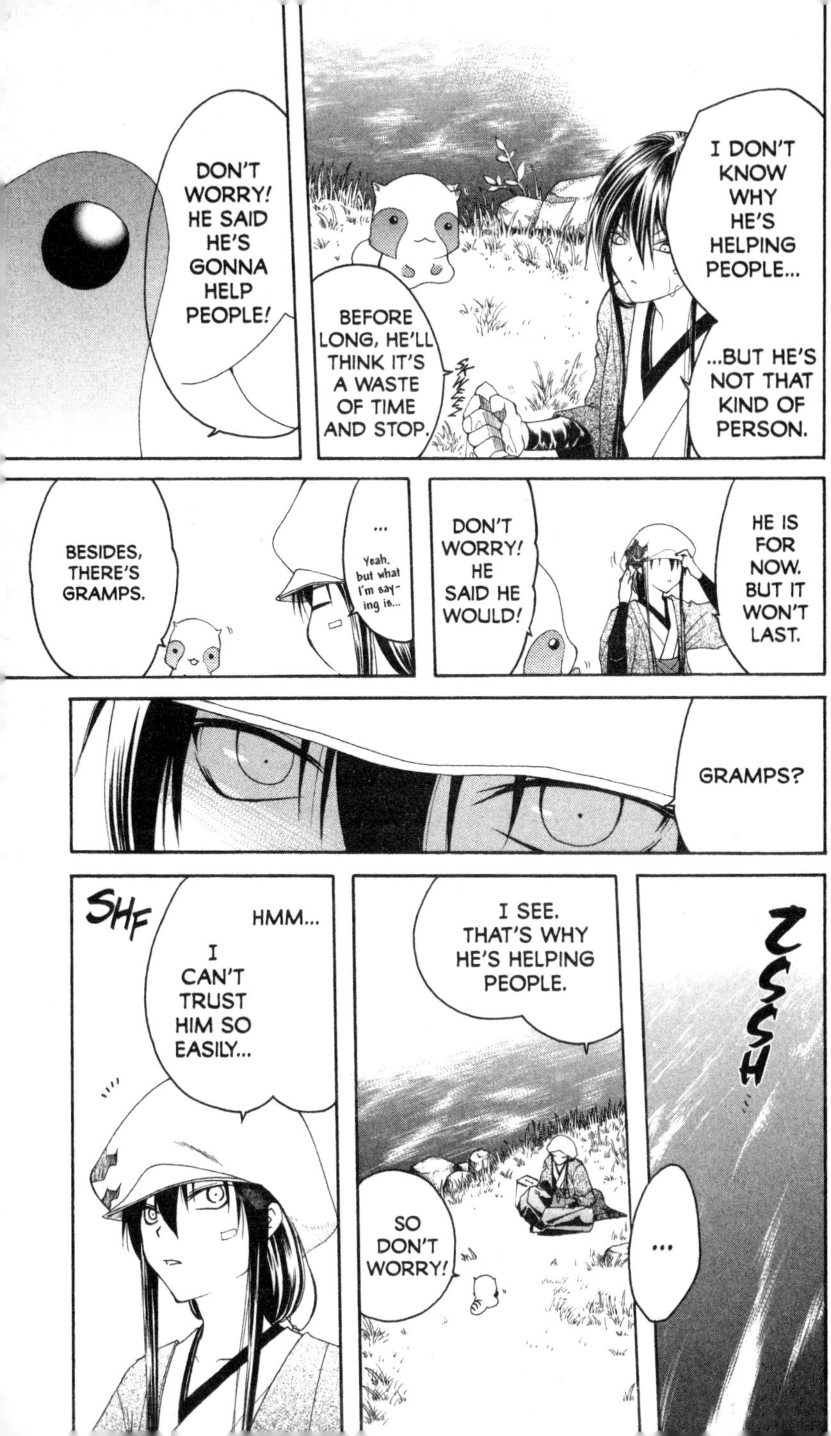
I DON'T KNOW WHY HE'S HELPING PEOPLE...
...BUT HE'S NOT THAT KIND OF PERSON.
BEFORE LONG, HE'LL THINK IT'S A WASTE OF TIME AND STOP.
DON'T WORRY! HE SAID HE'S GONNA HELP PEOPLE!
HE IS FOR NOW. BUT IT WON'T LAST.
DON'T WORRY! HE SAID HE WOULD!
...
Yeah, but what I'm saying is...
BESIDES, THERE'S GRAMPS.
GRAMPS?
ZSSSH
...
I SEE. THAT'S WHY HE'S HELPING PEOPLE.
SO DON'T WORRY!
SHF
HMM...
I CAN'T TRUST HIM SO EASILY...

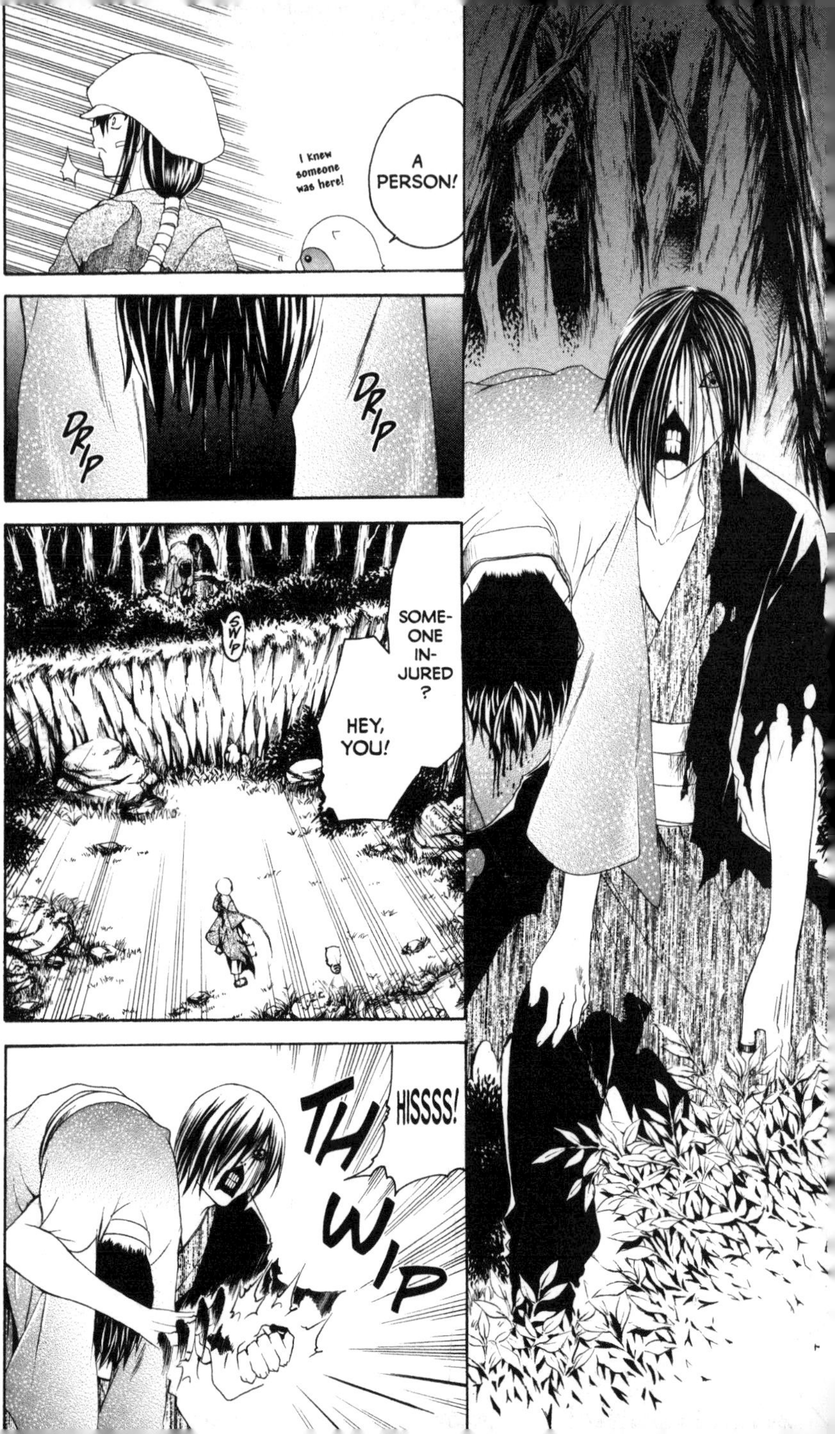
A PERSON!
I knew someone was here!
DRIP
DRIP
SOME-ONE IN-JURED?
HEY, YOU!
SWIP
HISSSS!
THWIP

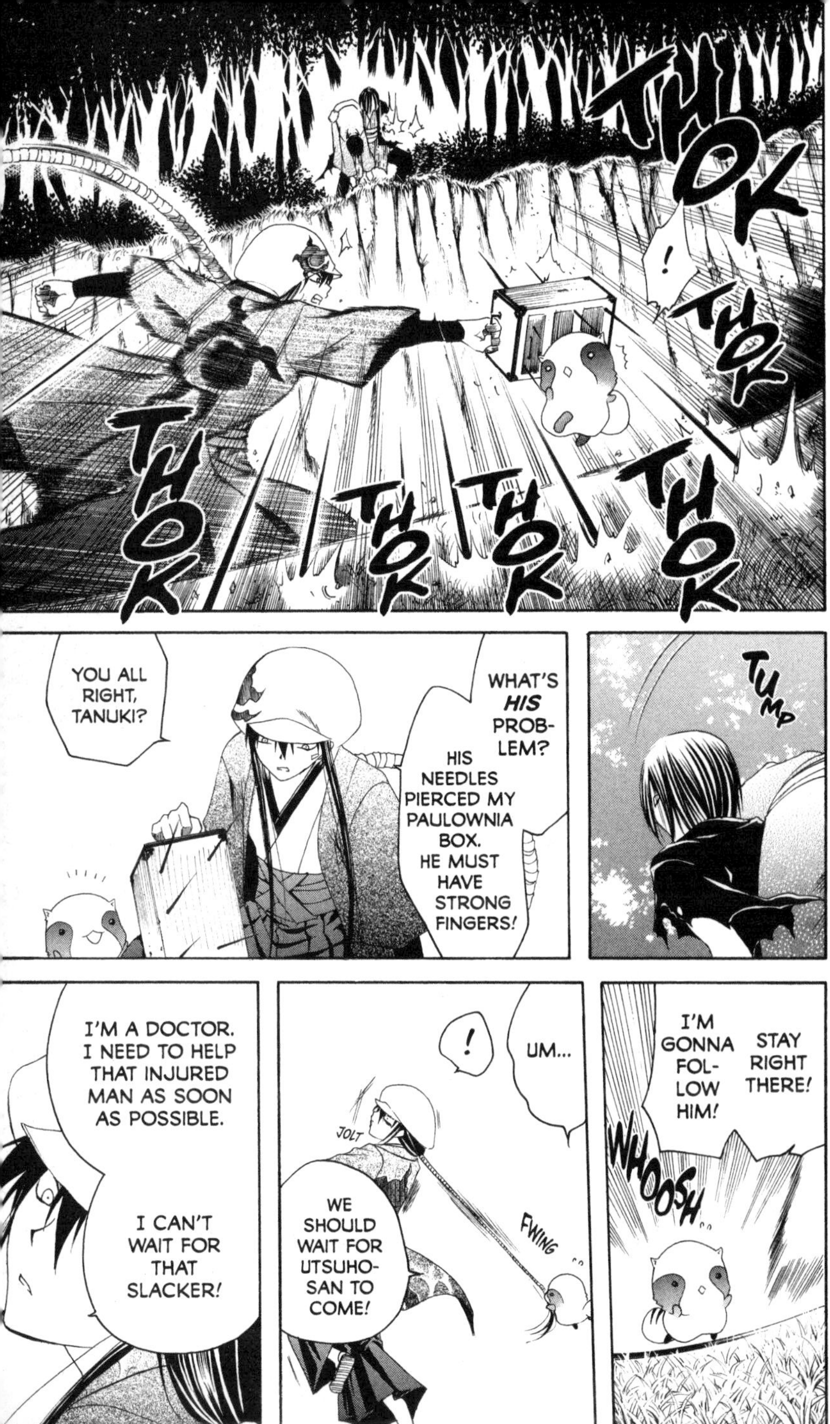
THOK
!
THOK
THOK
THOK
THOK
THOK
TUMP
WHAT'S *HIS* PROBLEM?
HIS NEEDLES PIERCED MY PAULOWNIA BOX. HE MUST HAVE STRONG FINGERS!
YOU ALL RIGHT, TANUKI?
STAY RIGHT THERE!
I'M GONNA FOLLOW HIM!
WHOOSH
UM...
!
JOLT
WE SHOULD WAIT FOR UTSUHO-SAN TO COME!
FWING
I'M A DOCTOR. I NEED TO HELP THAT INJURED MAN AS SOON AS POSSIBLE.
I CAN'T WAIT FOR THAT SLACKER!

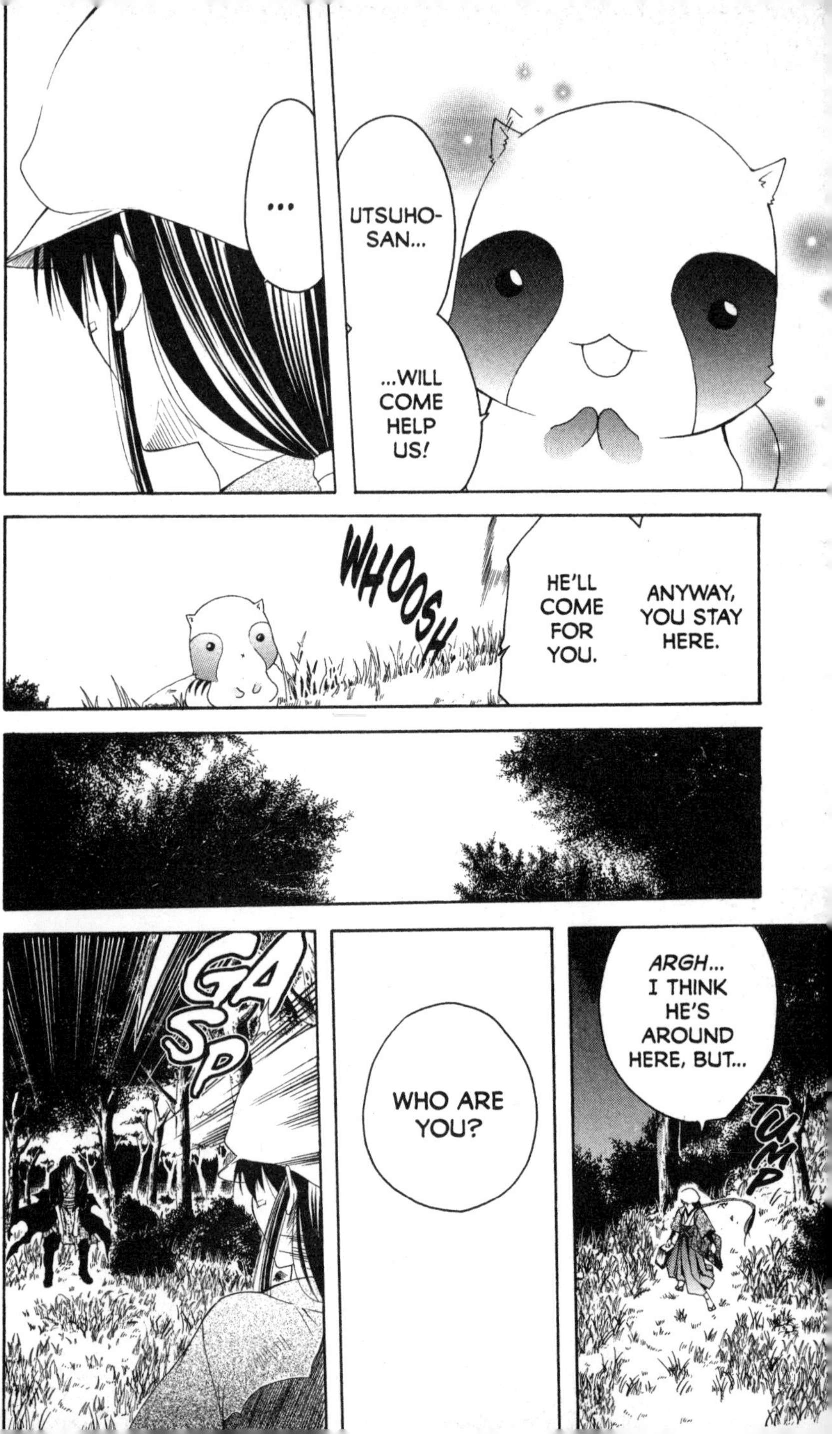
UTSUHO-SAN...
...WILL COME HELP US!
...
ANYWAY, YOU STAY HERE.
HE'LL COME FOR YOU.
WHOOSH
ARGH... I THINK HE'S AROUND HERE, BUT...
TUMP
WHO ARE YOU?
GASP

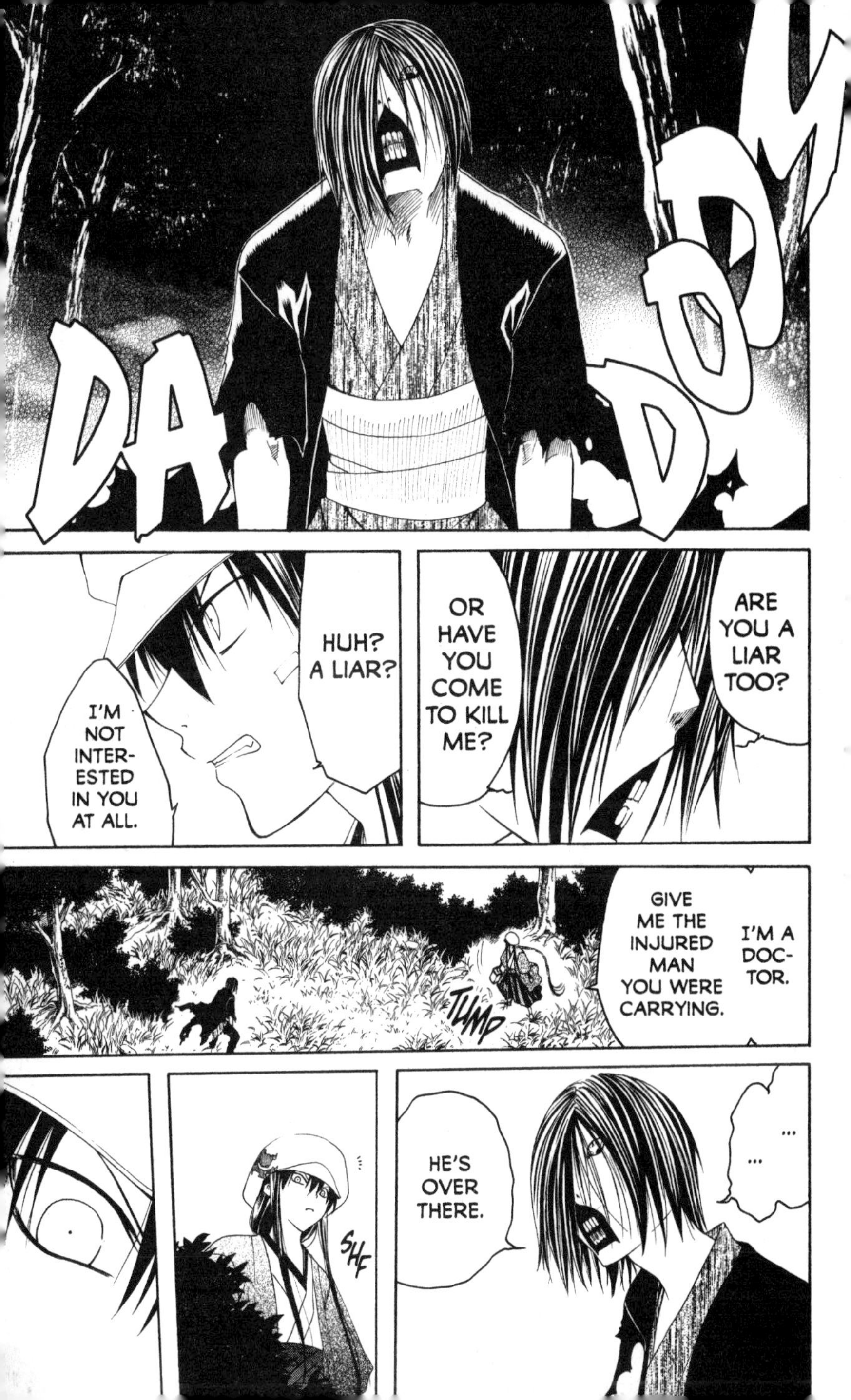
DA
ARE YOU A LIAR TOO?
OR HAVE YOU COME TO KILL ME?
HUH? A LIAR?
I'M NOT INTERESTED IN YOU AT ALL.
I'M A DOCTOR.
GIVE ME THE INJURED MAN YOU WERE CARRYING.
TUMP
...
...
HE'S OVER THERE.
SHF

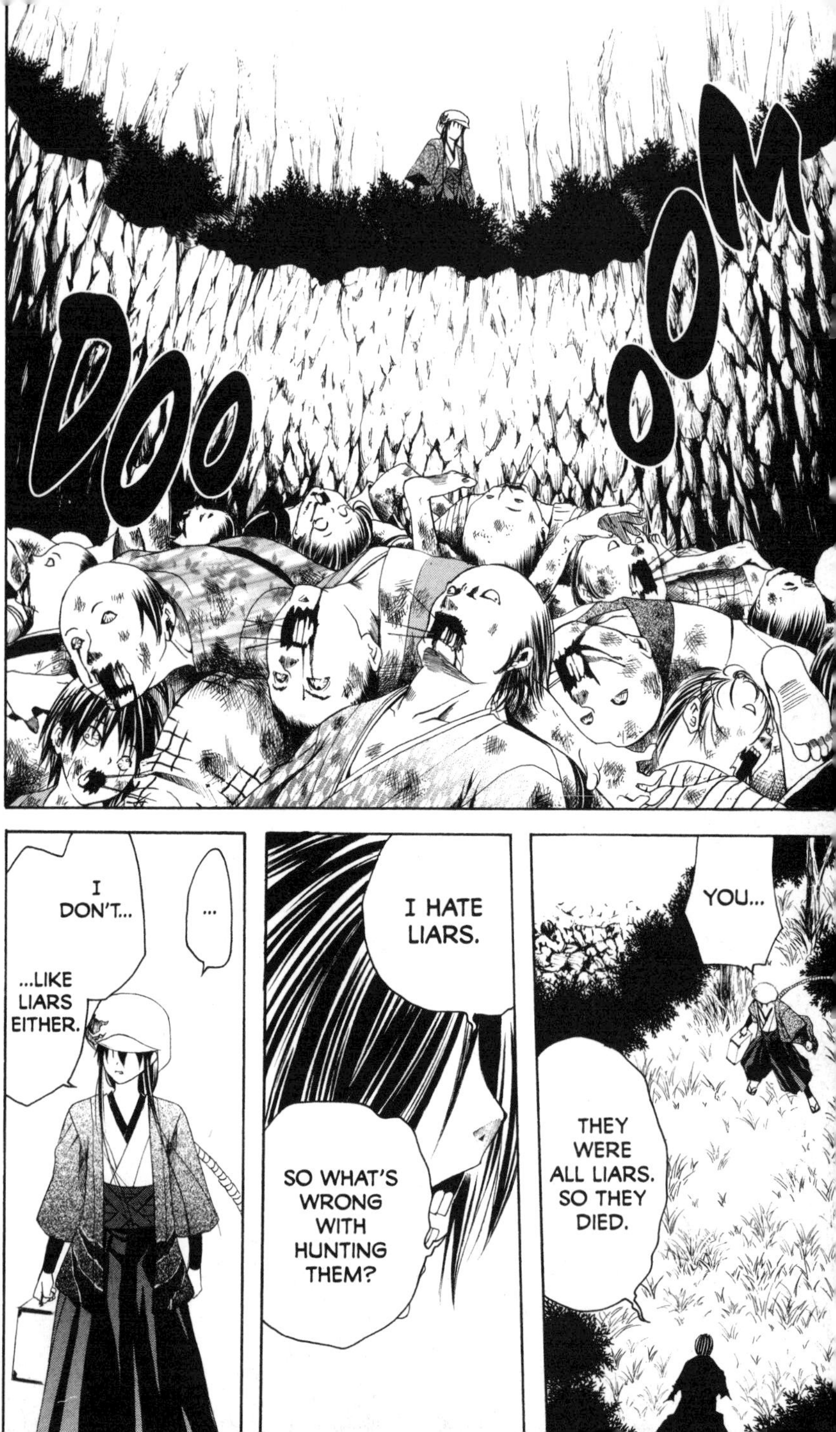
DOOOOOM
YOU...
THEY WERE ALL LIARS. SO THEY DIED.
I HATE LIARS.
SO WHAT'S WRONG WITH HUNTING THEM?
...
I DON'T...
...LIKE LIARS EITHER.

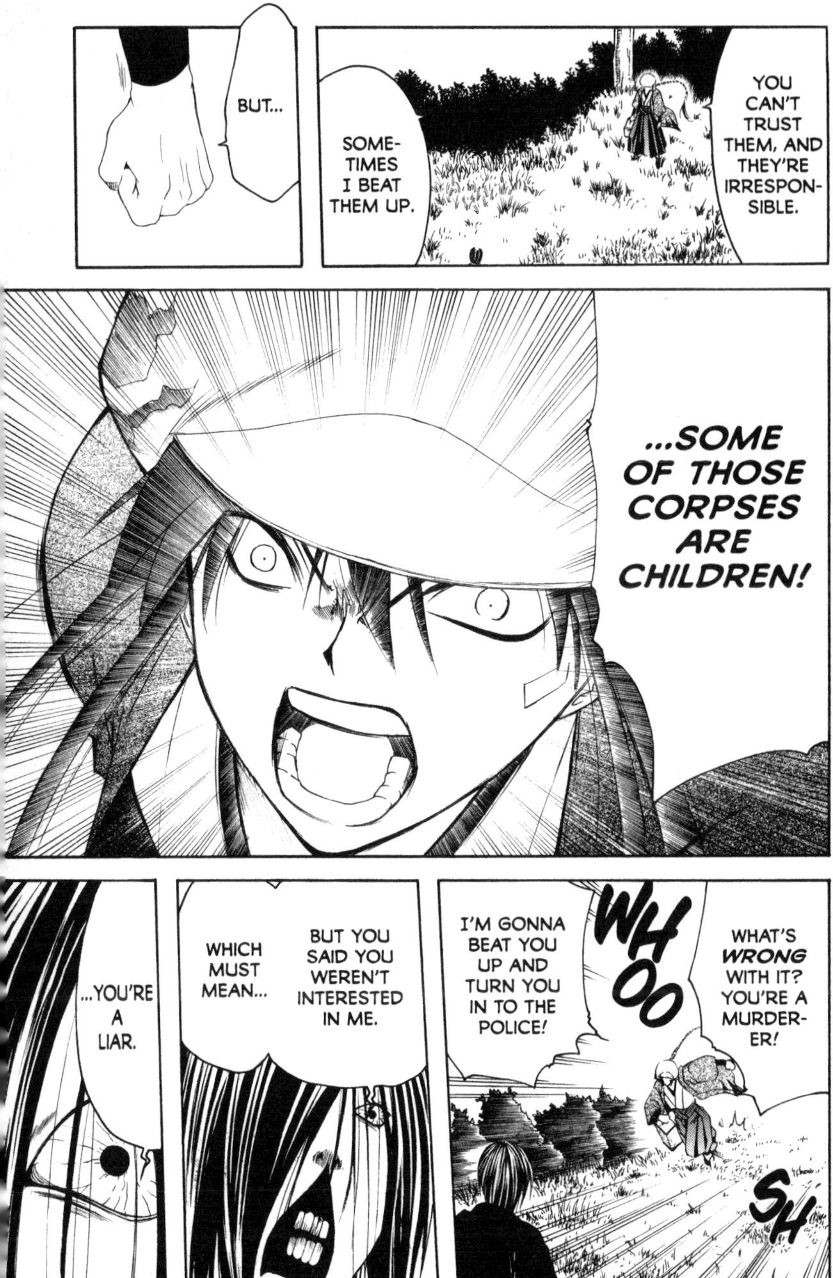
YOU CAN'T TRUST THEM, AND THEY'RE IRRESPON-SIBLE.
SOME-TIMES I BEAT THEM UP.
BUT...
...SOME OF THOSE CORPSES ARE CHILDREN!
WHAT'S WRONG WITH IT? YOU'RE A MURDER-ER!
WHOO
I'M GONNA BEAT YOU UP AND TURN YOU IN TO THE POLICE!
SH
BUT YOU SAID YOU WEREN'T INTERESTED IN ME.
WHICH MUST MEAN...
...YOU'RE A LIAR.

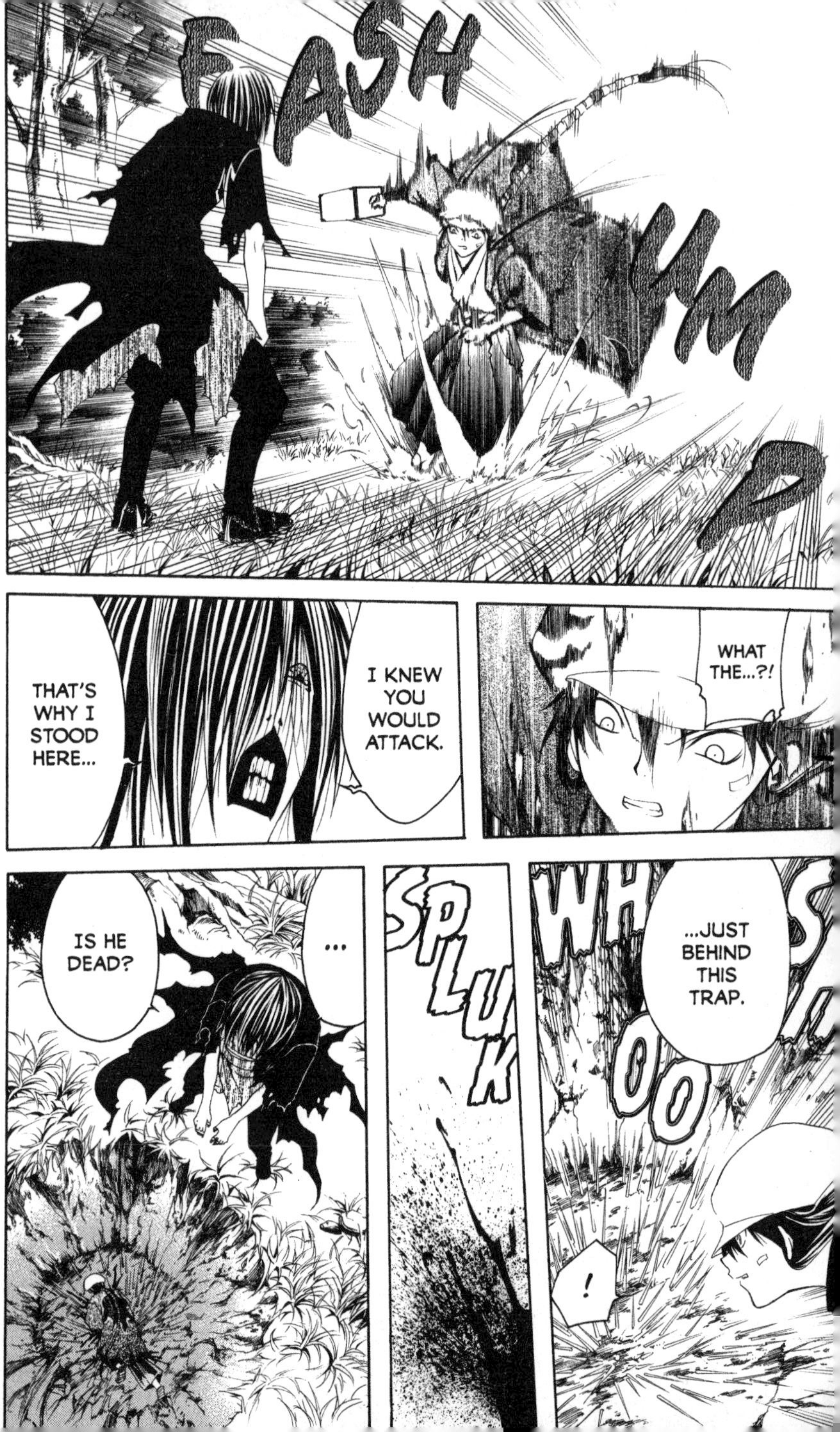
FASH
UMP
WHAT THE...?!
I KNEW YOU WOULD ATTACK.
THAT'S WHY I STOOD HERE...
...JUST BEHIND THIS TRAP.
!
SPLUK
...
IS HE DEAD?

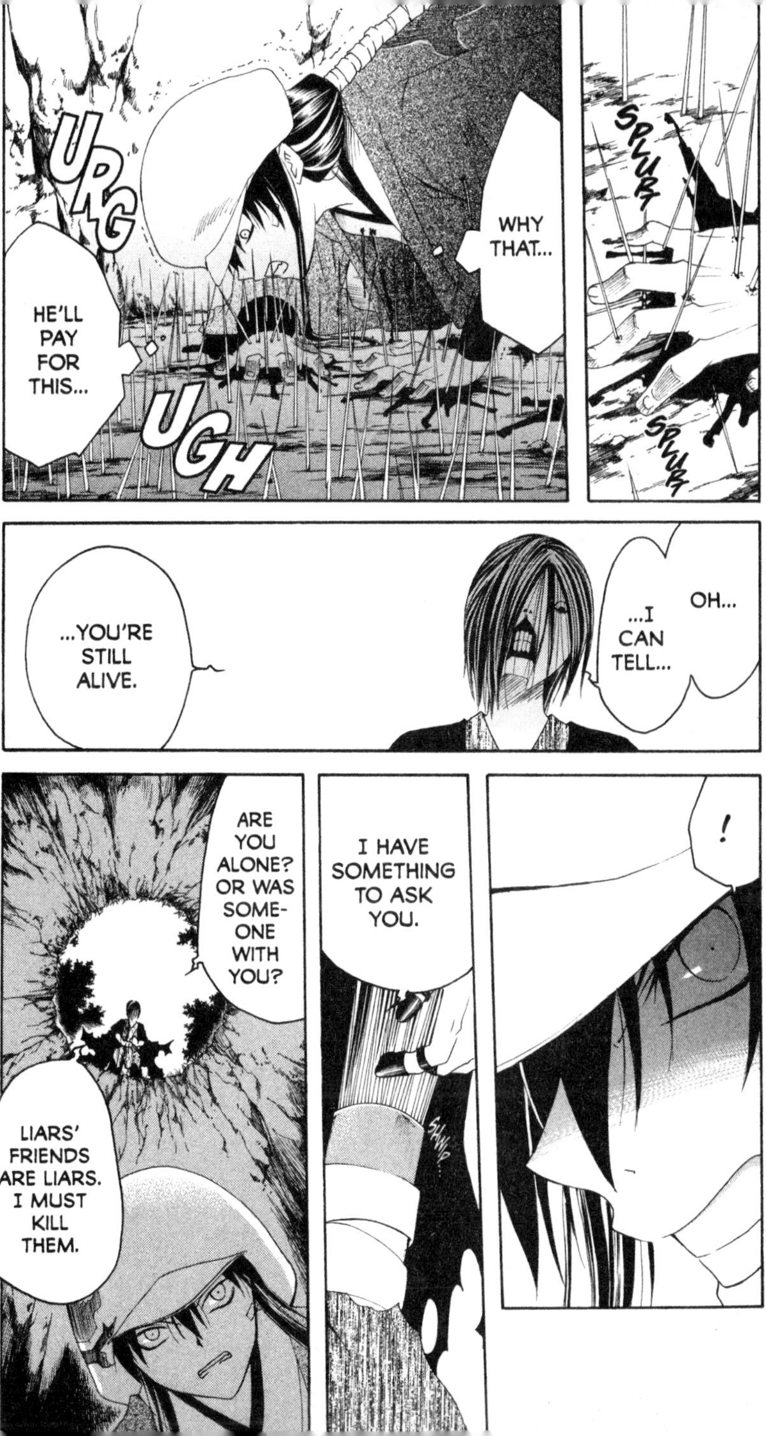
SPLURT
SPLURT
WHY THAT...
URG
HE'LL PAY FOR THIS...
UGH
OH...
...I CAN TELL...
...YOU'RE STILL ALIVE.
!
I HAVE SOMETHING TO ASK YOU.
SHWIP...
ARE YOU ALONE? OR WAS SOME-ONE WITH YOU?
LIARS' FRIENDS ARE LIARS. I MUST KILL THEM.

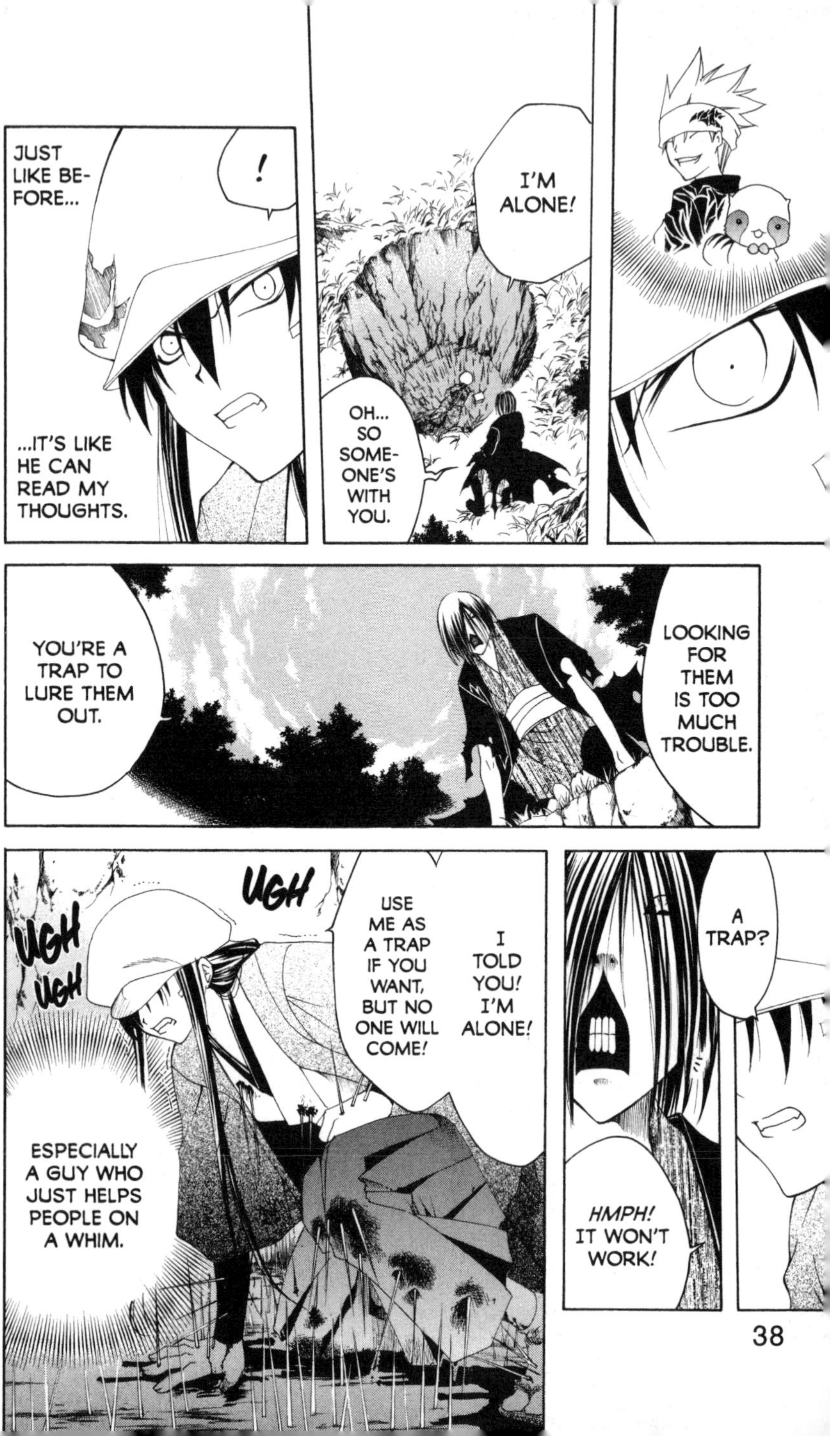
I'M ALONE!
OH... SO SOME-ONE'S WITH YOU.
!
JUST LIKE BE-FORE...
...IT'S LIKE HE CAN READ MY THOUGHTS.
LOOKING FOR THEM IS TOO MUCH TROUBLE.
YOU'RE A TRAP TO LURE THEM OUT.
A TRAP?
HMPH! IT WON'T WORK!
I TOLD YOU! I'M ALONE!
USE ME AS A TRAP IF YOU WANT, BUT NO ONE WILL COME!
UGH
UGH UGH
ESPECIALLY A GUY WHO JUST HELPS PEOPLE ON A WHIM.

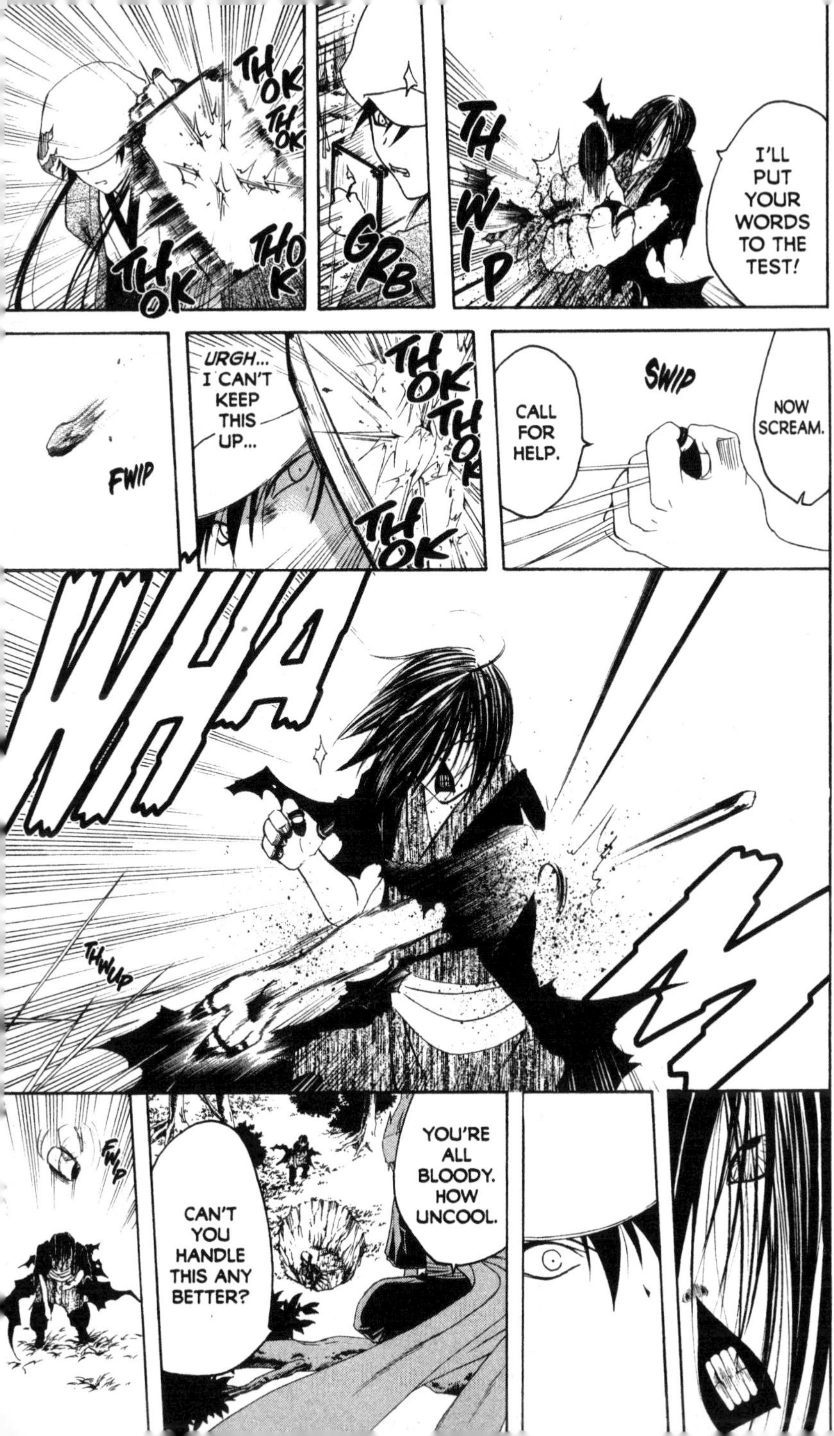
I'LL PUT YOUR WORDS TO THE TEST!
THWIP
GRB
THOK THOK
THOK
THOK
NOW SCREAM.
SWIP
CALL FOR HELP.
THOK THOK
THOK
URGH... I CAN'T KEEP THIS UP...
FWIP
WHAM
THWUP
YOU'RE ALL BLOODY. HOW UNCOOL.
CAN'T YOU HANDLE THIS ANY BETTER?
FWIP

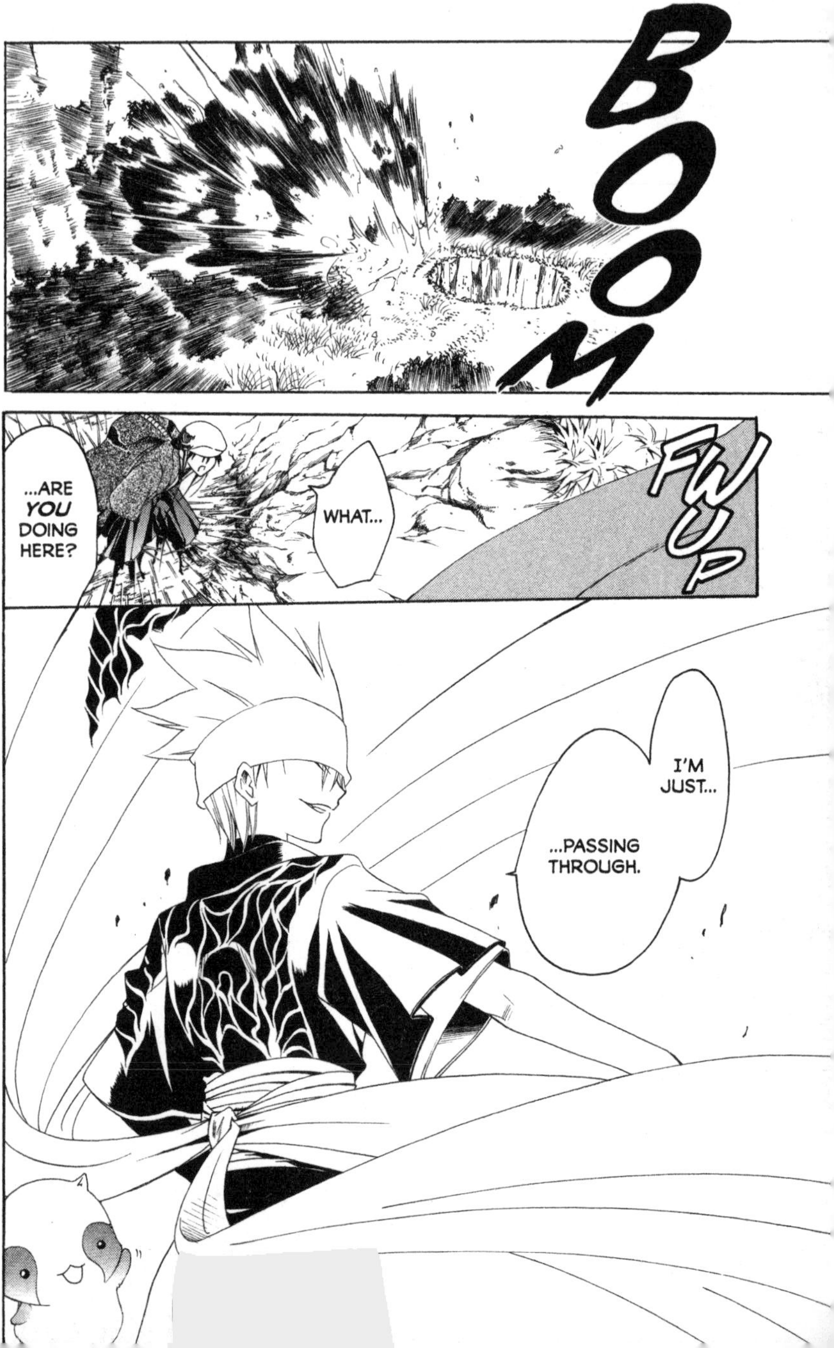
BOOM
FWUP
WHAT...
...ARE YOU DOING HERE?
I'M JUST...
...PASSING THROUGH.

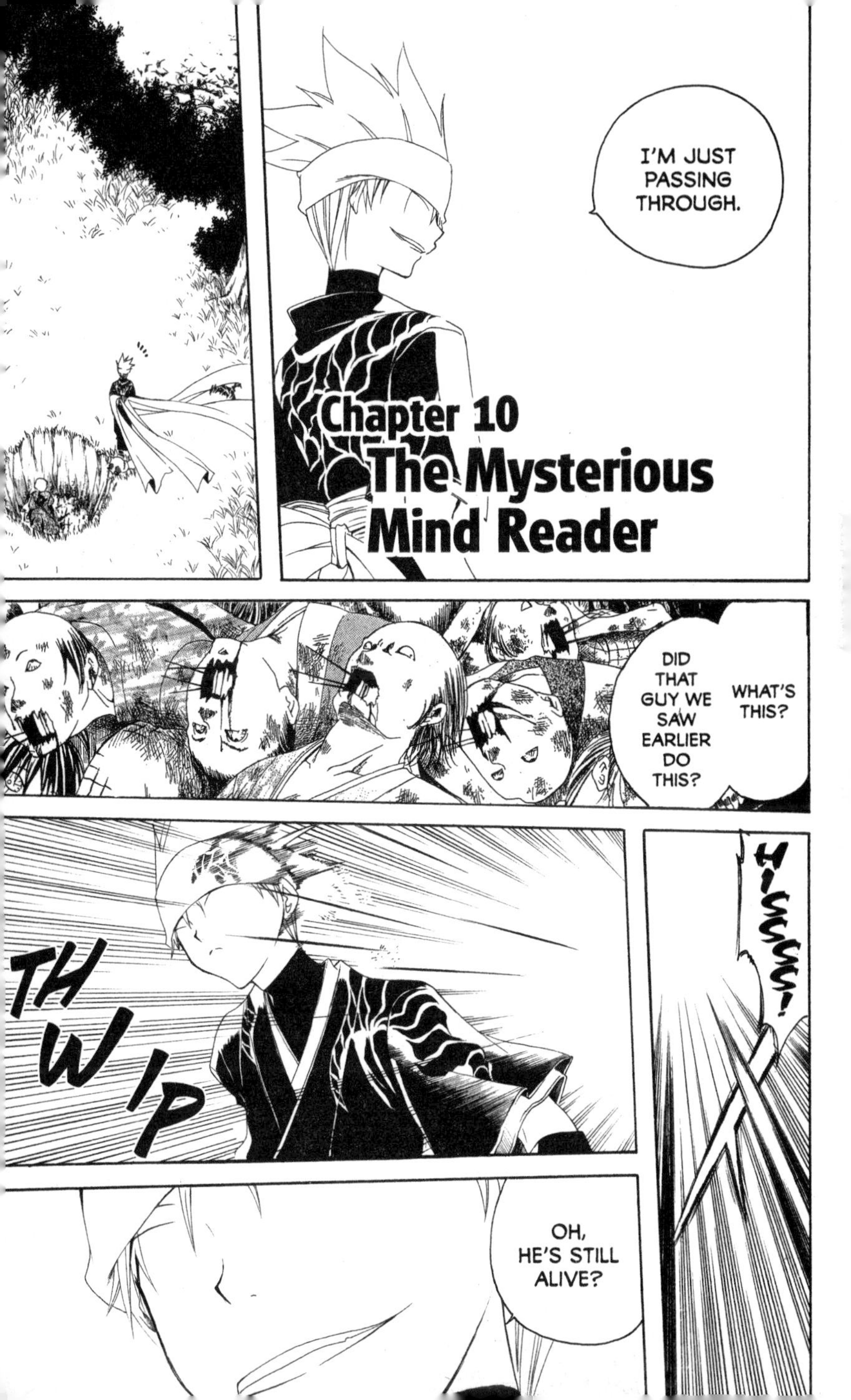
I'M JUST PASSING THROUGH.
Chapter 10
The Mysterious Mind Reader
WHAT'S THIS?
DID THAT GUY WE SAW EARLIER DO THIS?
HISSSSS!
THWIP
OH, HE'S STILL ALIVE?

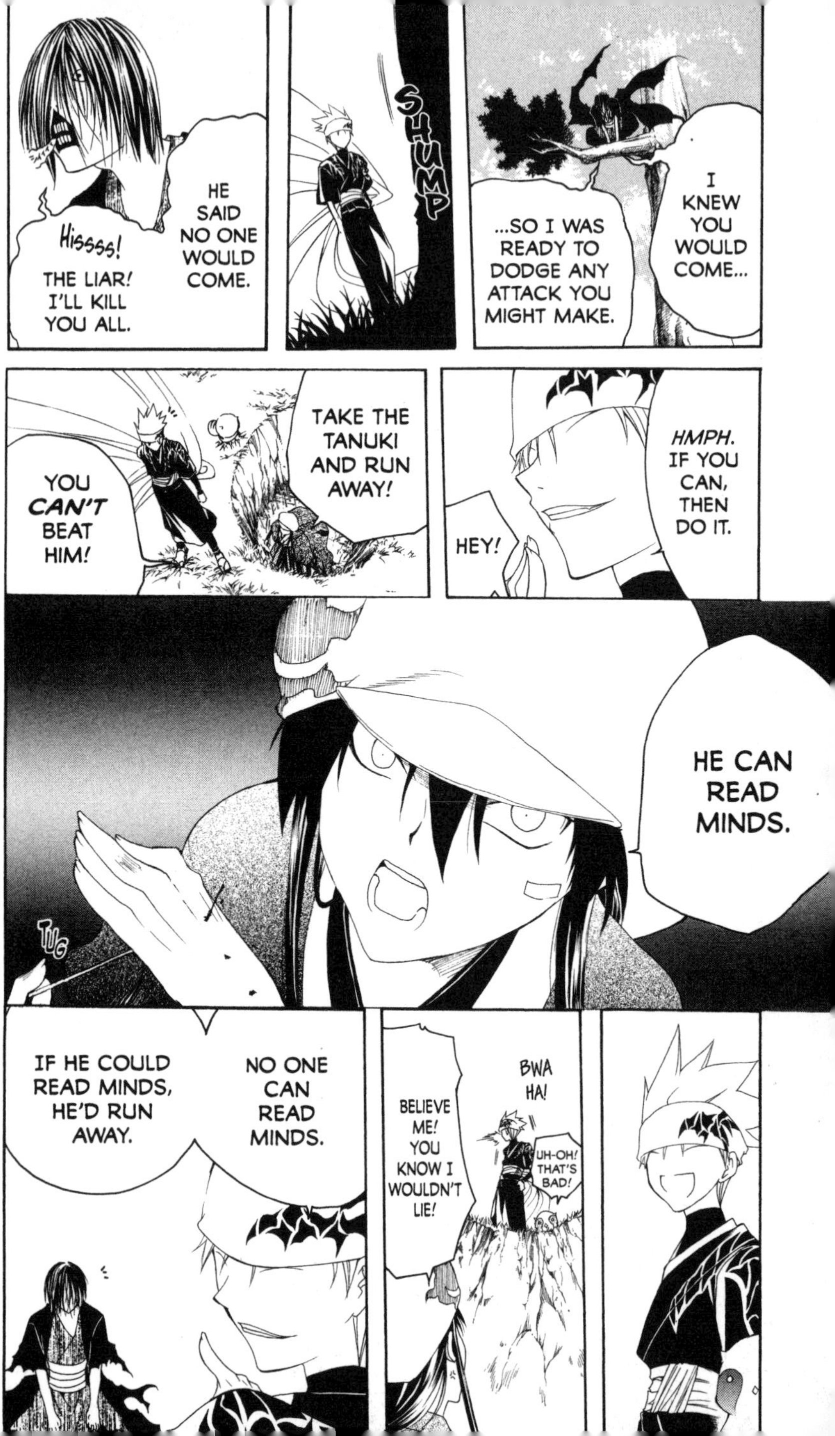
I KNEW YOU WOULD COME...
...SO I WAS READY TO DODGE ANY ATTACK YOU MIGHT MAKE.
SHUMP
HE SAID NO ONE WOULD COME.
Hissss!
THE LIAR! I'LL KILL YOU ALL.
HMPH. IF YOU CAN, THEN DO IT.
HEY!
TAKE THE TANUKI AND RUN AWAY!
YOU *CAN'T* BEAT HIM!
HE CAN READ MINDS.
TUG
BWA HA!
BELIEVE ME! YOU KNOW I WOULDN'T LIE!
UH-OH! THAT'S BAD!
NO ONE CAN READ MINDS.
IF HE COULD READ MINDS, HE'D RUN AWAY.

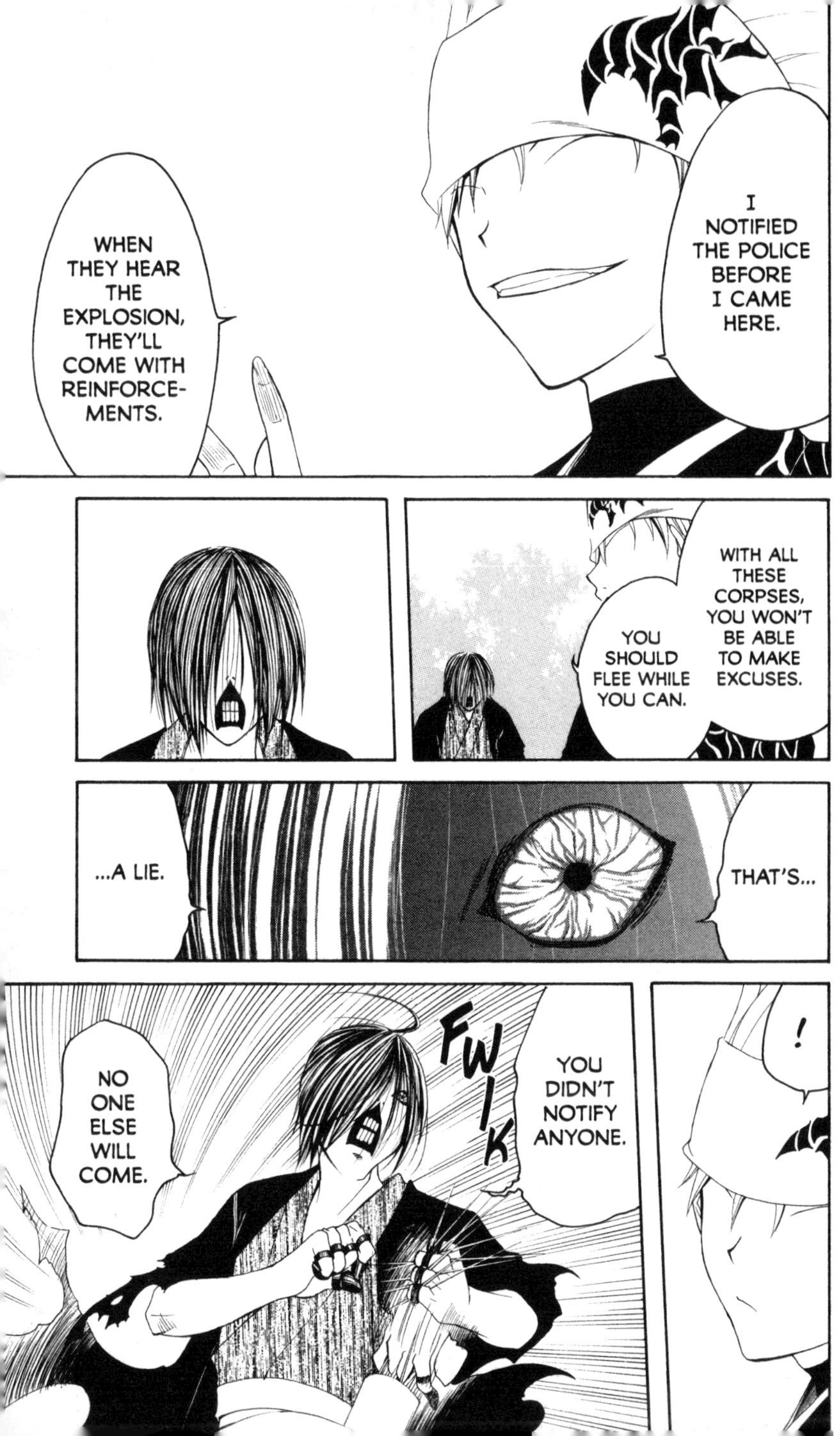
I NOTIFIED THE POLICE BEFORE I CAME HERE.
WHEN THEY HEAR THE EXPLOSION, THEY'LL COME WITH REINFORCE-MENTS.
WITH ALL THESE CORPSES, YOU WON'T BE ABLE TO MAKE EXCUSES.
YOU SHOULD FLEE WHILE YOU CAN.
THAT'S...
...A LIE.
!
YOU DIDN'T NOTIFY ANYONE.
FWIK
NO ONE ELSE WILL COME.

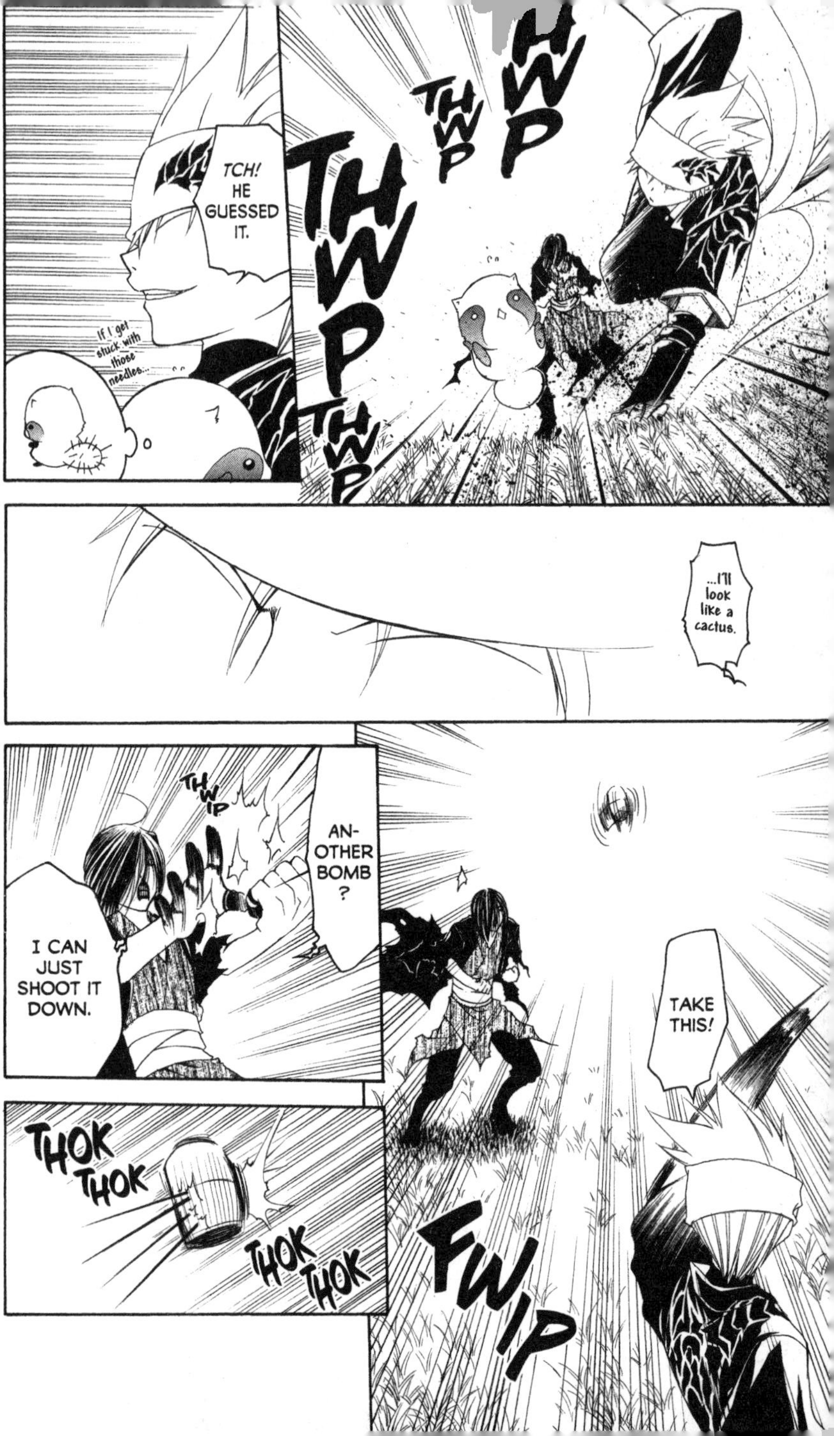
HWWP
THWP
THWP
THWP
TCH! HE GUESSED IT.
If I get stuck with those needles...
...I'll look like a cactus.
TAKE THIS!
FWIP
THWIP
AN-OTHER BOMB?
I CAN JUST SHOOT IT DOWN.
THOK THOK
THOK THOK

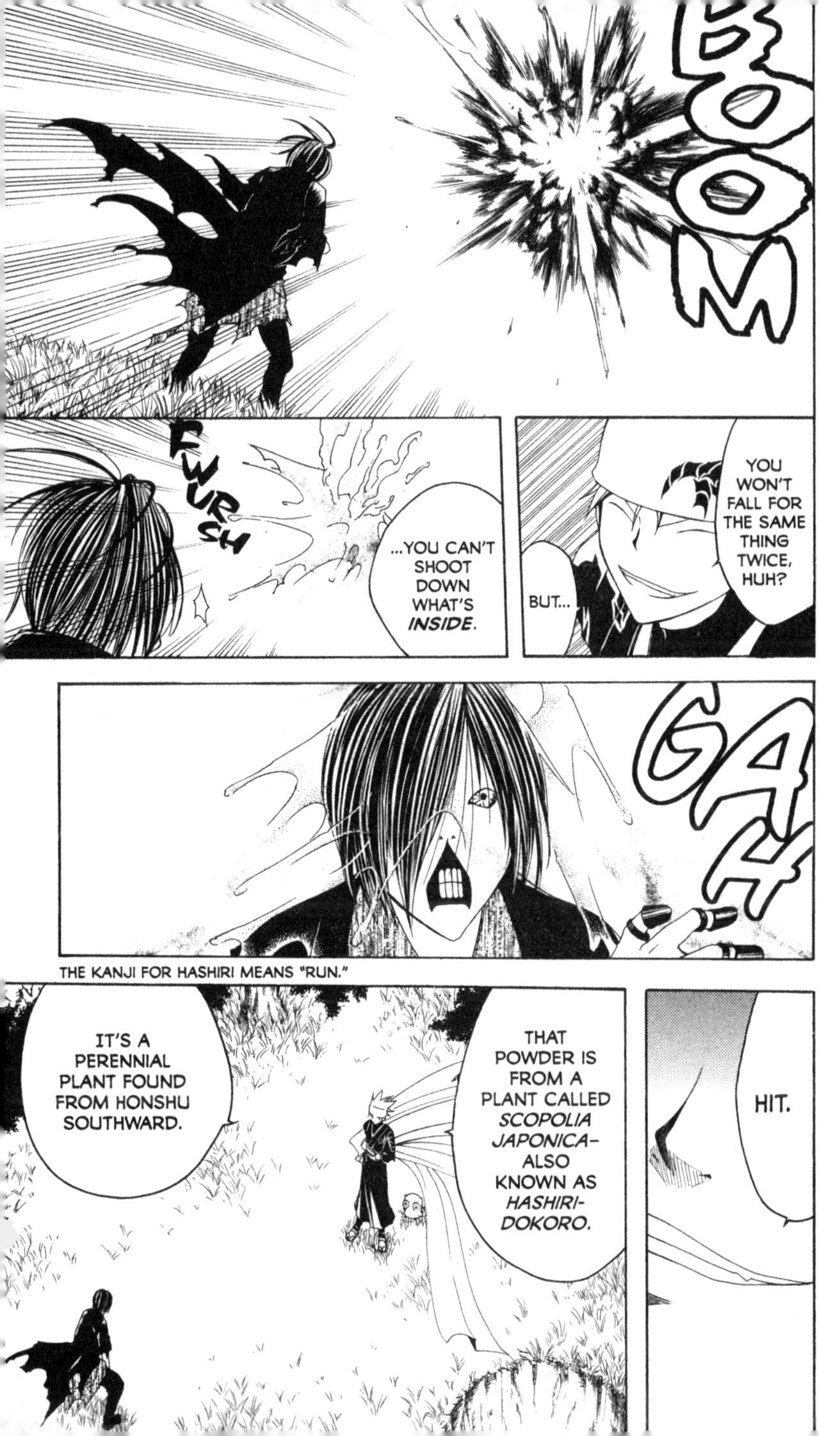
BOOM
YOU WON'T FALL FOR THE SAME THING TWICE, HUH?
BUT...
FWURSH
...YOU CAN'T SHOOT DOWN WHAT'S *INSIDE*.
GAAH
THE KANJI FOR HASHIRI MEANS "RUN."
HIT.
THAT POWDER IS FROM A PLANT CALLED *SCOPOLIA JAPONICA*—ALSO KNOWN AS *HASHIRI-DOKORO*.
IT'S A PERENNIAL PLANT FOUND FROM HONSHU SOUTHWARD.

SHAK SHAK SHAK

...

IT GOT ITS NAME BECAUSE...

...THOSE WHO INGEST IT GO CRAZY AND RUN AROUND LIKE MAD.

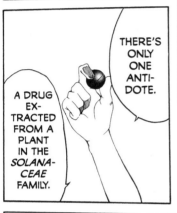

THERE'S ONLY ONE ANTIDOTE.

A DRUG EXTRACTED FROM A PLANT IN THE *SOLANACEAE* FAMILY.

TNK

BOL BOL

PICK IT UP.

FWIP

I'LL GIVE IT TO YOU.

SILENCE

...

TMP

THERE'S NO WAY HE CAN READ MINDS.

NOW I'LL PULL YAKUMA FROM THE PIT.

WHOOSH

...

MO

BO

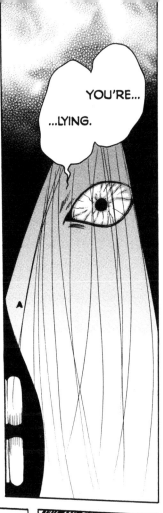

YOU'RE...

...LYING.

YOU'RE TRYING TO BLOW ME UP.

HEY!

HMM, YOU'RE RIGHT.

I *WAS* LYING.

YOU LIAR...

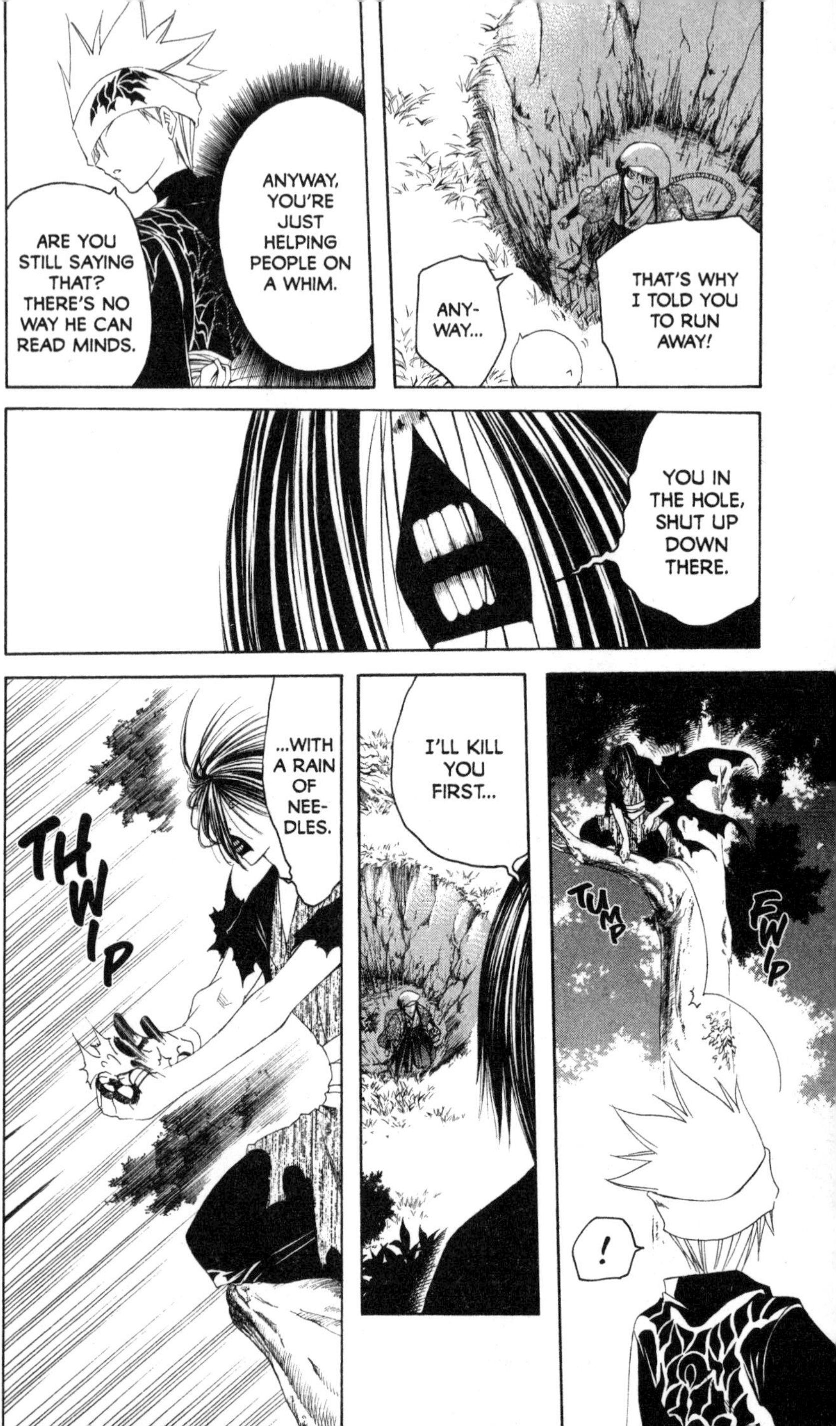
THAT'S WHY I TOLD YOU TO RUN AWAY!
ANY-WAY...
ANYWAY, YOU'RE JUST HELPING PEOPLE ON A WHIM.
ARE YOU STILL SAYING THAT? THERE'S NO WAY HE CAN READ MINDS.
YOU IN THE HOLE, SHUT UP DOWN THERE.
TUMP
FWIP
!
I'LL KILL YOU FIRST...
...WITH A RAIN OF NEE-DLES.
THWIP

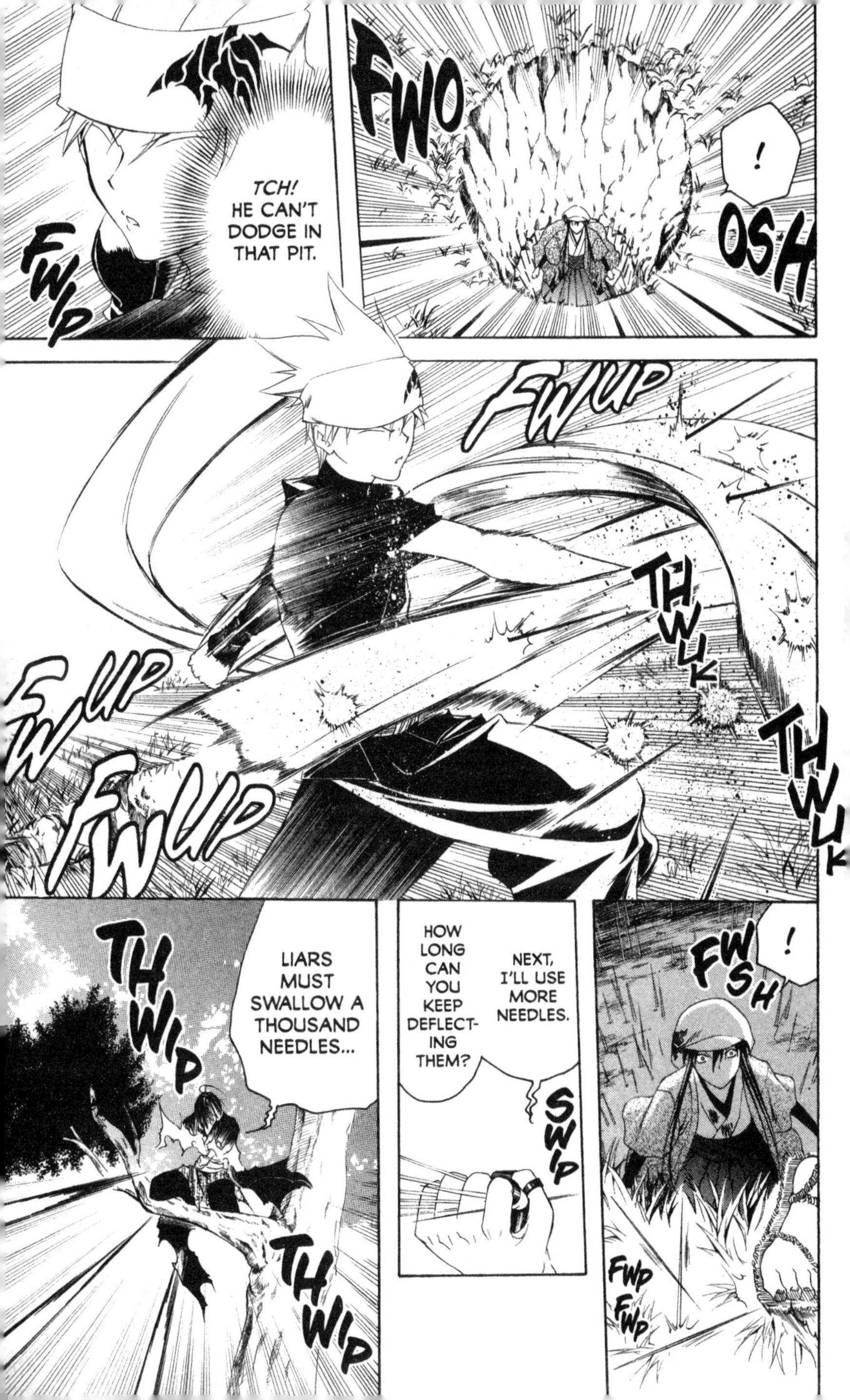
FWO
OSH
!
TCH! HE CAN'T DODGE IN THAT PIT.
FWIP
FWUP
THWUK
THWUK
FWUP
FWUP
!
FWSH
FWP
FWP
NEXT, I'LL USE MORE NEEDLES.
HOW LONG CAN YOU KEEP DEFLECTING THEM?
SWIP
LIARS MUST SWALLOW A THOUSAND NEEDLES...
THWIP
THWIP

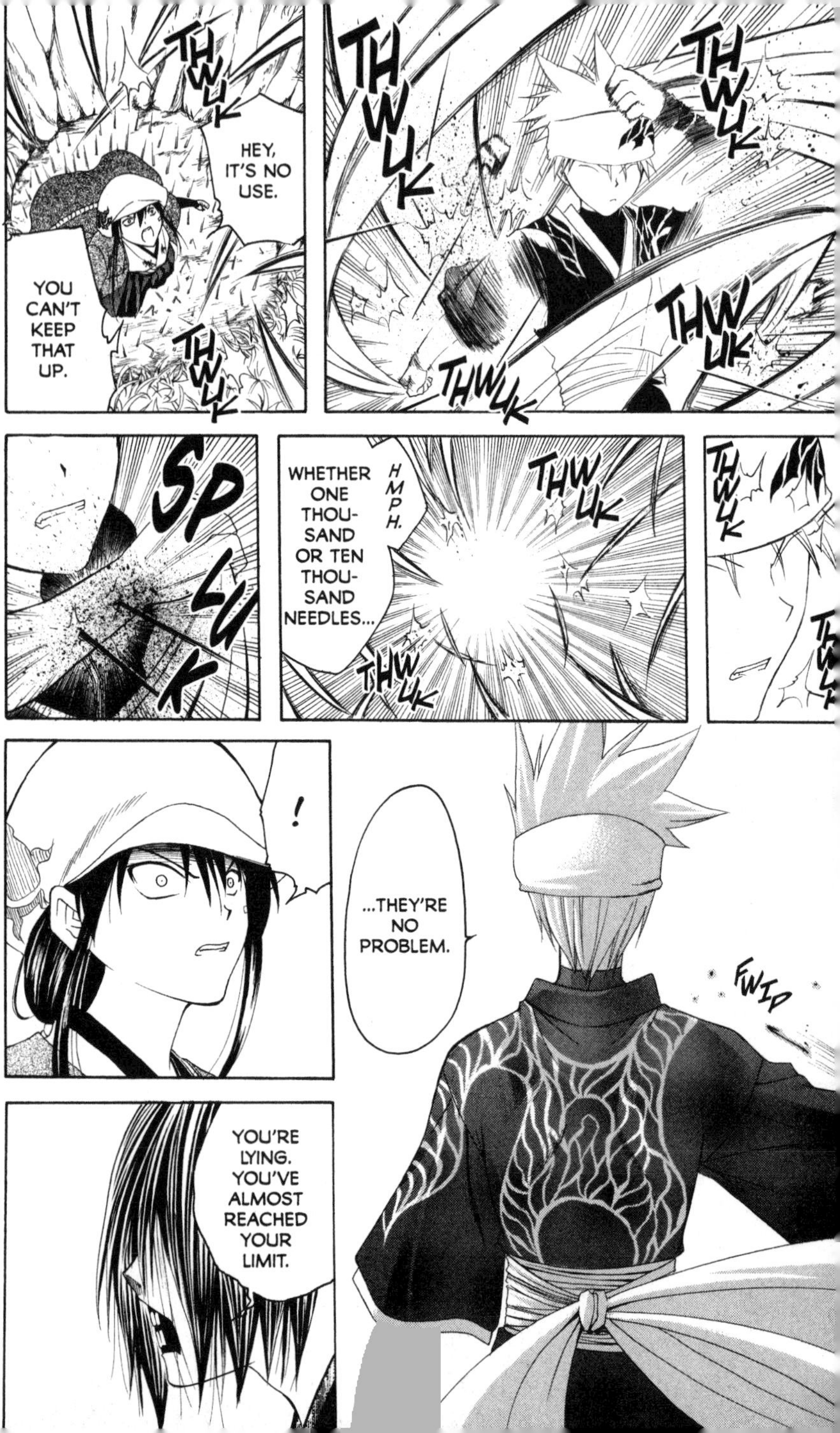
THWUK
THWUK
THWUK
THWUK
THWUK
HEY, IT'S NO USE.
YOU CAN'T KEEP THAT UP.
THWUK
THWUK
THWUK
THWUK
HMPH.
WHETHER ONE THOUSAND OR TEN THOUSAND NEEDLES...
THWUK
SPLUK
...THEY'RE NO PROBLEM.
FWIP
!
YOU'RE LYING. YOU'VE ALMOST REACHED YOUR LIMIT.

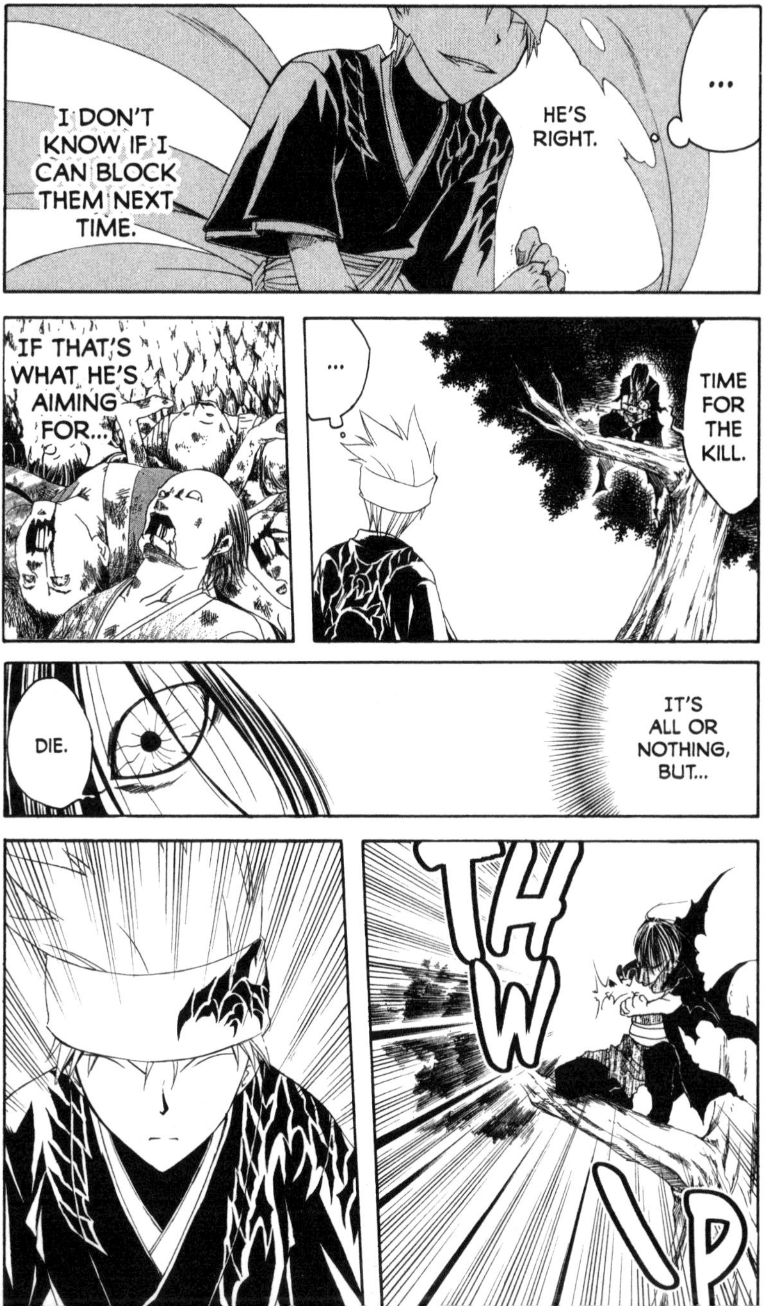
...
HE'S RIGHT.
I DON'T KNOW IF I CAN BLOCK THEM NEXT TIME.
TIME FOR THE KILL.
...
IF THAT'S WHAT HE'S AIMING FOR...
IT'S ALL OR NOTHING, BUT...
DIE.
THWIP

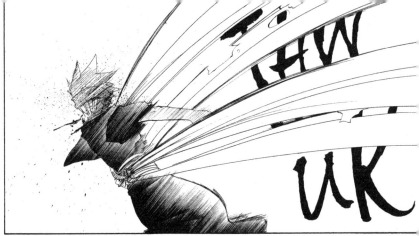

UTSU-
HO!

...

I...

MY
HAND
SLIPPED
...?

...

FWSH

TAKE
THAT...

STAGGER

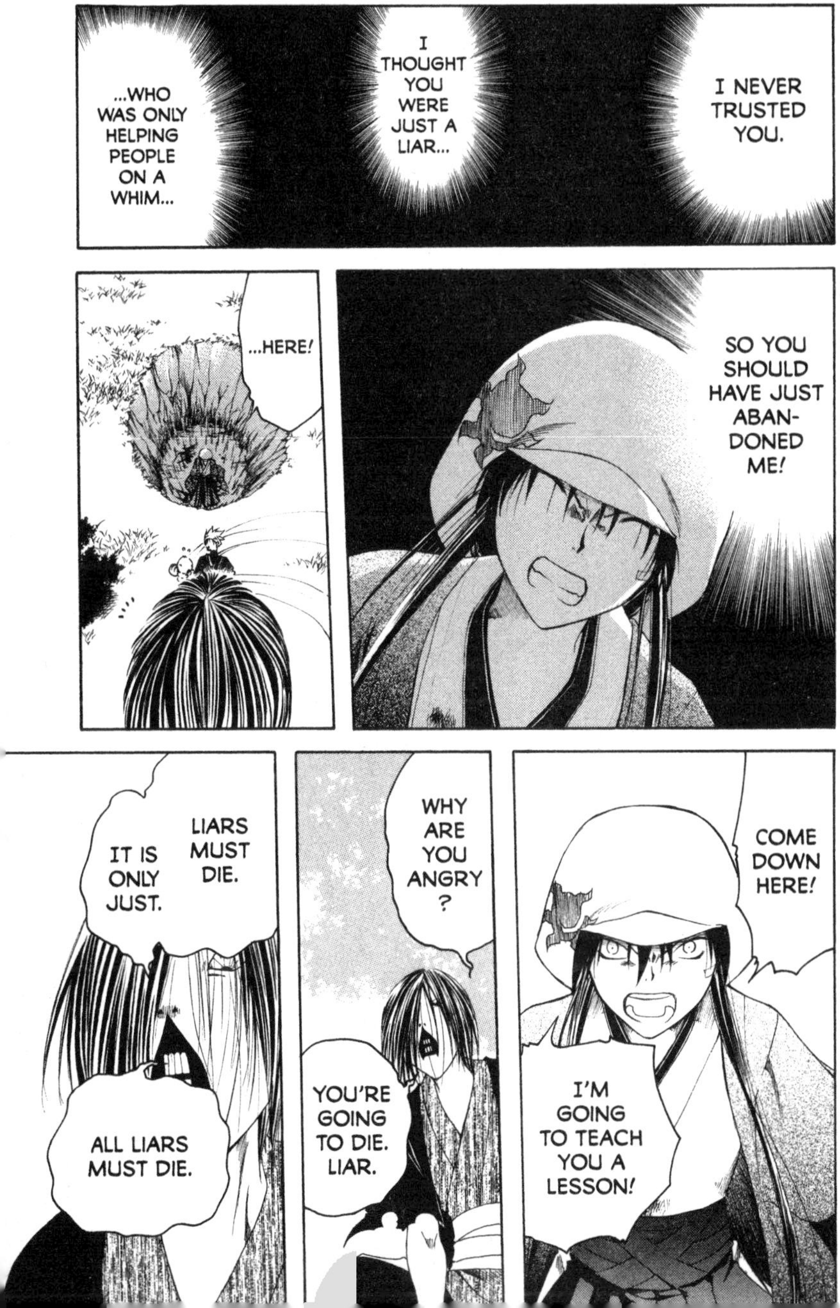
I NEVER TRUSTED YOU.
I THOUGHT YOU WERE JUST A LIAR...
...WHO WAS ONLY HELPING PEOPLE ON A WHIM...
SO YOU SHOULD HAVE JUST ABAN-DONED ME!
...HERE!
COME DOWN HERE!
I'M GOING TO TEACH YOU A LESSON!
WHY ARE YOU ANGRY?
YOU'RE GOING TO DIE. LIAR.
LIARS MUST DIE.
IT IS ONLY JUST.
ALL LIARS MUST DIE.

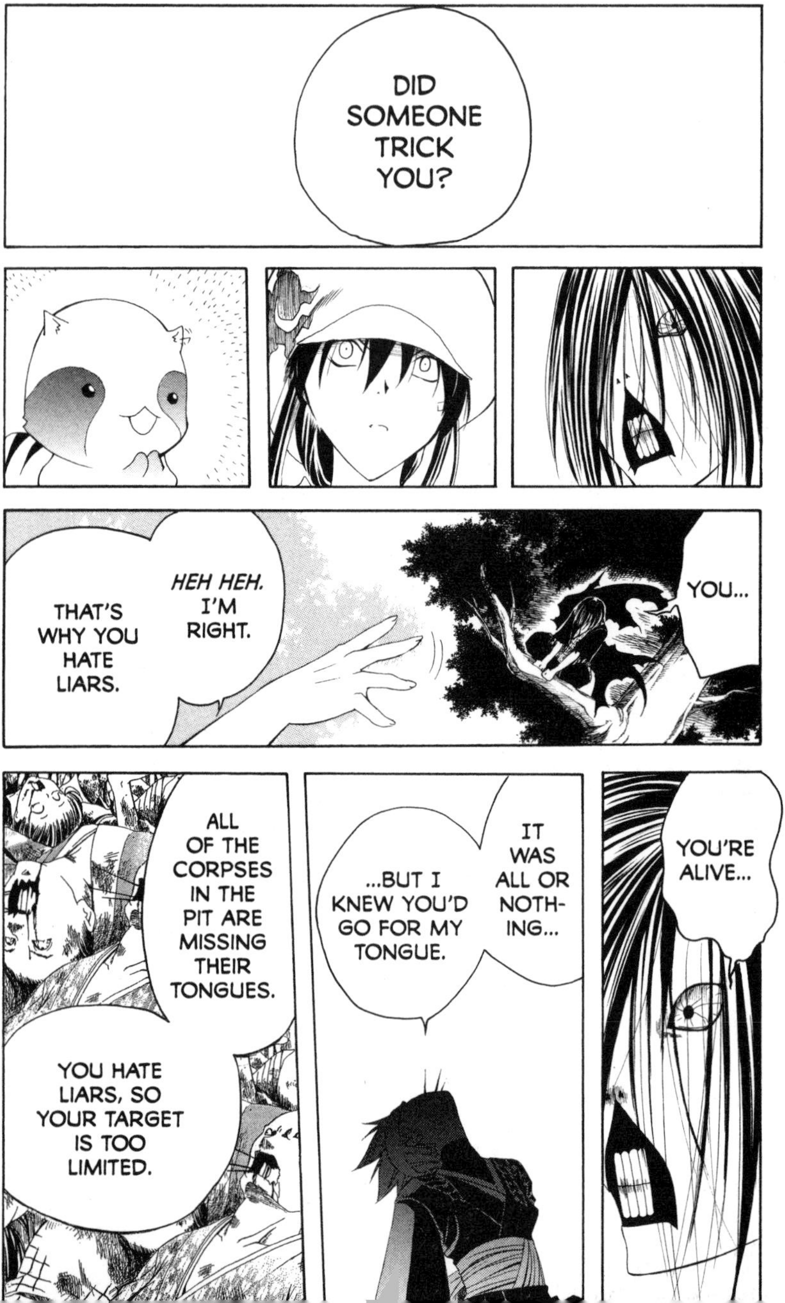
DID SOMEONE TRICK YOU?
YOU...
HEH HEH. I'M RIGHT.
THAT'S WHY YOU HATE LIARS.
YOU'RE ALIVE...
IT WAS ALL OR NOTH-ING...
...BUT I KNEW YOU'D GO FOR MY TONGUE.
ALL OF THE CORPSES IN THE PIT ARE MISSING THEIR TONGUES.
YOU HATE LIARS, SO YOUR TARGET IS TOO LIMITED.

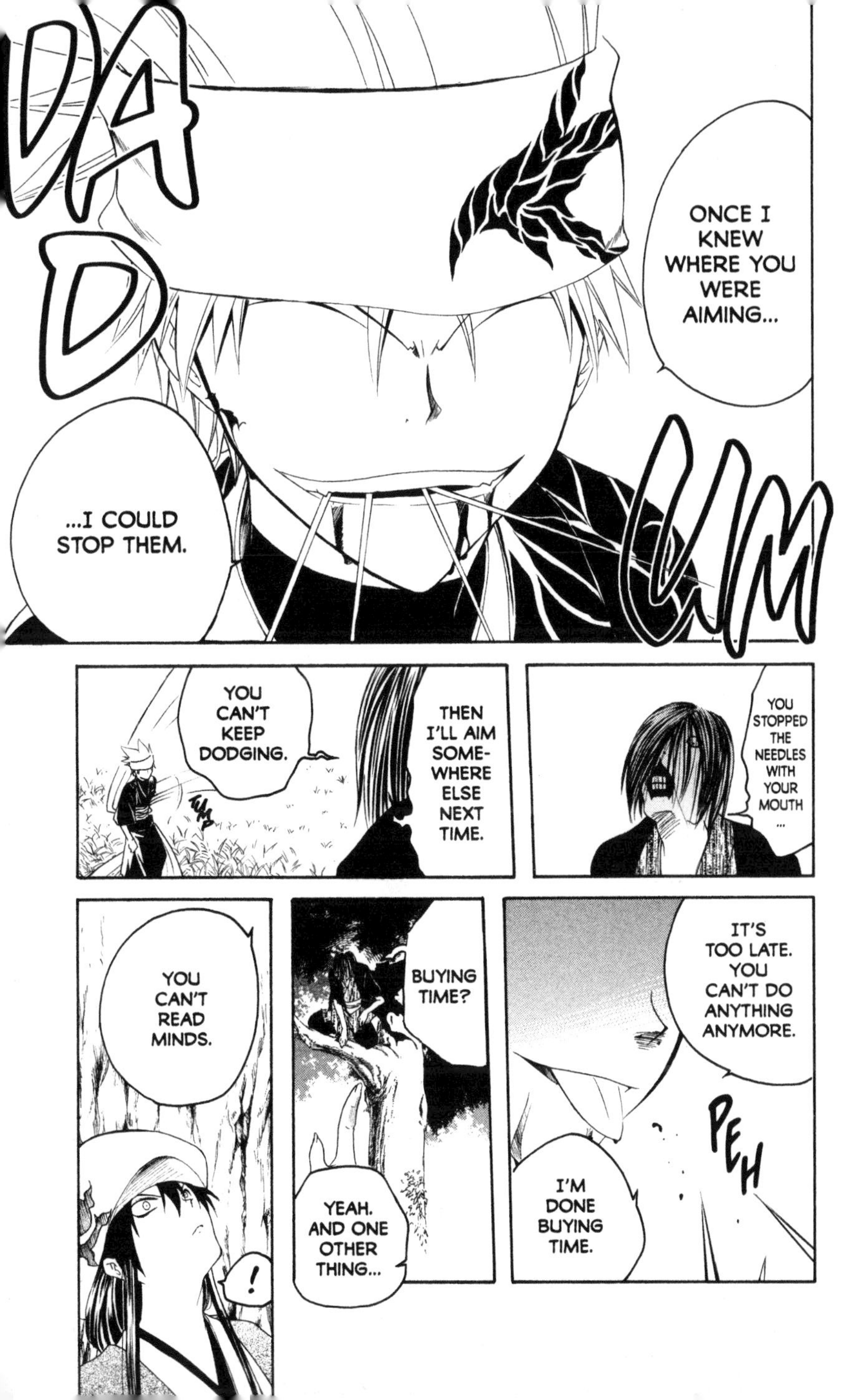
ONCE I KNEW WHERE YOU WERE AIMING...
...I COULD STOP THEM.
YOU STOPPED THE NEEDLES WITH YOUR MOUTH...
THEN I'LL AIM SOME-WHERE ELSE NEXT TIME.
YOU CAN'T KEEP DODGING.
IT'S TOO LATE. YOU CAN'T DO ANYTHING ANYMORE.
PEH
I'M DONE BUYING TIME.
BUYING TIME?
YEAH. AND ONE OTHER THING...
YOU CAN'T READ MINDS.
!

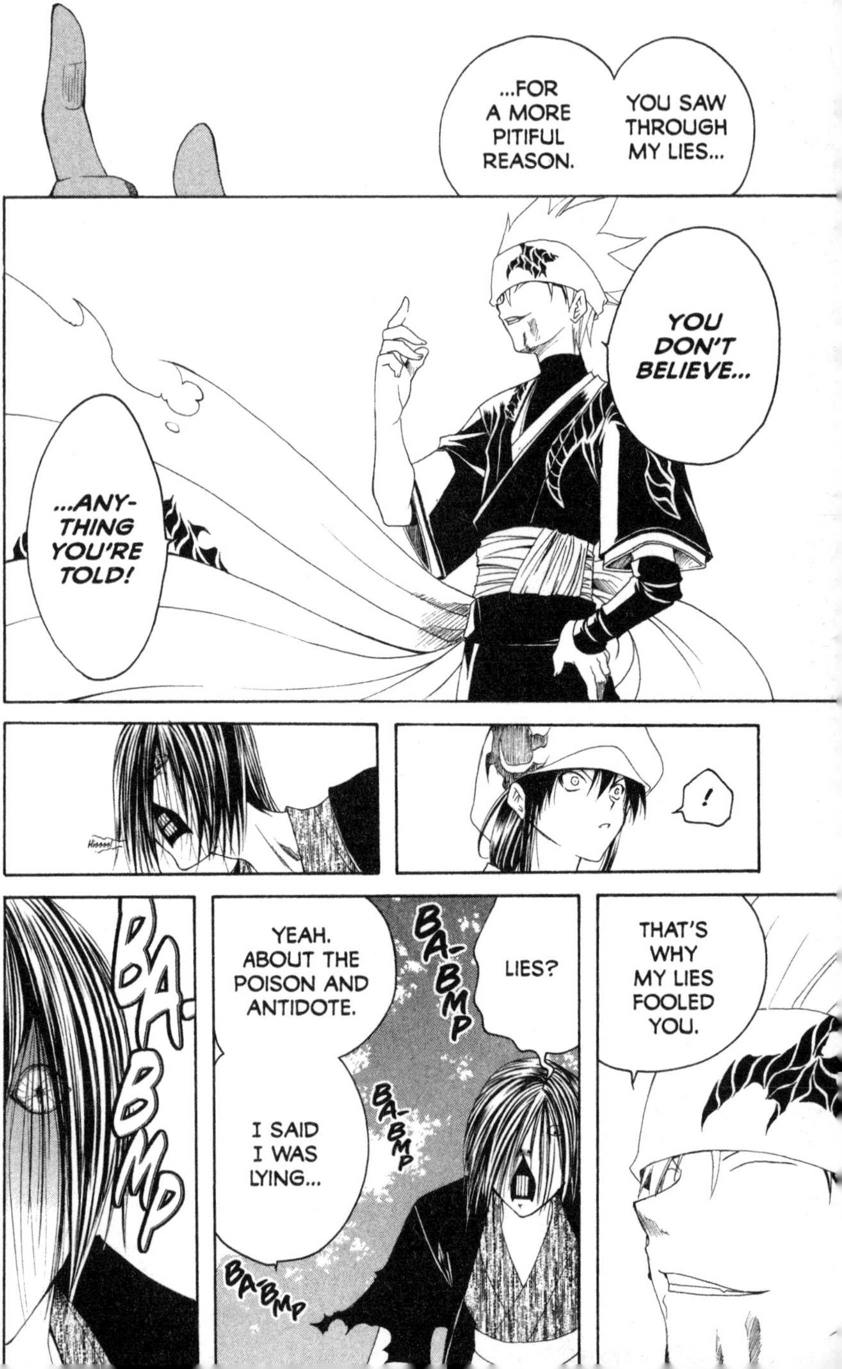
YOU SAW THROUGH MY LIES...
...FOR A MORE PITIFUL REASON.
YOU DON'T BELIEVE...
...ANY-THING YOU'RE TOLD!
!
THAT'S WHY MY LIES FOOLED YOU.
LIES?
BA-BMP
YEAH. ABOUT THE POISON AND ANTIDOTE.
BA-BMP
I SAID I WAS LYING...
BA-BMP
BA-BMP

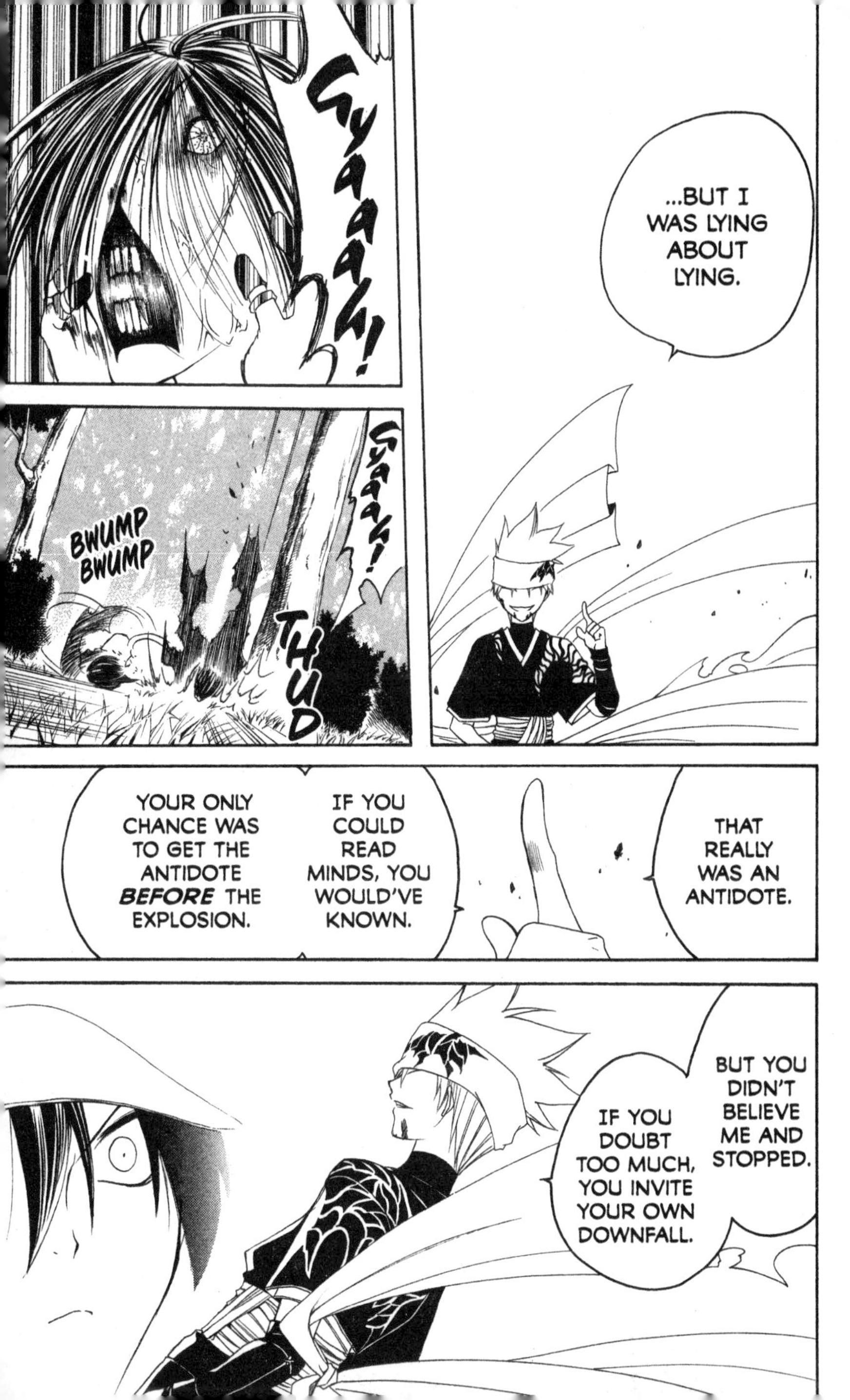
...BUT I WAS LYING ABOUT LYING.
GYAAAAAH!
GYAAAAH!
BWUMP BWUMP
THUD
THAT REALLY WAS AN ANTIDOTE.
IF YOU COULD READ MINDS, YOU WOULD'VE KNOWN.
YOUR ONLY CHANCE WAS TO GET THE ANTIDOTE *BEFORE* THE EXPLOSION.
BUT YOU DIDN'T BELIEVE ME AND STOPPED.
IF YOU DOUBT TOO MUCH, YOU INVITE YOUR OWN DOWNFALL.

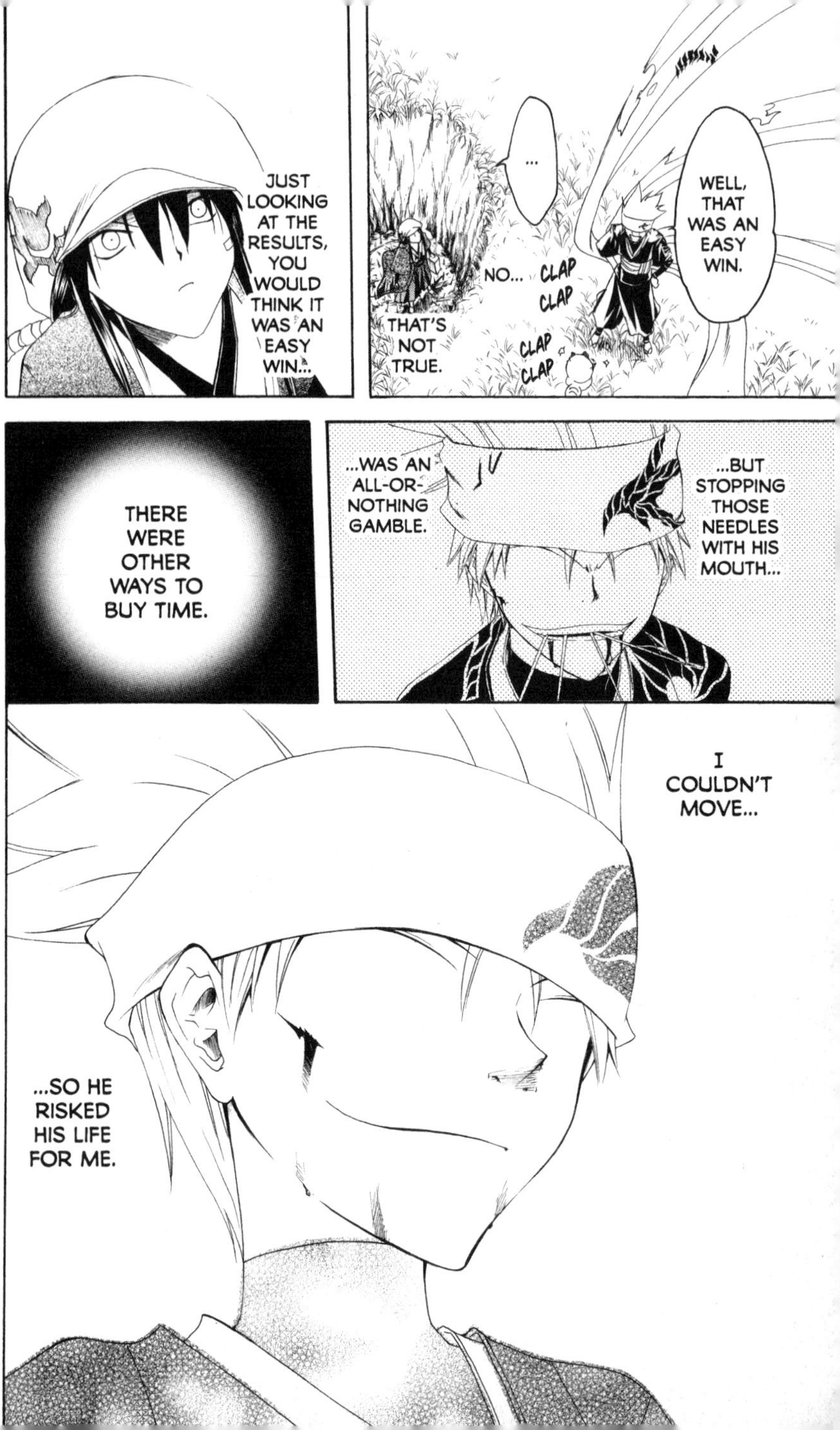
WELL, THAT WAS AN EASY WIN.
...
CLAP CLAP
NO... THAT'S NOT TRUE.
CLAP CLAP
JUST LOOKING AT THE RESULTS, YOU WOULD THINK IT WAS AN EASY WIN...
...BUT STOPPING THOSE NEEDLES WITH HIS MOUTH...
...WAS AN ALL-OR-NOTHING GAMBLE.
THERE WERE OTHER WAYS TO BUY TIME.
I COULDN'T MOVE...
...SO HE RISKED HIS LIFE FOR ME.

Chapter 11 If You Believe

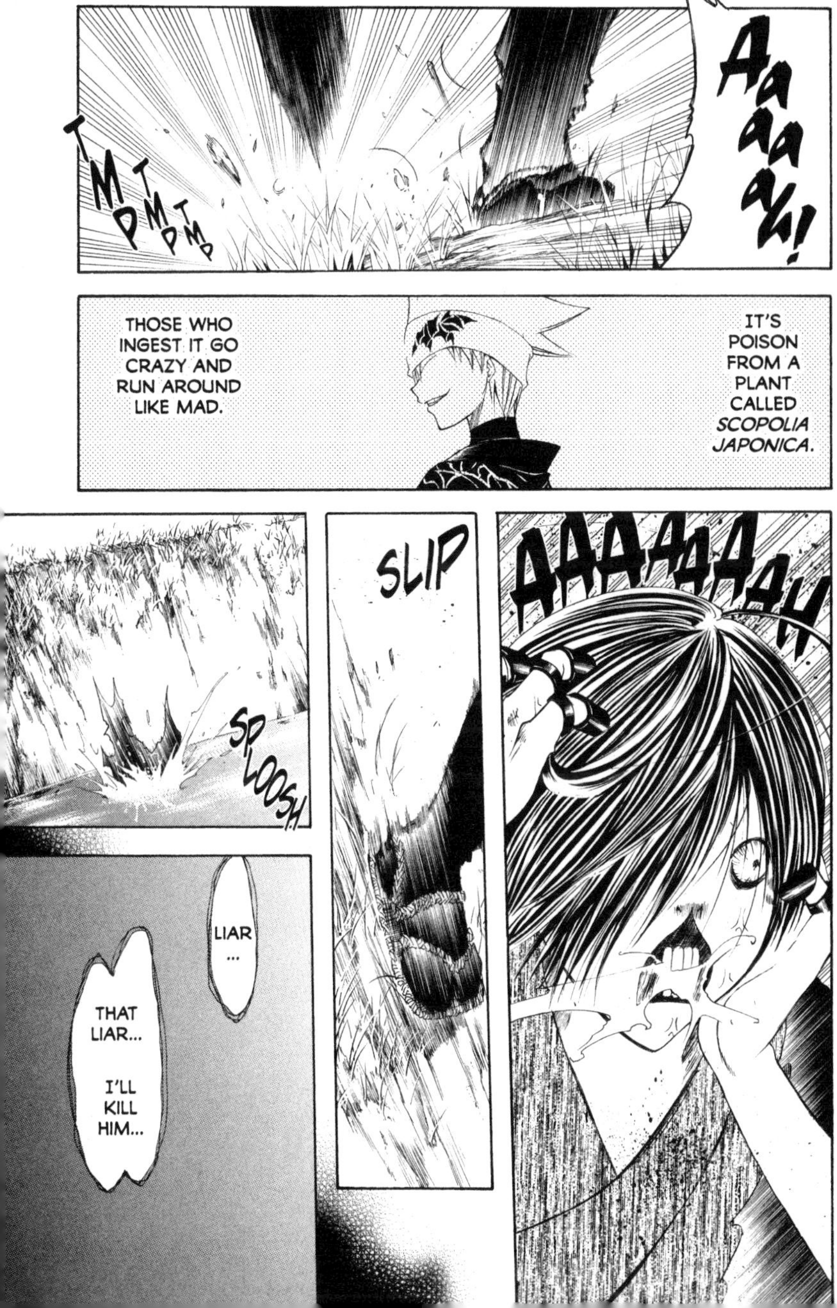
Aaaaaah!
TMP TMP TMP TMP
IT'S POISON FROM A PLANT CALLED *SCOPOLIA JAPONICA*.
THOSE WHO INGEST IT GO CRAZY AND RUN AROUND LIKE MAD.
AAAAAAAH
SLIP
SPLOOSH
LIAR...
THAT LIAR...
I'LL KILL HIM...

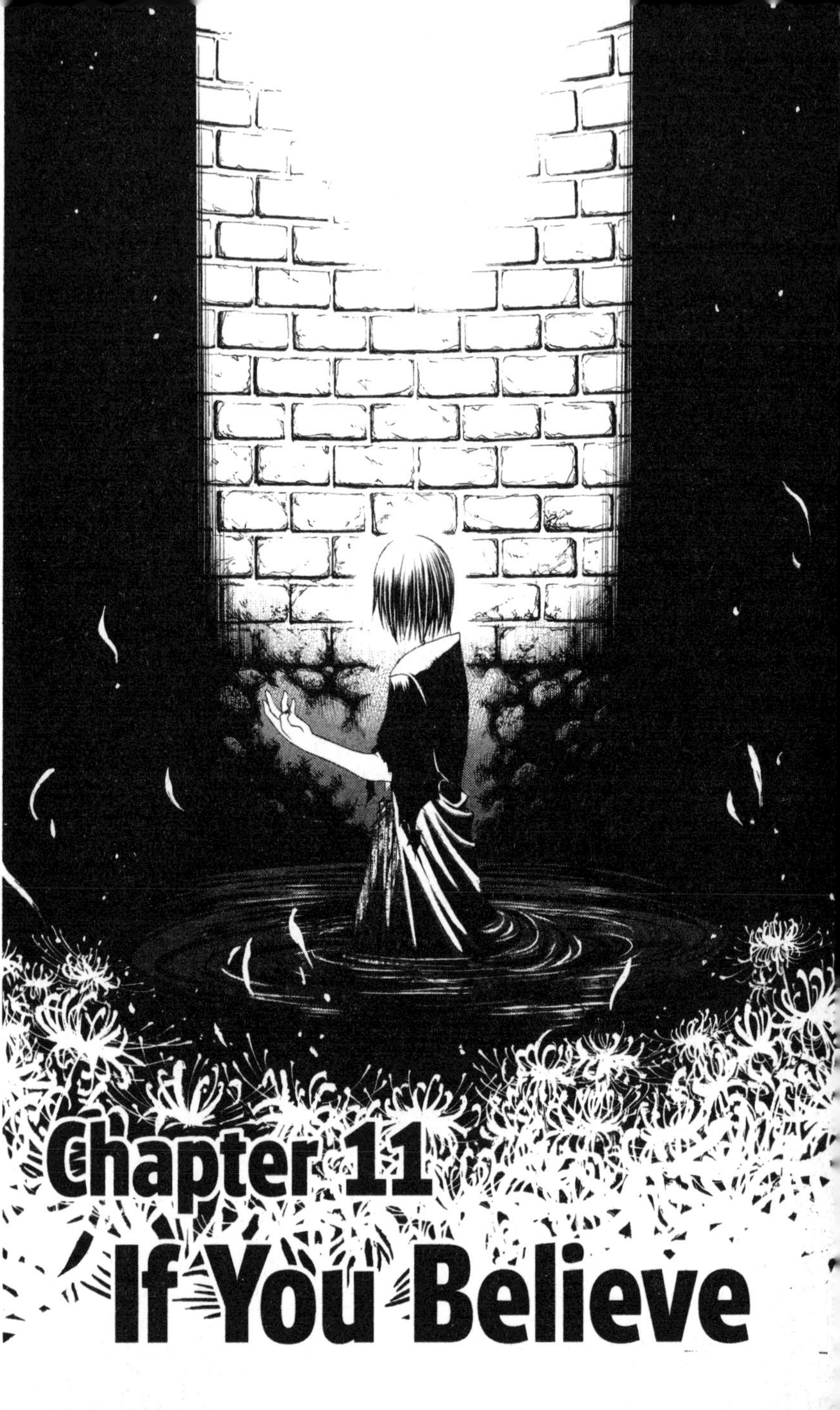
Chapter 11
If You Believe

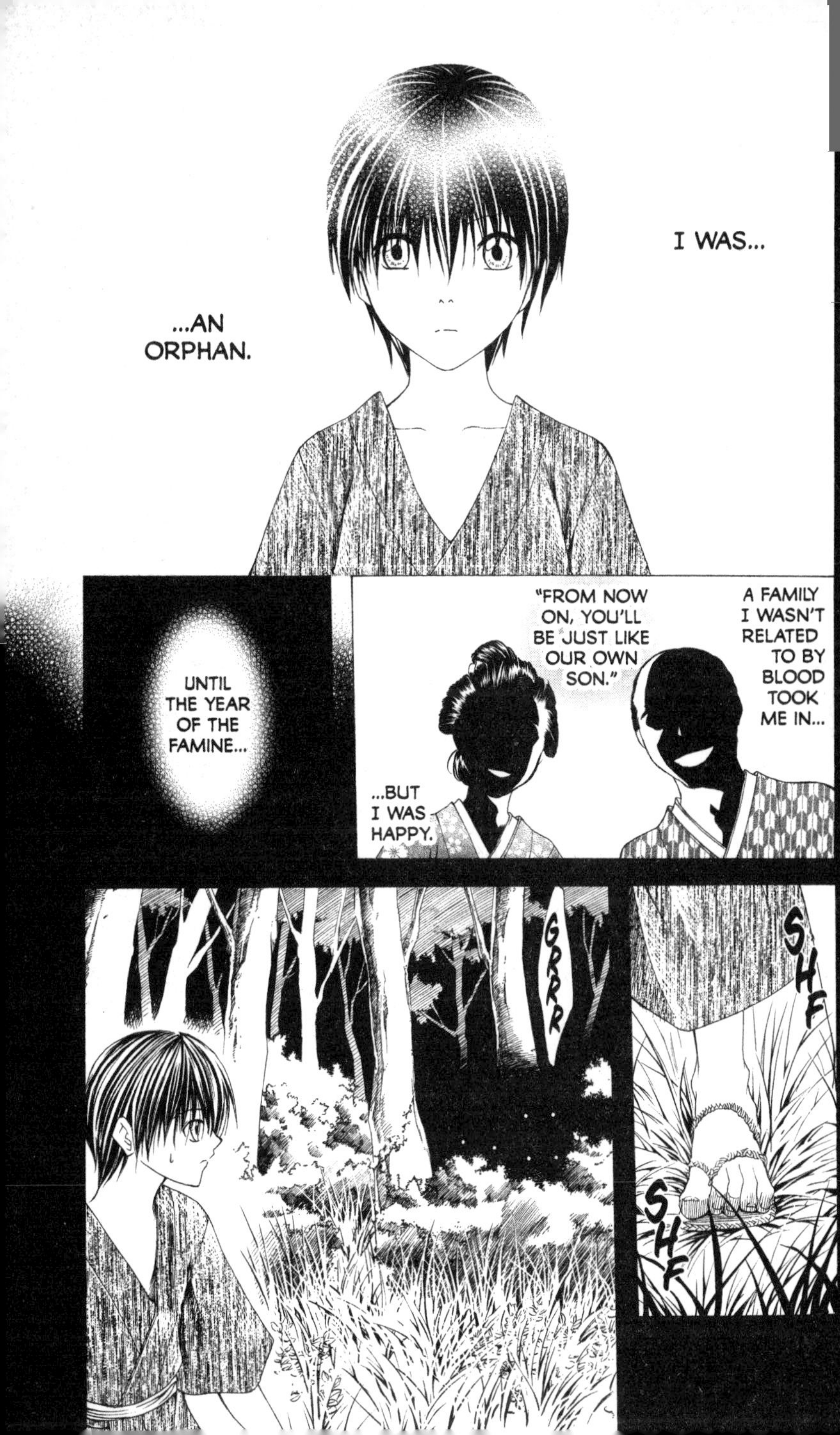
I WAS...
...AN ORPHAN.
A FAMILY I WASN'T RELATED TO BY BLOOD TOOK ME IN...
"FROM NOW ON, YOU'LL BE JUST LIKE OUR OWN SON."
...BUT I WAS HAPPY.
UNTIL THE YEAR OF THE FAMINE...
SHF
SHF
GRRR

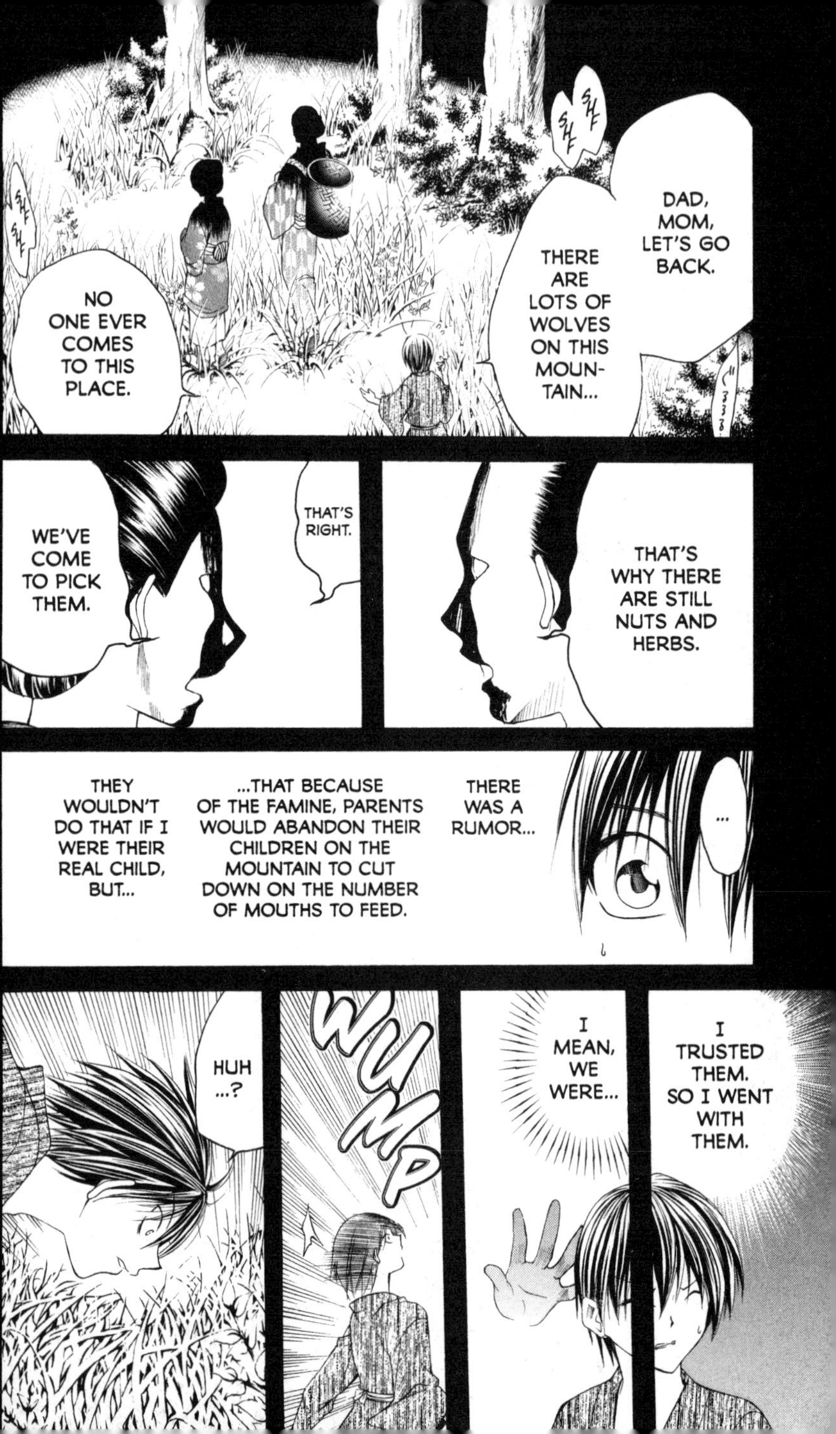
SHF SHF
DAD, MOM, LET'S GO BACK.
THERE ARE LOTS OF WOLVES ON THIS MOUN- TAIN...
NO ONE EVER COMES TO THIS PLACE.
SHF SHF
THAT'S WHY THERE ARE STILL NUTS AND HERBS.
THAT'S RIGHT.
WE'VE COME TO PICK THEM.
...
THERE WAS A RUMOR...
...THAT BECAUSE OF THE FAMINE, PARENTS WOULD ABANDON THEIR CHILDREN ON THE MOUNTAIN TO CUT DOWN ON THE NUMBER OF MOUTHS TO FEED.
THEY WOULDN'T DO THAT IF I WERE THEIR REAL CHILD, BUT...
I TRUSTED THEM. SO I WENT WITH THEM.
I MEAN, WE WERE...
WUMP
HUH ...?

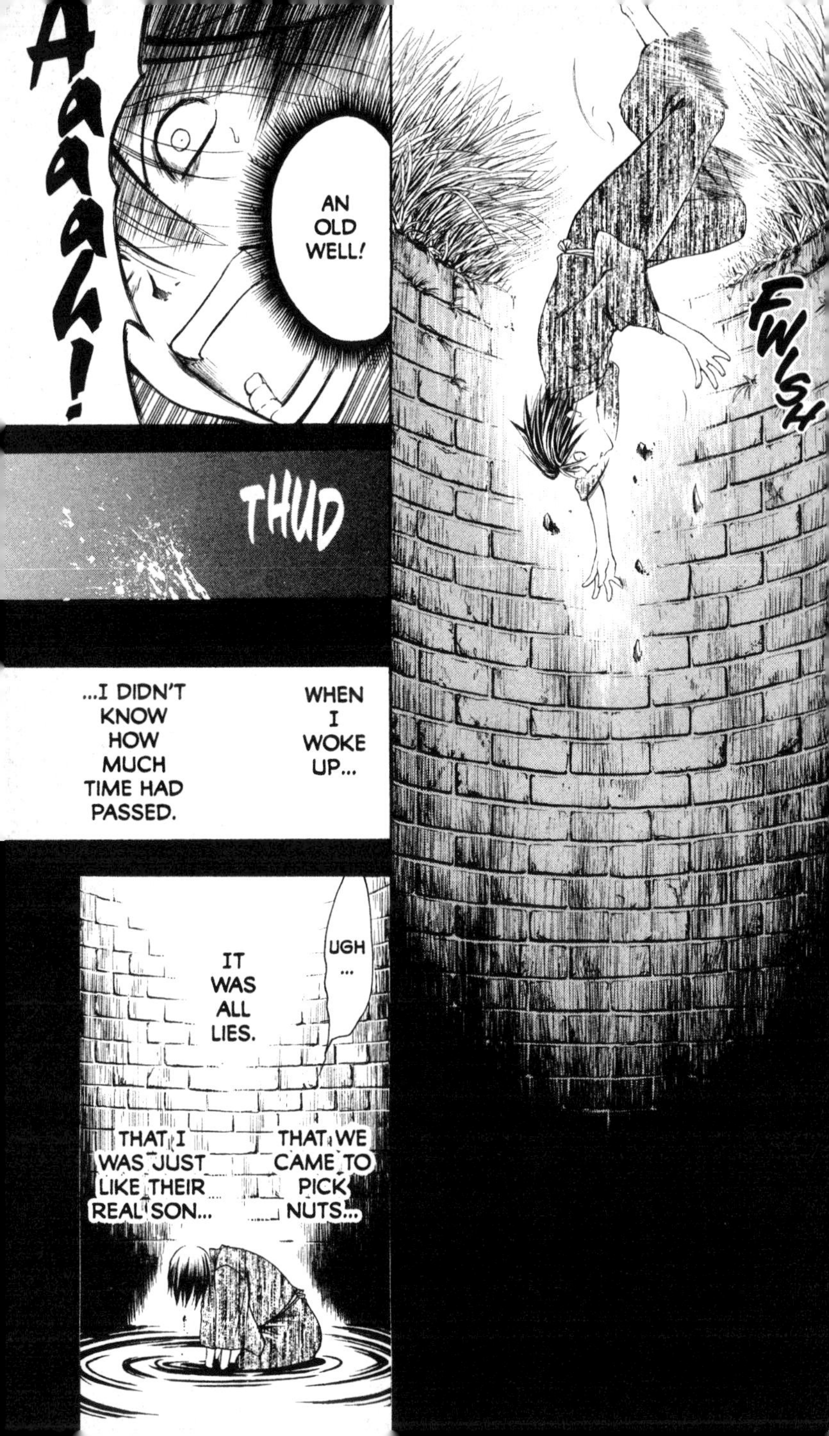
FWISH
AN OLD WELL!
Aaaah!
THUD
WHEN I WOKE UP...
...I DIDN'T KNOW HOW MUCH TIME HAD PASSED.
UGH...
IT WAS ALL LIES.
THAT WE CAME TO PICK NUTS...
THAT I WAS JUST LIKE THEIR REAL SON...

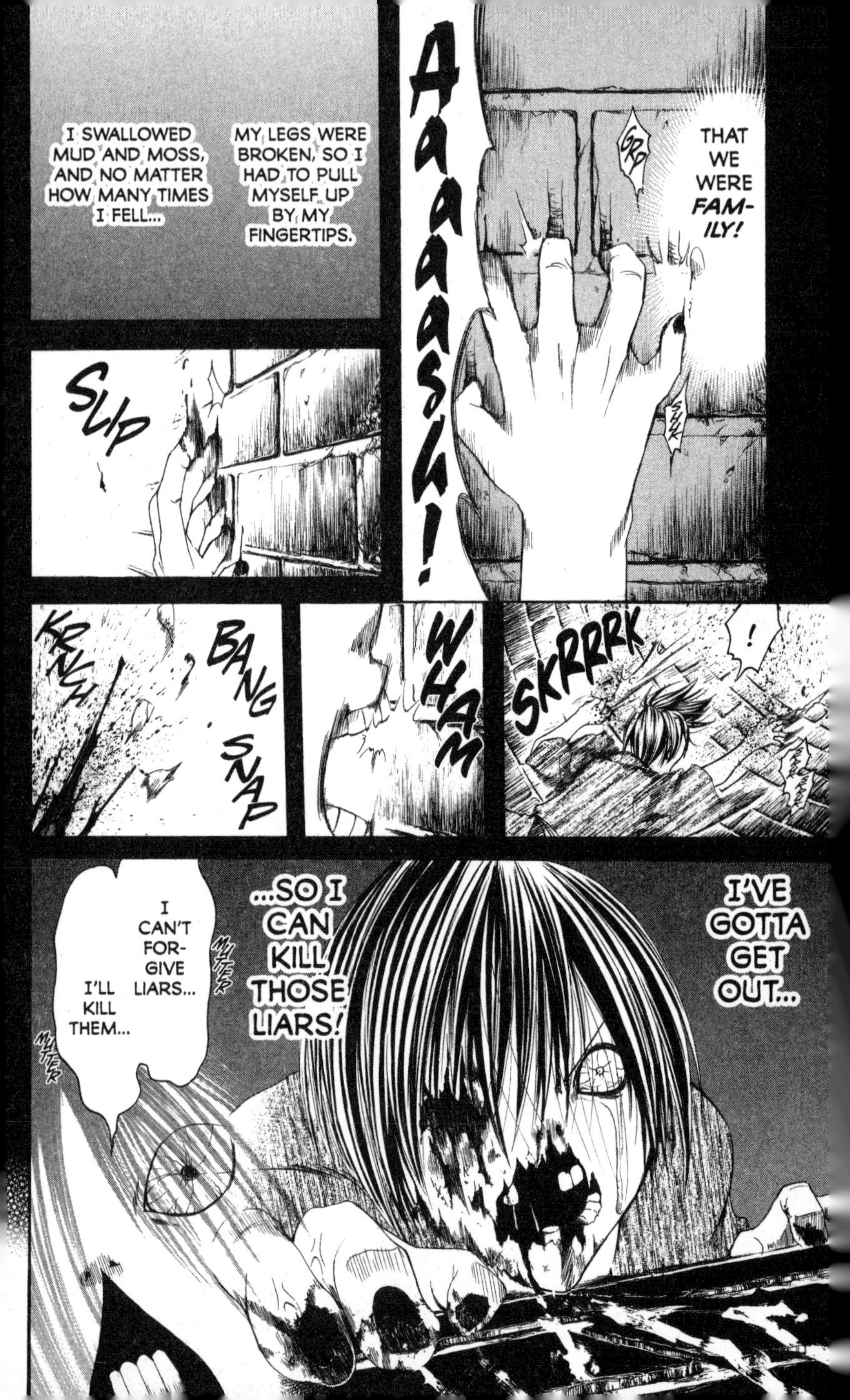
THAT WE WERE FAM-ILY!
GRP
AAAAASH!
MY LEGS WERE BROKEN, SO I HAD TO PULL MYSELF UP BY MY FINGERTIPS.
I SWALLOWED MUD AND MOSS, AND NO MATTER HOW MANY TIMES I FELL...
SLIP
!
SKRRRK
WHAM
BANG
SNAP
KRUNCH
I'VE GOTTA GET OUT...
...SO I CAN KILL THOSE LIARS!
MUTTER
I CAN'T FOR-GIVE LIARS...
I'LL KILL THEM...
MUTTER

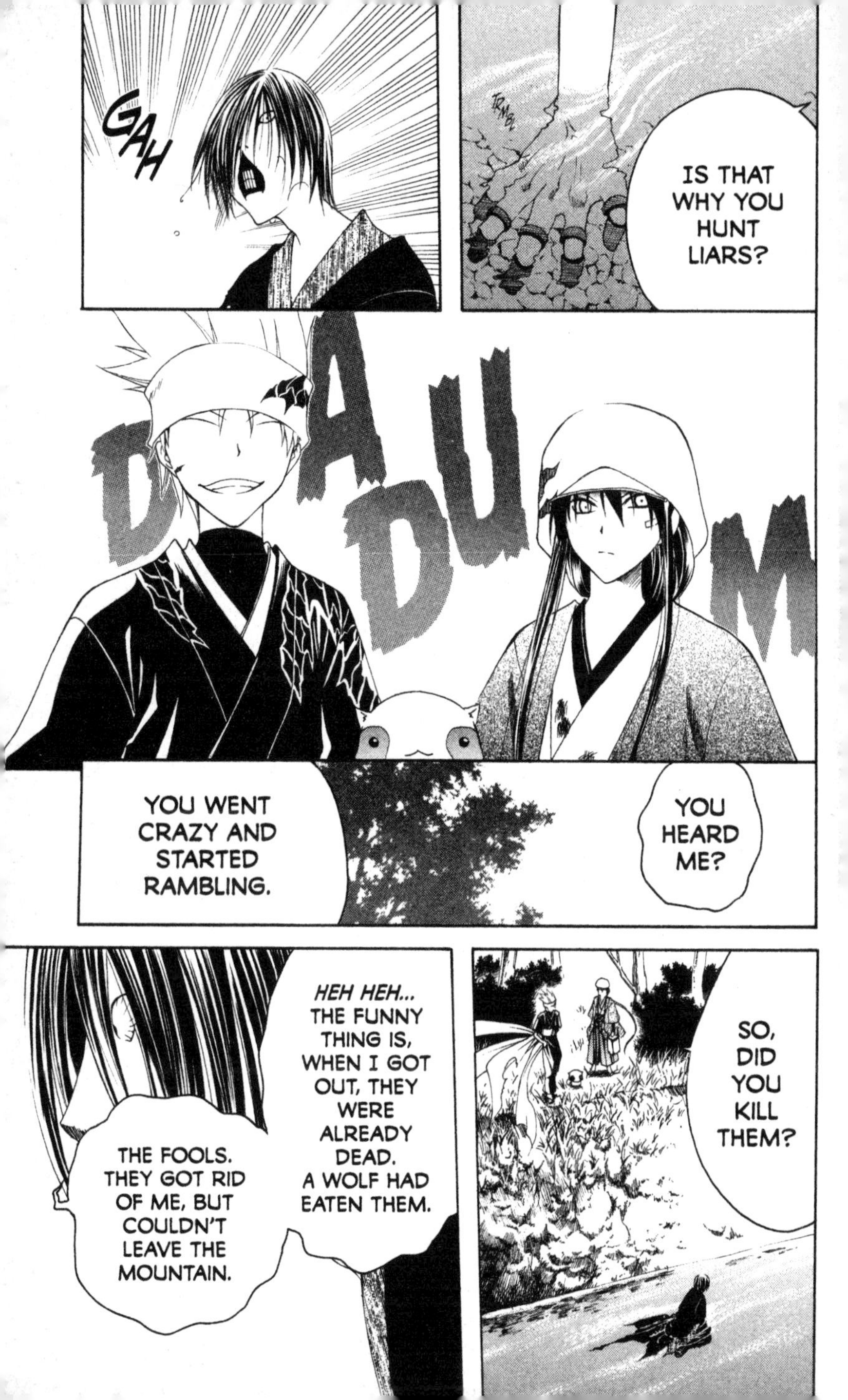
IS THAT WHY YOU HUNT LIARS?
GAH
DA DUM
YOU HEARD ME?
YOU WENT CRAZY AND STARTED RAMBLING.
SO, DID YOU KILL THEM?
HEH HEH... THE FUNNY THING IS, WHEN I GOT OUT, THEY WERE ALREADY DEAD. A WOLF HAD EATEN THEM.
THE FOOLS. THEY GOT RID OF ME, BUT COULDN'T LEAVE THE MOUNTAIN.

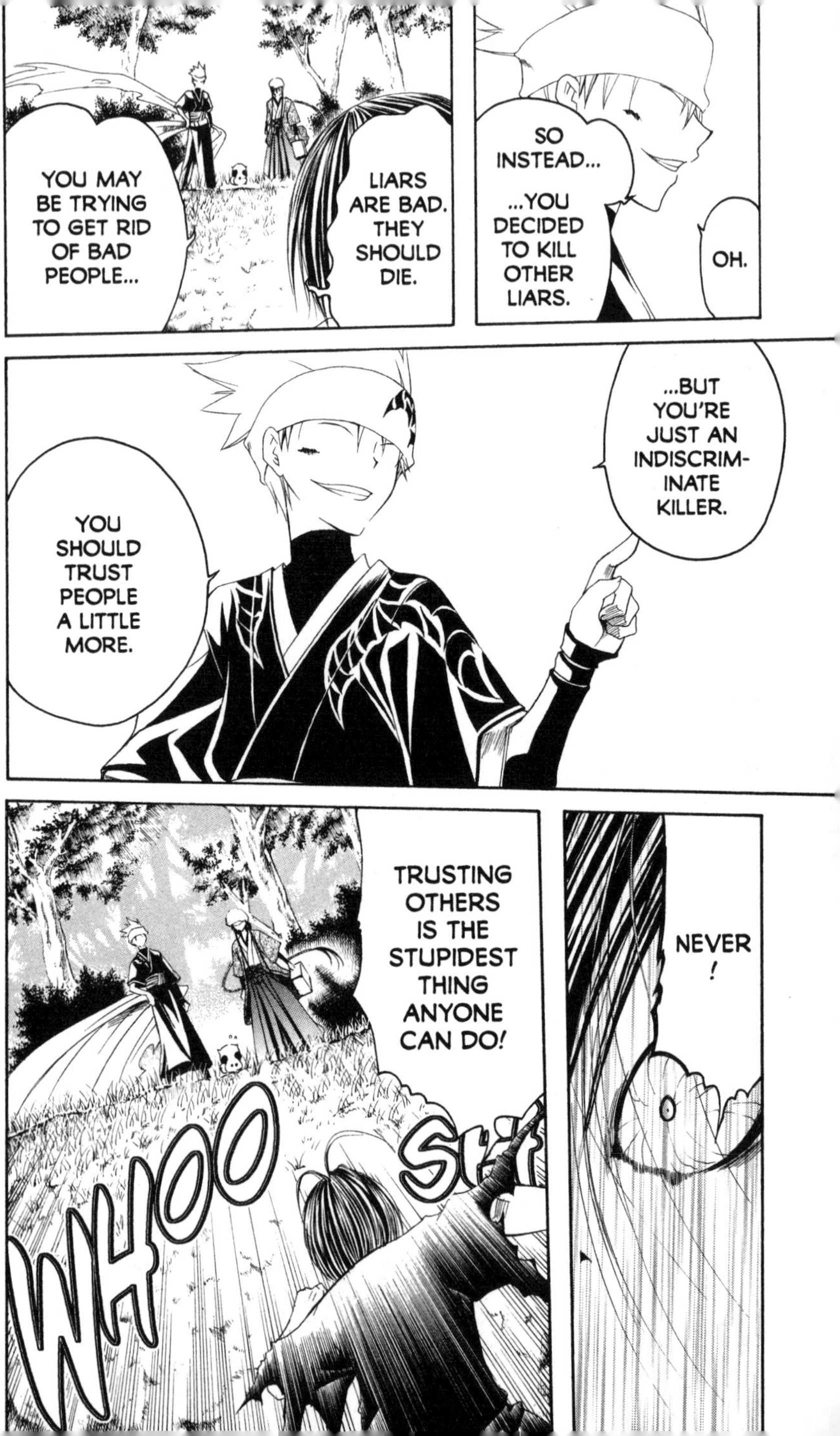
OH.
SO INSTEAD...
...YOU DECIDED TO KILL OTHER LIARS.
LIARS ARE BAD. THEY SHOULD DIE.
YOU MAY BE TRYING TO GET RID OF BAD PEOPLE...
...BUT YOU'RE JUST AN INDISCRIM-INATE KILLER.
YOU SHOULD TRUST PEOPLE A LITTLE MORE.
NEVER!
TRUSTING OTHERS IS THE STUPIDEST THING ANYONE CAN DO!
WHOO

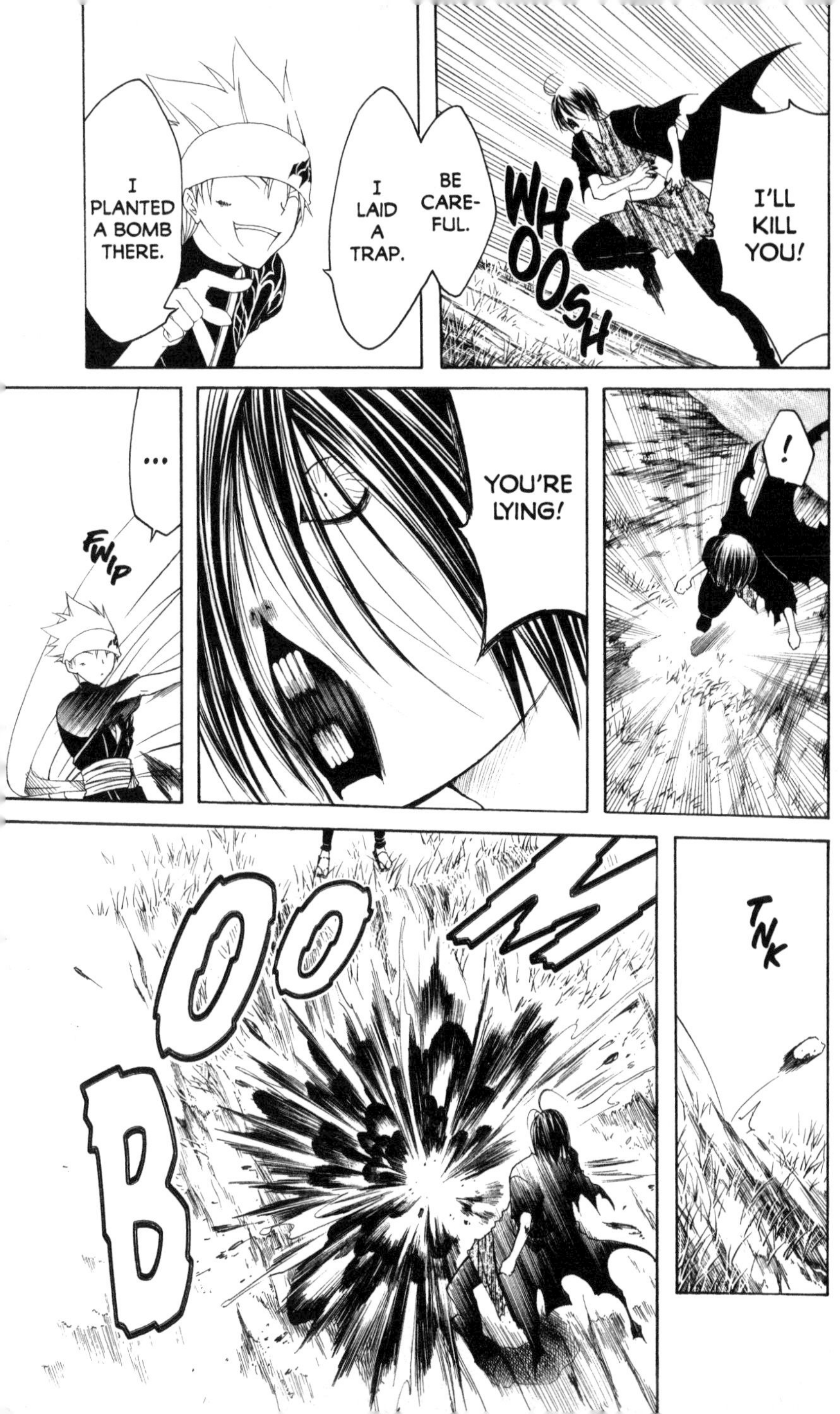
I'LL KILL YOU!
WHOOOSH
BE CARE-FUL.
I LAID A TRAP.
I PLANTED A BOMB THERE.
!
YOU'RE LYING!
...
FWIP
TNK
BOOOM

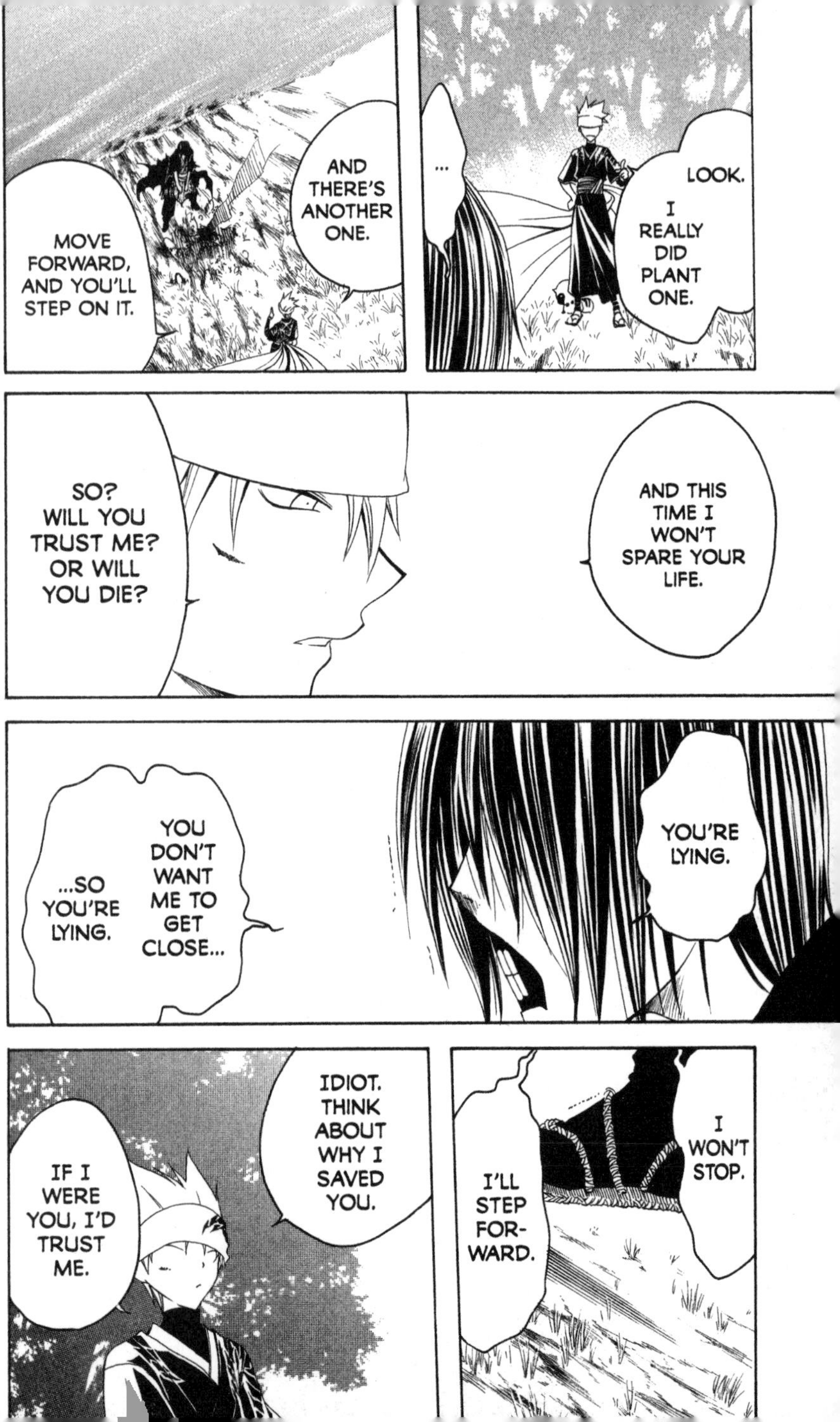
LOOK.
I REALLY DID PLANT ONE.
...
AND THERE'S ANOTHER ONE.
MOVE FORWARD, AND YOU'LL STEP ON IT.
AND THIS TIME I WON'T SPARE YOUR LIFE.
SO? WILL YOU TRUST ME? OR WILL YOU DIE?
YOU'RE LYING.
YOU DON'T WANT ME TO GET CLOSE...
...SO YOU'RE LYING.
I WON'T STOP.
I'LL STEP FOR-WARD.
IDIOT. THINK ABOUT WHY I SAVED YOU.
IF I WERE YOU, I'D TRUST ME.

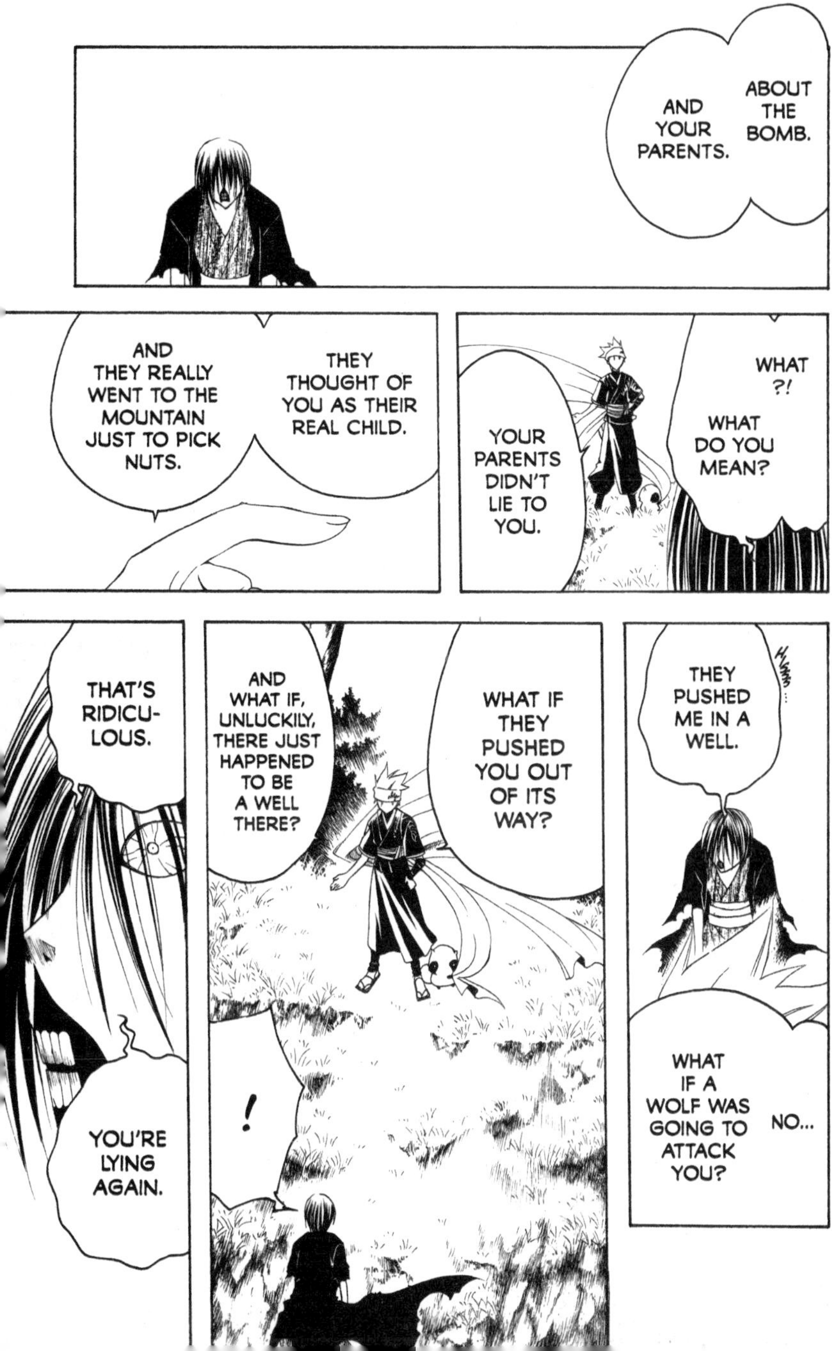
ABOUT THE BOMB.
AND YOUR PARENTS.
WHAT?!
WHAT DO YOU MEAN?
YOUR PARENTS DIDN'T LIE TO YOU.
THEY THOUGHT OF YOU AS THEIR REAL CHILD.
AND THEY REALLY WENT TO THE MOUNTAIN JUST TO PICK NUTS.
THEY PUSHED ME IN A WELL.
NO...
WHAT IF A WOLF WAS GOING TO ATTACK YOU?
WHAT IF THEY PUSHED YOU OUT OF ITS WAY?
AND WHAT IF, UNLUCKILY, THERE JUST HAPPENED TO BE A WELL THERE?
!
THAT'S RIDICU-LOUS.
YOU'RE LYING AGAIN.

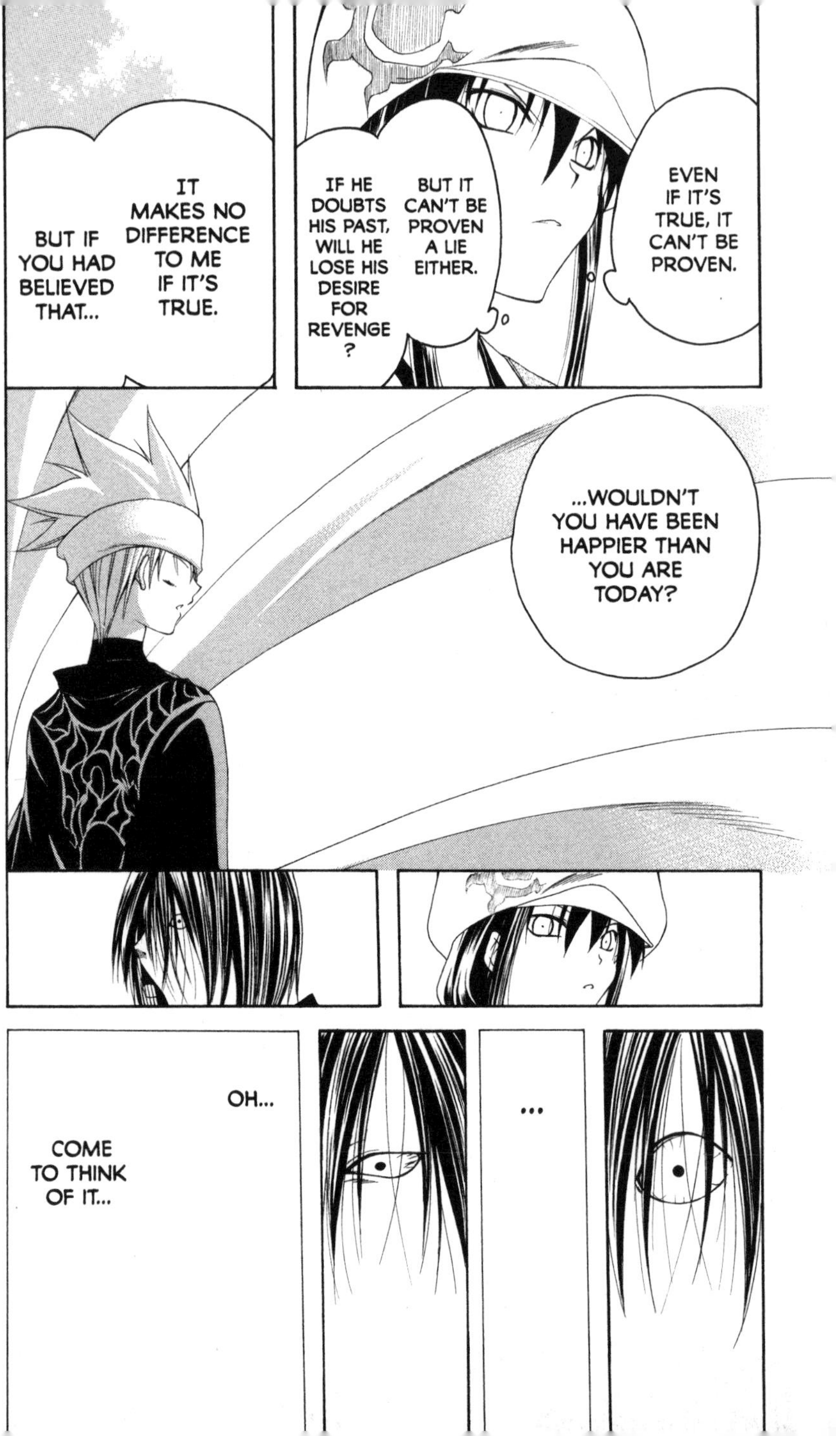
EVEN IF IT'S TRUE, IT CAN'T BE PROVEN.
BUT IT CAN'T BE PROVEN A LIE EITHER.
IF HE DOUBTS HIS PAST, WILL HE LOSE HIS DESIRE FOR REVENGE ?
IT MAKES NO DIFFERENCE TO ME IF IT'S TRUE.
BUT IF YOU HAD BELIEVED THAT...
...WOULDN'T YOU HAVE BEEN HAPPIER THAN YOU ARE TODAY?
...
OH...
COME TO THINK OF IT...

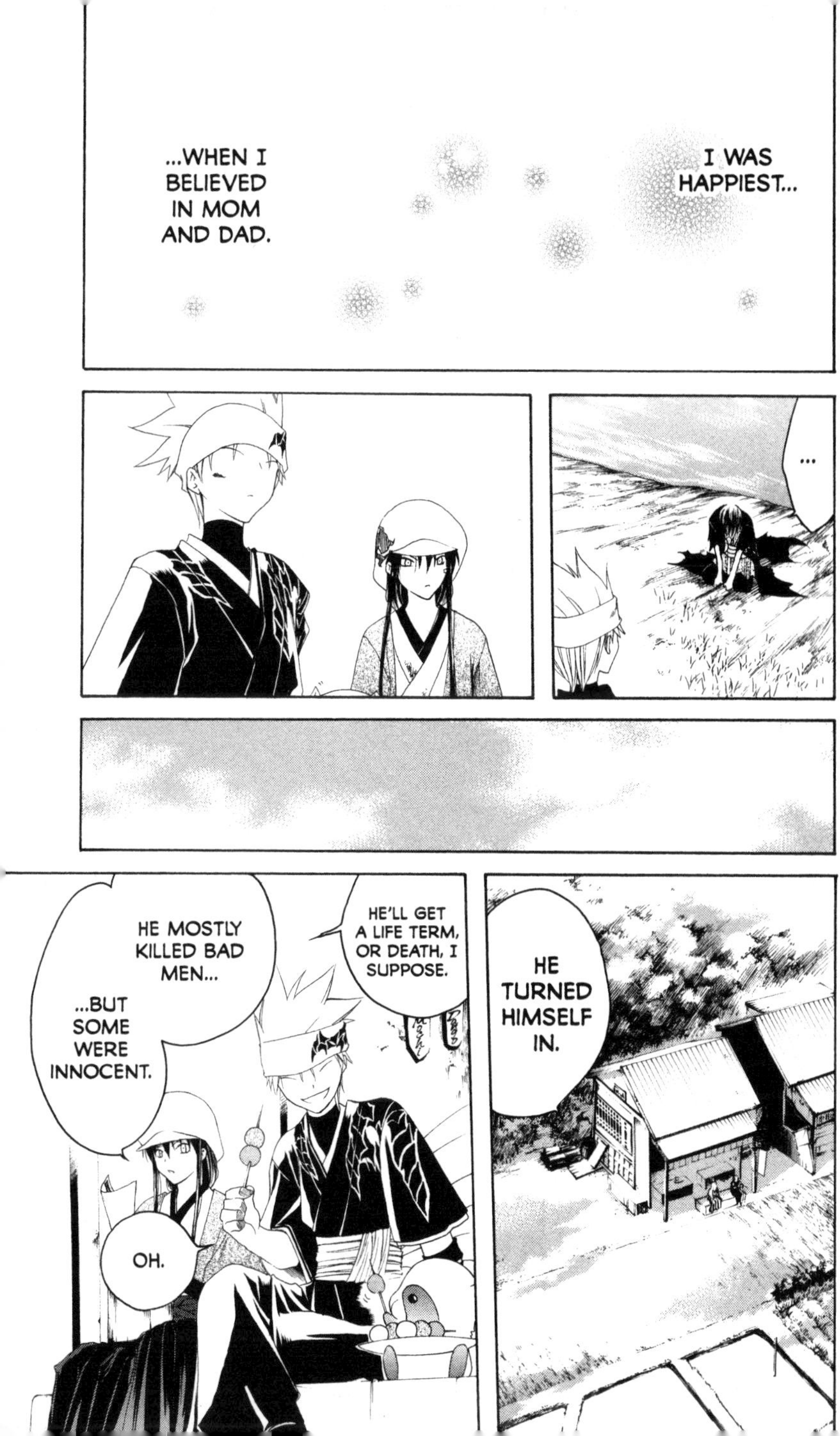
I WAS HAPPIEST...
...WHEN I BELIEVED IN MOM AND DAD.
...
HE TURNED HIMSELF IN.
HE'LL GET A LIFE TERM, OR DEATH, I SUPPOSE.
HE MOSTLY KILLED BAD MEN...
...BUT SOME WERE INNOCENT.
OH.

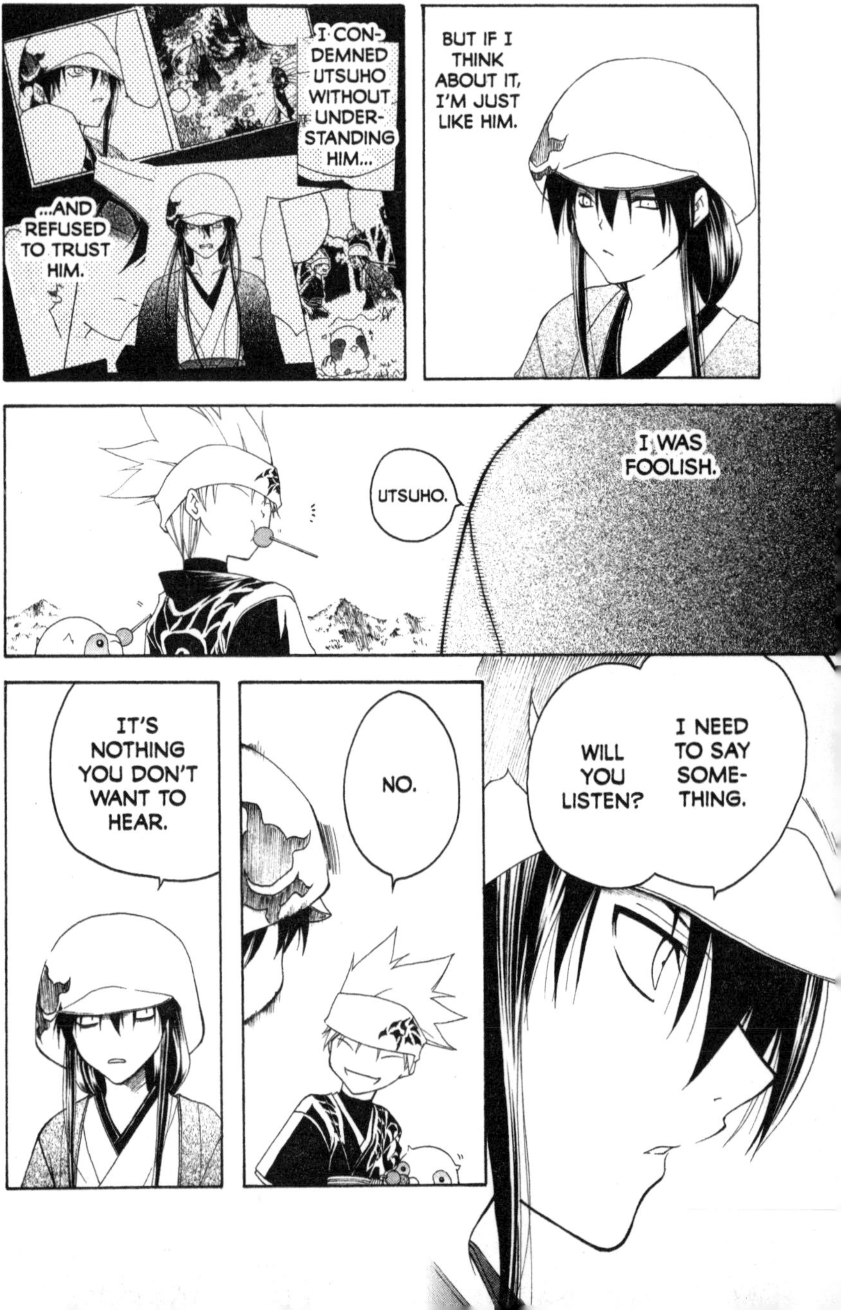
BUT IF I THINK ABOUT IT, I'M JUST LIKE HIM.
I CON-DEMNED UTSUHO WITHOUT UNDER-STANDING HIM...
...AND REFUSED TO TRUST HIM.
I WAS FOOLISH.
UTSUHO.
I NEED TO SAY SOME-THING.
WILL YOU LISTEN?
NO.
IT'S NOTHING YOU DON'T WANT TO HEAR.

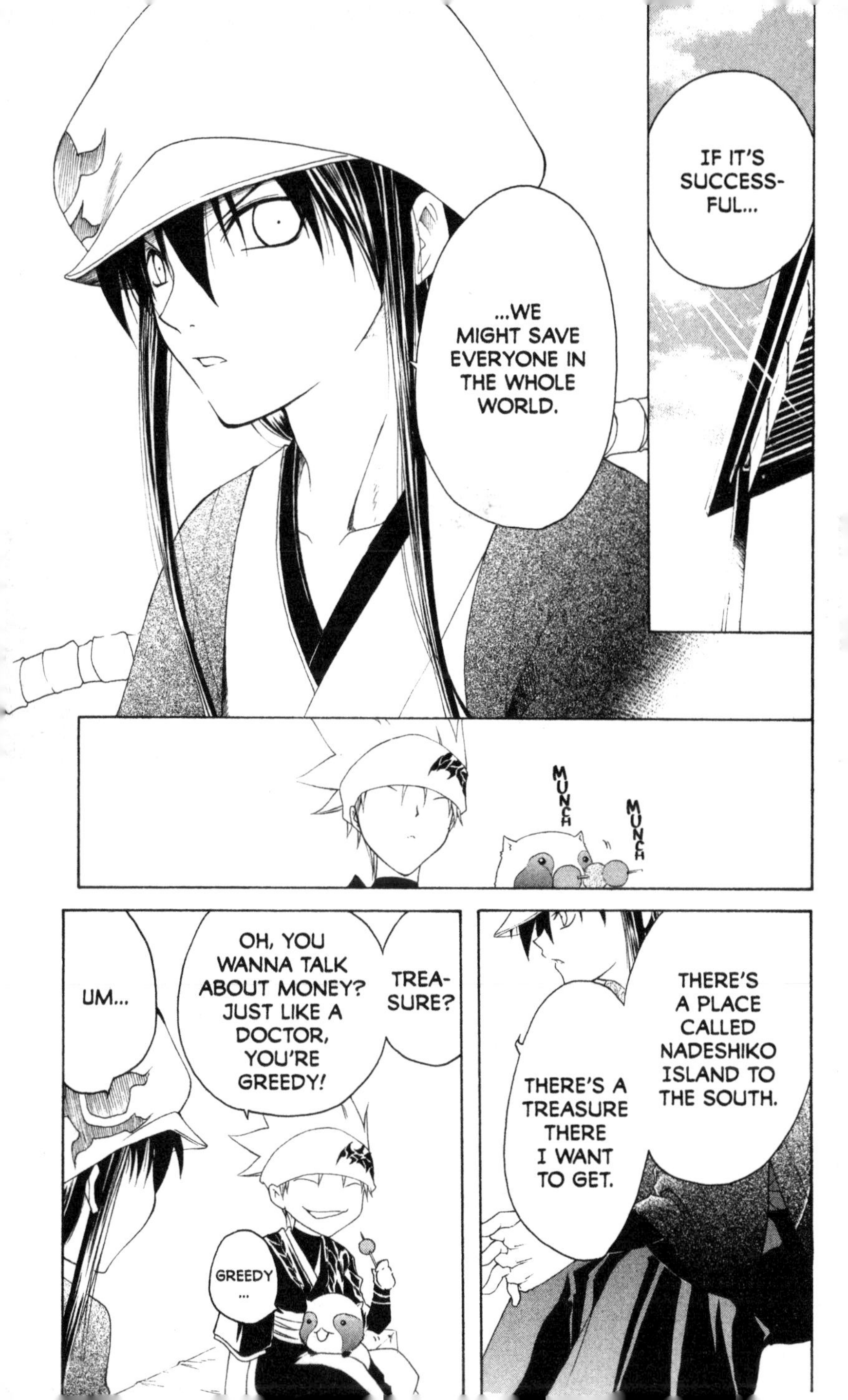
IF IT'S SUCCESS-FUL...
...WE MIGHT SAVE EVERYONE IN THE WHOLE WORLD.
MUNCH
MUNCH
THERE'S A PLACE CALLED NADESHIKO ISLAND TO THE SOUTH.
THERE'S A TREASURE THERE I WANT TO GET.
TREA-SURE?
OH, YOU WANNA TALK ABOUT MONEY? JUST LIKE A DOCTOR, YOU'RE GREEDY!
UM...
GREEDY...

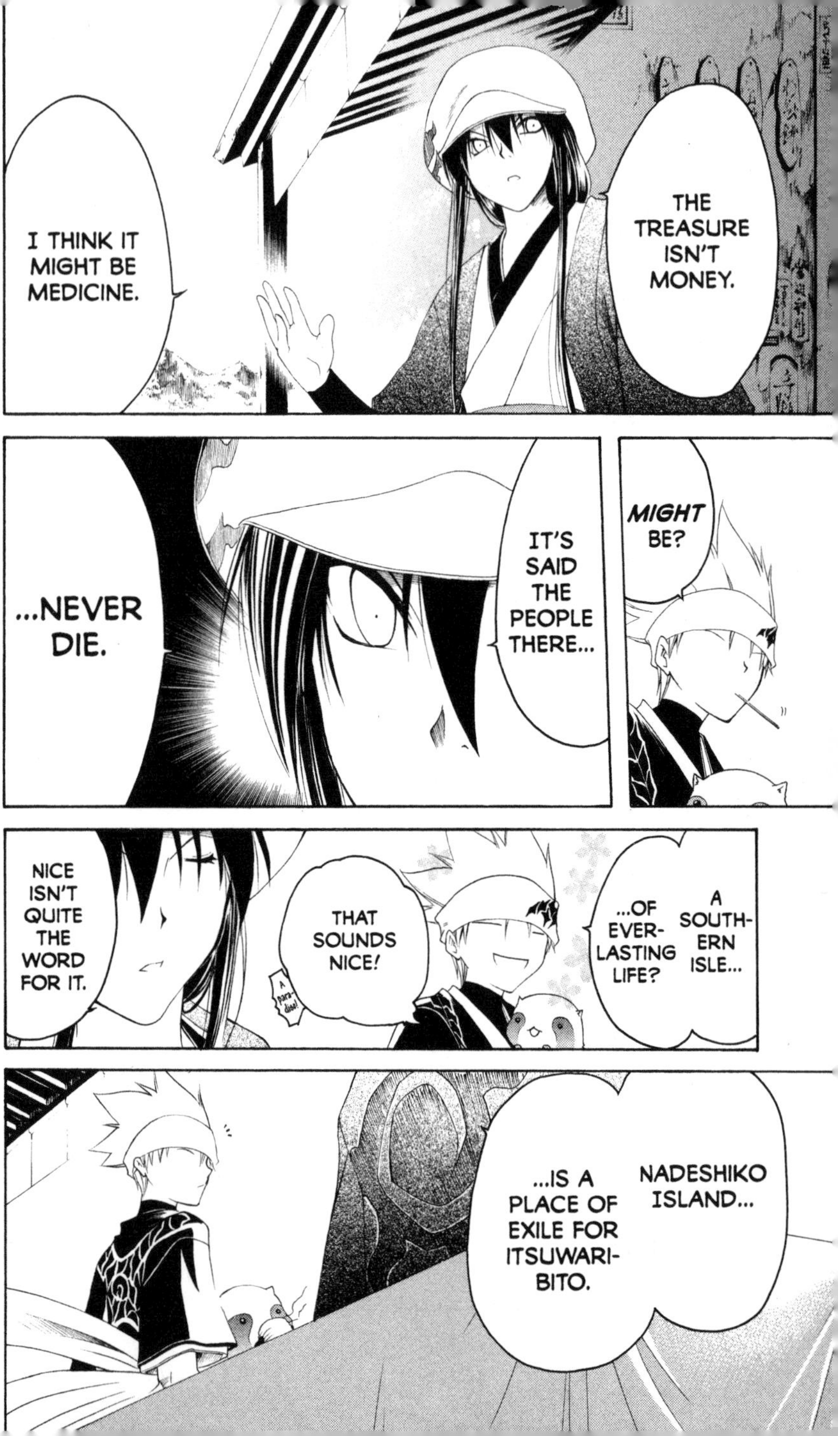
THE TREASURE ISN'T MONEY.
I THINK IT MIGHT BE MEDICINE.
MIGHT BE?
IT'S SAID THE PEOPLE THERE...
...NEVER DIE.
A SOUTH-ERN ISLE...
...OF EVER-LASTING LIFE?
THAT SOUNDS NICE!
A para-dise!
NICE ISN'T QUITE THE WORD FOR IT.
NADESHIKO ISLAND...
...IS A PLACE OF EXILE FOR ITSUWARI-BITO.

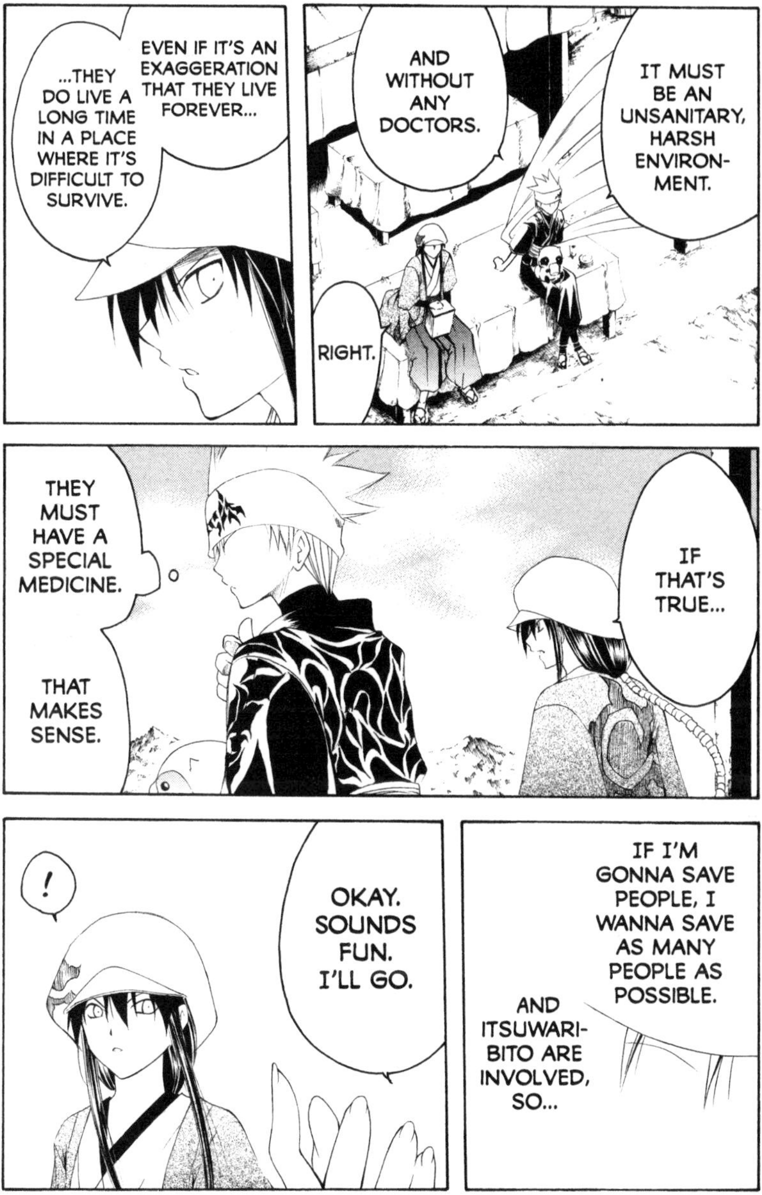
IT MUST BE AN UNSANITARY, HARSH ENVIRON-MENT.
AND WITHOUT ANY DOCTORS.
RIGHT.
EVEN IF IT'S AN EXAGGERATION THAT THEY LIVE FOREVER...
...THEY DO LIVE A LONG TIME IN A PLACE WHERE IT'S DIFFICULT TO SURVIVE.
IF THAT'S TRUE...
THEY MUST HAVE A SPECIAL MEDICINE.
THAT MAKES SENSE.
IF I'M GONNA SAVE PEOPLE, I WANNA SAVE AS MANY PEOPLE AS POSSIBLE.
AND ITSUWARI-BITO ARE INVOLVED, SO...
OKAY. SOUNDS FUN. I'LL GO.
!

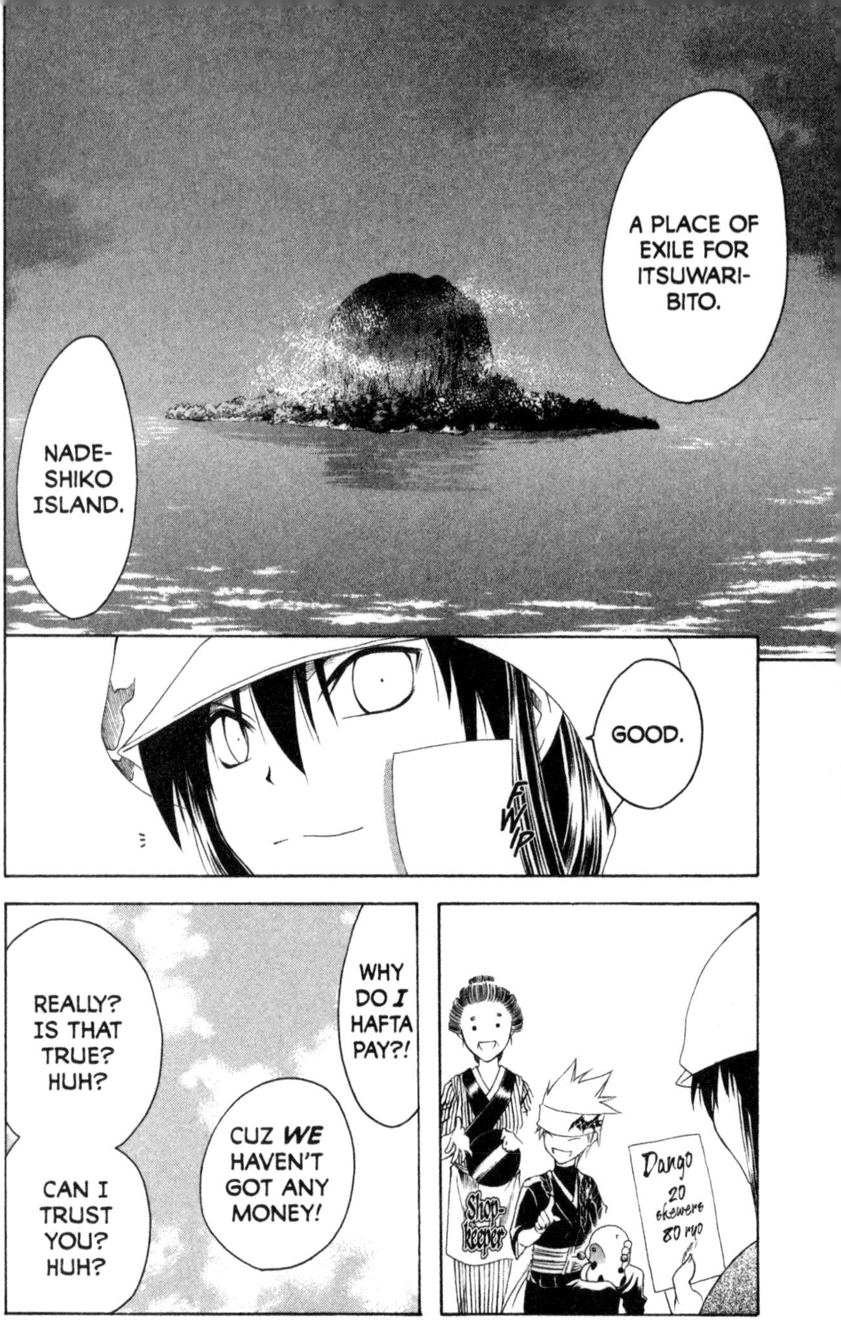
A PLACE OF EXILE FOR ITSUWARI-BITO.
NADE-SHIKO ISLAND.
FWIP
GOOD.
Shop-keeper
Dango
20 skewers 80 ryo
WHY DO *I* HAFTA PAY?!
CUZ ***WE*** HAVEN'T GOT ANY MONEY!
REALLY? IS THAT TRUE? HUH?
CAN I TRUST YOU? HUH?

RYO WAS A FORM OF CURRENCY BEFORE YEN.

Itsuwaribito・空・

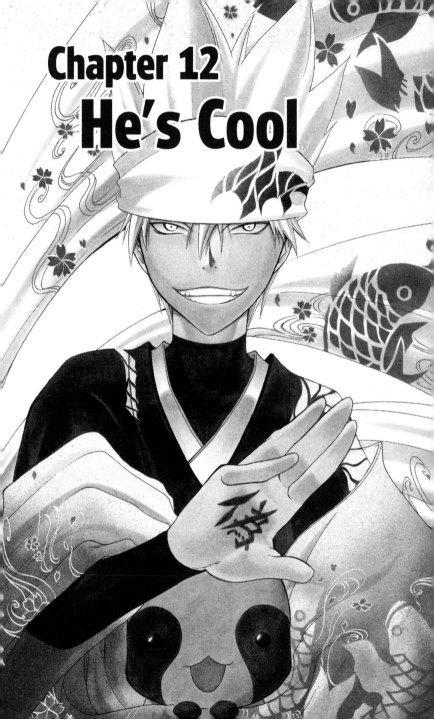

Chapter 12
He's Cool

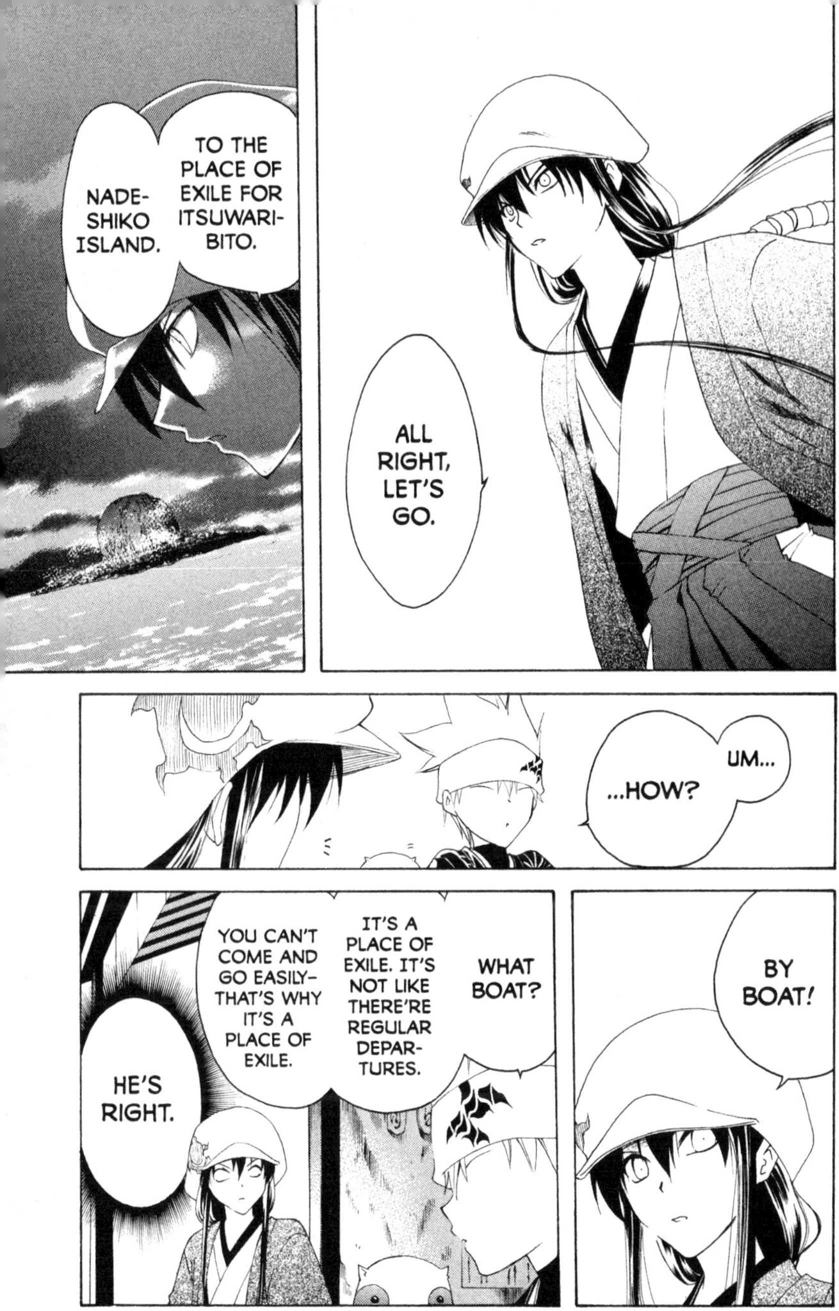
ALL RIGHT, LET'S GO.
TO THE PLACE OF EXILE FOR ITSUWARI-BITO.
NADE-SHIKO ISLAND.
UM...
...HOW?
BY BOAT!
WHAT BOAT?
IT'S A PLACE OF EXILE. IT'S NOT LIKE THERE'RE REGULAR DEPAR-TURES.
YOU CAN'T COME AND GO EASILY—THAT'S WHY IT'S A PLACE OF EXILE.
HE'S RIGHT.

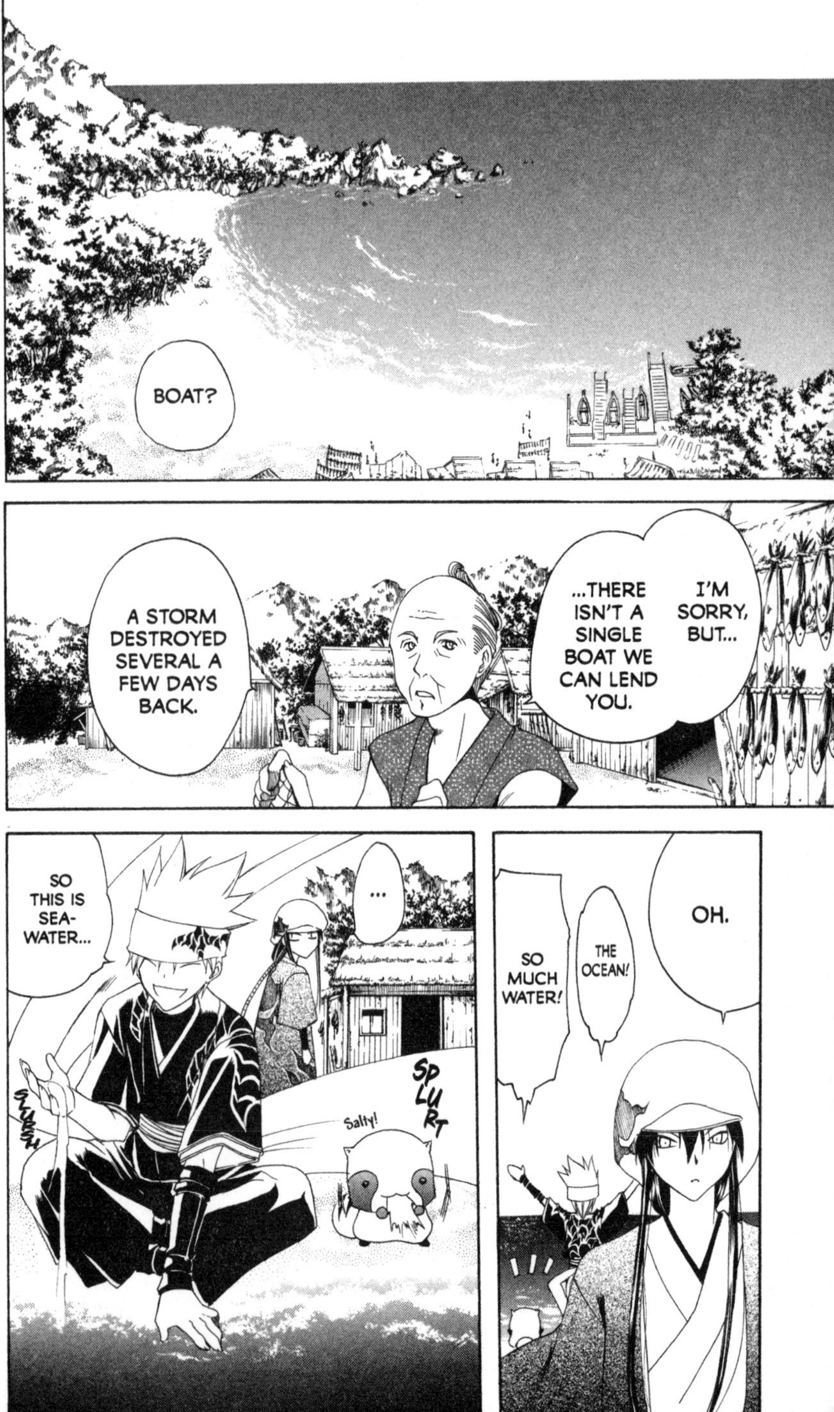
BOAT?
I'M SORRY, BUT...
...THERE ISN'T A SINGLE BOAT WE CAN LEND YOU.
A STORM DESTROYED SEVERAL A FEW DAYS BACK.
OH.
THE OCEAN!
SO MUCH WATER!
...
SO THIS IS SEA-WATER...
SPLURT
Salty!
SLURSH

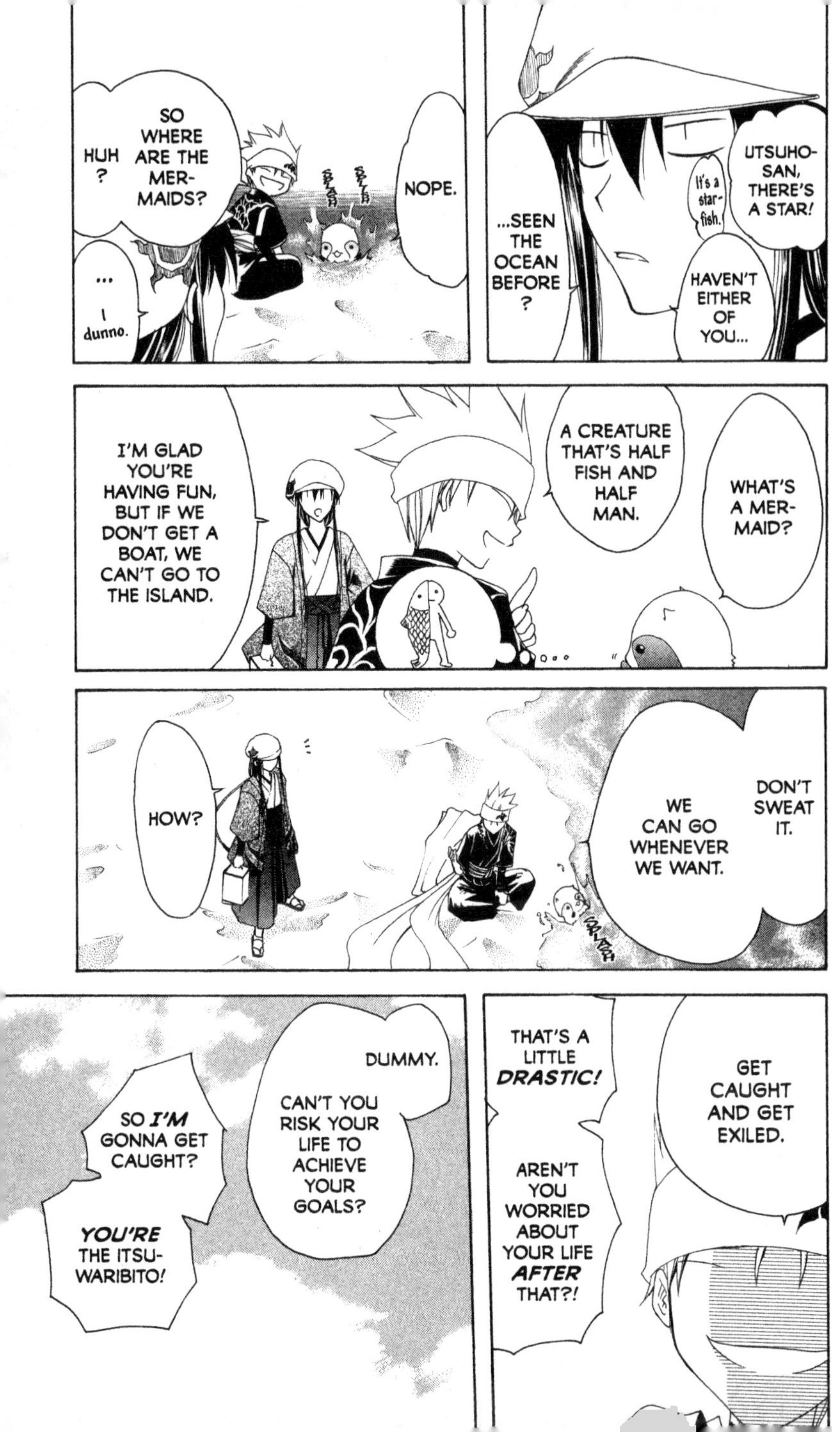
UTSUHO-SAN, THERE'S A STAR!
It's a star-fish.
HAVEN'T EITHER OF YOU...
...SEEN THE OCEAN BEFORE?
NOPE.
SO WHERE ARE THE MER-MAIDS?
HUH?
... I dunno.
WHAT'S A MER-MAID?
A CREATURE THAT'S HALF FISH AND HALF MAN.
I'M GLAD YOU'RE HAVING FUN, BUT IF WE DON'T GET A BOAT, WE CAN'T GO TO THE ISLAND.
DON'T SWEAT IT.
WE CAN GO WHENEVER WE WANT.
HOW?
GET CAUGHT AND GET EXILED.
THAT'S A LITTLE *DRASTIC!*
AREN'T YOU WORRIED ABOUT YOUR LIFE *AFTER* THAT?!
DUMMY.
CAN'T YOU RISK YOUR LIFE TO ACHIEVE YOUR GOALS?
SO *I'M* GONNA GET CAUGHT?
YOU'RE THE ITSU-WARIBITO!

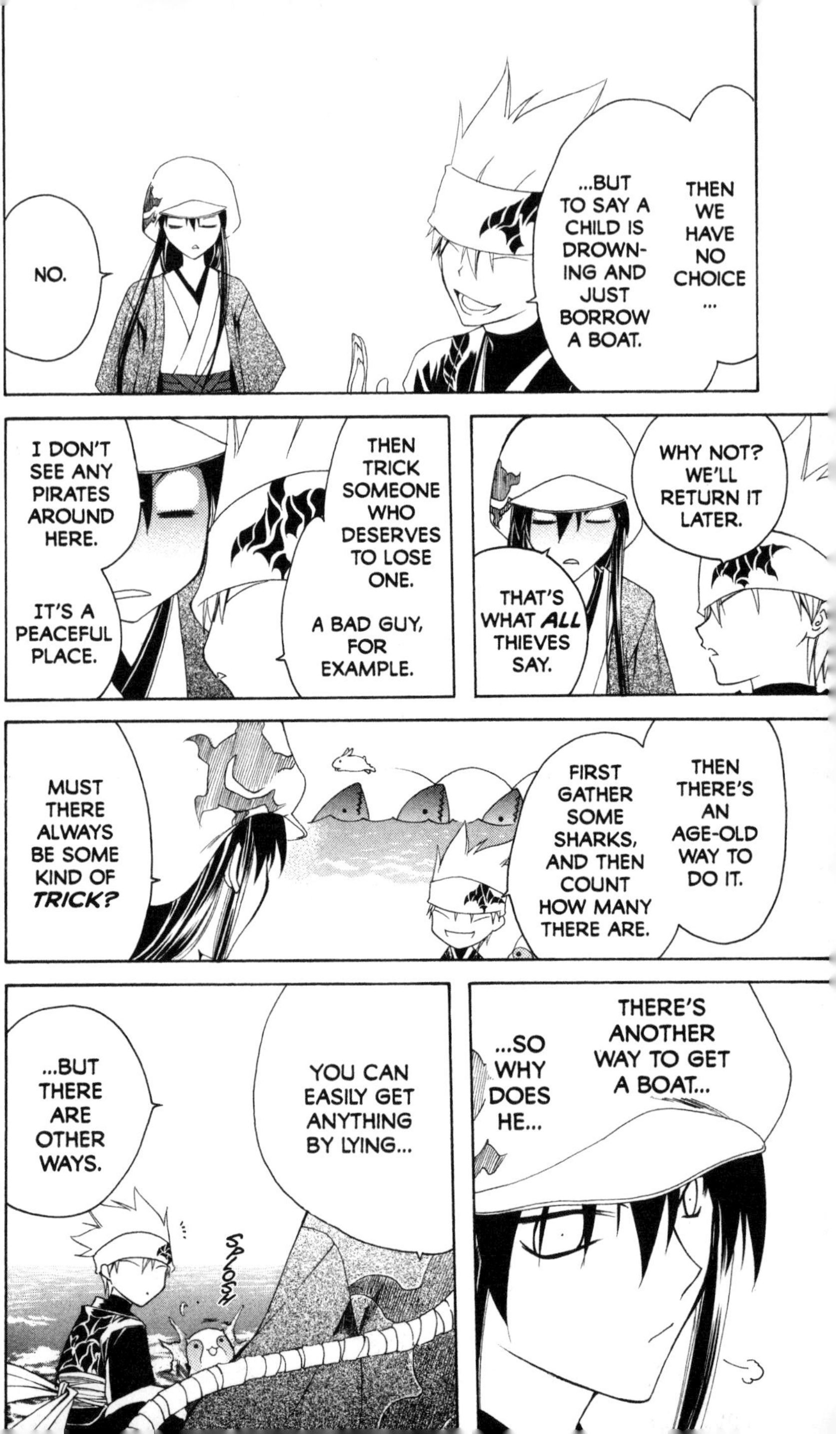
THEN WE HAVE NO CHOICE ...
...BUT TO SAY A CHILD IS DROWNING AND JUST BORROW A BOAT.
NO.
WHY NOT? WE'LL RETURN IT LATER.
THAT'S WHAT *ALL* THIEVES SAY.
THEN TRICK SOMEONE WHO DESERVES TO LOSE ONE.
A BAD GUY, FOR EXAMPLE.
I DON'T SEE ANY PIRATES AROUND HERE.
IT'S A PEACEFUL PLACE.
THEN THERE'S AN AGE-OLD WAY TO DO IT.
FIRST GATHER SOME SHARKS, AND THEN COUNT HOW MANY THERE ARE.
MUST THERE ALWAYS BE SOME KIND OF *TRICK?*
THERE'S ANOTHER WAY TO GET A BOAT...
...SO WHY DOES HE...
YOU CAN EASILY GET ANYTHING BY LYING...
...BUT THERE ARE OTHER WAYS.
SPLOOSH

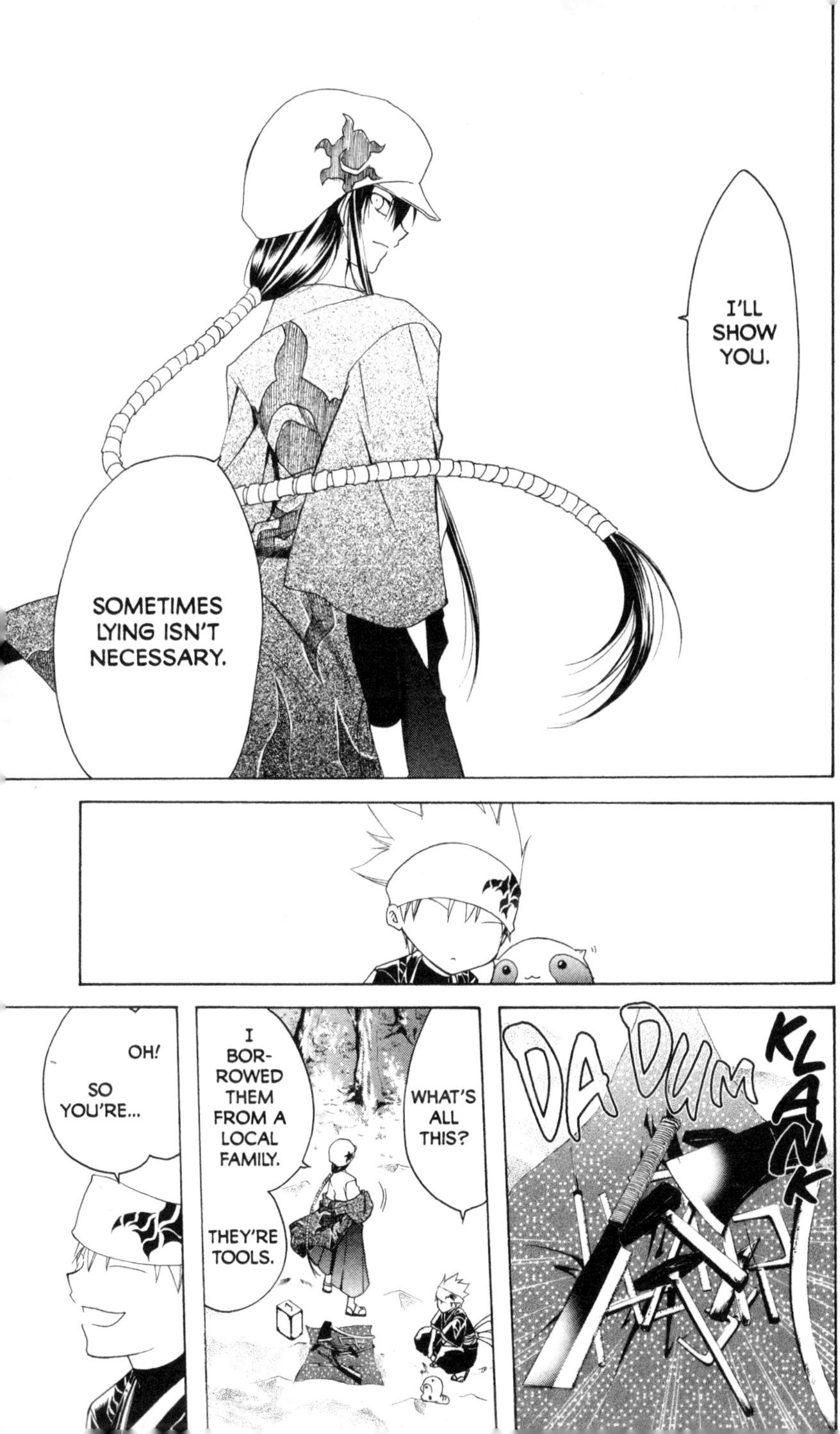
I'LL SHOW YOU.
SOMETIMES LYING ISN'T NECESSARY.
KLANK
DA DUM
WHAT'S ALL THIS?
I BOR-ROWED THEM FROM A LOCAL FAMILY.
THEY'RE TOOLS.
OH! SO YOU'RE...

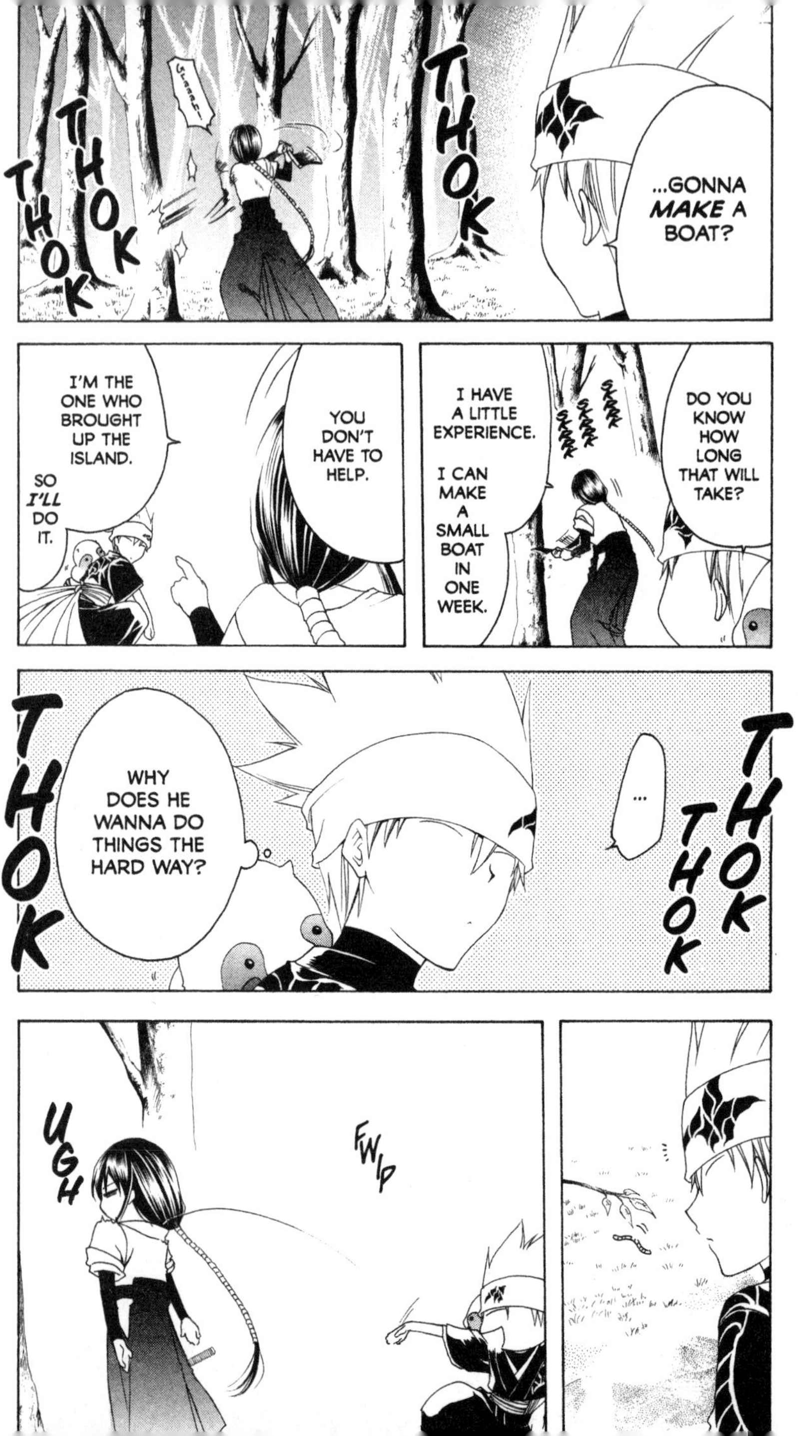
...GONNA *MAKE* A BOAT?
THOK
THOK
THOK
DO YOU KNOW HOW LONG THAT WILL TAKE?
SKRRK SKRRK SKRRK
I HAVE A LITTLE EXPERIENCE.
I CAN MAKE A SMALL BOAT IN ONE WEEK.
YOU DON'T HAVE TO HELP.
I'M THE ONE WHO BROUGHT UP THE ISLAND.
SO *I'LL* DO IT.
THOK
THOK
...
WHY DOES HE WANNA DO THINGS THE HARD WAY?
THOK
...
FWIP
UGH

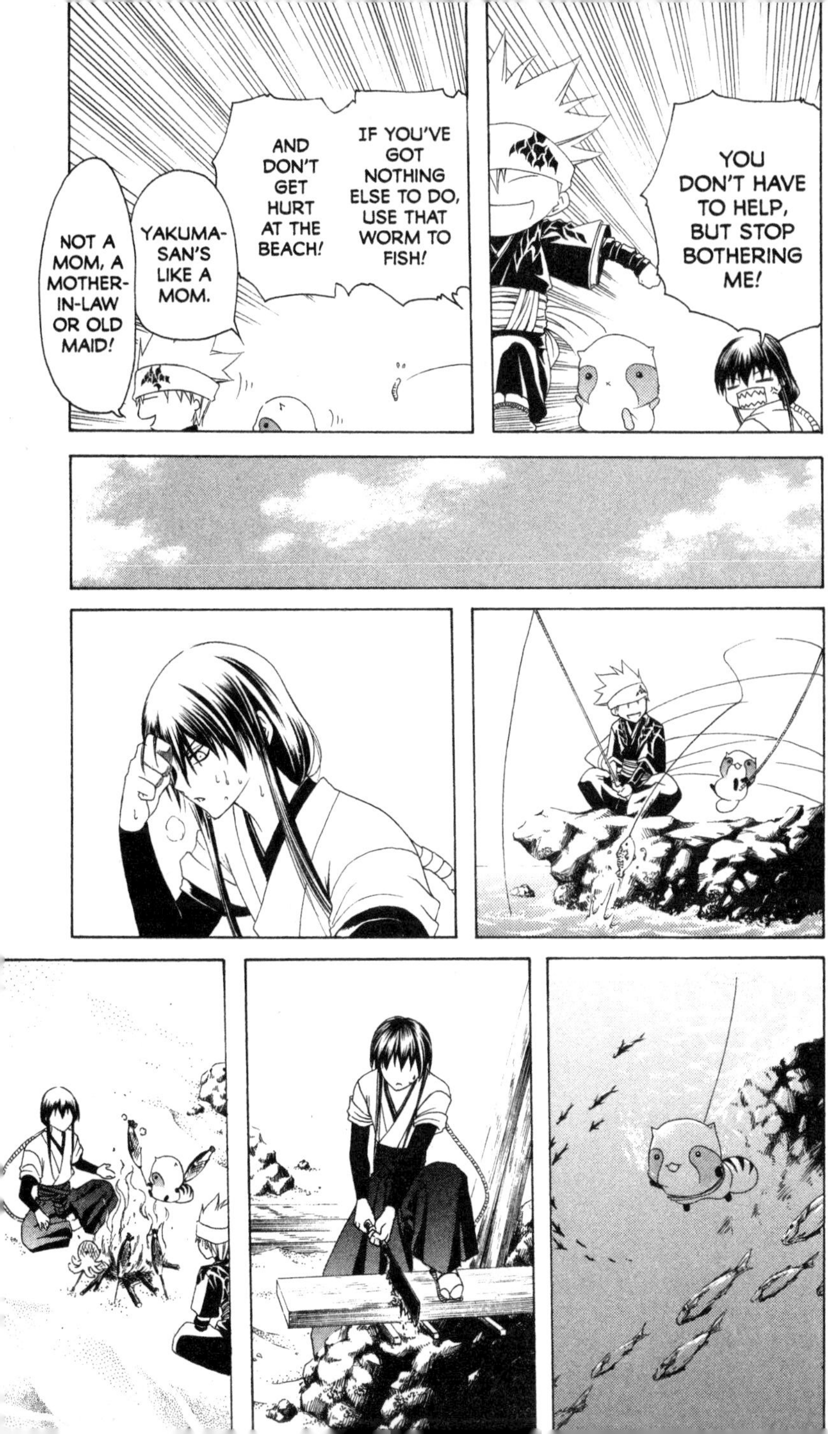
YOU DON'T HAVE TO HELP, BUT STOP BOTHERING ME!
IF YOU'VE GOT NOTHING ELSE TO DO, USE THAT WORM TO FISH!
AND DON'T GET HURT AT THE BEACH!
YAKUMA-SAN'S LIKE A MOM.
NOT A MOM, A MOTHER-IN-LAW OR OLD MAID!

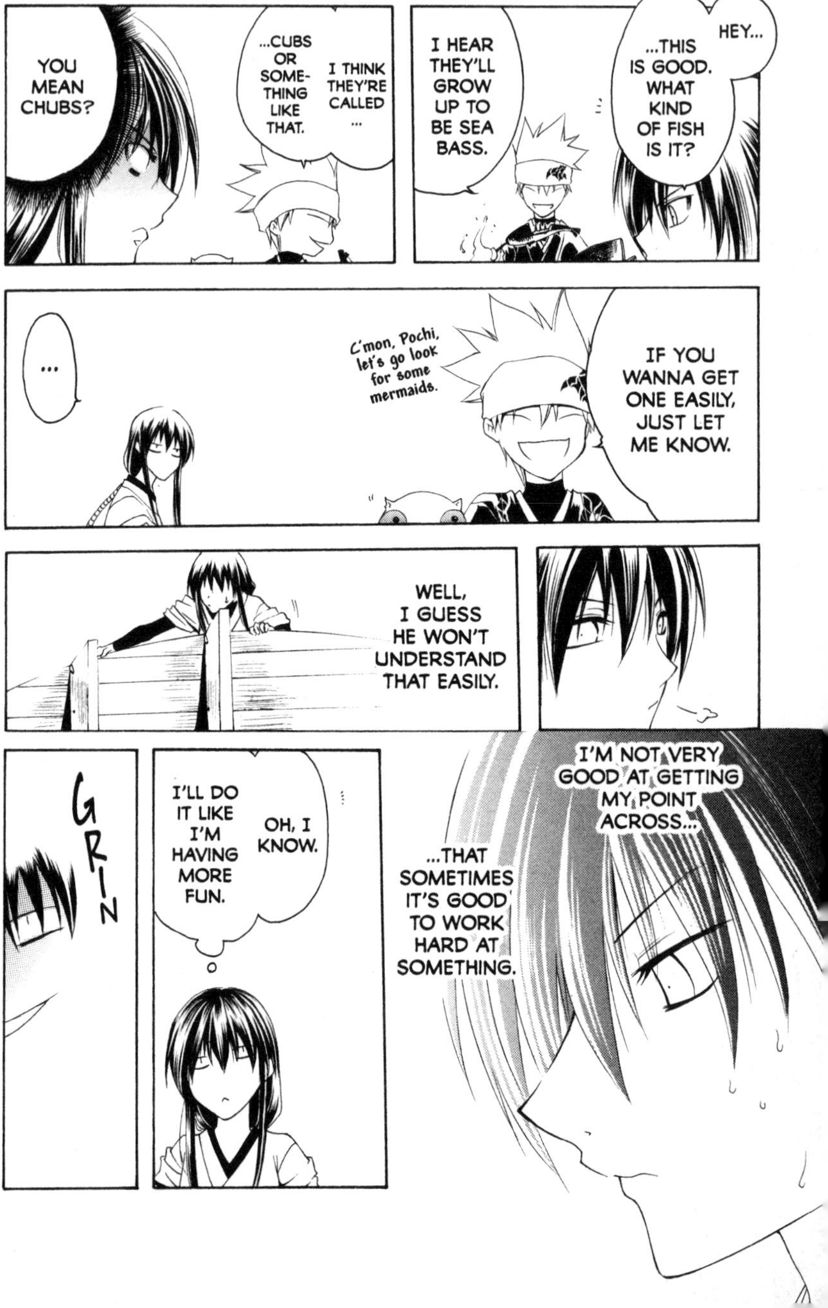
HEY...
...THIS IS GOOD. WHAT KIND OF FISH IS IT?
I HEAR THEY'LL GROW UP TO BE SEA BASS.
I THINK THEY'RE CALLED ...
...CUBS OR SOME-THING LIKE THAT.
YOU MEAN CHUBS?
IF YOU WANNA GET ONE EASILY, JUST LET ME KNOW.
C'mon, Pochi, let's go look for some mermaids.
...
WELL, I GUESS HE WON'T UNDERSTAND THAT EASILY.
I'M NOT VERY GOOD AT GETTING MY POINT ACROSS...
...THAT SOMETIMES IT'S GOOD TO WORK HARD AT SOMETHING.
OH, I KNOW.
I'LL DO IT LIKE I'M HAVING MORE FUN.
GRIN

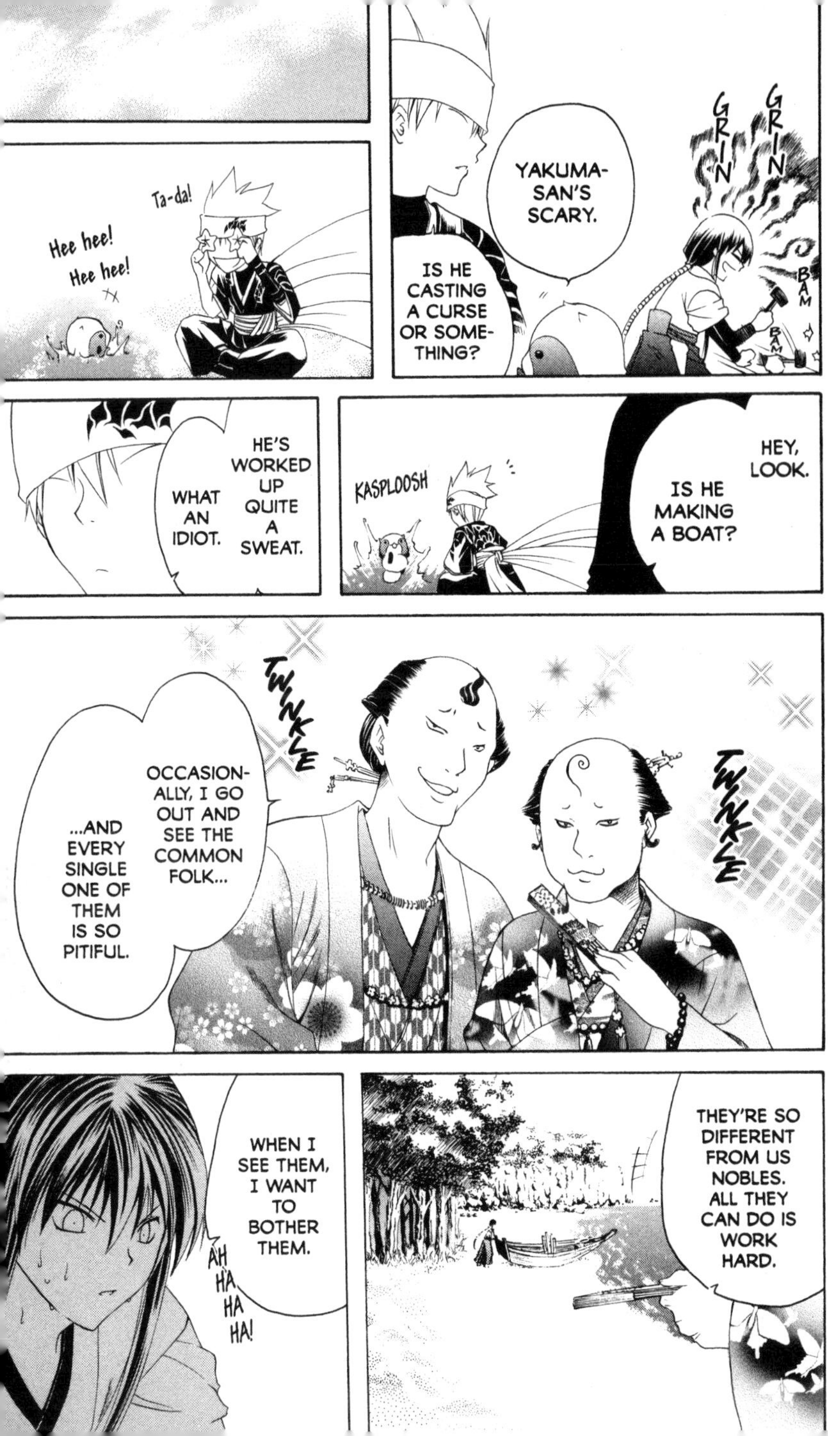
GRIN GRIN
YAKUMA-SAN'S SCARY.
IS HE CASTING A CURSE OR SOME-THING?
BAM BAM
Ta-da!
Hee hee! Hee hee!
HEY, LOOK.
IS HE MAKING A BOAT?
KASPLOOSH
HE'S WORKED UP QUITE A SWEAT.
WHAT AN IDIOT.
TWINKLE
TWINKLE
OCCASION-ALLY, I GO OUT AND SEE THE COMMON FOLK...
...AND EVERY SINGLE ONE OF THEM IS SO PITIFUL.
THEY'RE SO DIFFERENT FROM US NOBLES. ALL THEY CAN DO IS WORK HARD.
WHEN I SEE THEM, I WANT TO BOTHER THEM.
AH HA HA HA!

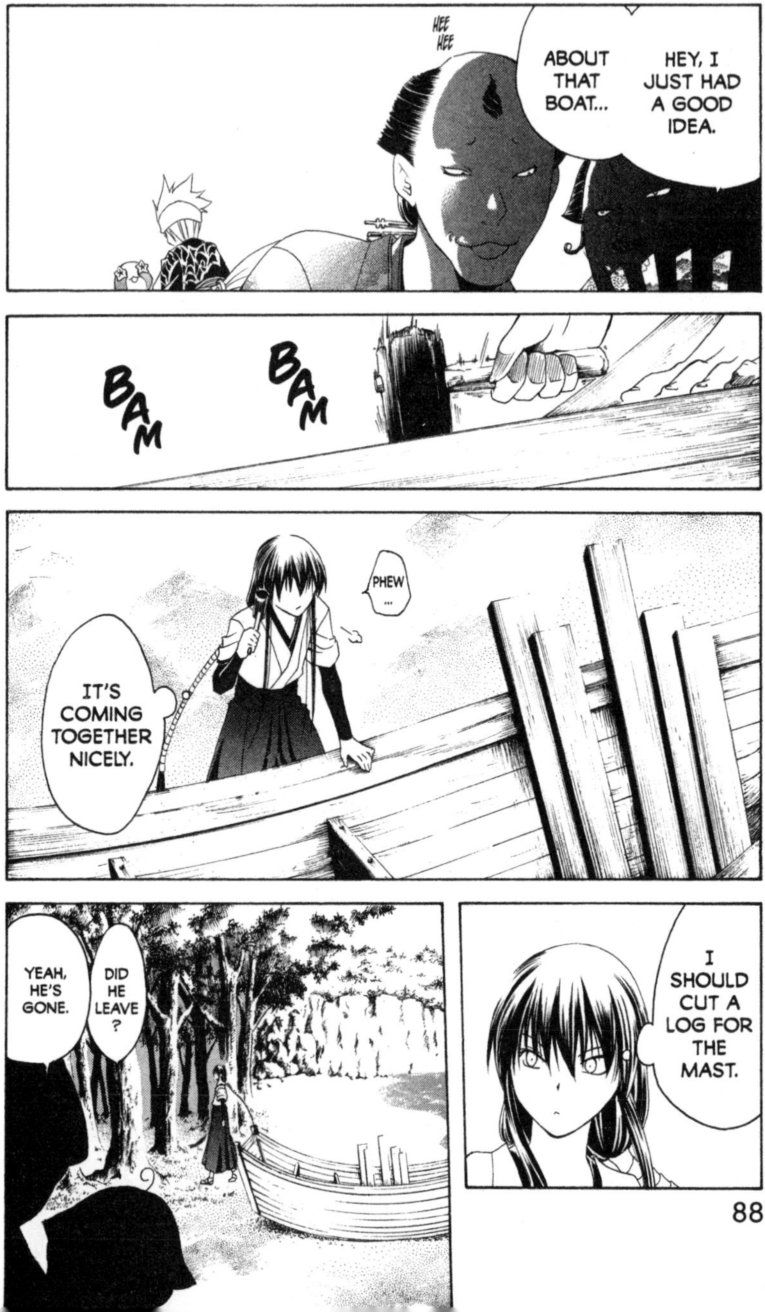
HEE HEE
HEY, I JUST HAD A GOOD IDEA.
ABOUT THAT BOAT...
BAM
BAM
PHEW...
IT'S COMING TOGETHER NICELY.
I SHOULD CUT A LOG FOR THE MAST.
DID HE LEAVE?
YEAH, HE'S GONE.

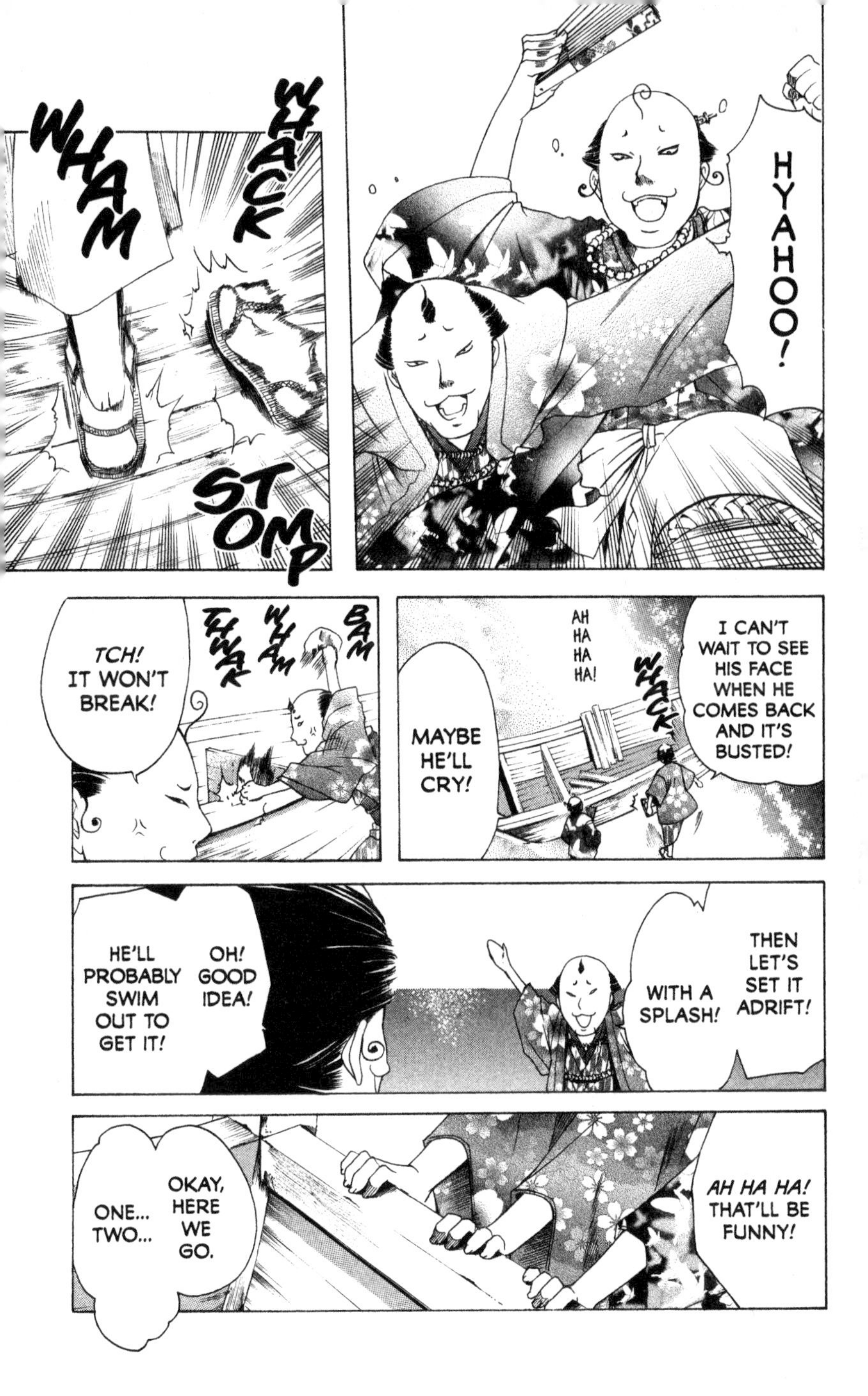
HYAHOO!
WHACK
WHAM
STOMP
I CAN'T WAIT TO SEE HIS FACE WHEN HE COMES BACK AND IT'S BUSTED!
AH HA HA HA!
WHACK
MAYBE HE'LL CRY!
BAM
WHAM
THWAK
TCH! IT WON'T BREAK!
THEN LET'S SET IT ADRIFT!
WITH A SPLASH!
OH! GOOD IDEA!
HE'LL PROBABLY SWIM OUT TO GET IT!
AH HA HA! THAT'LL BE FUNNY!
OKAY, HERE WE GO.
ONE... TWO...

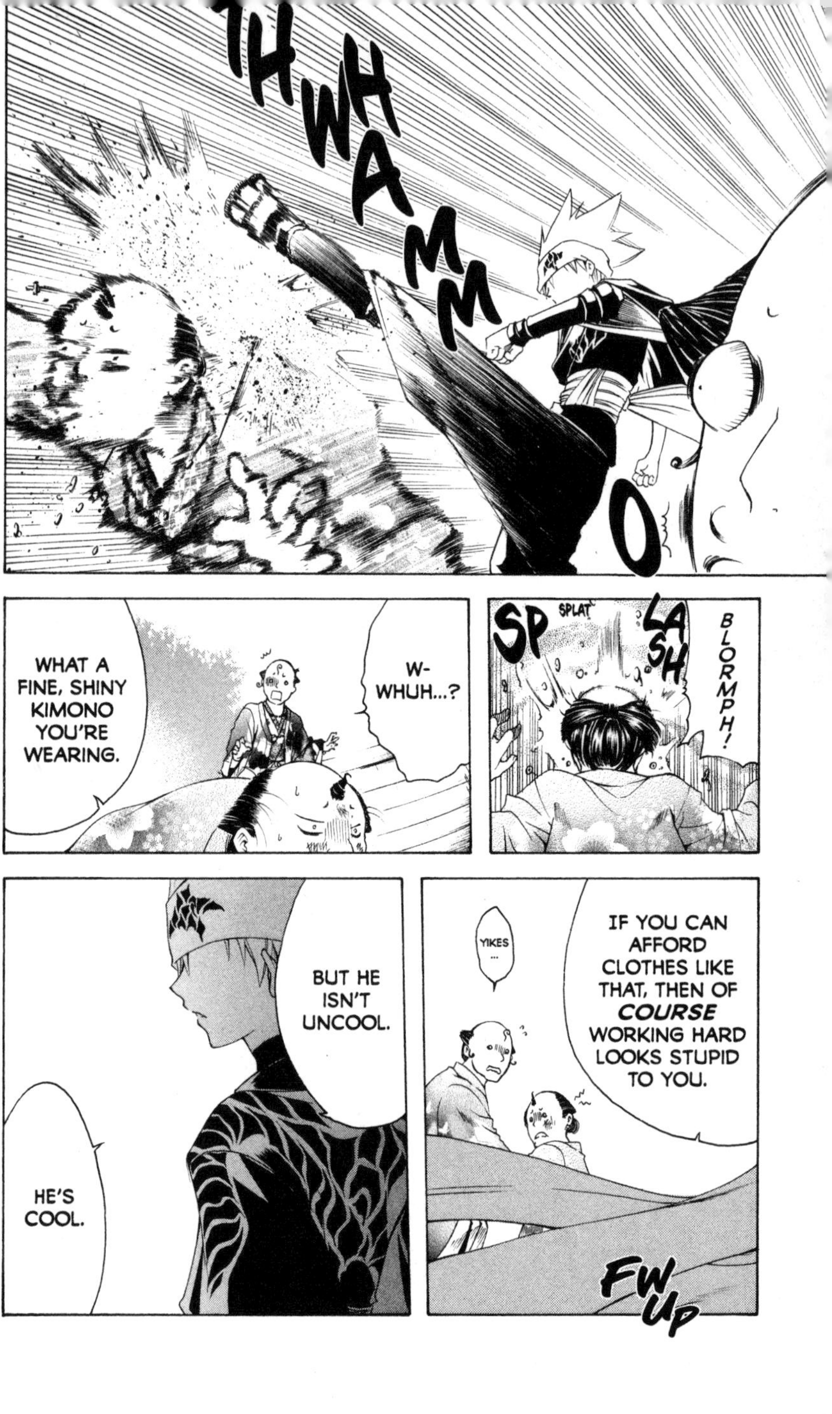
THWHAMM
O
SPLASH
SPLAT
BLORMPH!
W-WHUH...?
WHAT A FINE, SHINY KIMONO YOU'RE WEARING.
IF YOU CAN AFFORD CLOTHES LIKE THAT, THEN OF *COURSE* WORKING HARD LOOKS STUPID TO YOU.
YIKES...
FWUP
BUT HE ISN'T UNCOOL.
HE'S COOL.

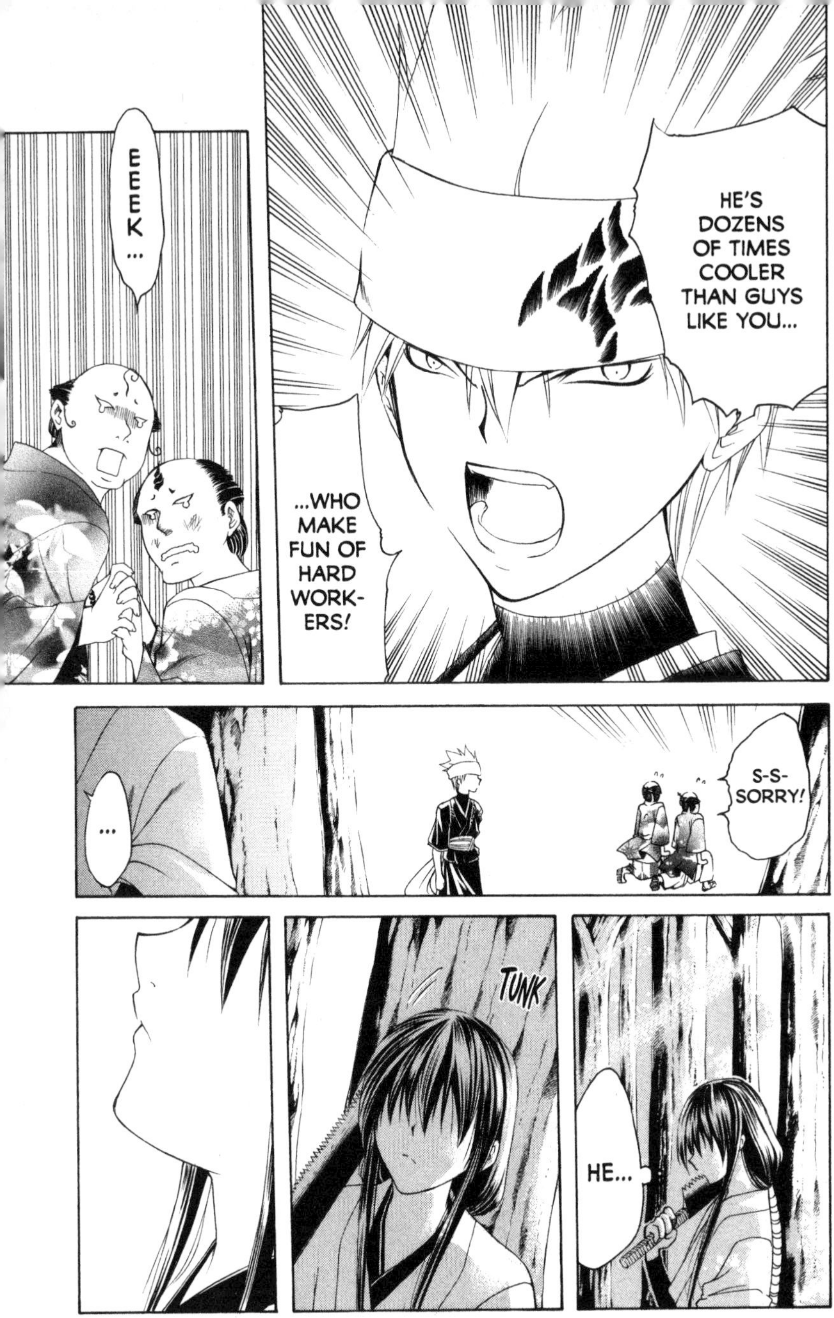
HE'S DOZENS OF TIMES COOLER THAN GUYS LIKE YOU...
...WHO MAKE FUN OF HARD WORK-ERS!
EEEK...
S-S-SORRY!
...
HE...
TUNK

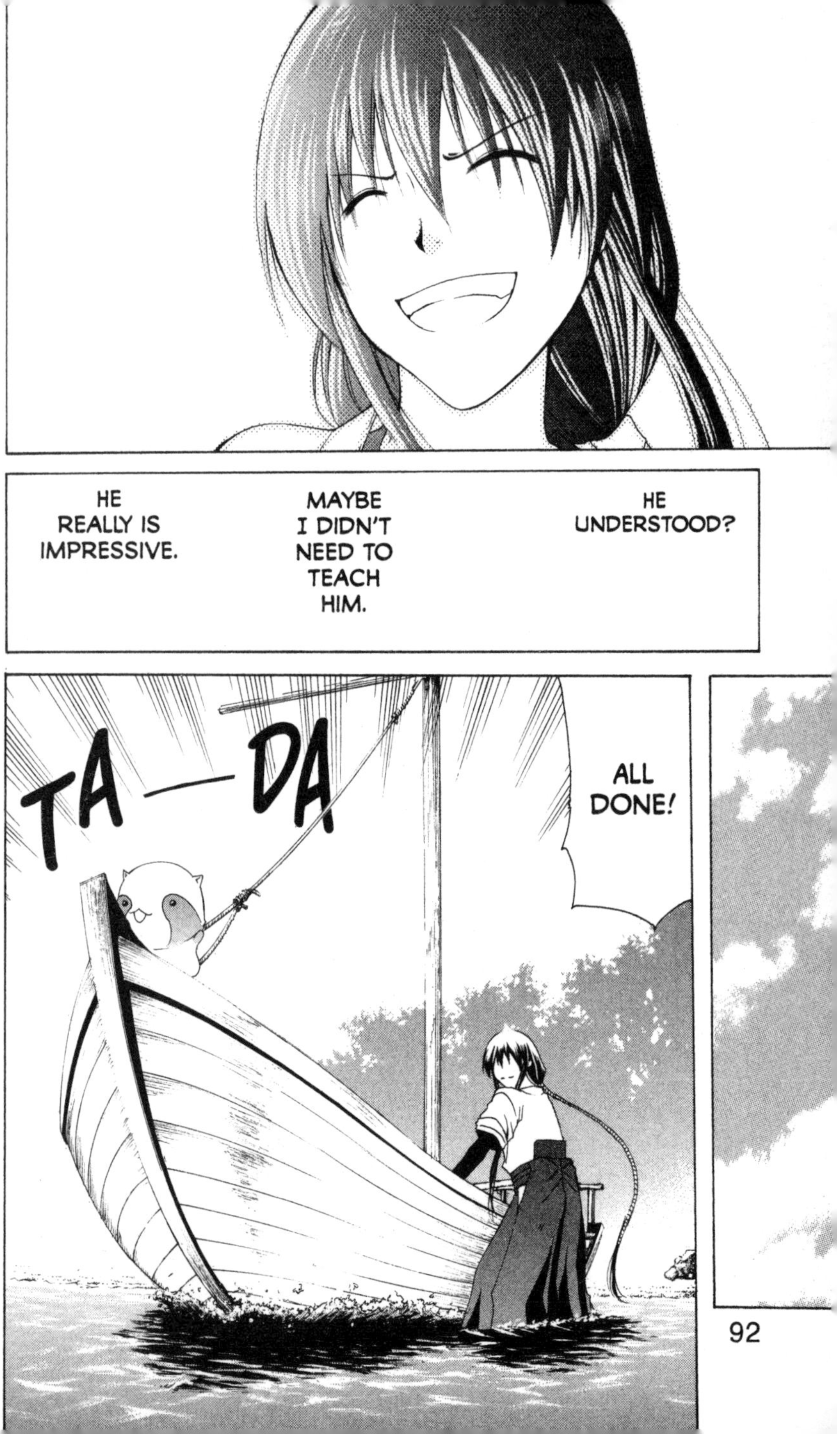
HE UNDERSTOOD?
MAYBE I DIDN'T NEED TO TEACH HIM.
HE REALLY IS IMPRESSIVE.
ALL DONE!
TA—DA

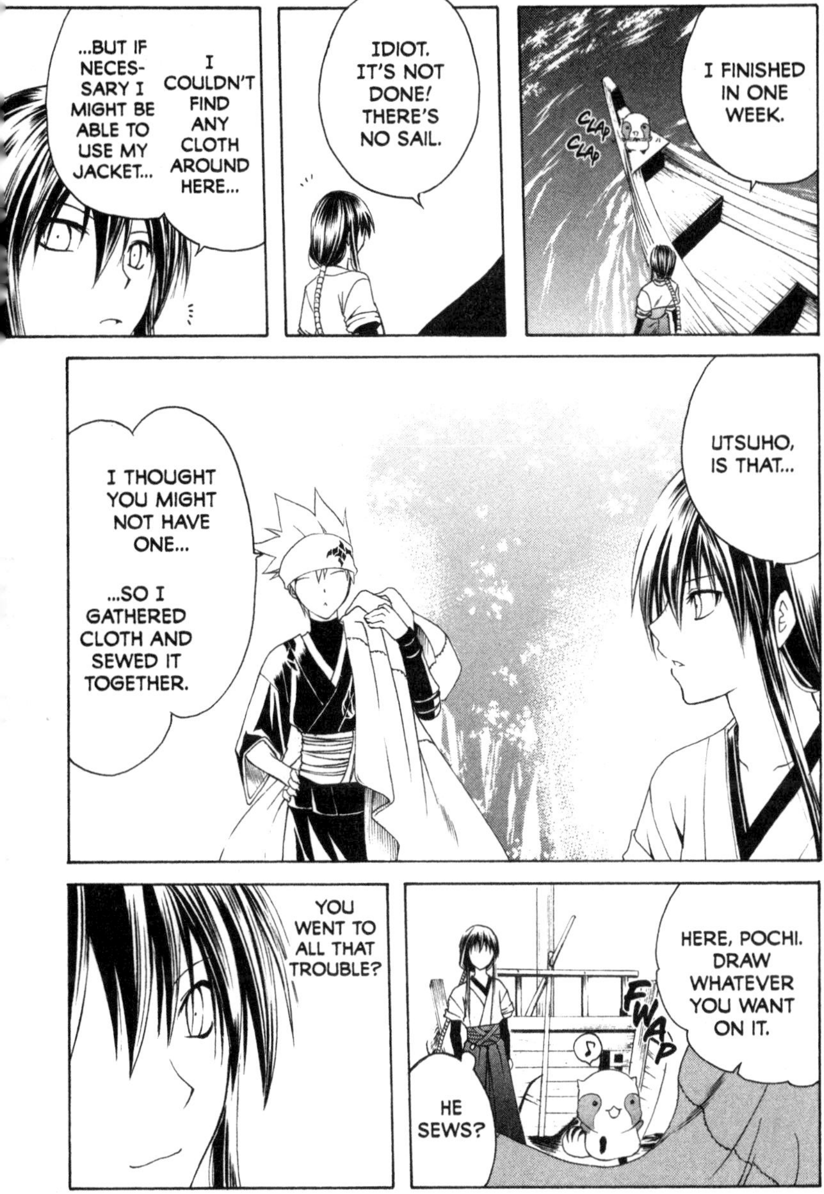
I FINISHED IN ONE WEEK.
CLAP CLAP
IDIOT. IT'S NOT DONE! THERE'S NO SAIL.
I COULDN'T FIND ANY CLOTH AROUND HERE...
...BUT IF NECES-SARY I MIGHT BE ABLE TO USE MY JACKET...
UTSUHO, IS THAT...
I THOUGHT YOU MIGHT NOT HAVE ONE...
...SO I GATHERED CLOTH AND SEWED IT TOGETHER.
HERE, POCHI. DRAW WHATEVER YOU WANT ON IT.
FWAP
HE SEWS?
YOU WENT TO ALL THAT TROUBLE?

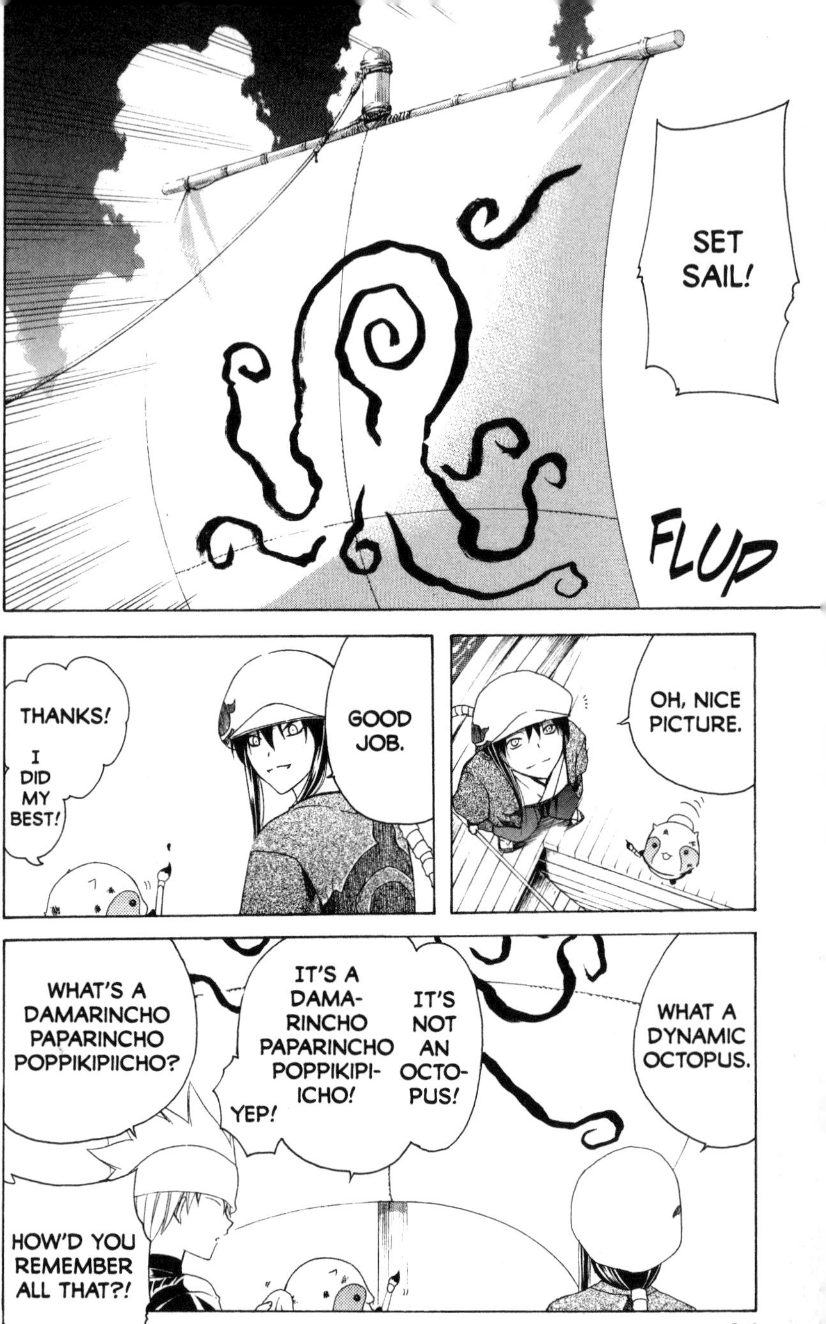
SET SAIL!
FLUP
OH, NICE PICTURE.
GOOD JOB.
THANKS!
I DID MY BEST!
WHAT A DYNAMIC OCTOPUS.
IT'S NOT AN OCTOPUS!
IT'S A DAMARINCHO PAPARINCHO POPPIKIPIICHO!
YEP!
WHAT'S A DAMARINCHO PAPARINCHO POPPIKIPIICHO?
HOW'D YOU REMEMBER ALL THAT?!

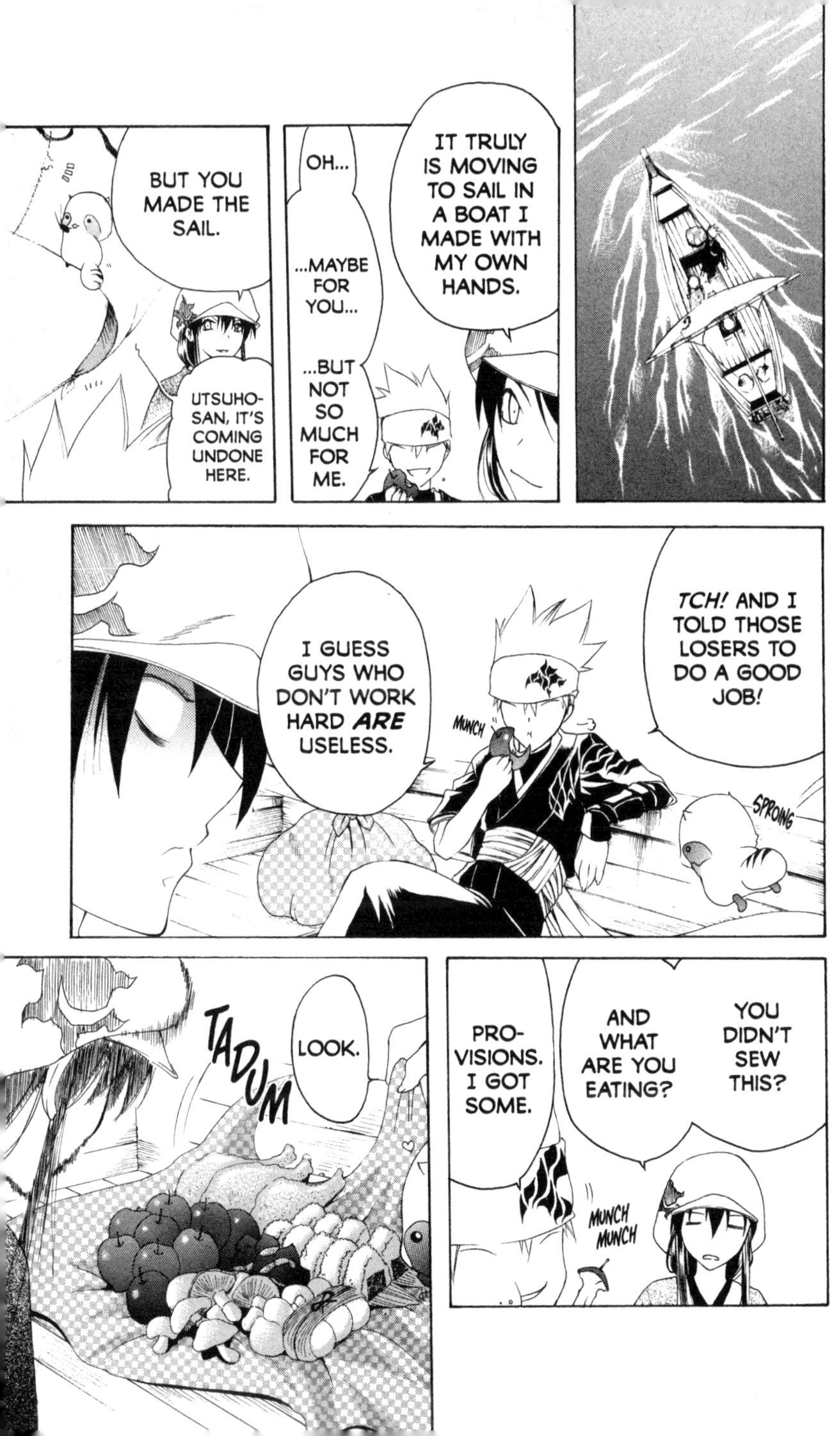
IT TRULY IS MOVING TO SAIL IN A BOAT I MADE WITH MY OWN HANDS.
OH...
...MAYBE FOR YOU...
...BUT NOT SO MUCH FOR ME.
BUT YOU MADE THE SAIL.
UTSUHO-SAN, IT'S COMING UNDONE HERE.
TCH! AND I TOLD THOSE LOSERS TO DO A GOOD JOB!
SPROING
MUNCH
I GUESS GUYS WHO DON'T WORK HARD ***ARE*** USELESS.
YOU DIDN'T SEW THIS?
AND WHAT ARE YOU EATING?
PRO-VISIONS. I GOT SOME.
MUNCH MUNCH
LOOK.
TADUM

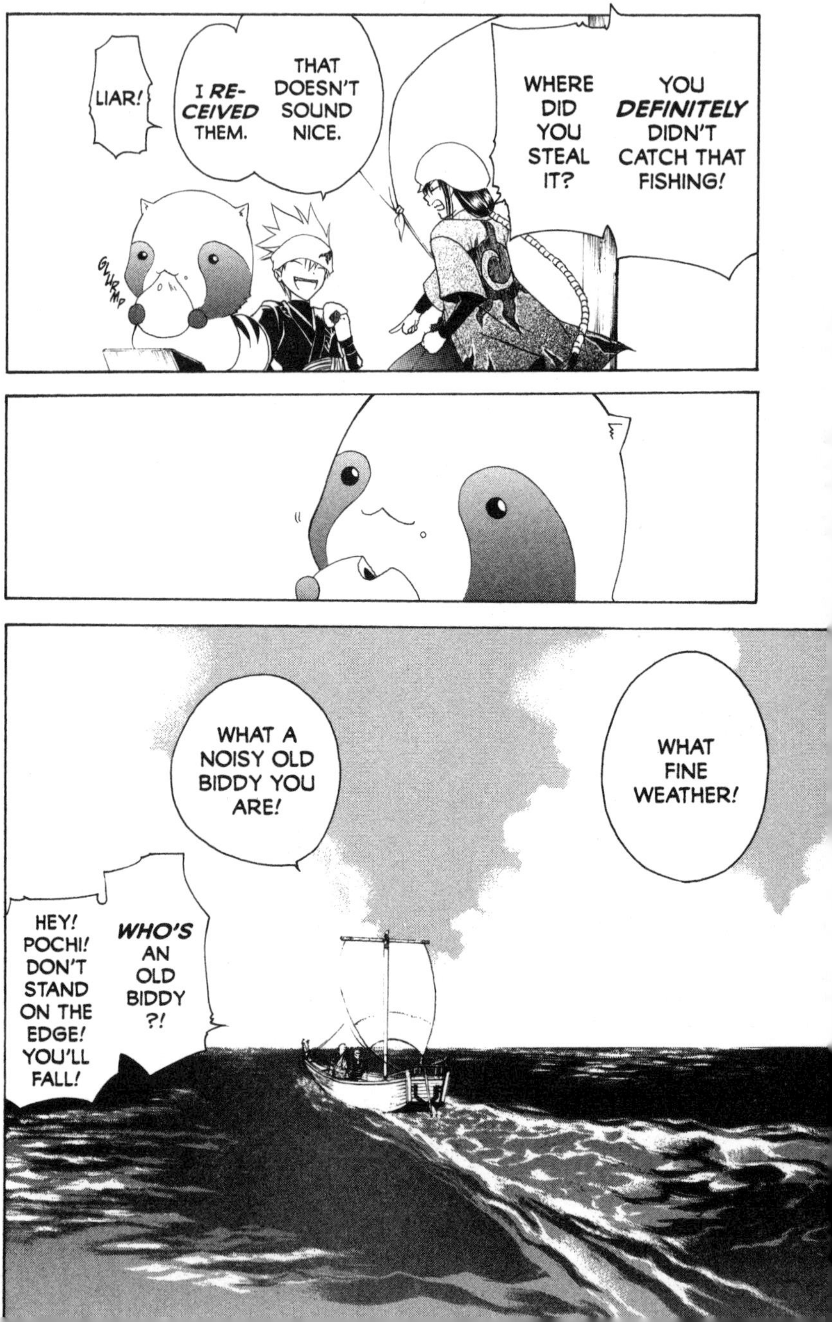
YOU DEFINITELY DIDN'T CATCH THAT FISHING!
WHERE DID YOU STEAL IT?
THAT DOESN'T SOUND NICE.
I RECEIVED THEM.
LIAR!
WHAT FINE WEATHER!
WHAT A NOISY OLD BIDDY YOU ARE!
WHO'S AN OLD BIDDY?!
HEY! POCHI! DON'T STAND ON THE EDGE! YOU'LL FALL!

Chapter 13 Utsuho Is Human After All

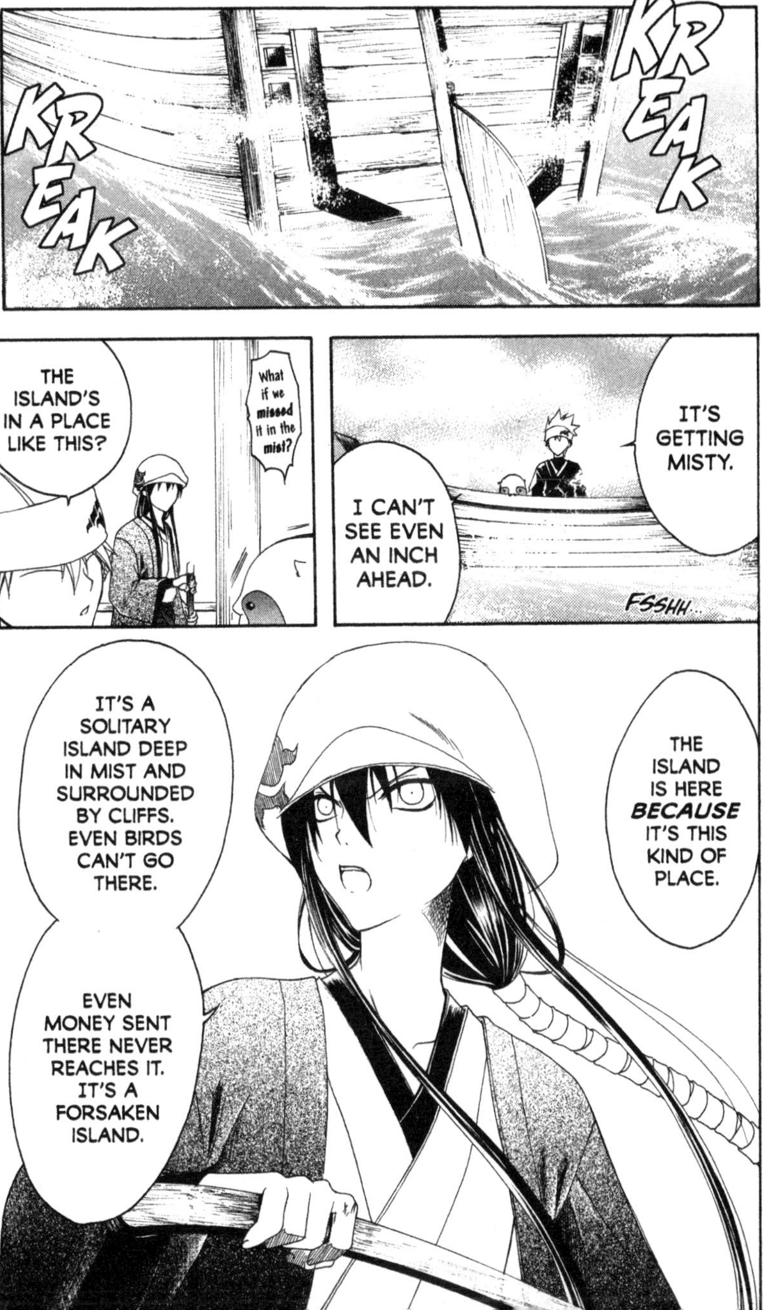
KREAK
KREAK
IT'S GETTING MISTY.
I CAN'T SEE EVEN AN INCH AHEAD.
FSSHH...
What if we **missed** it in the **mist?**
THE ISLAND'S IN A PLACE LIKE THIS?
THE ISLAND IS HERE ***BECAUSE*** IT'S THIS KIND OF PLACE.
IT'S A SOLITARY ISLAND DEEP IN MIST AND SURROUNDED BY CLIFFS. EVEN BIRDS CAN'T GO THERE.
EVEN MONEY SENT THERE NEVER REACHES IT. IT'S A FORSAKEN ISLAND.

Chapter 13
Utsuho Is Human After All

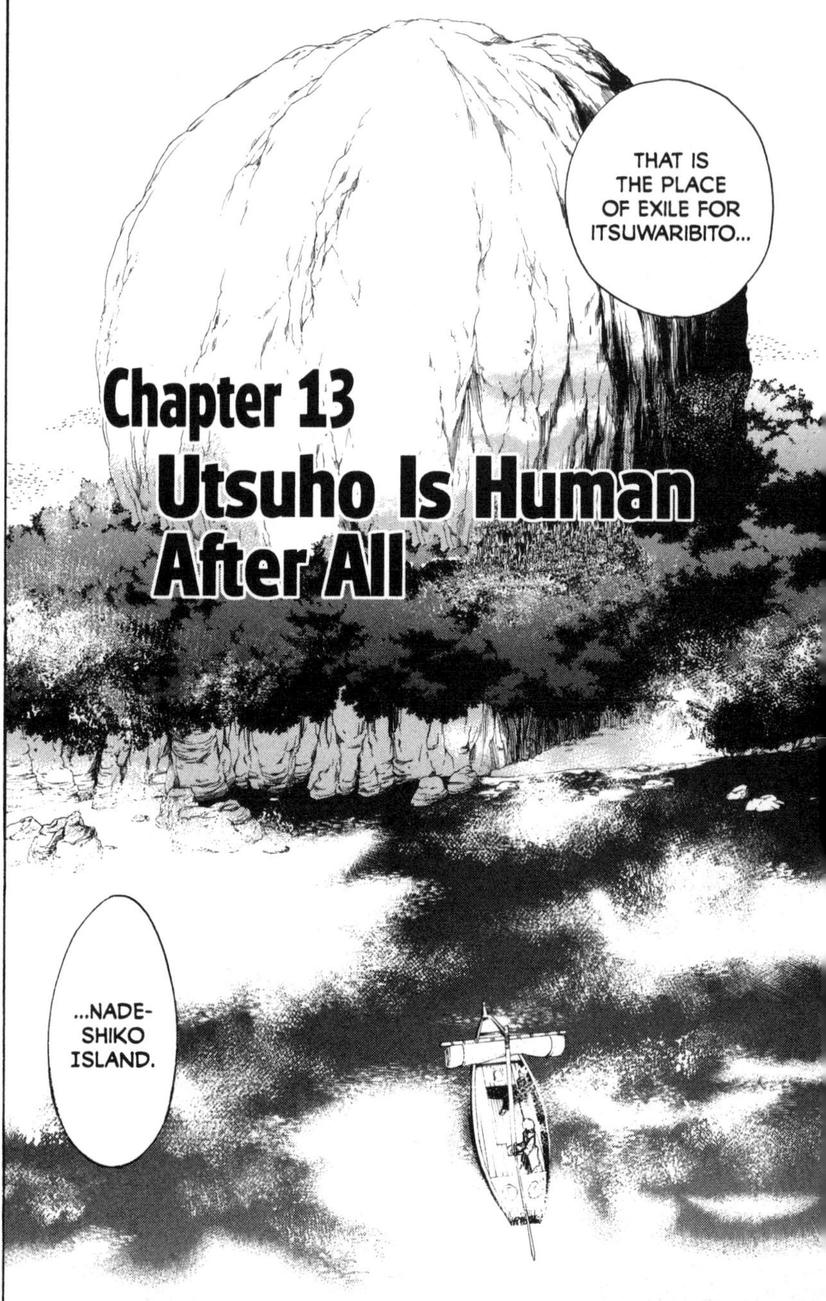
THAT IS THE PLACE OF EXILE FOR ITSUWARIBITO...
...NADE-SHIKO ISLAND.

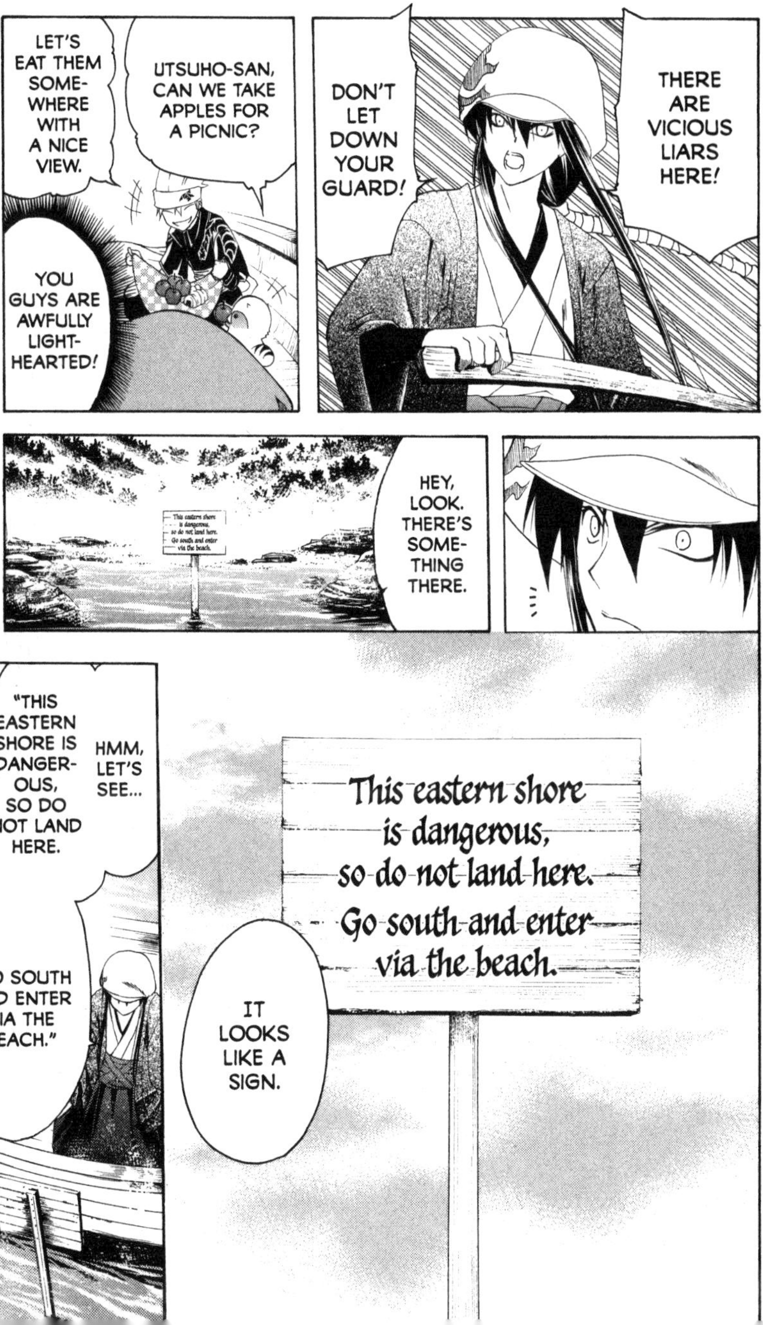
THERE ARE VICIOUS LIARS HERE!
DON'T LET DOWN YOUR GUARD!
UTSUHO-SAN, CAN WE TAKE APPLES FOR A PICNIC?
LET'S EAT THEM SOMEWHERE WITH A NICE VIEW.
YOU GUYS ARE AWFULLY LIGHT-HEARTED!
HEY, LOOK. THERE'S SOMETHING THERE.
This eastern shore is dangerous, so do not land here. Go south and enter via the beach.
IT LOOKS LIKE A SIGN.
HMM, LET'S SEE...
"THIS EASTERN SHORE IS DANGEROUS, SO DO NOT LAND HERE.
"GO SOUTH AND ENTER VIA THE BEACH."

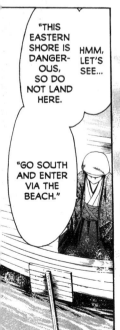

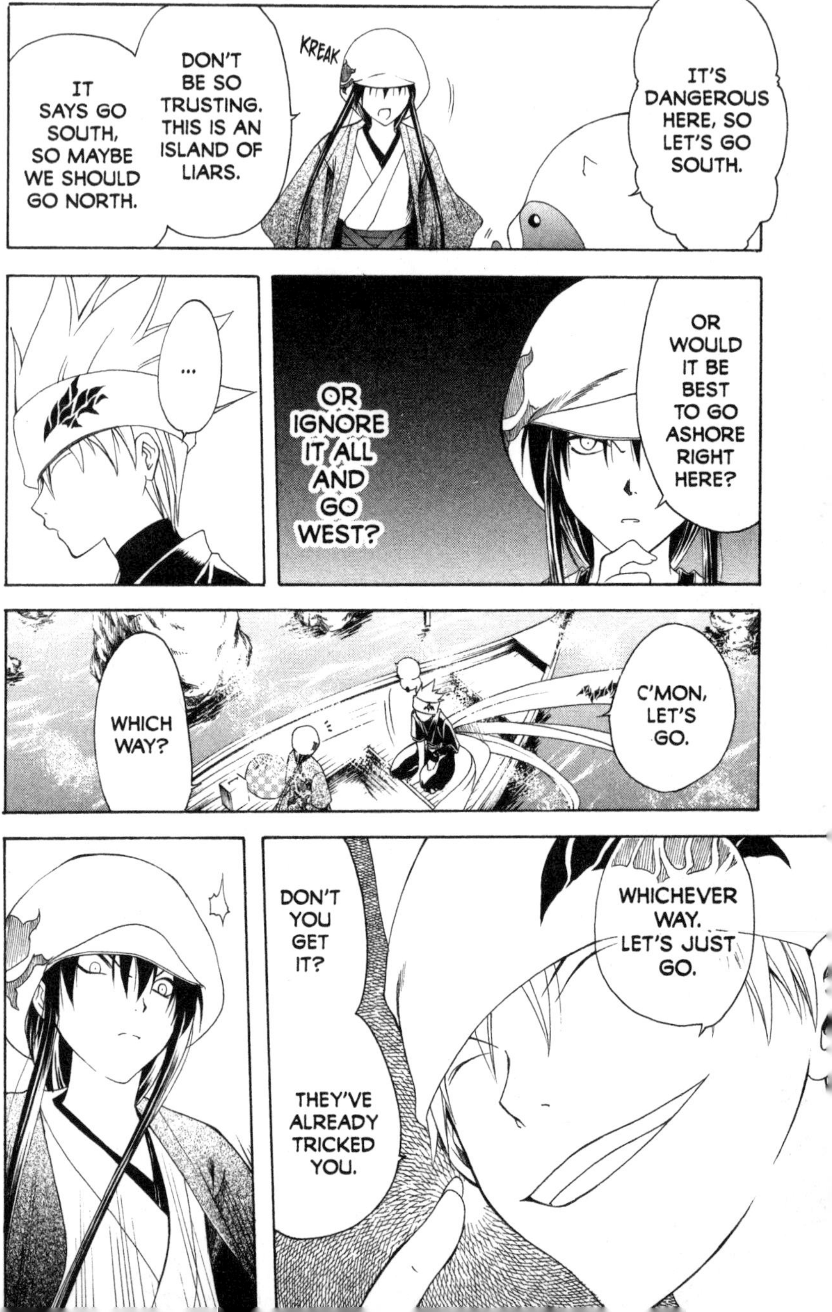
IT'S DANGEROUS HERE, SO LET'S GO SOUTH.
KREAK
DON'T BE SO TRUSTING. THIS IS AN ISLAND OF LIARS.
IT SAYS GO SOUTH, SO MAYBE WE SHOULD GO NORTH.
OR WOULD IT BE BEST TO GO ASHORE RIGHT HERE?
OR IGNORE IT ALL AND GO WEST?
...
C'MON, LET'S GO.
WHICH WAY?
WHICHEVER WAY. LET'S JUST GO.
DON'T YOU GET IT?
THEY'VE ALREADY TRICKED YOU.

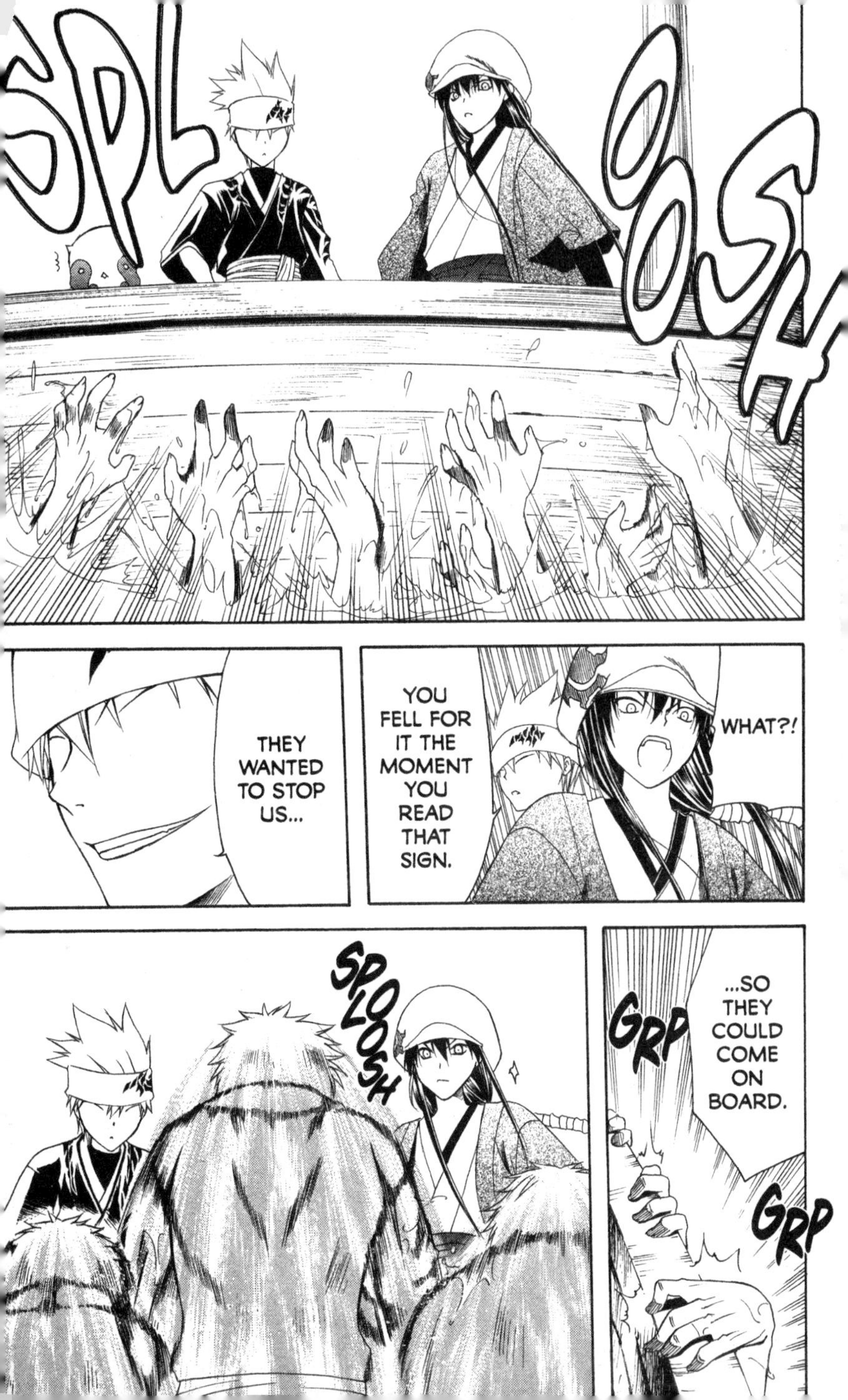
SPLOOSH
YOU FELL FOR IT THE MOMENT YOU READ THAT SIGN.
WHAT?!
THEY WANTED TO STOP US...
...SO THEY COULD COME ON BOARD.
GRP
GRP
SPLOOSH

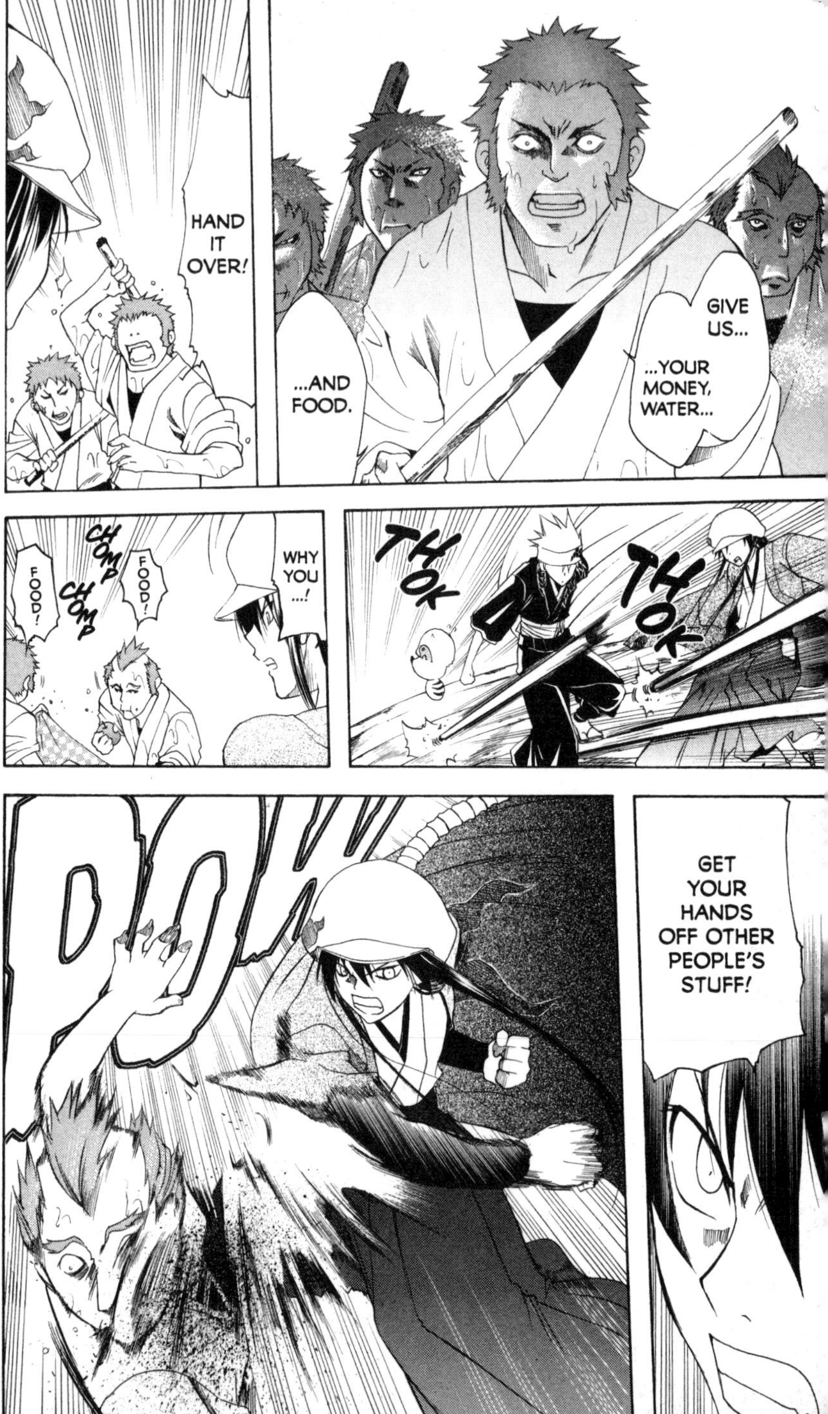
GIVE US...
...YOUR MONEY, WATER...
...AND FOOD.
HAND IT OVER!
THOK
THOK
WHY YOU ...!
FOOD!
CHOMP CHOMP
FOOD!
GET YOUR HANDS OFF OTHER PEOPLE'S STUFF!

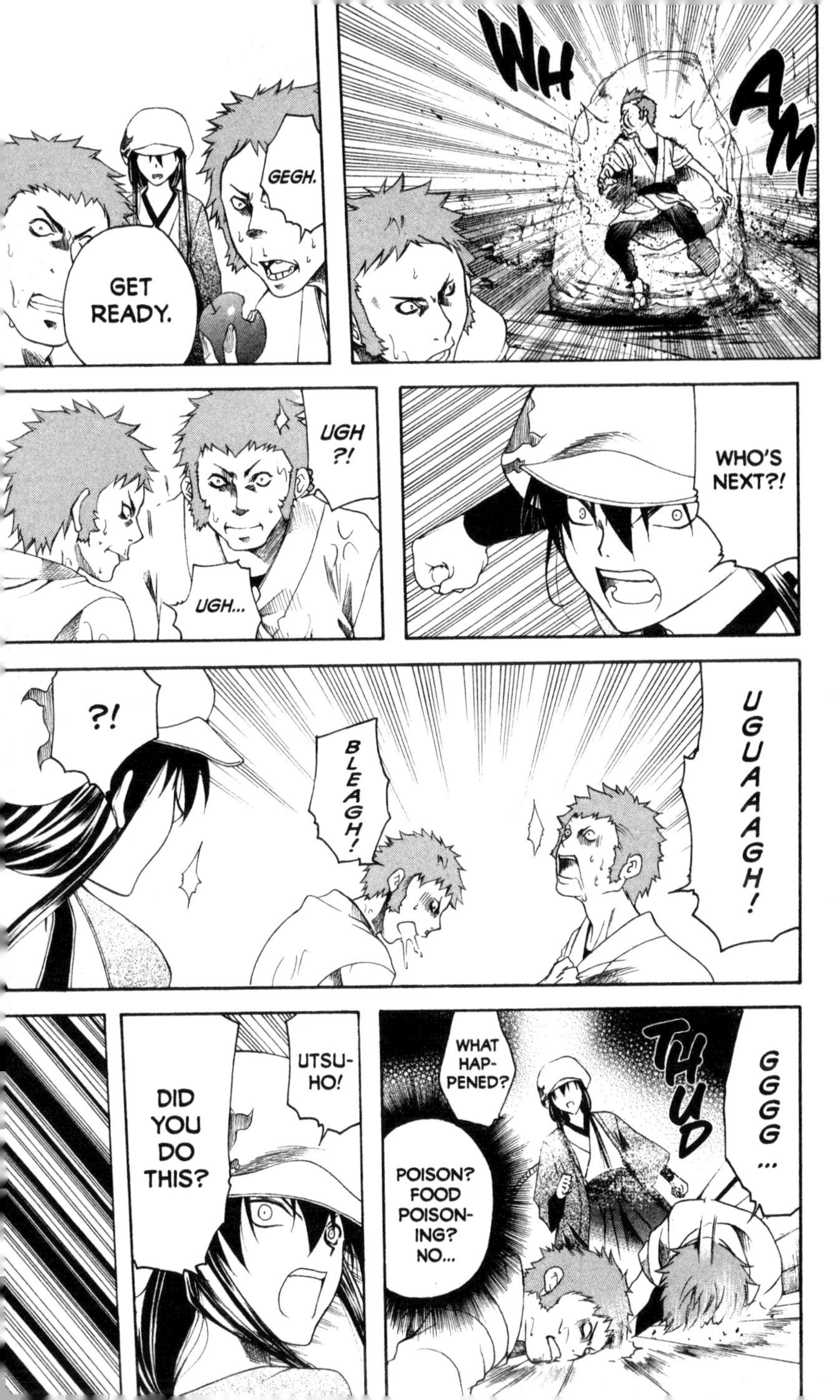
WHAM
GEGH.
GET READY.
WHO'S NEXT?!
UGH ?!
UGH...
UGUAAAAGH!
BLEAAGH!
?!
GGGG...
THUD
WHAT HAP-PENED?
POISON? FOOD POISON-ING? NO...
UTSU-HO!
DID YOU DO THIS?

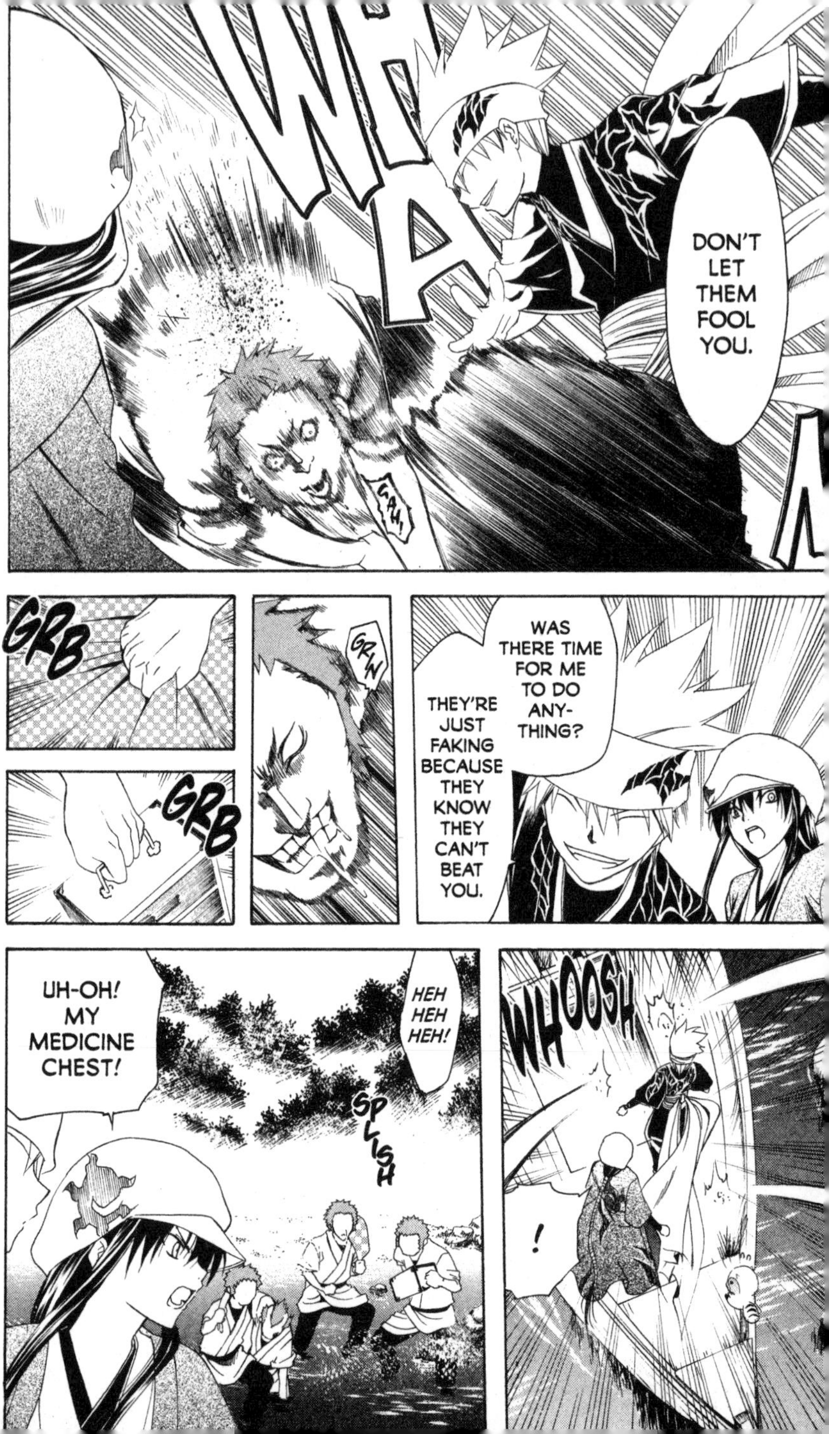
WHAM
DON'T LET THEM FOOL YOU.
GRAH!
WAS THERE TIME FOR ME TO DO ANY-THING?
THEY'RE JUST FAKING BECAUSE THEY KNOW THEY CAN'T BEAT YOU.
GRIN
GRB
GRB
WHOOSH
!
HEH HEH HEH!
SPLISH
UH-OH! MY MEDICINE CHEST!

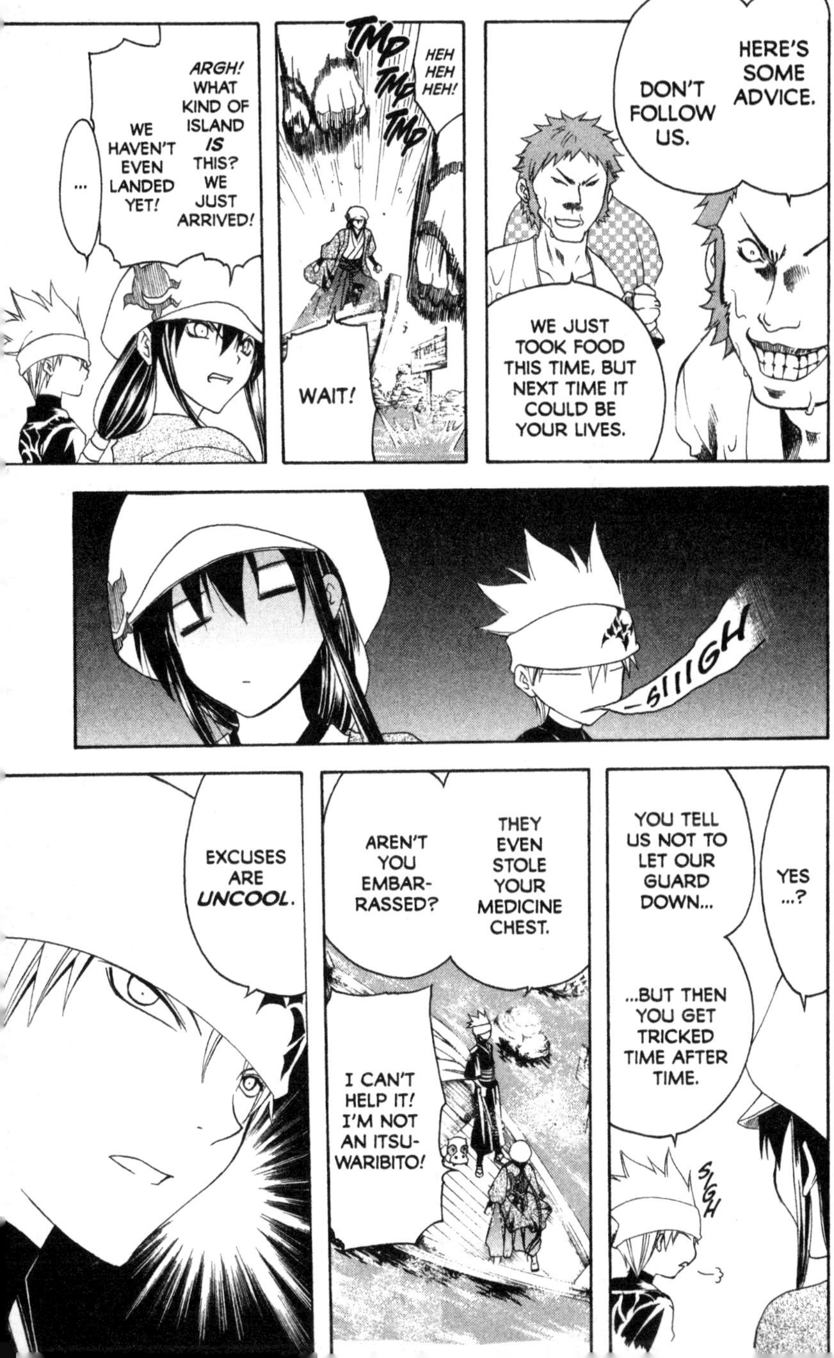
HERE'S SOME ADVICE.
DON'T FOLLOW US.
WE JUST TOOK FOOD THIS TIME, BUT NEXT TIME IT COULD BE YOUR LIVES.
HEH HEH HEH!
TMP TMP TMP TMP
WAIT!
ARGH! WHAT KIND OF ISLAND *IS* THIS? WE JUST ARRIVED!
WE HAVEN'T EVEN LANDED YET!
...
SIIIGH
YES ...?
YOU TELL US NOT TO LET OUR GUARD DOWN...
...BUT THEN YOU GET TRICKED TIME AFTER TIME.
SIGH
THEY EVEN STOLE YOUR MEDICINE CHEST.
AREN'T YOU EMBARRASSED?
I CAN'T HELP IT! I'M NOT AN ITSU-WARIBITO!
EXCUSES ARE *UNCOOL*.

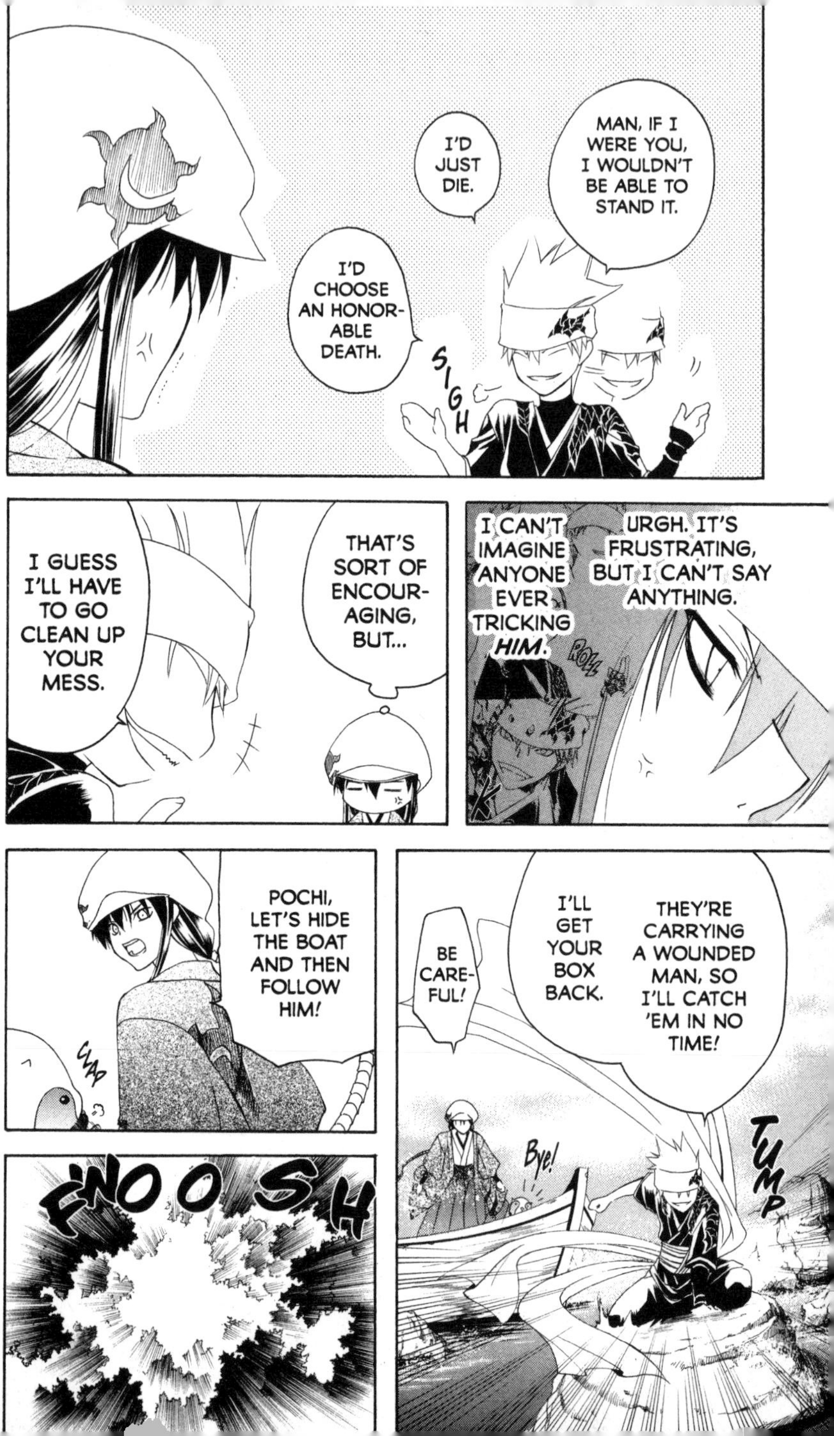
MAN, IF I WERE YOU, I WOULDN'T BE ABLE TO STAND IT.
I'D JUST DIE.
I'D CHOOSE AN HONORABLE DEATH.
SIGH
URGH. IT'S FRUSTRATING, BUT I CAN'T SAY ANYTHING.
I CAN'T IMAGINE ANYONE EVER TRICKING *HIM*.
THAT'S SORT OF ENCOURAGING, BUT...
I GUESS I'LL HAVE TO GO CLEAN UP YOUR MESS.
THEY'RE CARRYING A WOUNDED MAN, SO I'LL CATCH 'EM IN NO TIME!
I'LL GET YOUR BOX BACK.
BE CAREFUL!
Bye!
TUMP
POCHI, LET'S HIDE THE BOAT AND THEN FOLLOW HIM!
FWOOSH

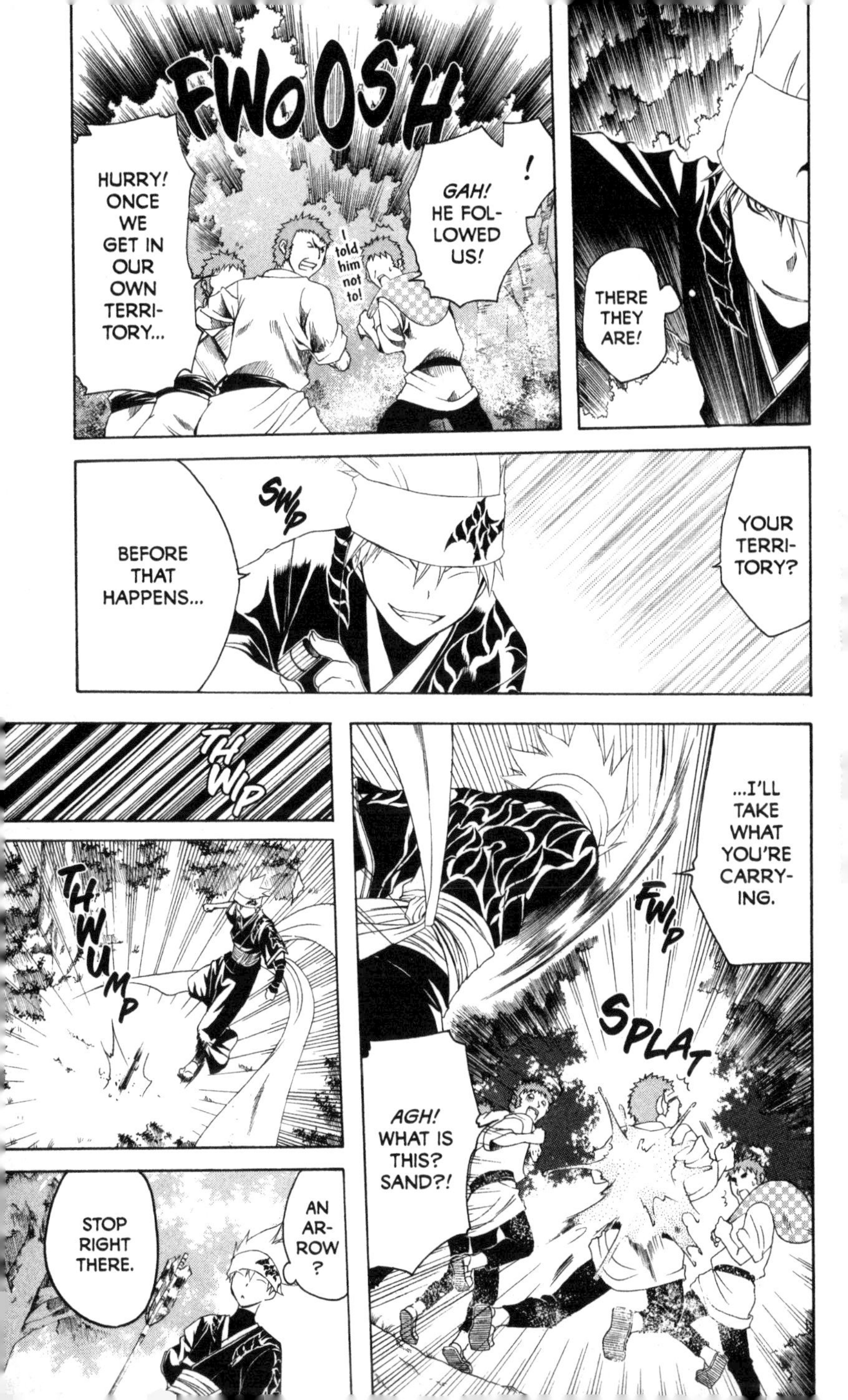
THERE THEY ARE!
FWOOSH
!
GAH! HE FOLLOWED US!
I told him not to!
HURRY! ONCE WE GET IN OUR OWN TERRITORY...
YOUR TERRITORY?
SWIP
BEFORE THAT HAPPENS...
...I'LL TAKE WHAT YOU'RE CARRYING.
FWIP
SPLAT
AGH! WHAT IS THIS? SAND?!
THWIP
THWUMP
AN ARROW?
STOP RIGHT THERE.

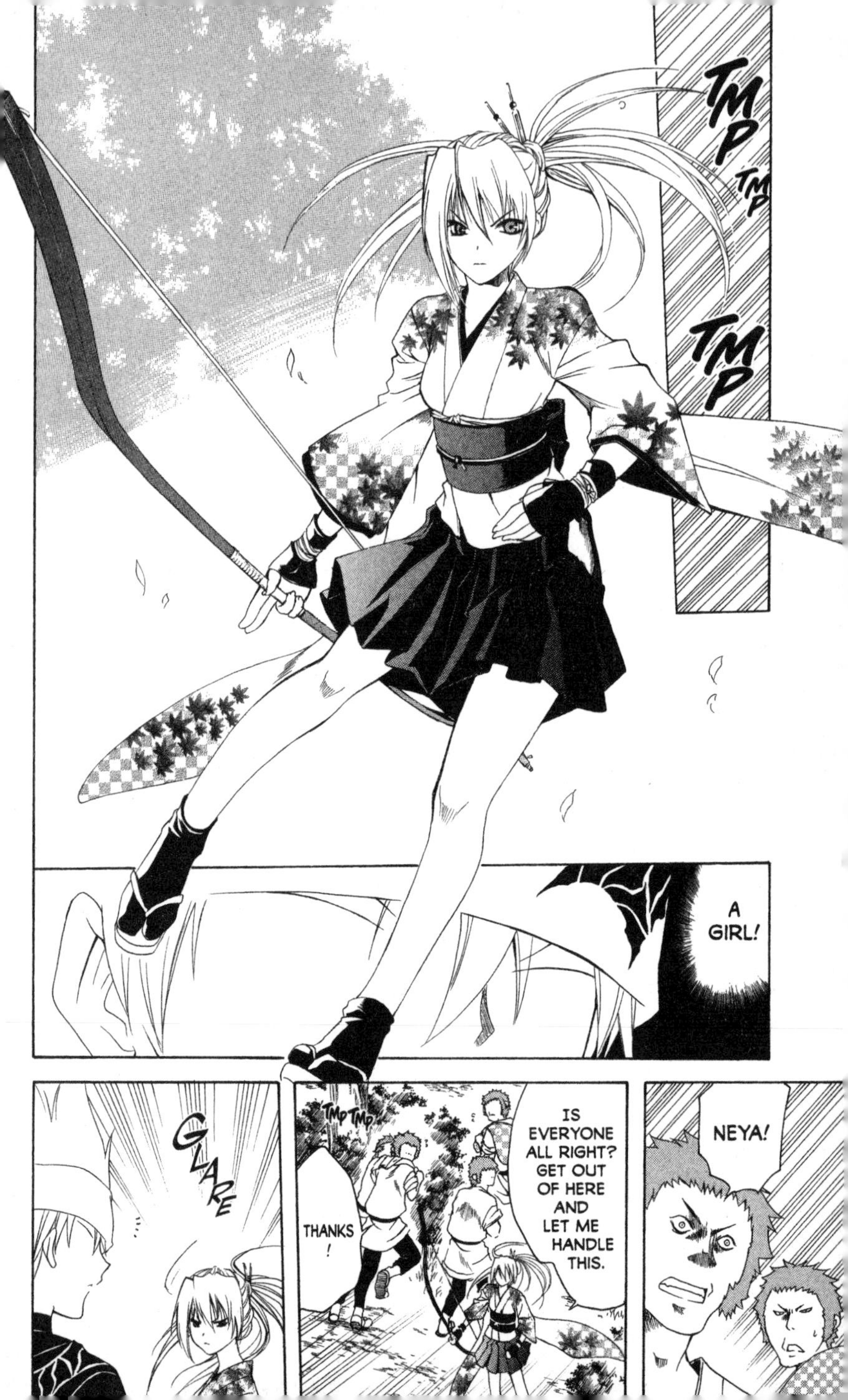
TMP
TMP
TMP
TMP
A GIRL!
NEYA!
IS EVERYONE ALL RIGHT? GET OUT OF HERE AND LET ME HANDLE THIS.
TMP TMP
THANKS!
GLARE
...

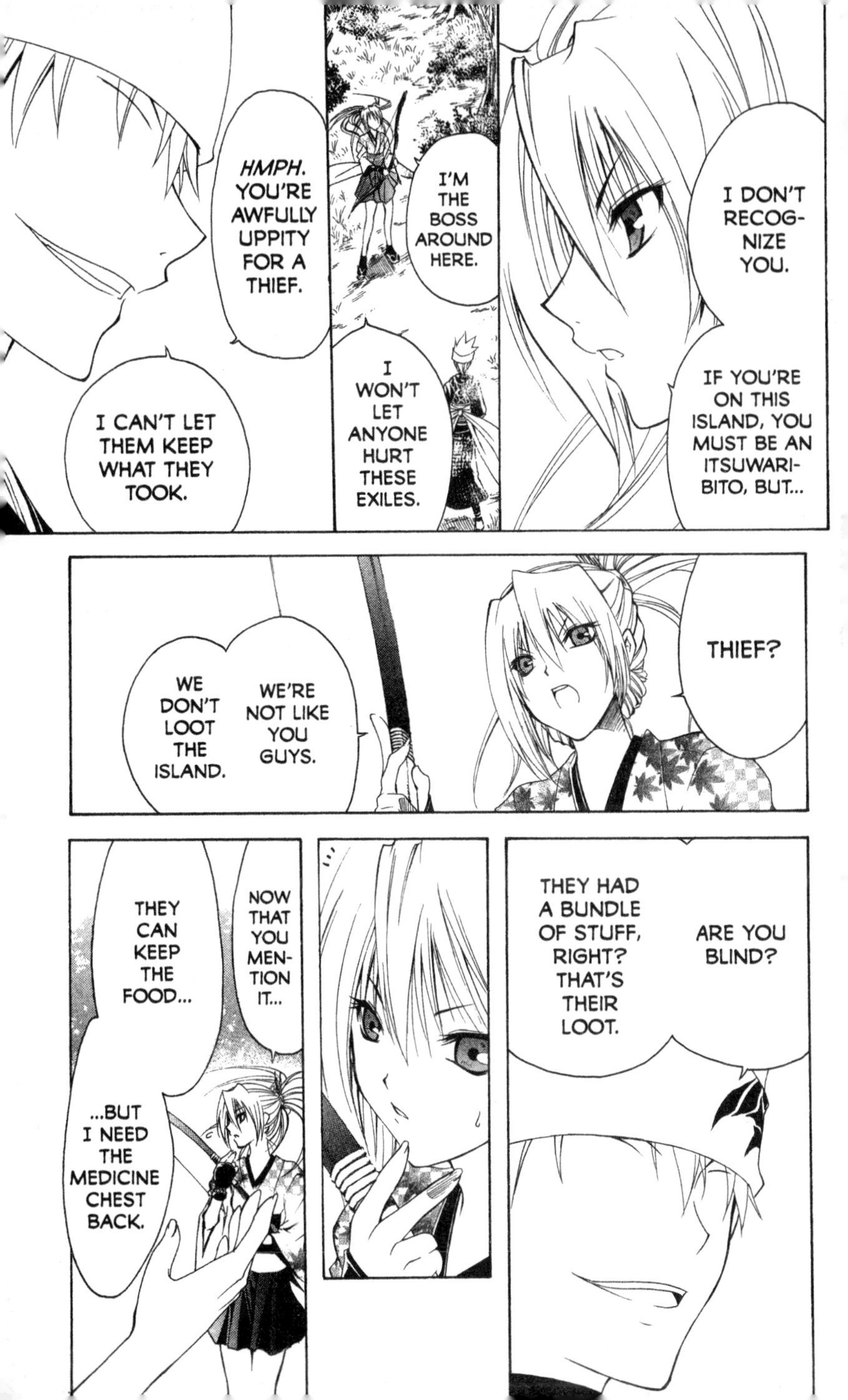
I DON'T RECOGNIZE YOU.
IF YOU'RE ON THIS ISLAND, YOU MUST BE AN ITSUWARIBITO, BUT...
I'M THE BOSS AROUND HERE.
I WON'T LET ANYONE HURT THESE EXILES.
HMPH. YOU'RE AWFULLY UPPITY FOR A THIEF.
I CAN'T LET THEM KEEP WHAT THEY TOOK.
THIEF?
WE'RE NOT LIKE YOU GUYS.
WE DON'T LOOT THE ISLAND.
ARE YOU BLIND?
THEY HAD A BUNDLE OF STUFF, RIGHT? THAT'S THEIR LOOT.
NOW THAT YOU MENTION IT...
THEY CAN KEEP THE FOOD...
...BUT I NEED THE MEDICINE CHEST BACK.

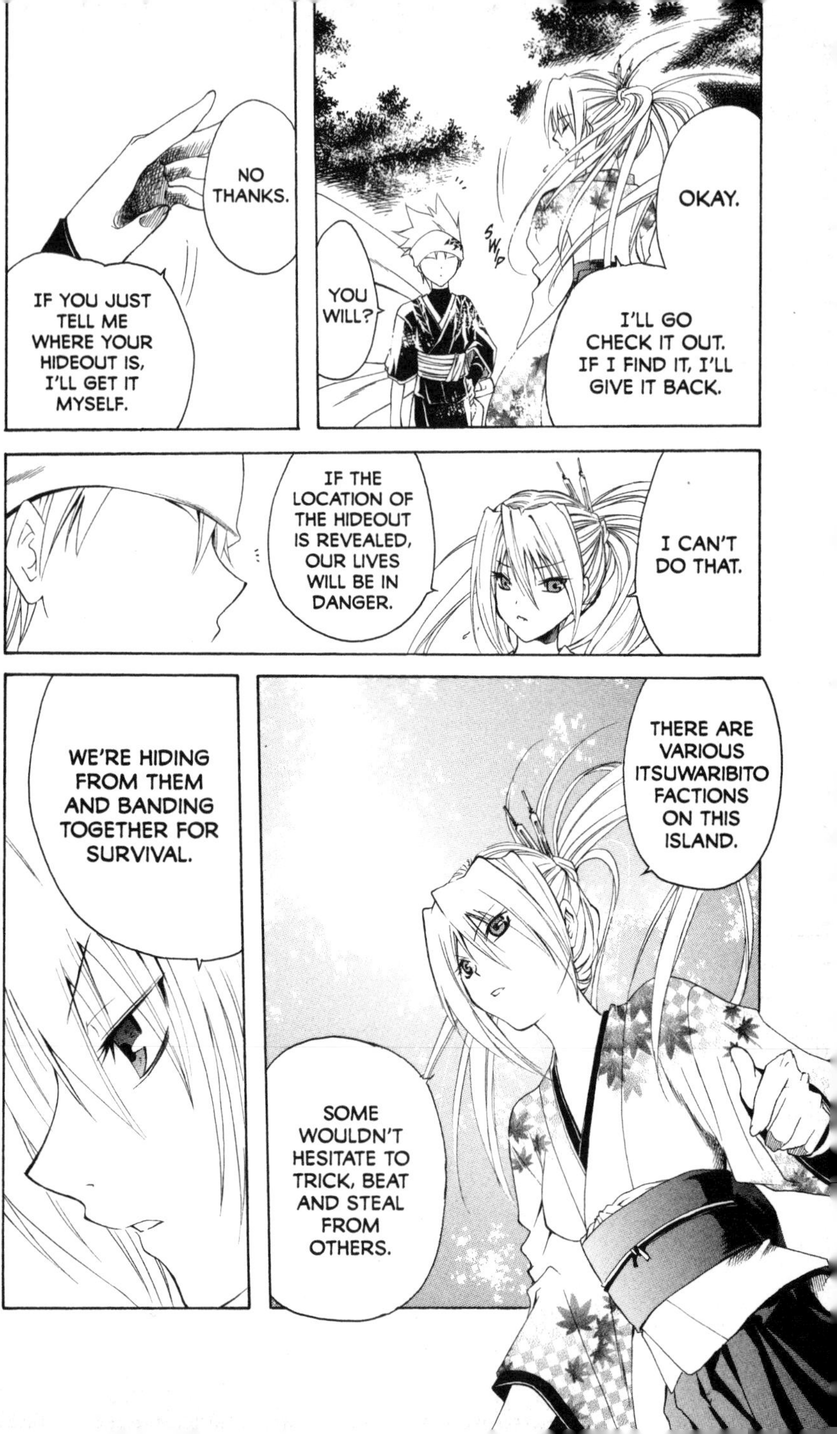
OKAY.
SWIP
I'LL GO CHECK IT OUT. IF I FIND IT, I'LL GIVE IT BACK.
YOU WILL?
NO THANKS.
IF YOU JUST TELL ME WHERE YOUR HIDEOUT IS, I'LL GET IT MYSELF.
I CAN'T DO THAT.
IF THE LOCATION OF THE HIDEOUT IS REVEALED, OUR LIVES WILL BE IN DANGER.
THERE ARE VARIOUS ITSUWARIBITO FACTIONS ON THIS ISLAND.
SOME WOULDN'T HESITATE TO TRICK, BEAT AND STEAL FROM OTHERS.
WE'RE HIDING FROM THEM AND BANDING TOGETHER FOR SURVIVAL.

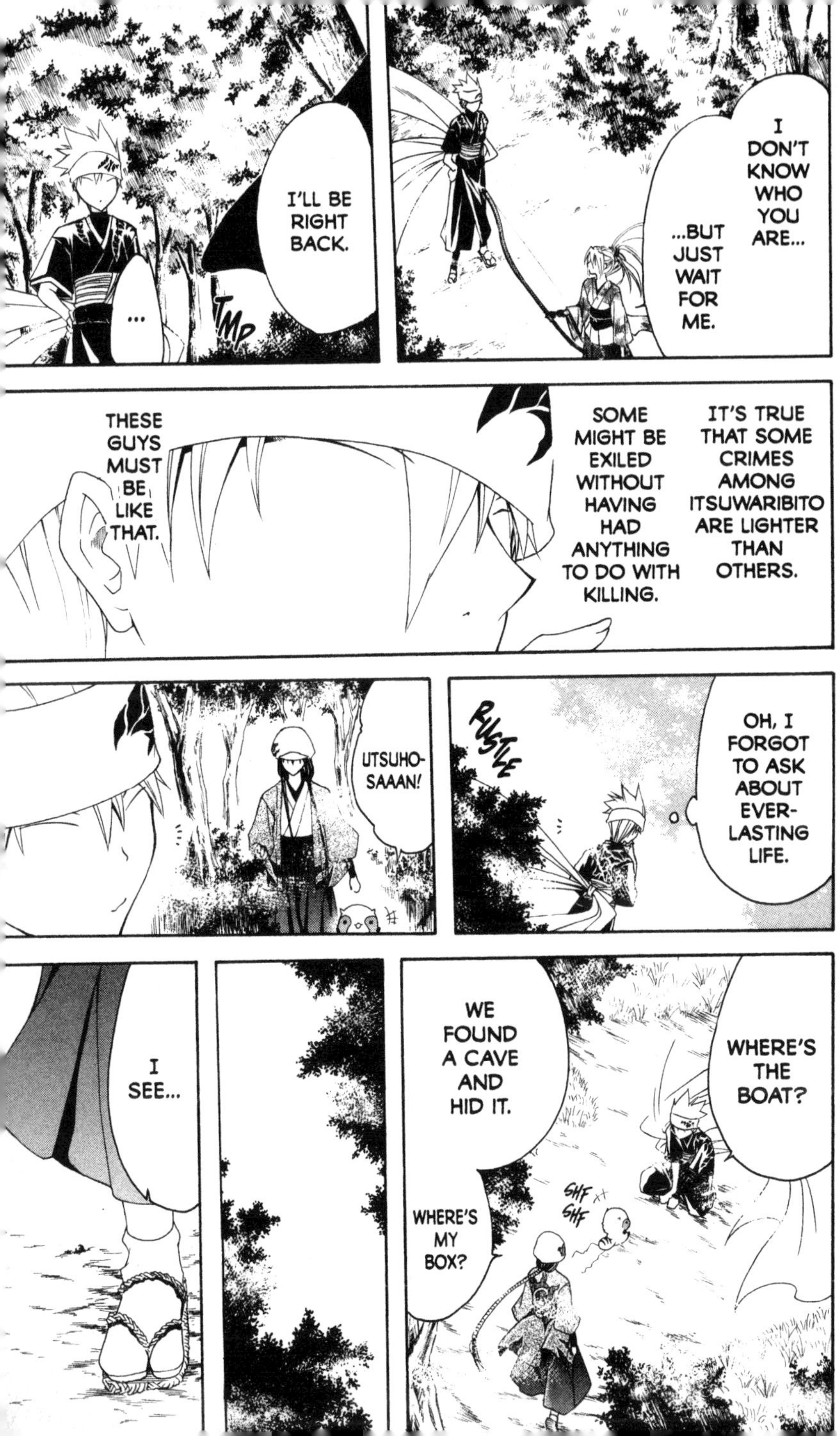
I DON'T KNOW WHO YOU ARE...
...BUT JUST WAIT FOR ME.
I'LL BE RIGHT BACK.
TMP
...
IT'S TRUE THAT SOME CRIMES AMONG ITSUWARIBITO ARE LIGHTER THAN OTHERS.
SOME MIGHT BE EXILED WITHOUT HAVING HAD ANYTHING TO DO WITH KILLING.
THESE GUYS MUST BE LIKE THAT.
OH, I FORGOT TO ASK ABOUT EVER-LASTING LIFE.
RUSTLE
UTSUHO-SAAAN!
WHERE'S THE BOAT?
WE FOUND A CAVE AND HID IT.
SHF SHF
WHERE'S MY BOX?
I SEE...

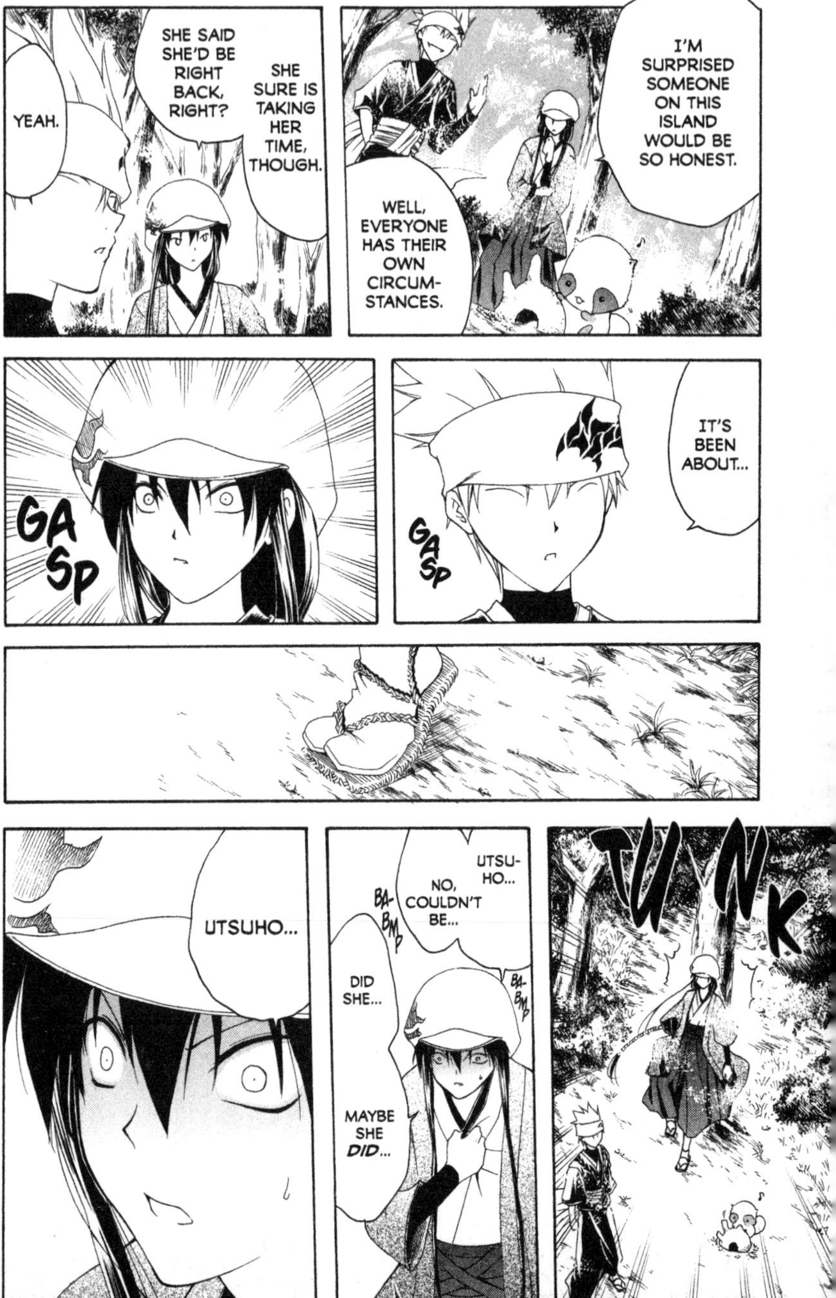
I'M SURPRISED SOMEONE ON THIS ISLAND WOULD BE SO HONEST.
WELL, EVERYONE HAS THEIR OWN CIRCUMSTANCES.
SHE SAID SHE'D BE RIGHT BACK, RIGHT?
SHE SURE IS TAKING HER TIME, THOUGH.
YEAH.
IT'S BEEN ABOUT...
GASP
GASP
TUNK
UTSU-HO...
NO, COULDN'T BE...
BA-BMP
BA-BMP
DID SHE...
MAYBE SHE *DID*...
UTSUHO...

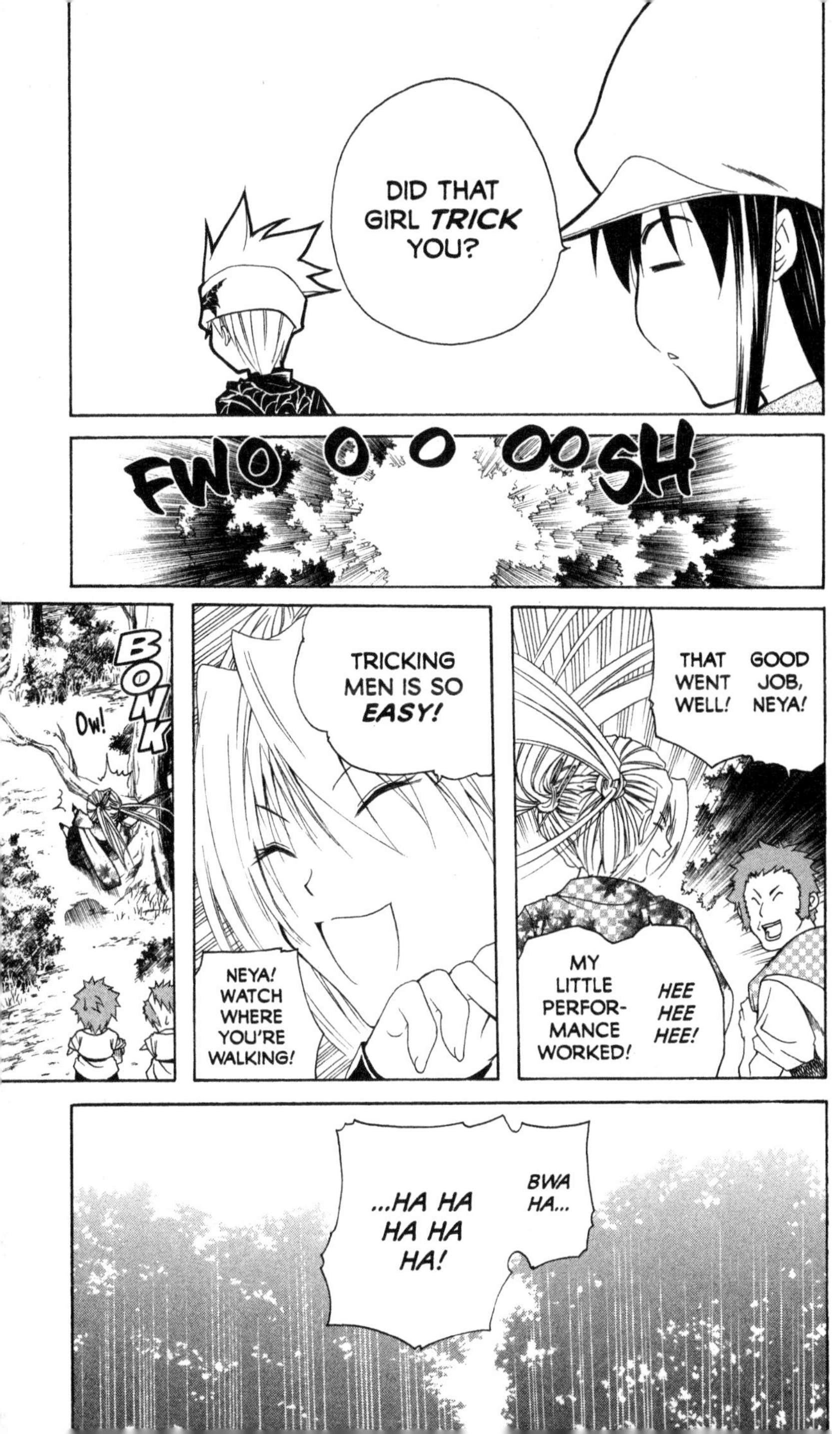
DID THAT GIRL TRICK YOU?
FWO O O OOSH
GOOD JOB, NEYA!
THAT WENT WELL!
HEE HEE HEE!
MY LITTLE PERFORMANCE WORKED!
TRICKING MEN IS SO EASY!
NEYA! WATCH WHERE YOU'RE WALKING!
BONK
Ow!
BWA HA...
...HA HA HA HA HA!

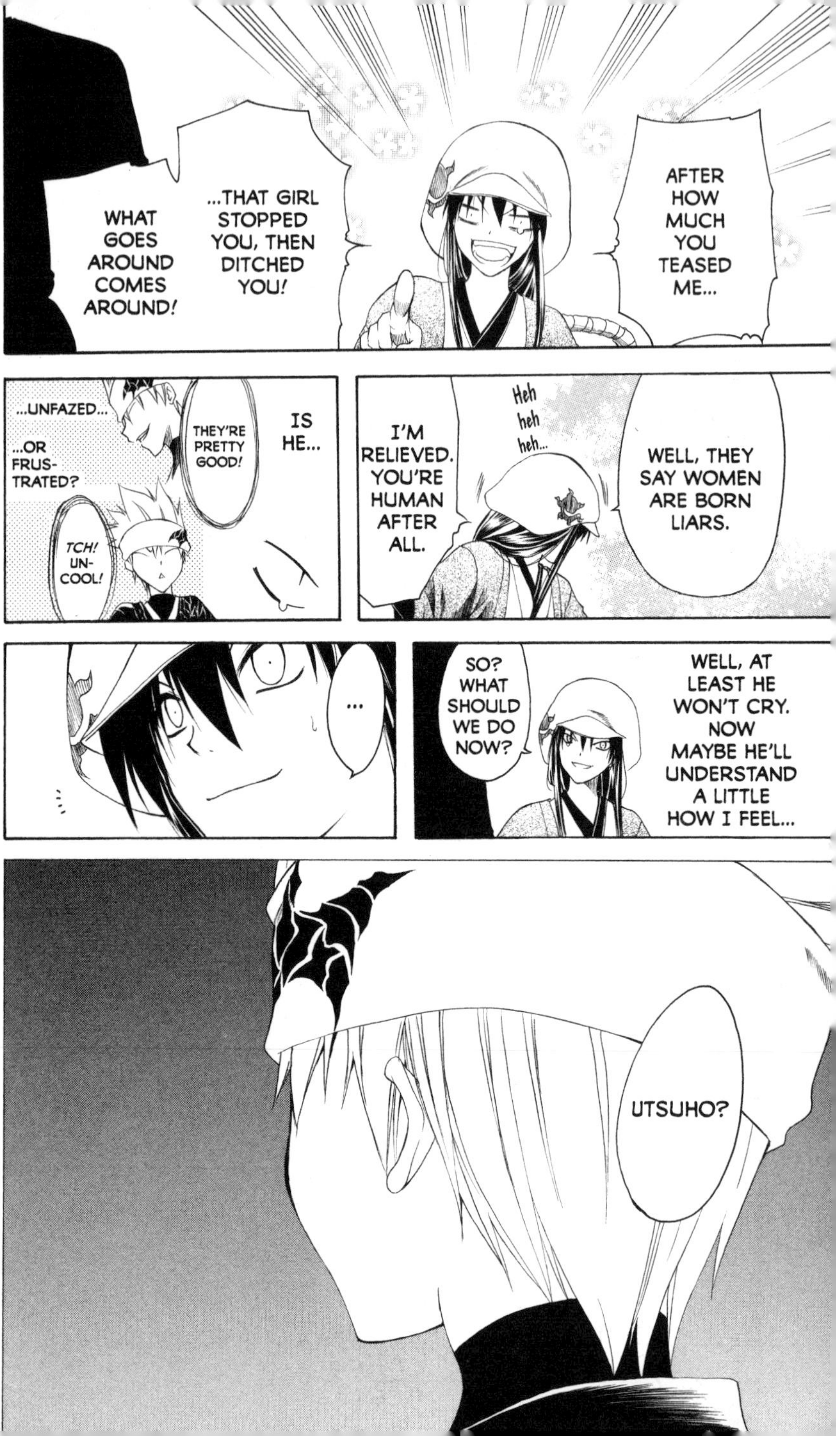
AFTER HOW MUCH YOU TEASED ME...
...THAT GIRL STOPPED YOU, THEN DITCHED YOU!
WHAT GOES AROUND COMES AROUND!
WELL, THEY SAY WOMEN ARE BORN LIARS.
Heh heh heh...
I'M RELIEVED. YOU'RE HUMAN AFTER ALL.
IS HE...
THEY'RE PRETTY GOOD!
...UNFAZED...
...OR FRUS-TRATED?
TCH! UN-COOL!
WELL, AT LEAST HE WON'T CRY. NOW MAYBE HE'LL UNDERSTAND A LITTLE HOW I FEEL...
SO? WHAT SHOULD WE DO NOW?
...
UTSUHO?

Chapter 14 Utsuho Gets Tricked

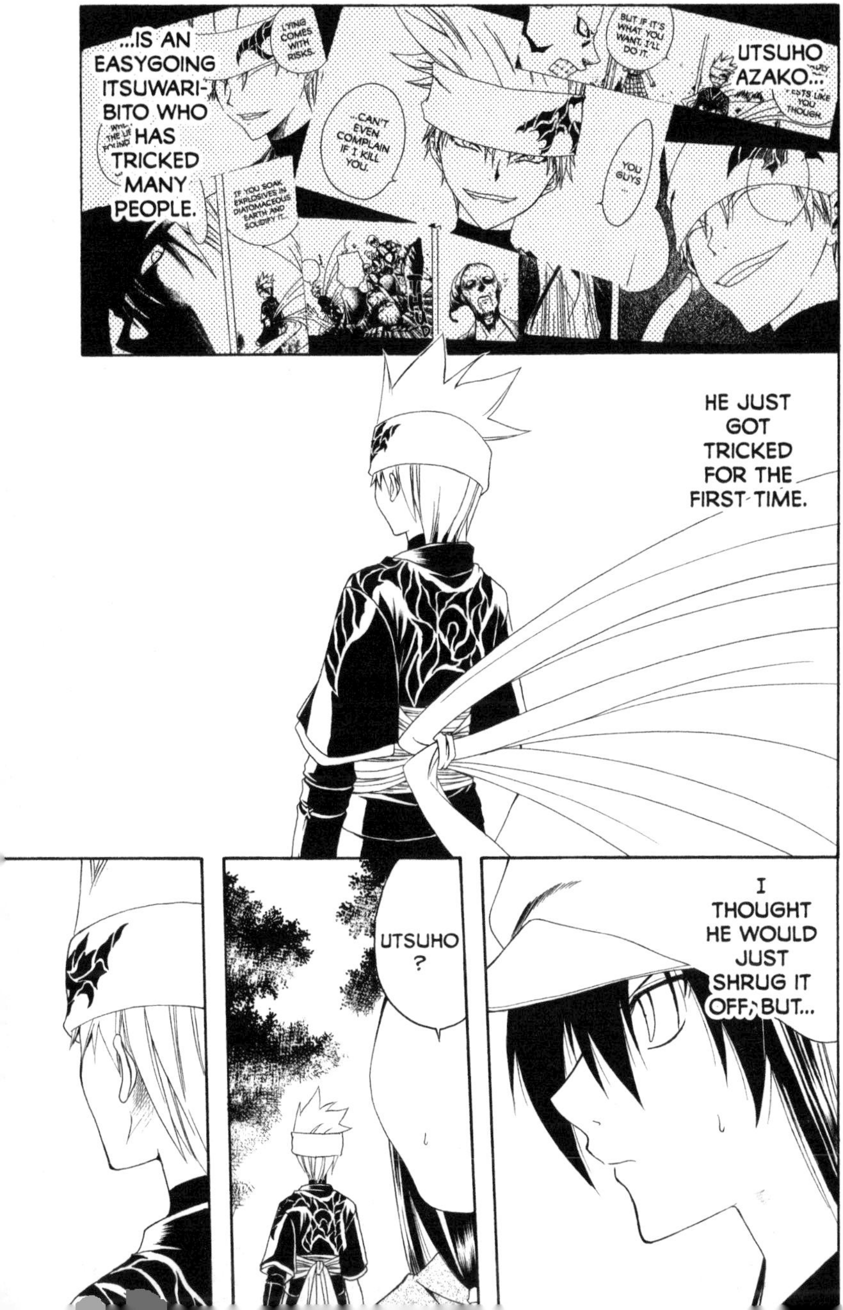

UTSUHO AZAKO...
BUT IF IT'S WHAT YOU WANT, I'LL DO IT.
YOU GUYS...
...CAN'T EVEN COMPLAIN IF I KILL YOU.
LYING COMES WITH RISKS.
...IS AN EASYGOING ITSUWARIBITO WHO HAS TRICKED MANY PEOPLE.
IF YOU SOAK EXPLOSIVES IN DIATOMACEOUS EARTH AND SOLIDIFY IT...
HE JUST GOT TRICKED FOR THE FIRST TIME.
I THOUGHT HE WOULD JUST SHRUG IT OFF, BUT...
UTSUHO?

Chapter 14
Utsuho Gets Tricked

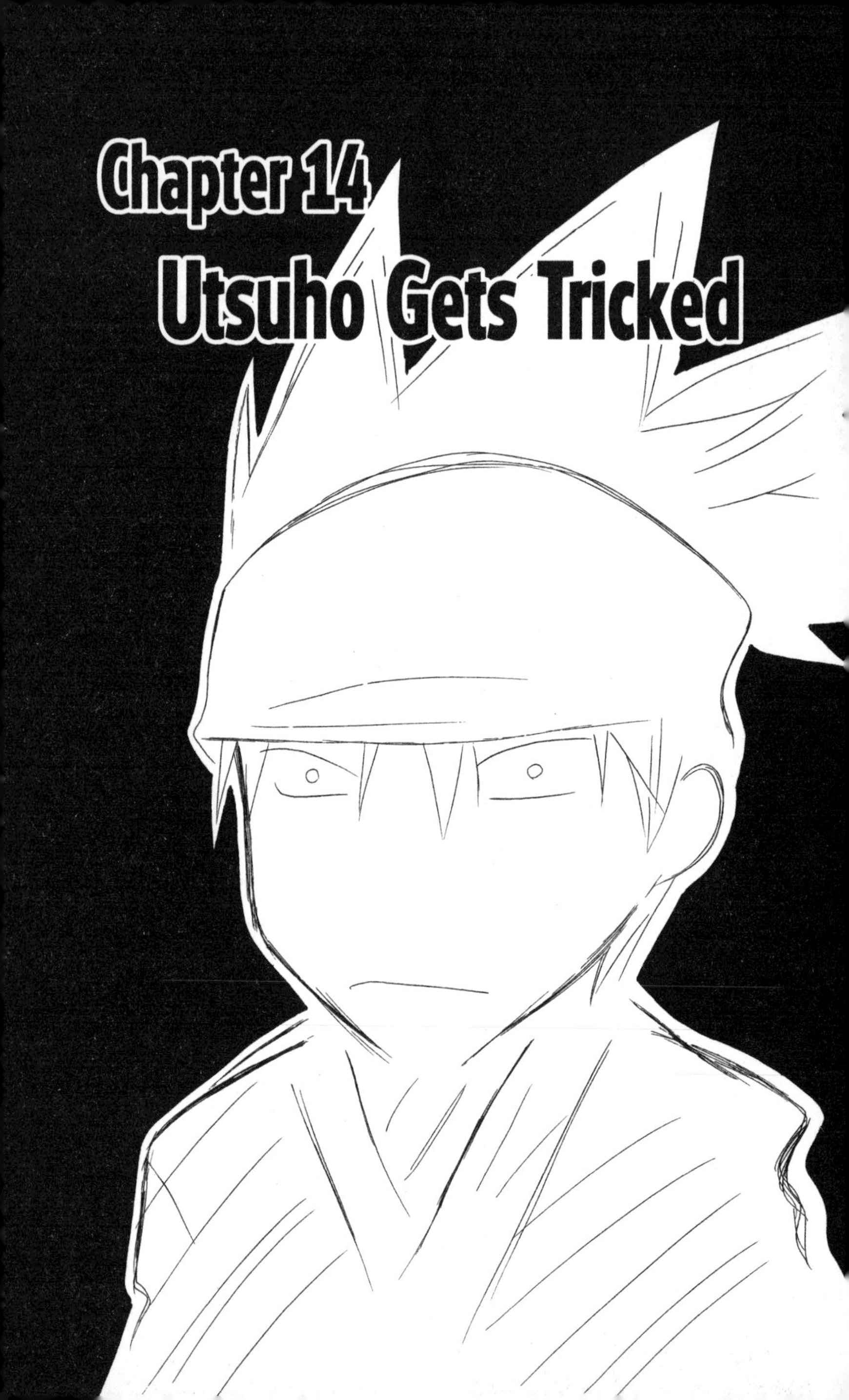

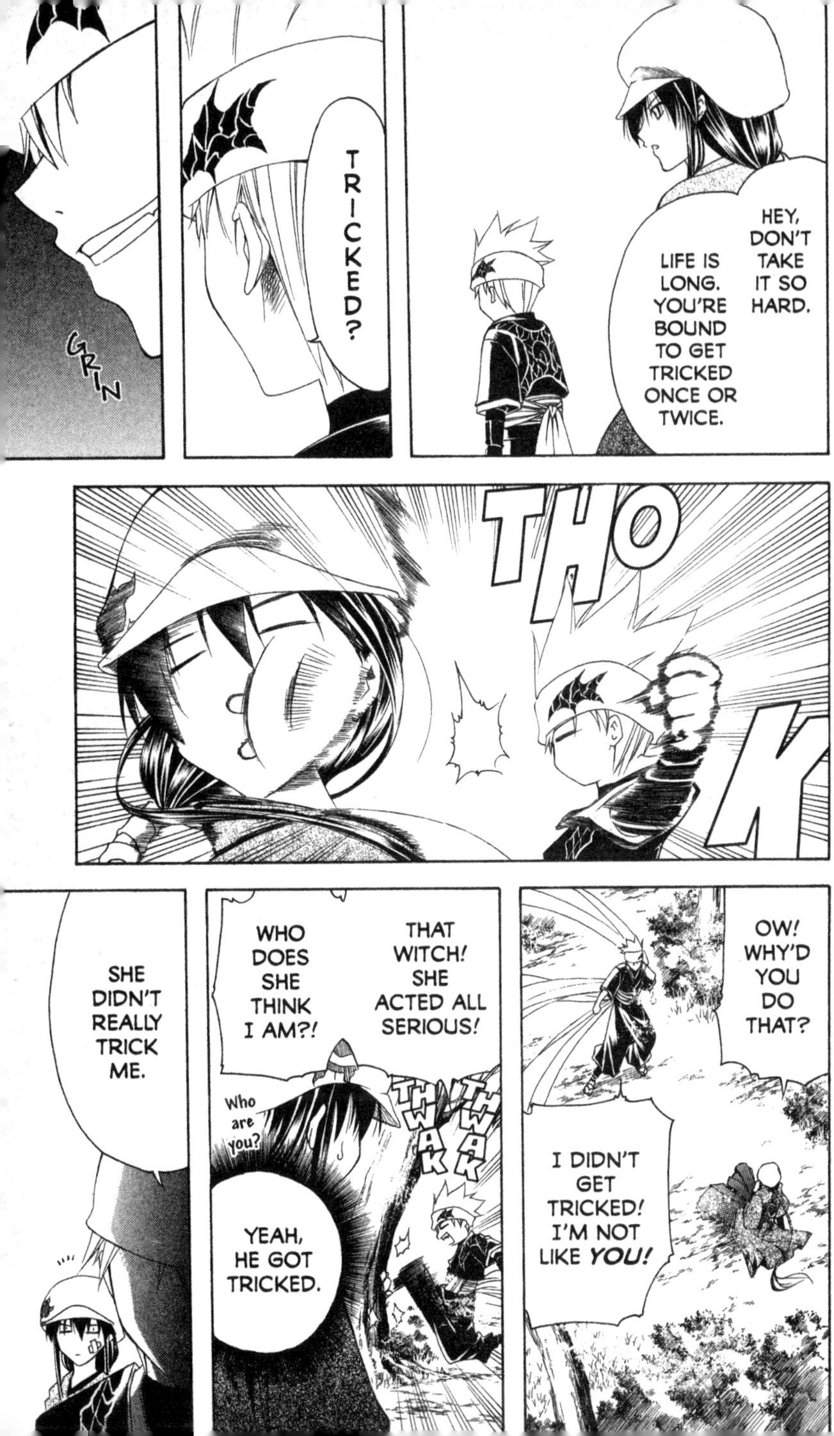
HEY, DON'T TAKE IT SO HARD.
LIFE IS LONG. YOU'RE BOUND TO GET TRICKED ONCE OR TWICE.
TRICKED?
GRIN
THOK
OW! WHY'D YOU DO THAT?
I DIDN'T GET TRICKED! I'M NOT LIKE *YOU!*
THAT WITCH! SHE ACTED ALL SERIOUS!
WHO DOES SHE THINK I AM?!
THWAK
THWAK
Who are you?
YEAH, HE GOT TRICKED.
SHE DIDN'T REALLY TRICK ME.

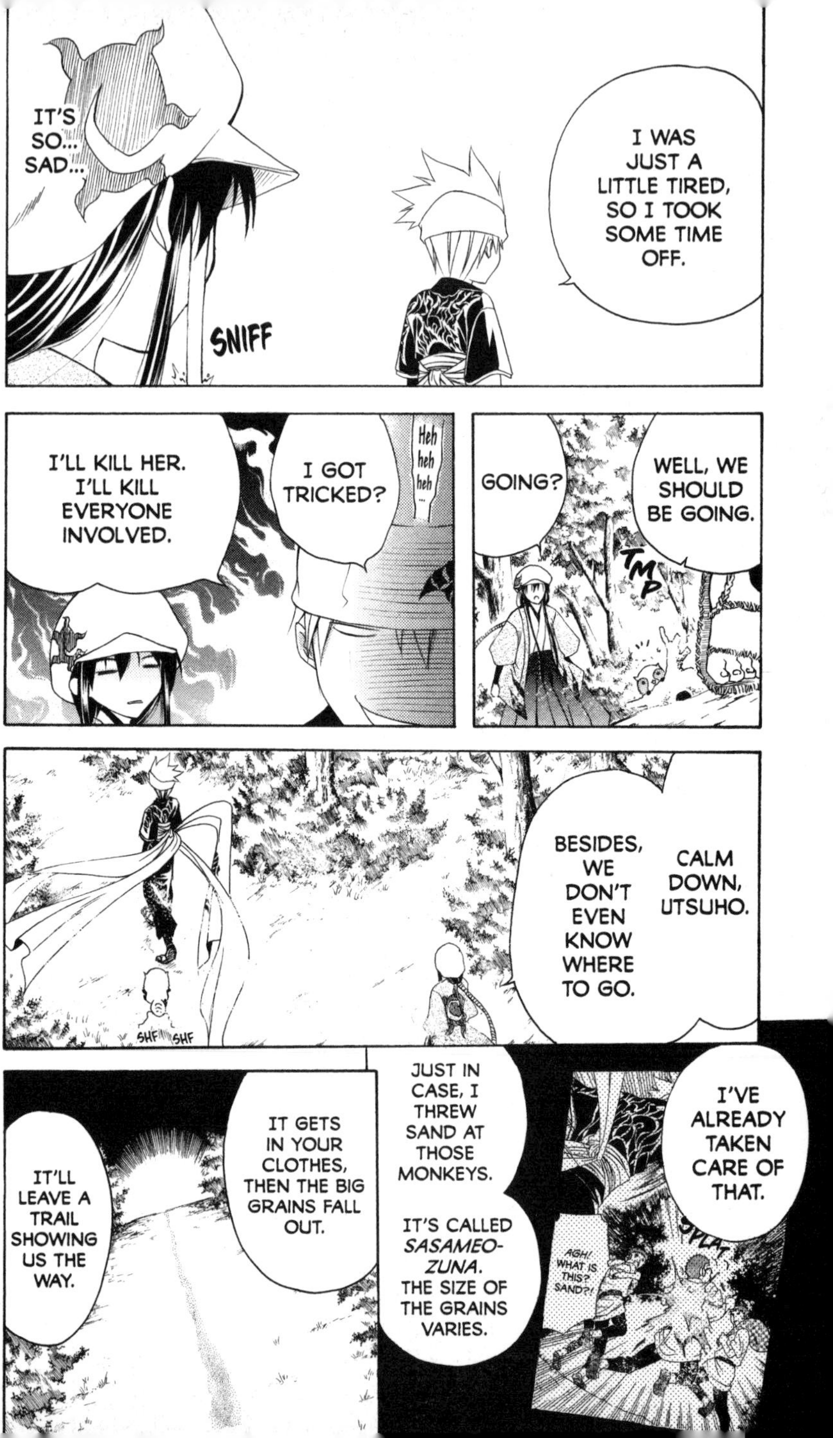
I WAS JUST A LITTLE TIRED, SO I TOOK SOME TIME OFF.
IT'S SO... SAD...
SNIFF
WELL, WE SHOULD BE GOING.
GOING?
TMP
Heh heh heh...
I GOT TRICKED?
I'LL KILL HER. I'LL KILL EVERYONE INVOLVED.
CALM DOWN, UTSUHO.
BESIDES, WE DON'T EVEN KNOW WHERE TO GO.
SHF SHF
I'VE ALREADY TAKEN CARE OF THAT.
AGH! WHAT IS THIS? SAND?!
JUST IN CASE, I THREW SAND AT THOSE MONKEYS.
IT'S CALLED *SASAMEO-ZUNA*. THE SIZE OF THE GRAINS VARIES.
IT GETS IN YOUR CLOTHES, THEN THE BIG GRAINS FALL OUT.
IT'LL LEAVE A TRAIL SHOWING US THE WAY.

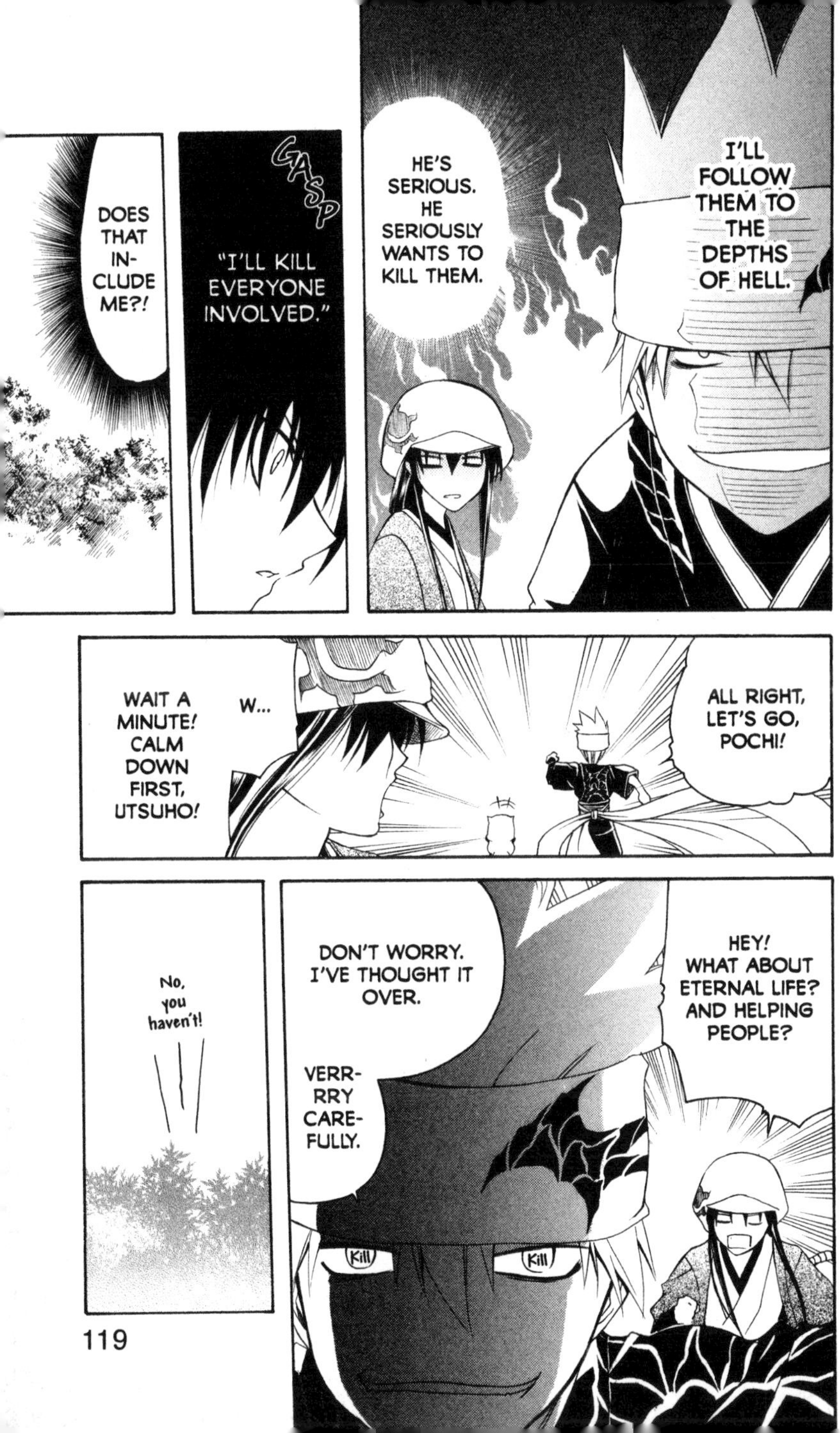
I'LL FOLLOW THEM TO THE DEPTHS OF HELL.
HE'S SERIOUS. HE SERIOUSLY WANTS TO KILL THEM.
GASP
"I'LL KILL EVERYONE INVOLVED."
DOES THAT IN-CLUDE ME?!
ALL RIGHT, LET'S GO, POCHI!
W...
WAIT A MINUTE! CALM DOWN FIRST, UTSUHO!
HEY! WHAT ABOUT ETERNAL LIFE? AND HELPING PEOPLE?
DON'T WORRY. I'VE THOUGHT IT OVER.
VERR-RRY CARE-FULLY.
Kill
Kill
No, you haven't!

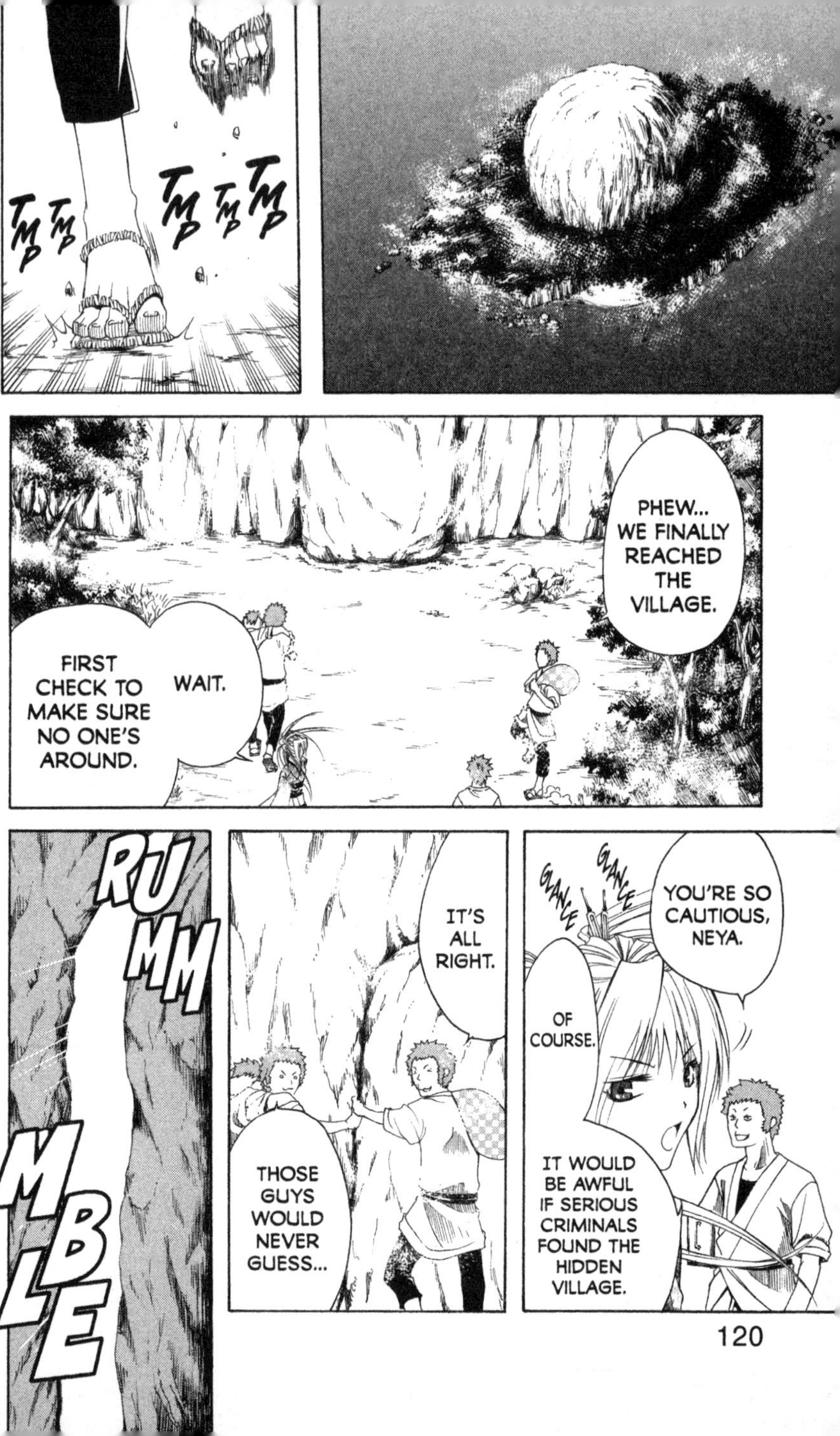
TMP TMP TMP
TMP TMP
PHEW... WE FINALLY REACHED THE VILLAGE.
WAIT.
FIRST CHECK TO MAKE SURE NO ONE'S AROUND.
GLANCE GLANCE
YOU'RE SO CAUTIOUS, NEYA.
OF COURSE.
IT WOULD BE AWFUL IF SERIOUS CRIMINALS FOUND THE HIDDEN VILLAGE.
IT'S ALL RIGHT.
THOSE GUYS WOULD NEVER GUESS...
RUMMMBLE

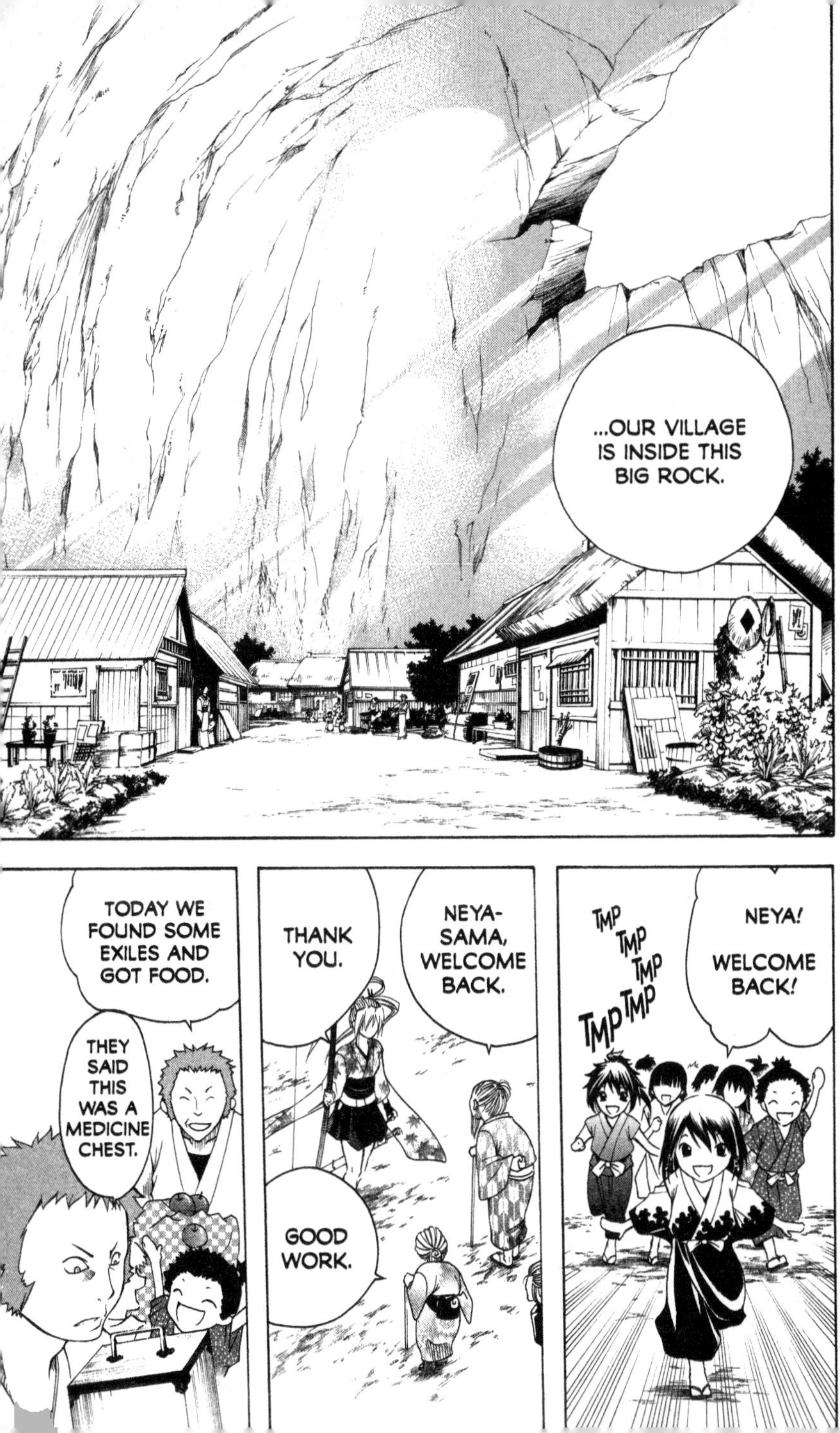
...OUR VILLAGE IS INSIDE THIS BIG ROCK.
TMP TMP TMP TMP TMP
NEYA!
WELCOME BACK!
NEYA-SAMA, WELCOME BACK.
THANK YOU.
GOOD WORK.
TODAY WE FOUND SOME EXILES AND GOT FOOD.
THEY SAID THIS WAS A MEDICINE CHEST.

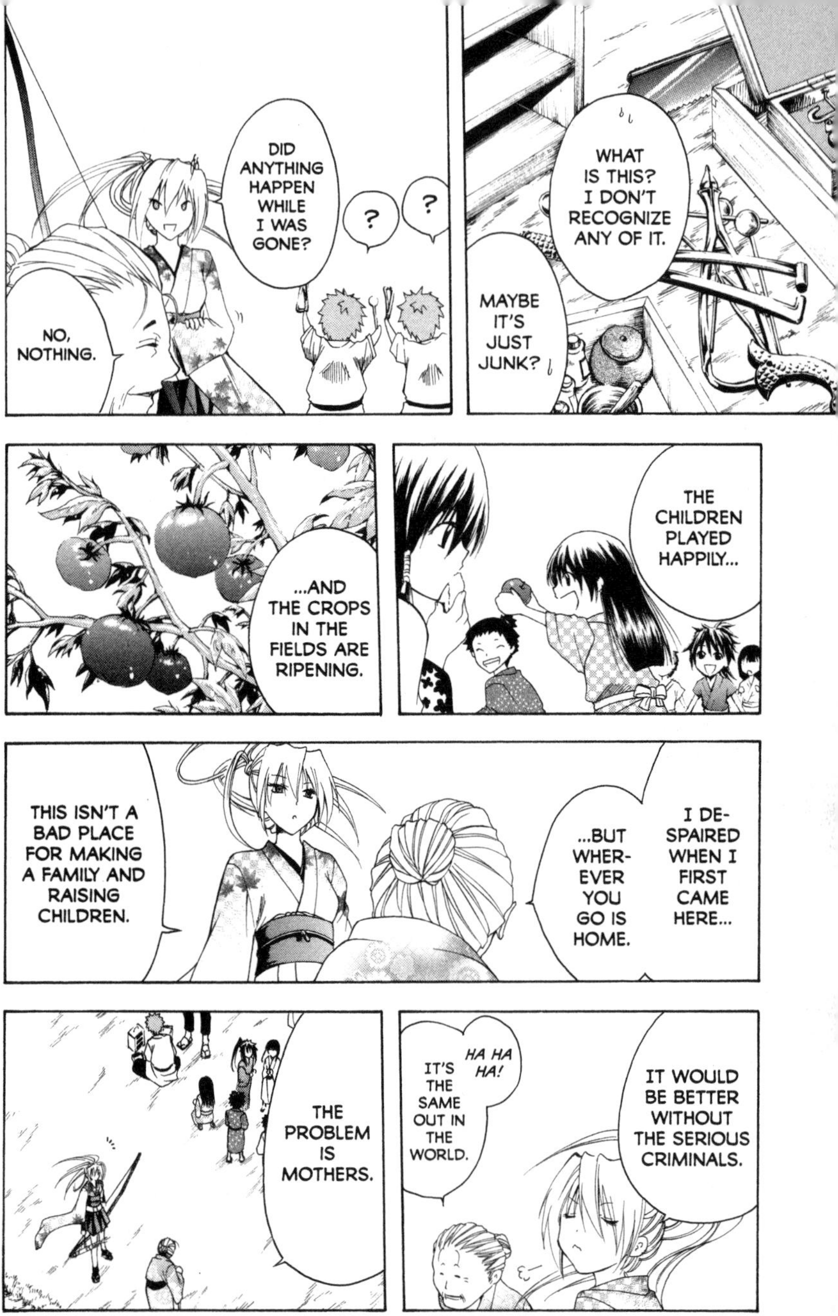
WHAT IS THIS? I DON'T RECOGNIZE ANY OF IT.
MAYBE IT'S JUST JUNK?
DID ANYTHING HAPPEN WHILE I WAS GONE?
?
?
NO, NOTHING.
THE CHILDREN PLAYED HAPPILY...
...AND THE CROPS IN THE FIELDS ARE RIPENING.
I DESPAIRED WHEN I FIRST CAME HERE...
...BUT WHEREVER YOU GO IS HOME.
THIS ISN'T A BAD PLACE FOR MAKING A FAMILY AND RAISING CHILDREN.
IT WOULD BE BETTER WITHOUT THE SERIOUS CRIMINALS.
HA HA HA!
IT'S THE SAME OUT IN THE WORLD.
THE PROBLEM IS MOTHERS.

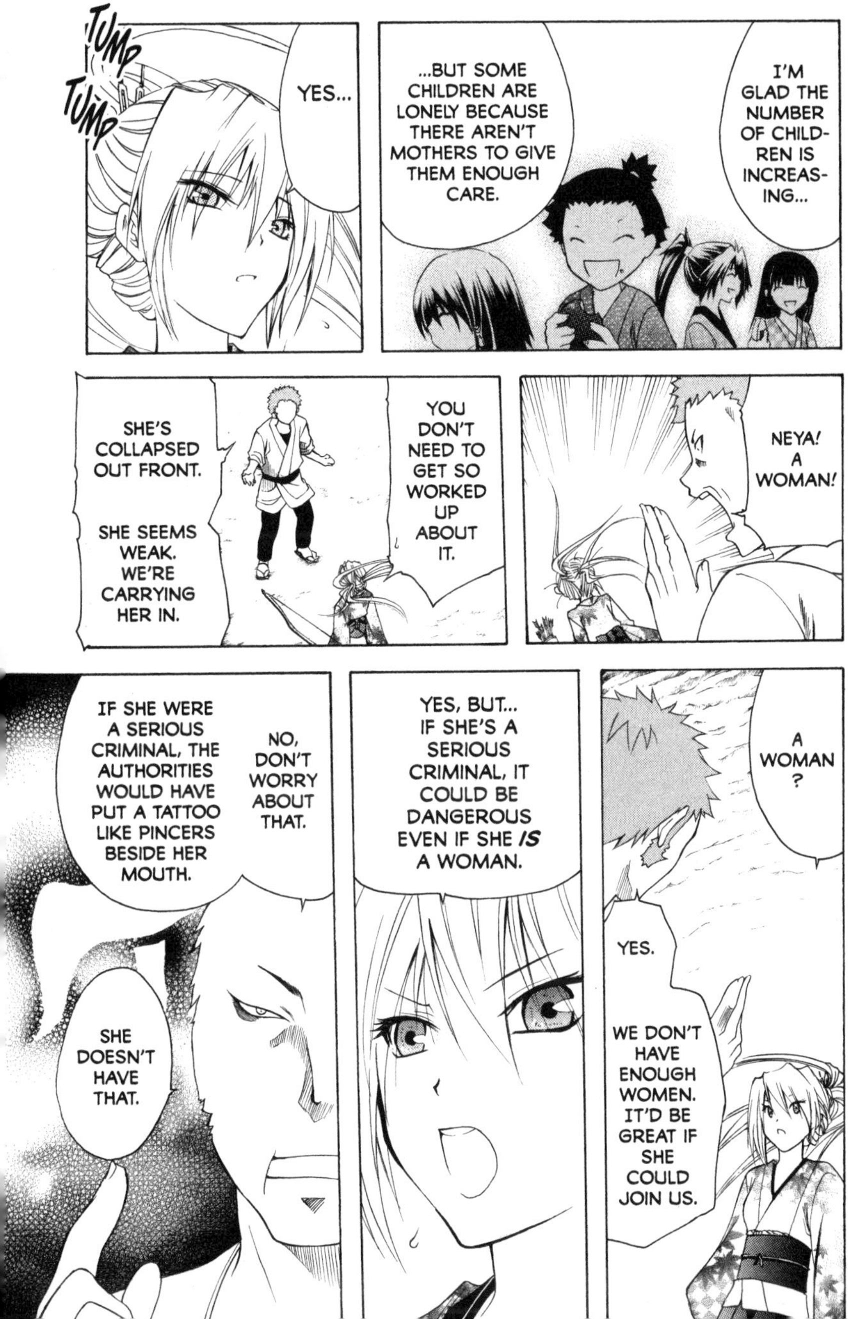
I'M GLAD THE NUMBER OF CHILD-REN IS INCREAS-ING...
...BUT SOME CHILDREN ARE LONELY BECAUSE THERE AREN'T MOTHERS TO GIVE THEM ENOUGH CARE.
TUMP TUMP
YES...
NEYA! A WOMAN!
YOU DON'T NEED TO GET SO WORKED UP ABOUT IT.
SHE'S COLLAPSED OUT FRONT.
SHE SEEMS WEAK. WE'RE CARRYING HER IN.
A WOMAN?
YES.
WE DON'T HAVE ENOUGH WOMEN. IT'D BE GREAT IF SHE COULD JOIN US.
YES, BUT... IF SHE'S A SERIOUS CRIMINAL, IT COULD BE DANGEROUS EVEN IF SHE *IS* A WOMAN.
NO, DON'T WORRY ABOUT THAT.
IF SHE WERE A SERIOUS CRIMINAL, THE AUTHORITIES WOULD HAVE PUT A TATTOO LIKE PINCERS BESIDE HER MOUTH.
SHE DOESN'T HAVE THAT.

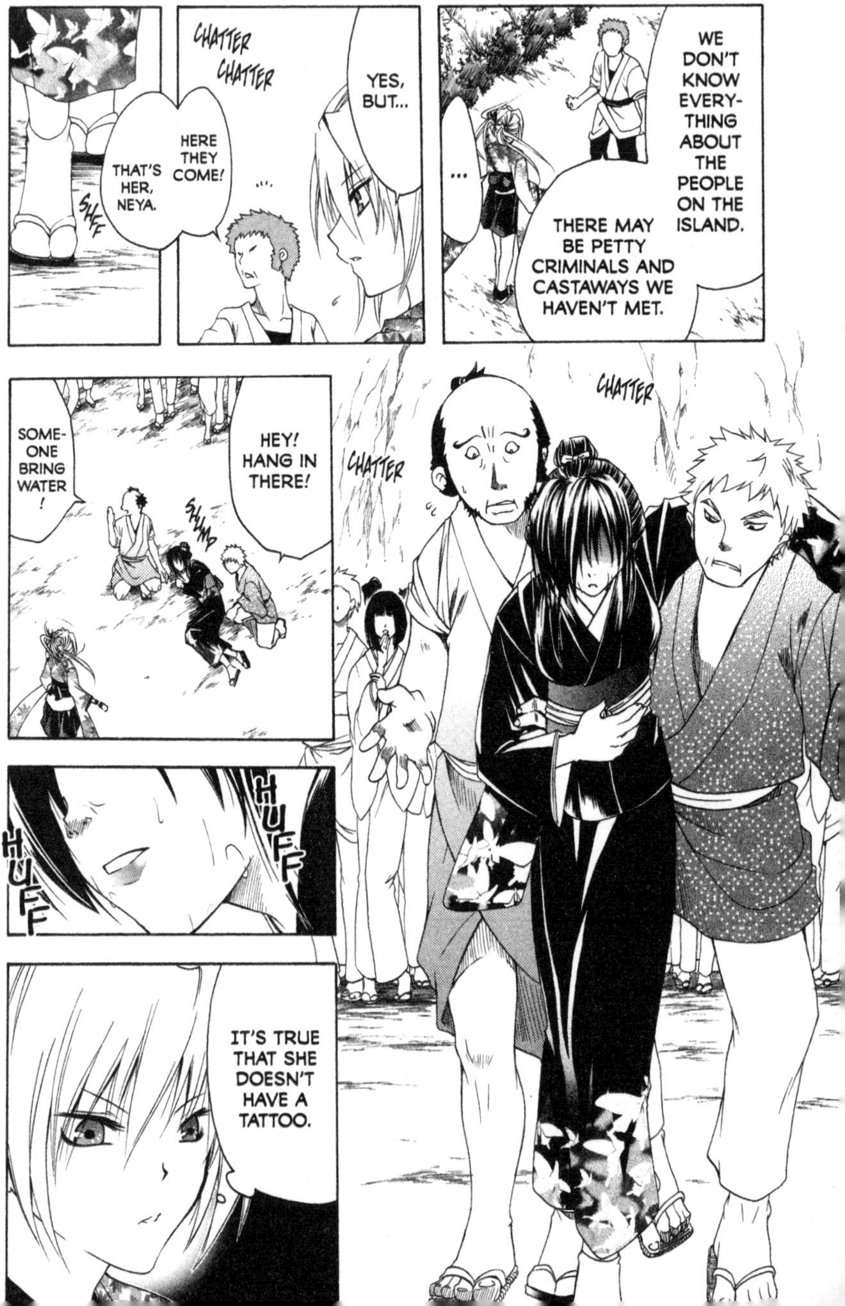
WE DON'T KNOW EVERYTHING ABOUT THE PEOPLE ON THE ISLAND.
...
THERE MAY BE PETTY CRIMINALS AND CASTAWAYS WE HAVEN'T MET.
YES, BUT...
CHATTER CHATTER
HERE THEY COME!
THAT'S HER, NEYA.
...
SHFF
CHATTER
CHATTER
HEY! HANG IN THERE!
SOME-ONE BRING WATER!
SHUMP
HUFF
HUFF
IT'S TRUE THAT SHE DOESN'T HAVE A TATTOO.

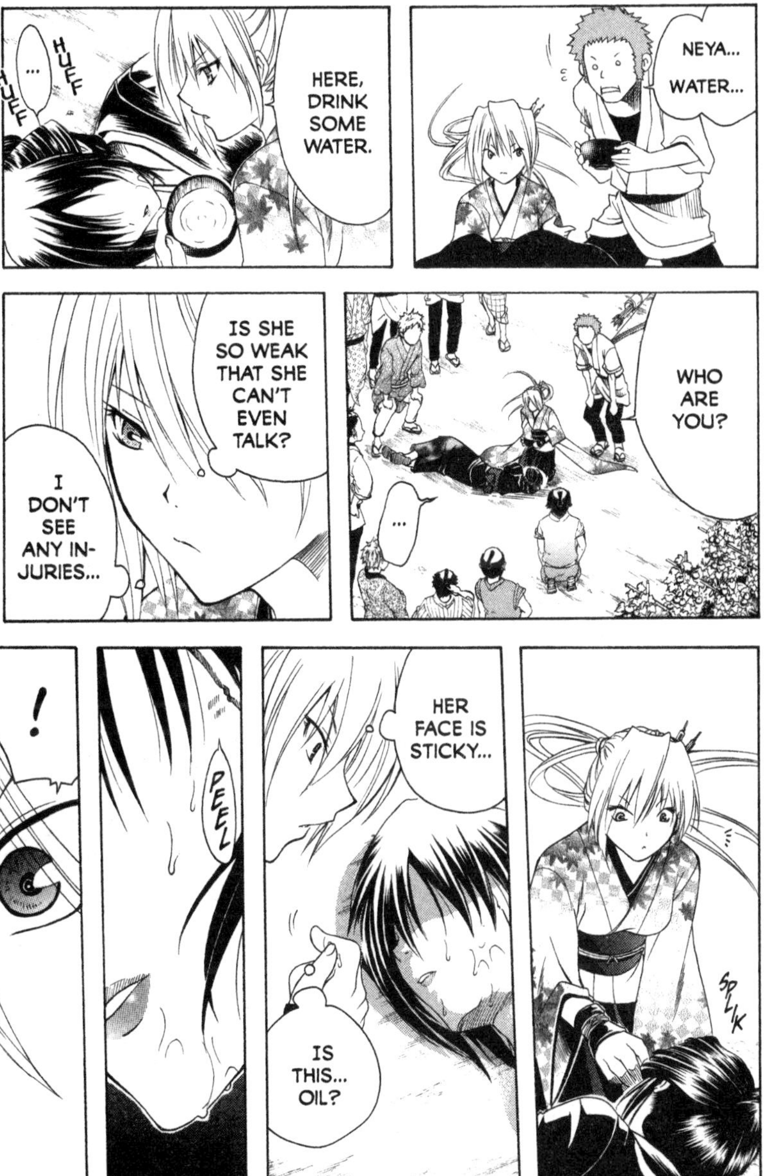
NEYA...
WATER...
HUFF
HUFF
...
HERE, DRINK SOME WATER.
WHO ARE YOU?
...
IS SHE SO WEAK THAT SHE CAN'T EVEN TALK?
I DON'T SEE ANY INJURIES...
SPLIK
HER FACE IS STICKY...
IS THIS... OIL?
PEEL
!

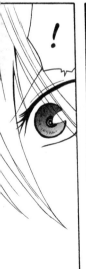

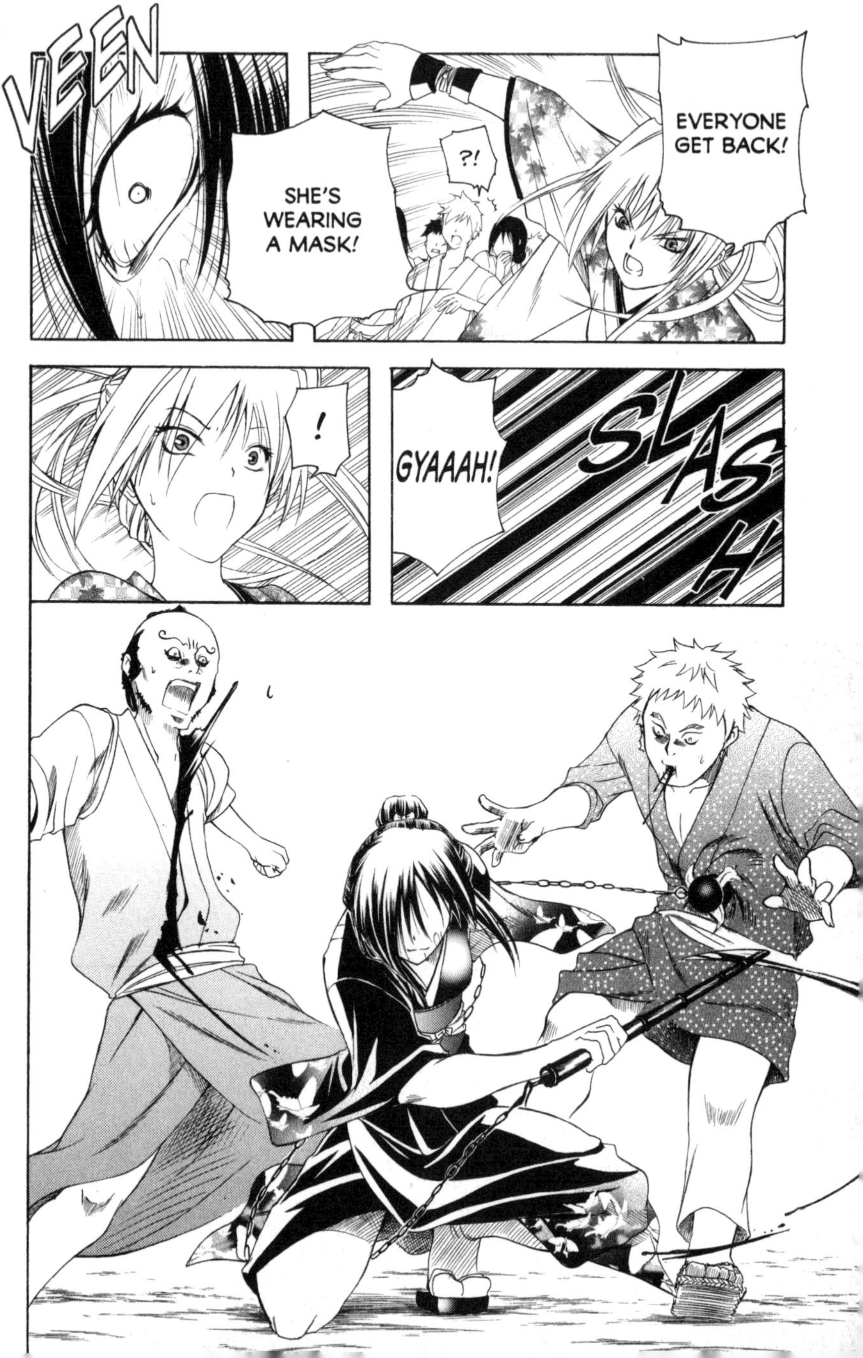
EVERYONE GET BACK!
?!
SHE'S WEARING A MASK!
VEEN
GYAAAH!
SLASH
!

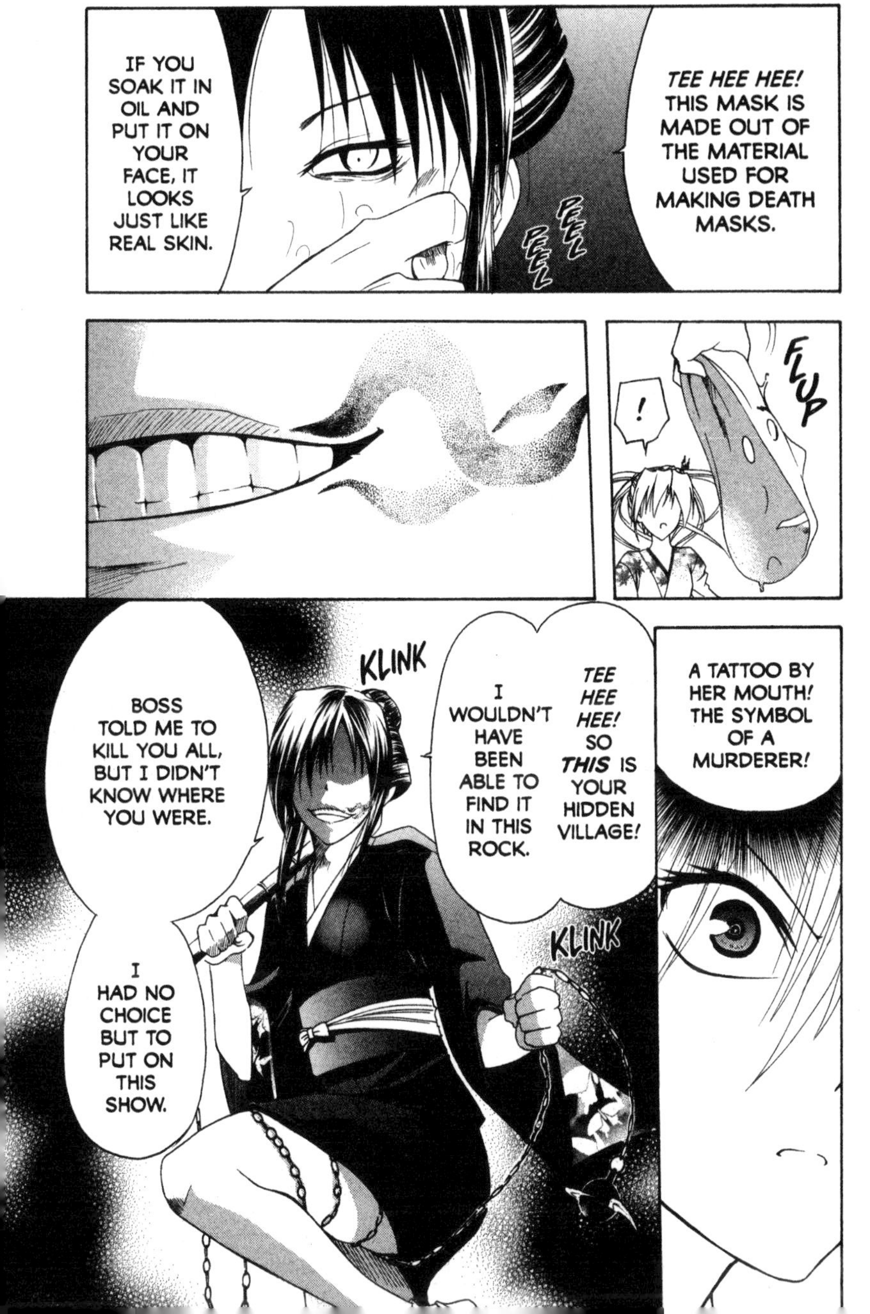
TEE HEE HEE! THIS MASK IS MADE OUT OF THE MATERIAL USED FOR MAKING DEATH MASKS.
PEEL PEEL
IF YOU SOAK IT IN OIL AND PUT IT ON YOUR FACE, IT LOOKS JUST LIKE REAL SKIN.
FLUP
!
A TATTOO BY HER MOUTH! THE SYMBOL OF A MURDERER!
TEE HEE HEE! SO THIS IS YOUR HIDDEN VILLAGE!
I WOULDN'T HAVE BEEN ABLE TO FIND IT IN THIS ROCK.
KLINK
BOSS TOLD ME TO KILL YOU ALL, BUT I DIDN'T KNOW WHERE YOU WERE.
KLINK
I HAD NO CHOICE BUT TO PUT ON THIS SHOW.

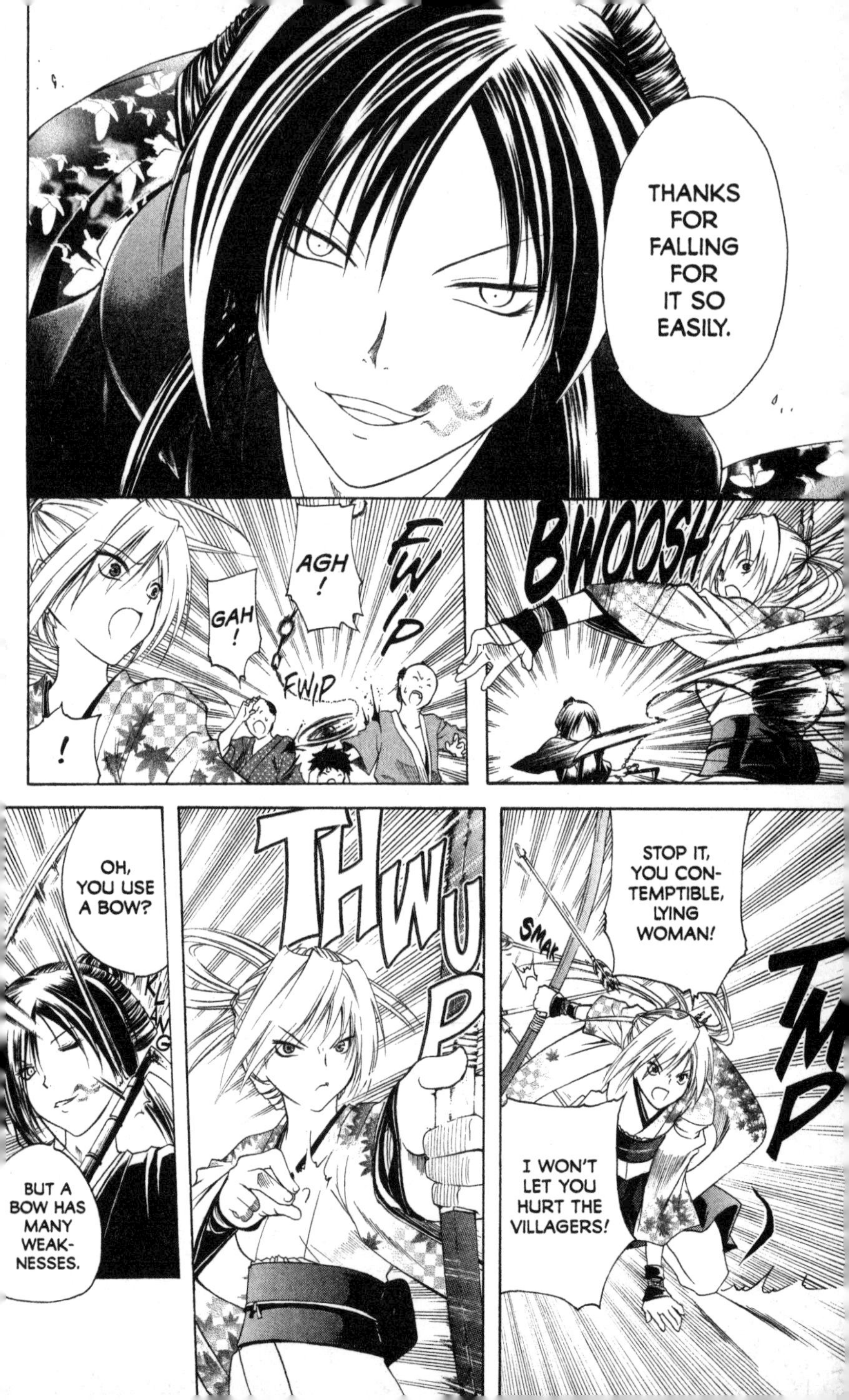
THANKS FOR FALLING FOR IT SO EASILY.
BWOOSH
FWIP
AGH!
GAH!
FWIP
!
STOP IT, YOU CON-TEMPTIBLE, LYING WOMAN!
SMAK
TMP
I WON'T LET YOU HURT THE VILLAGERS!
THWUMP
OH, YOU USE A BOW?
KLANG
BUT A BOW HAS MANY WEAK-NESSES.

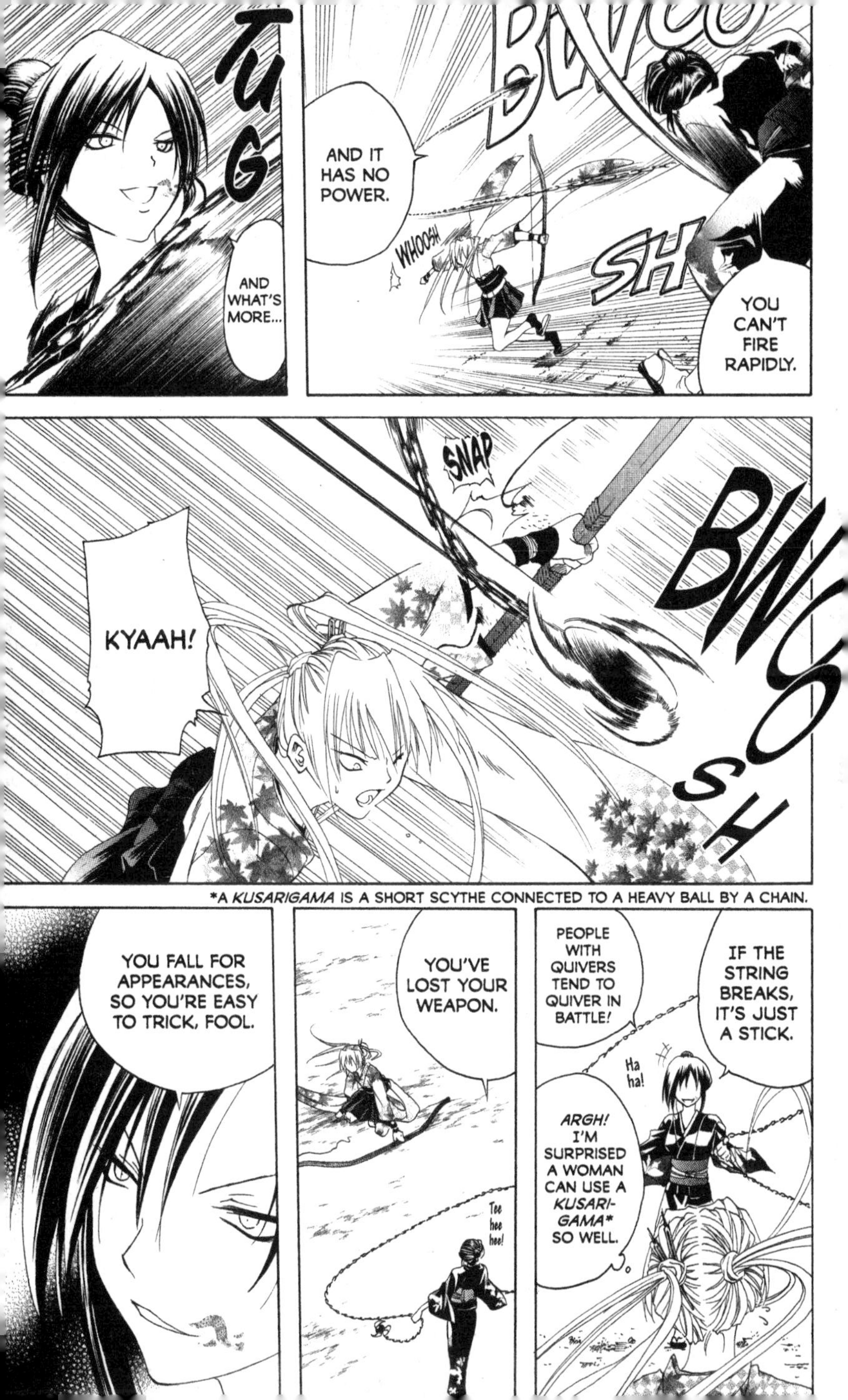
BWOO
SH
WHOOSH
YOU CAN'T FIRE RAPIDLY.
AND IT HAS NO POWER.
TUG
AND WHAT'S MORE...
SNAP
BWOOSH
KYAAH!
IF THE STRING BREAKS, IT'S JUST A STICK.
PEOPLE WITH QUIVERS TEND TO QUIVER IN BATTLE!
Ha ha!
ARGH! I'M SURPRISED A WOMAN CAN USE A *KUSARI-GAMA** SO WELL.
YOU'VE LOST YOUR WEAPON.
Tee hee hee!
YOU FALL FOR APPEARANCES, SO YOU'RE EASY TO TRICK, FOOL.

*A *KUSARIGAMA* IS A SHORT SCYTHE CONNECTED TO A HEAVY BALL BY A CHAIN.

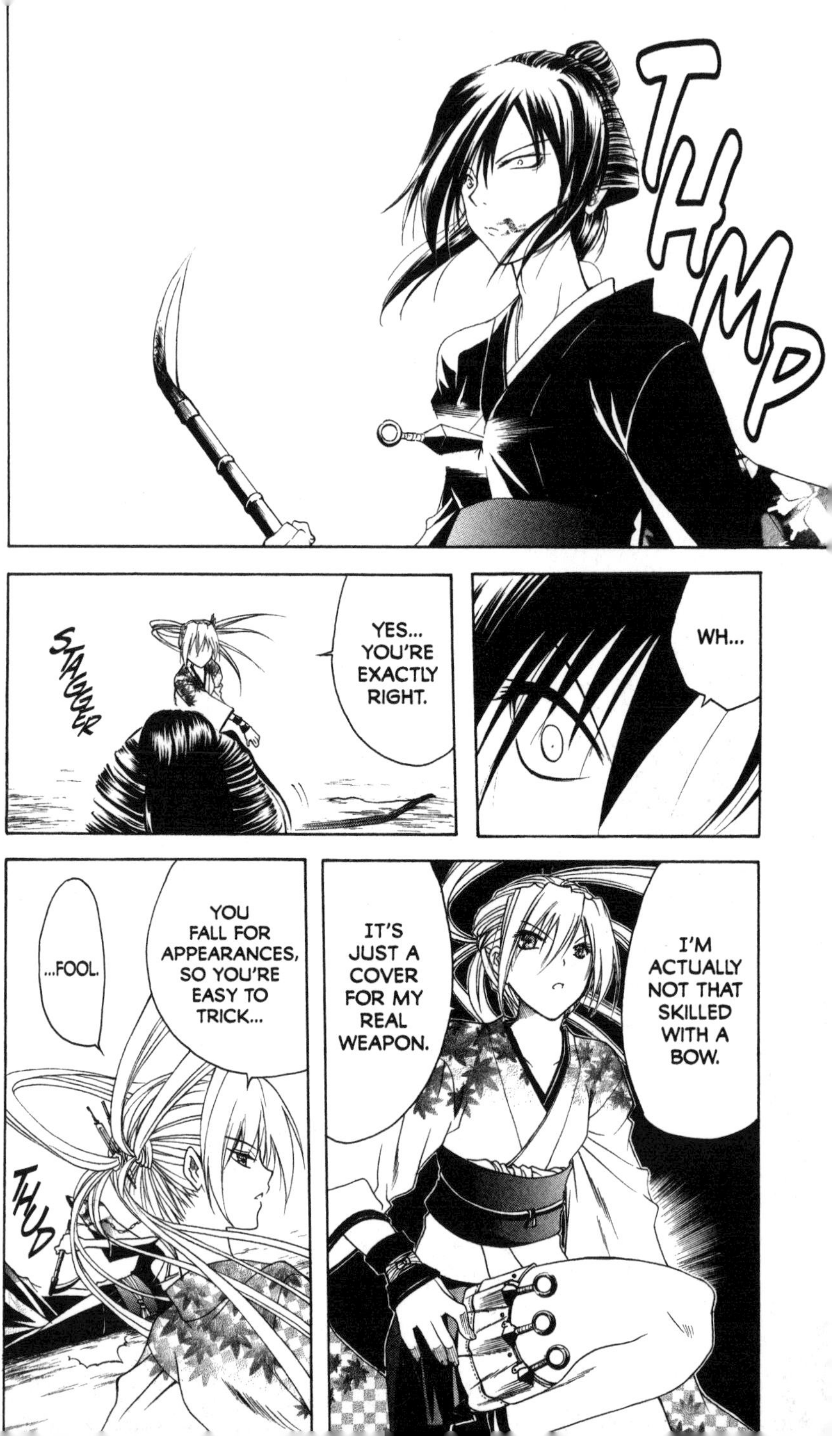
THMP
WH...
YES... YOU'RE EXACTLY RIGHT.
STAGGER
I'M ACTUALLY NOT THAT SKILLED WITH A BOW.
IT'S JUST A COVER FOR MY REAL WEAPON.
YOU FALL FOR APPEARANCES, SO YOU'RE EASY TO TRICK...
...FOOL.
THUD

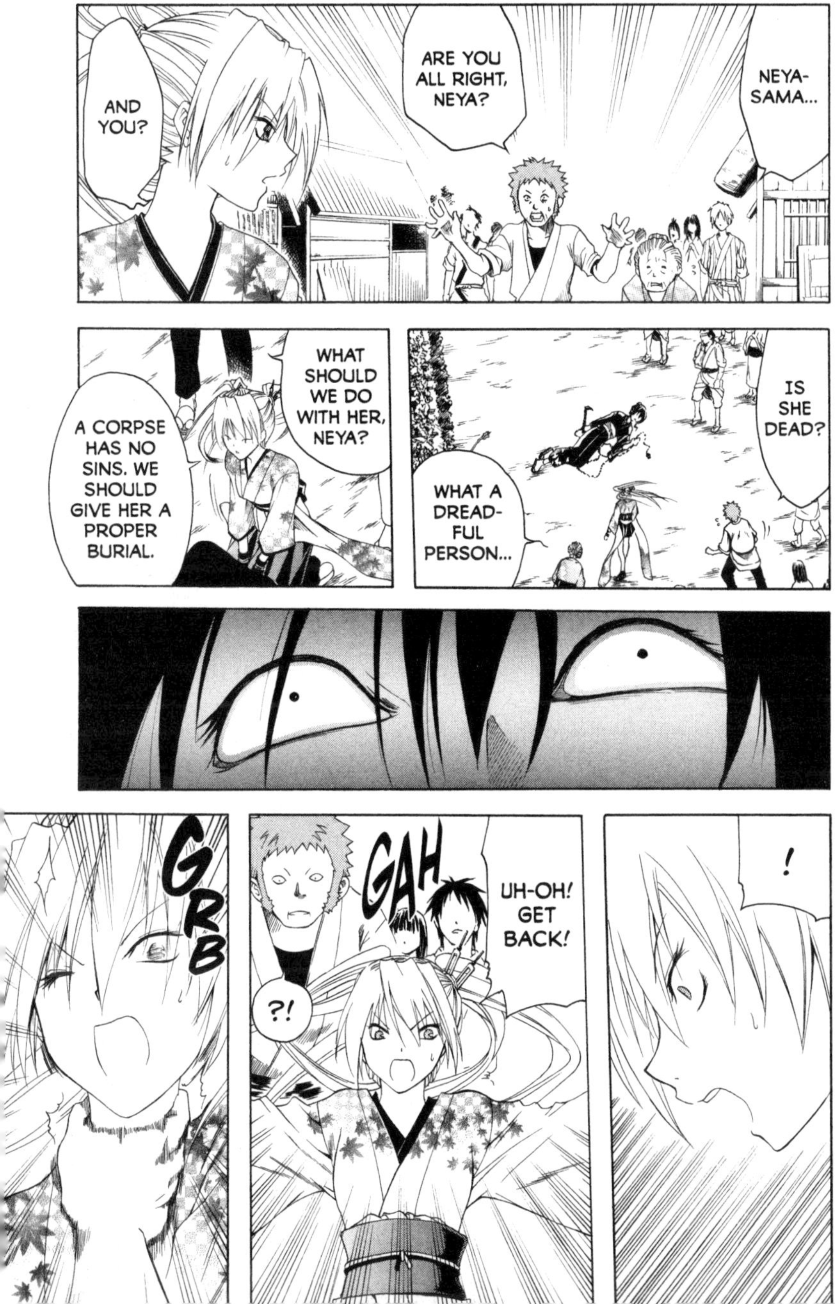
NEYA-SAMA...
ARE YOU ALL RIGHT, NEYA?
AND YOU?
IS SHE DEAD?
WHAT A DREAD-FUL PERSON...
WHAT SHOULD WE DO WITH HER, NEYA?
A CORPSE HAS NO SINS. WE SHOULD GIVE HER A PROPER BURIAL.
!
UH-OH! GET BACK!
GAH
?!
GRB

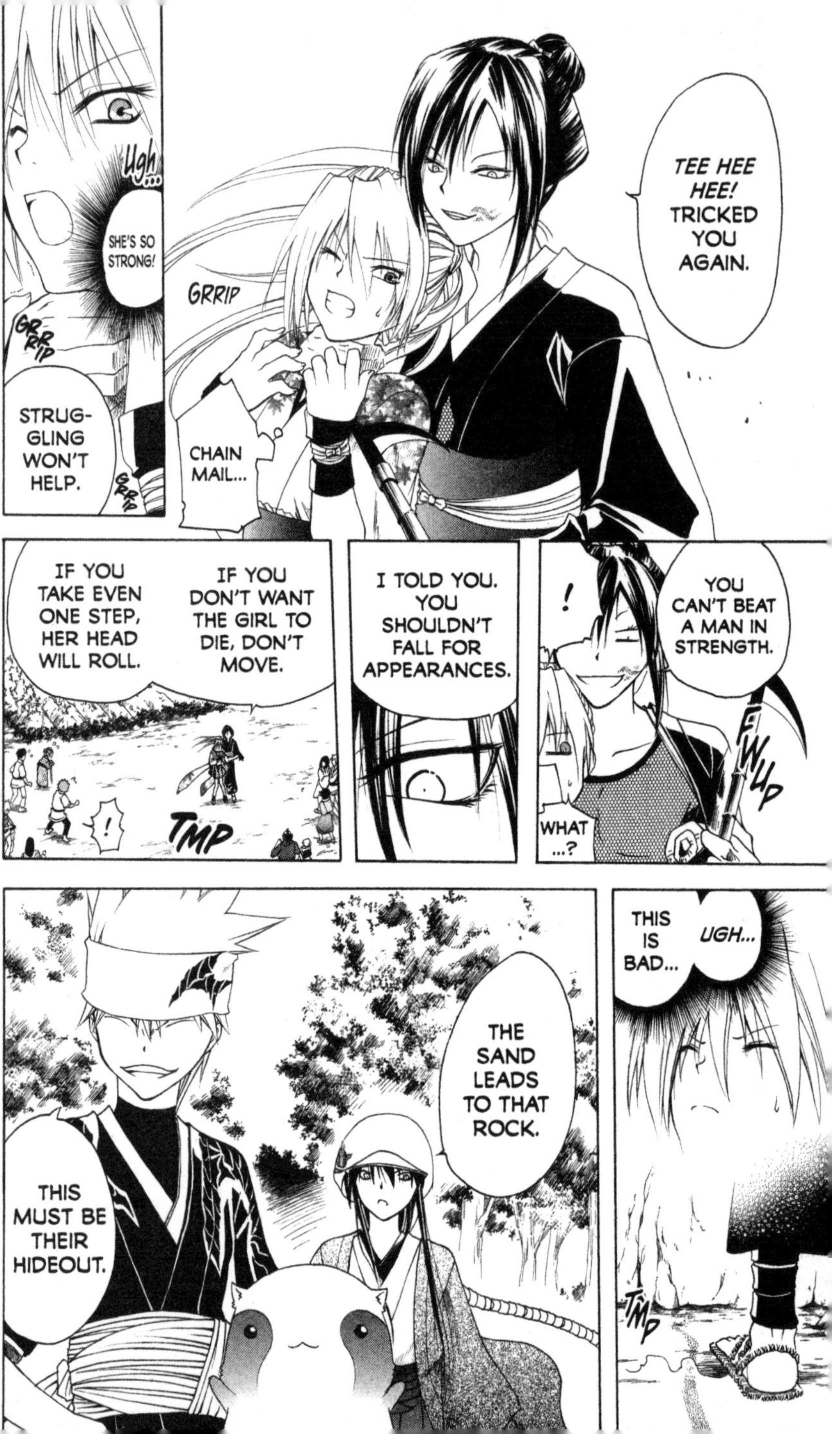
TEE HEE HEE! TRICKED YOU AGAIN.
...
GRRIP
CHAIN MAIL...
Ugh...
SHE'S SO STRONG!
GRRIP
STRUG-GLING WON'T HELP.
GRRIP
YOU CAN'T BEAT A MAN IN STRENGTH.
!
FWUP
WHAT ...?
I TOLD YOU. YOU SHOULDN'T FALL FOR APPEARANCES.
IF YOU DON'T WANT THE GIRL TO DIE, DON'T MOVE.
IF YOU TAKE EVEN ONE STEP, HER HEAD WILL ROLL.
TMP
!
THIS IS BAD...
UGH...
TMP
THE SAND LEADS TO THAT ROCK.
THIS MUST BE THEIR HIDEOUT.

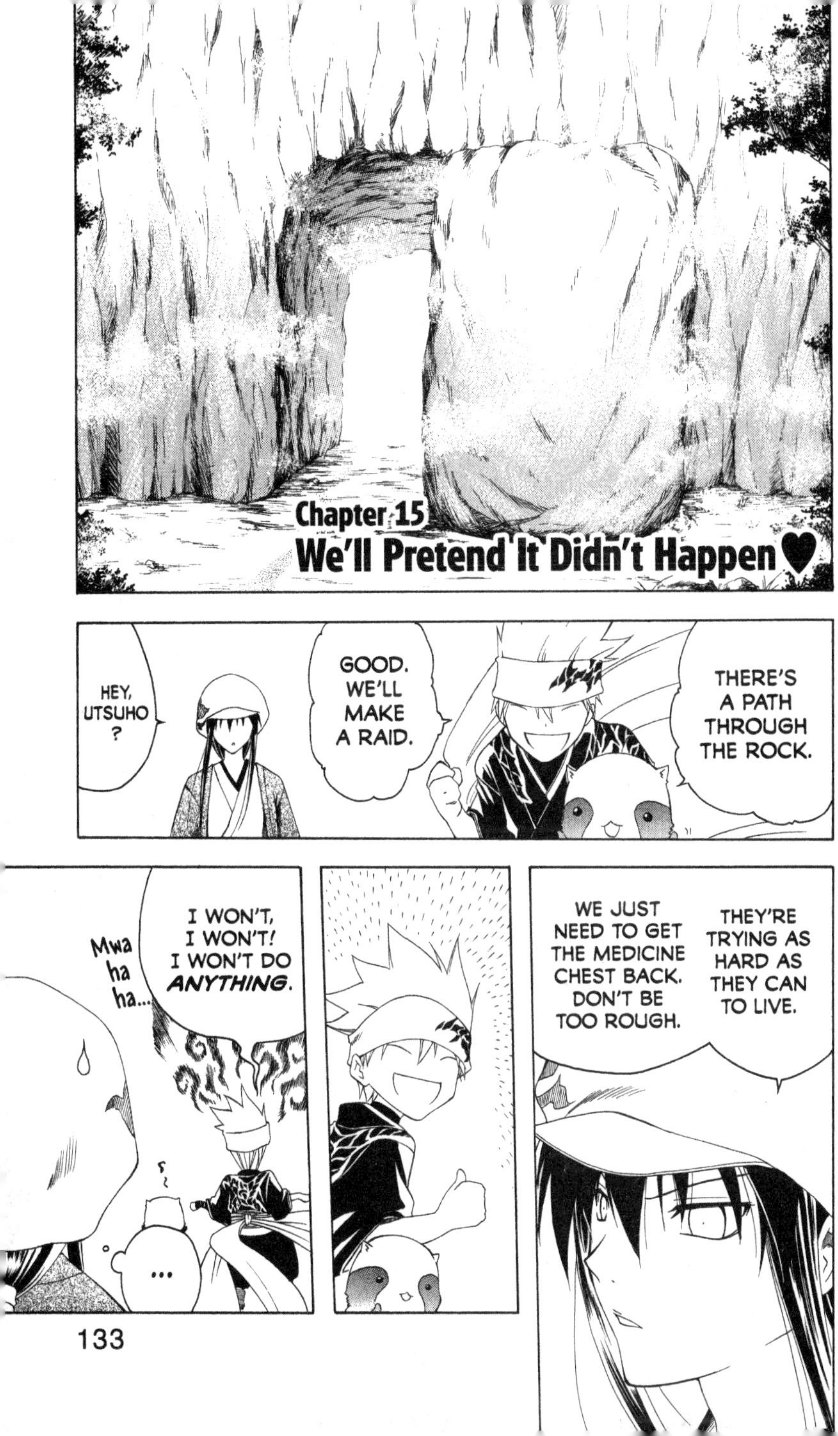
Chapter 15
We'll Pretend It Didn't Happen♥
THERE'S A PATH THROUGH THE ROCK.
GOOD. WE'LL MAKE A RAID.
HEY, UTSUHO?
THEY'RE TRYING AS HARD AS THEY CAN TO LIVE.
WE JUST NEED TO GET THE MEDICINE CHEST BACK. DON'T BE TOO ROUGH.
I WON'T, I WON'T! I WON'T DO *ANYTHING*.
Mwa ha ha...
...

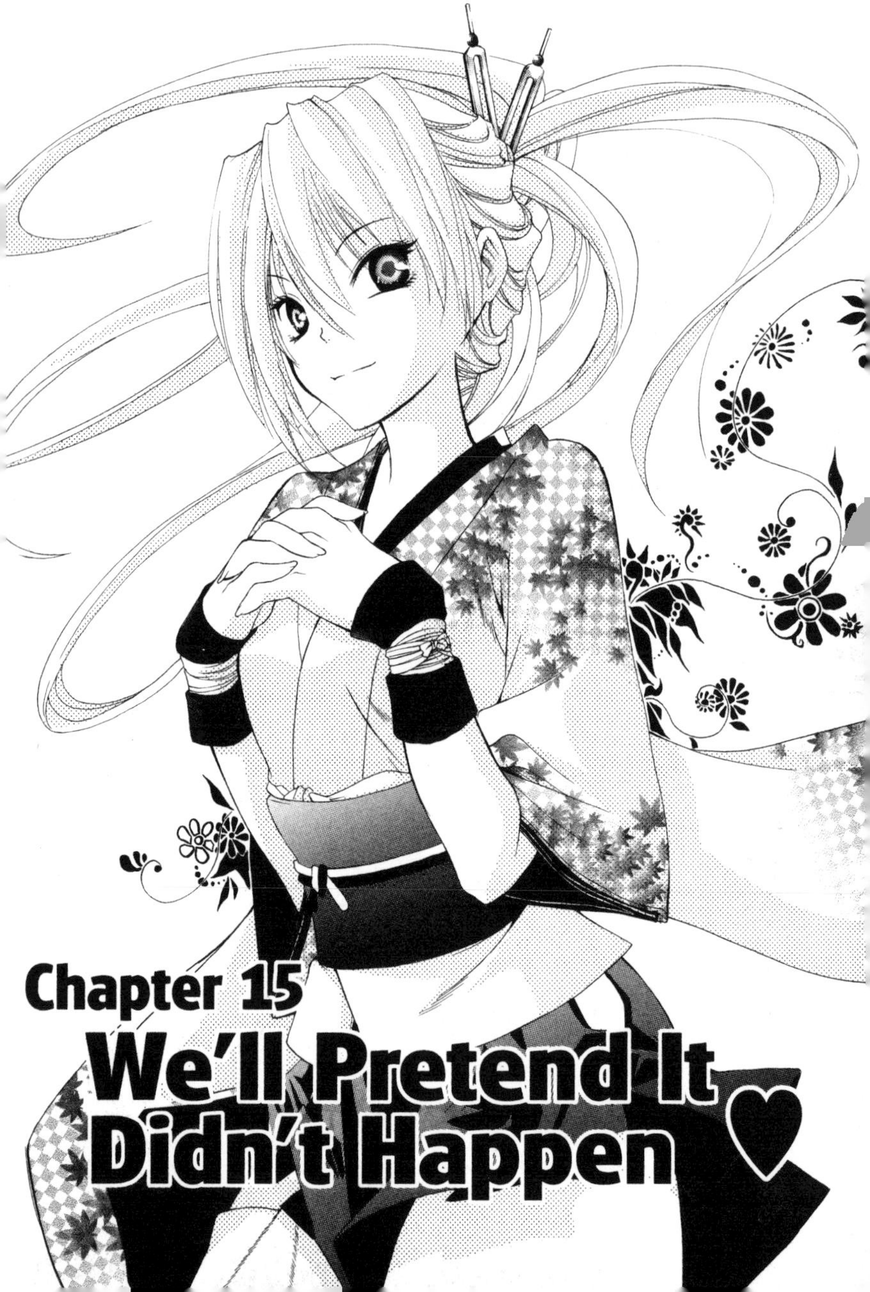
Chapter 15
We'll Pretend It Didn't Happen ♥

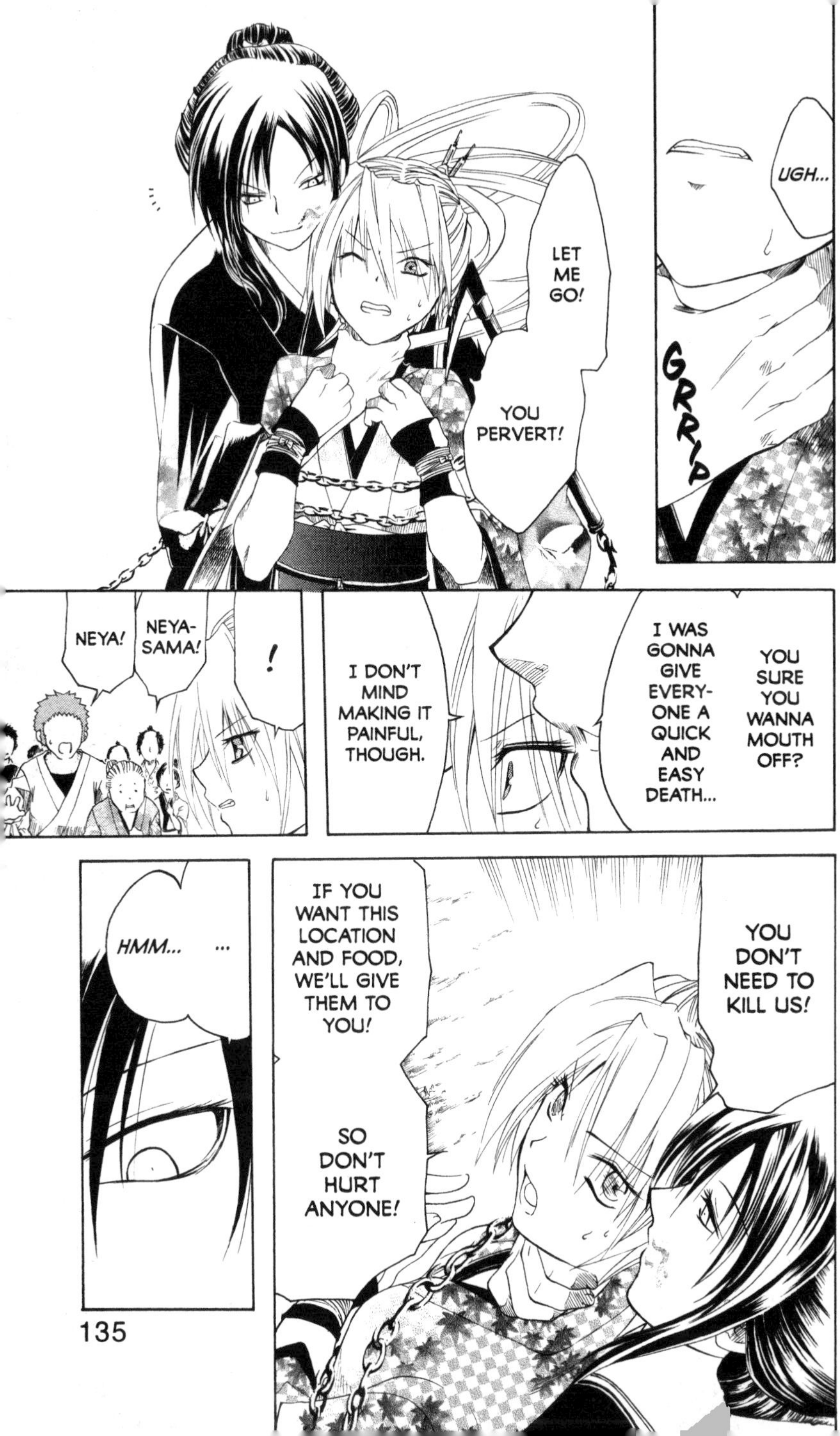
UGH...
GRRIP
LET ME GO!
YOU PERVERT!
YOU SURE YOU WANNA MOUTH OFF?
I WAS GONNA GIVE EVERY-ONE A QUICK AND EASY DEATH...
I DON'T MIND MAKING IT PAINFUL, THOUGH.
!
NEYA-SAMA!
NEYA!
YOU DON'T NEED TO KILL US!
IF YOU WANT THIS LOCATION AND FOOD, WE'LL GIVE THEM TO YOU!
SO DON'T HURT ANYONE!
HMM... ...

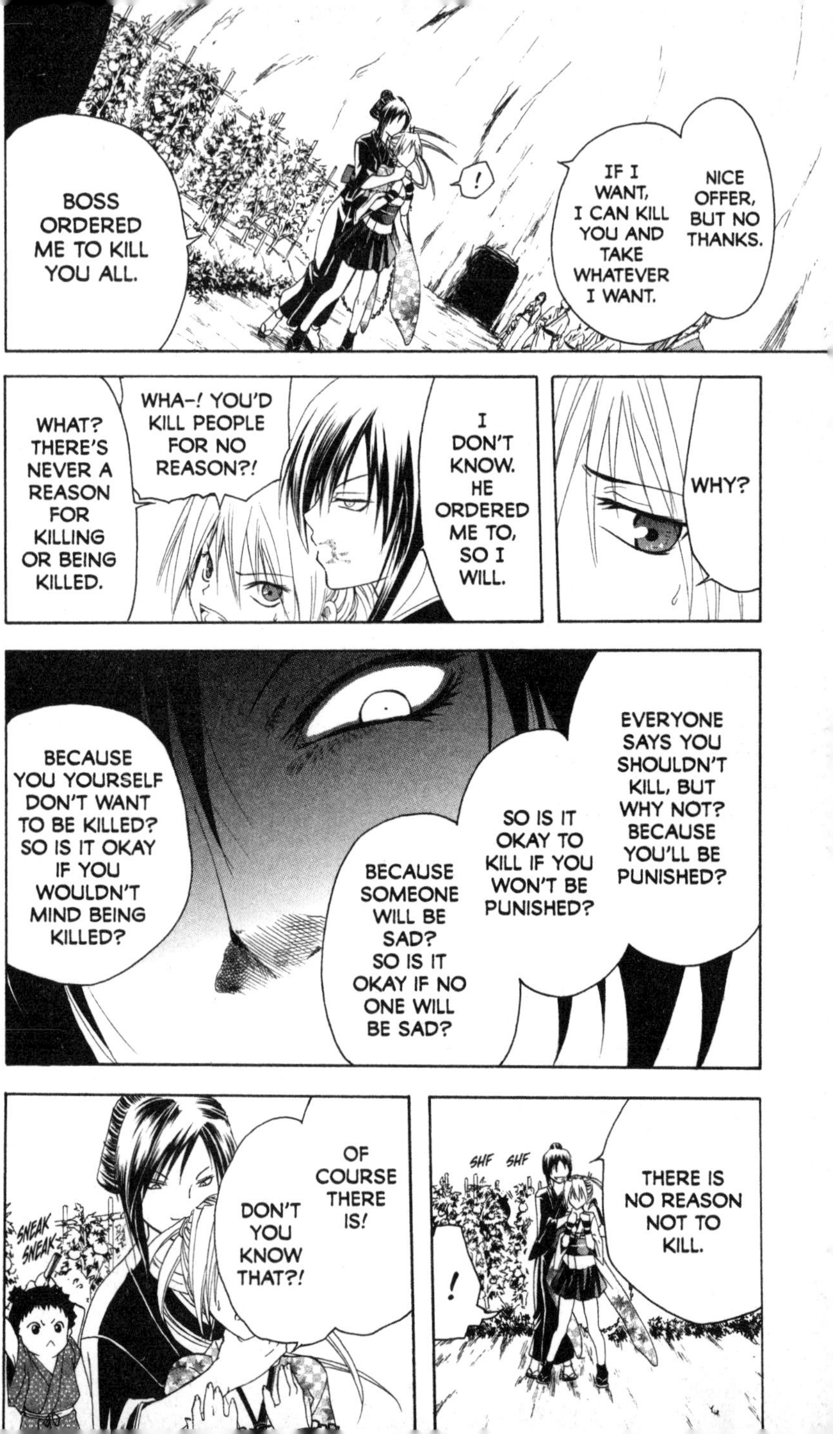
NICE OFFER, BUT NO THANKS.
IF I WANT, I CAN KILL YOU AND TAKE WHATEVER I WANT.
!
BOSS ORDERED ME TO KILL YOU ALL.
WHY?
I DON'T KNOW. HE ORDERED ME TO, SO I WILL.
WHA-! YOU'D KILL PEOPLE FOR NO REASON?!
WHAT? THERE'S NEVER A REASON FOR KILLING OR BEING KILLED.
EVERYONE SAYS YOU SHOULDN'T KILL, BUT WHY NOT? BECAUSE YOU'LL BE PUNISHED?
SO IS IT OKAY TO KILL IF YOU WON'T BE PUNISHED?
BECAUSE SOMEONE WILL BE SAD? SO IS IT OKAY IF NO ONE WILL BE SAD?
BECAUSE YOU YOURSELF DON'T WANT TO BE KILLED? SO IS IT OKAY IF YOU WOULDN'T MIND BEING KILLED?
SHF SHF
THERE IS NO REASON NOT TO KILL.
!
OF COURSE THERE IS!
DON'T YOU KNOW THAT?!
SNEAK SNEAK

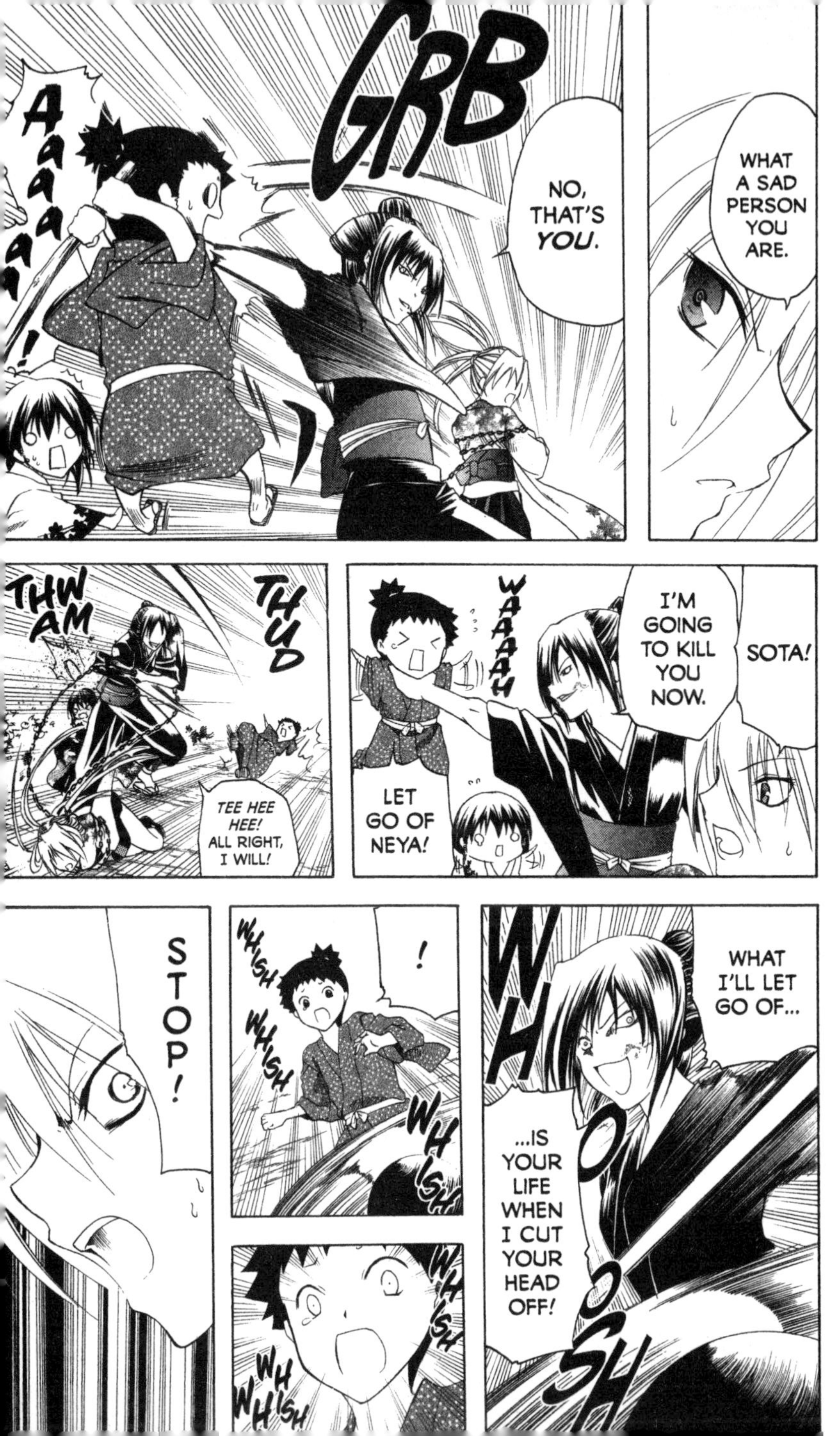
WHAT A SAD PERSON YOU ARE.
NO, THAT'S *YOU*.
GRB
Aaaaaaa!
SOTA!
I'M GOING TO KILL YOU NOW.
WAAAAAH
LET GO OF NEYA!
THUD
THWAM
TEE HEE HEE! ALL RIGHT, I WILL!
WHAT I'LL LET GO OF...
WHOOSH
...IS YOUR LIFE WHEN I CUT YOUR HEAD OFF!
!
WHISH
WHISH
WHISH
WHISH
WHISH
WHISH
STOP!

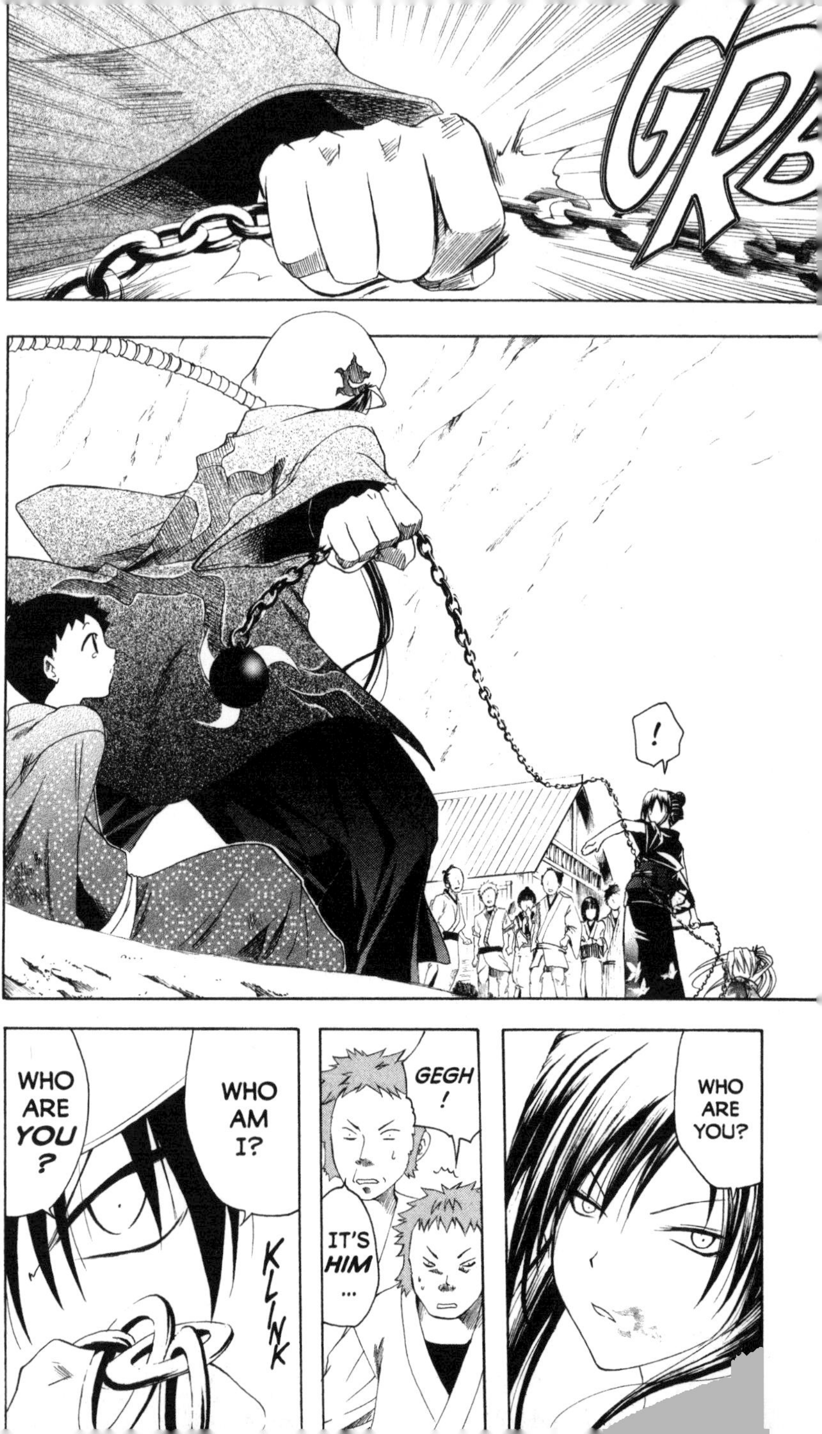
GRB
!
WHO ARE YOU?
GEGH!
IT'S HIM...
WHO AM I?
WHO ARE YOU?
KLINK

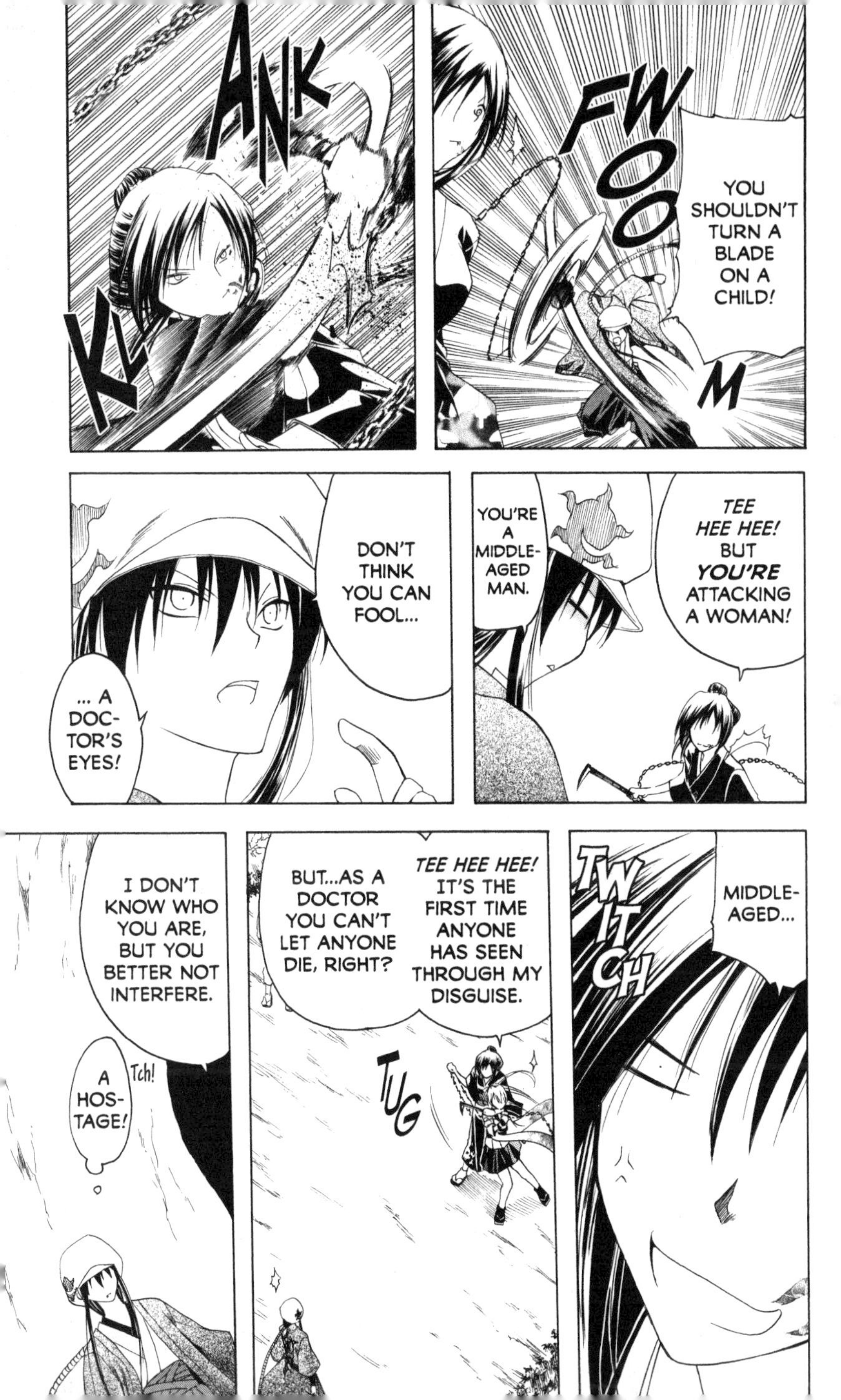
FWOOO
YOU SHOULDN'T TURN A BLADE ON A CHILD!
M
ANK
KL
TEE HEE HEE! BUT *YOU'RE* ATTACKING A WOMAN!
YOU'RE A MIDDLE-AGED MAN.
DON'T THINK YOU CAN FOOL...
... A DOCTOR'S EYES!
TWITCH
MIDDLE-AGED...
TEE HEE HEE! IT'S THE FIRST TIME ANYONE HAS SEEN THROUGH MY DISGUISE.
BUT...AS A DOCTOR YOU CAN'T LET ANYONE DIE, RIGHT?
TUG
I DON'T KNOW WHO YOU ARE, BUT YOU BETTER NOT INTERFERE.
Tch!
A HOSTAGE!

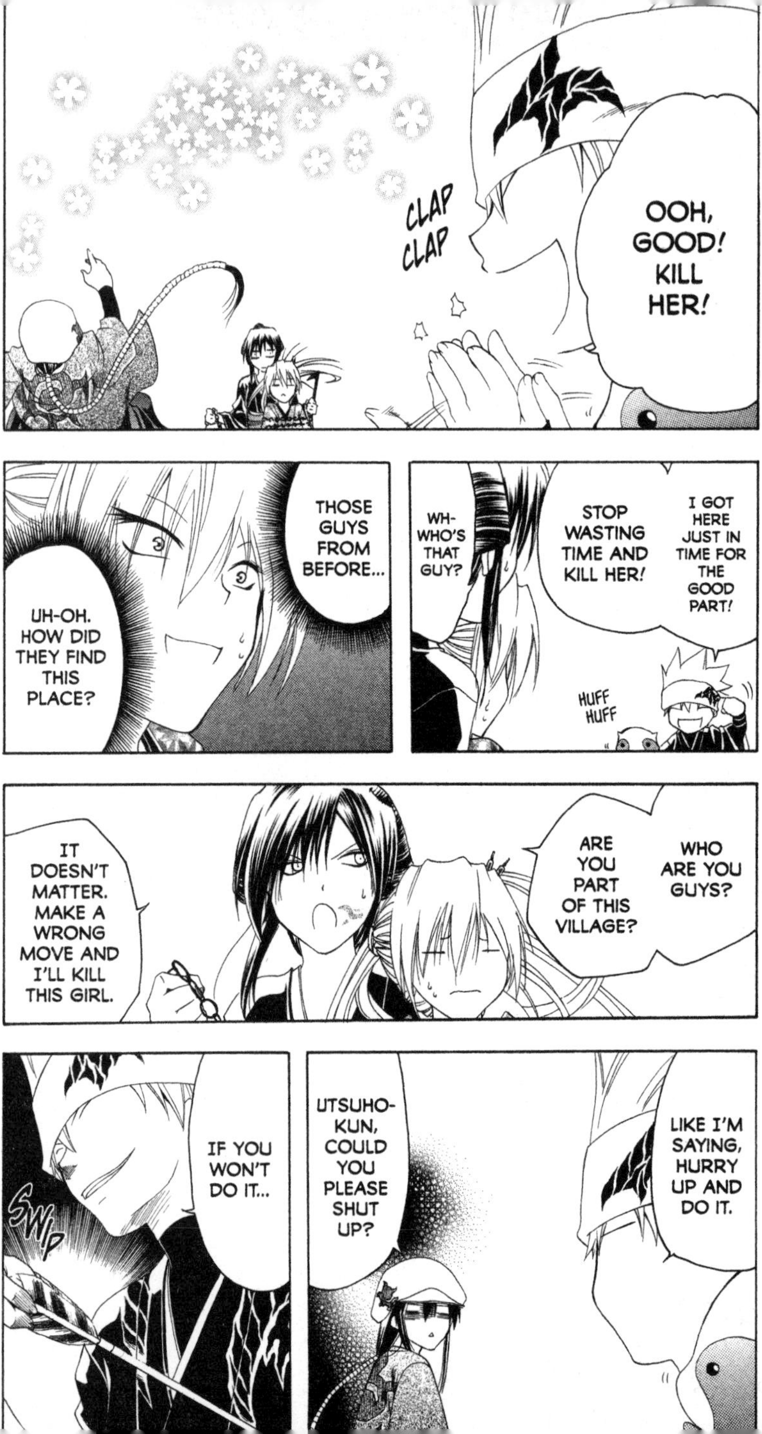
OOH, GOOD! KILL HER!
CLAP CLAP
I GOT HERE JUST IN TIME FOR THE GOOD PART!
STOP WASTING TIME AND KILL HER!
WH-WHO'S THAT GUY?
HUFF HUFF
THOSE GUYS FROM BEFORE...
UH-OH. HOW DID THEY FIND THIS PLACE?
WHO ARE YOU GUYS?
ARE YOU PART OF THIS VILLAGE?
IT DOESN'T MATTER. MAKE A WRONG MOVE AND I'LL KILL THIS GIRL.
LIKE I'M SAYING, HURRY UP AND DO IT.
UTSUHO-KUN, COULD YOU PLEASE SHUT UP?
IF YOU WON'T DO IT...
SWIP

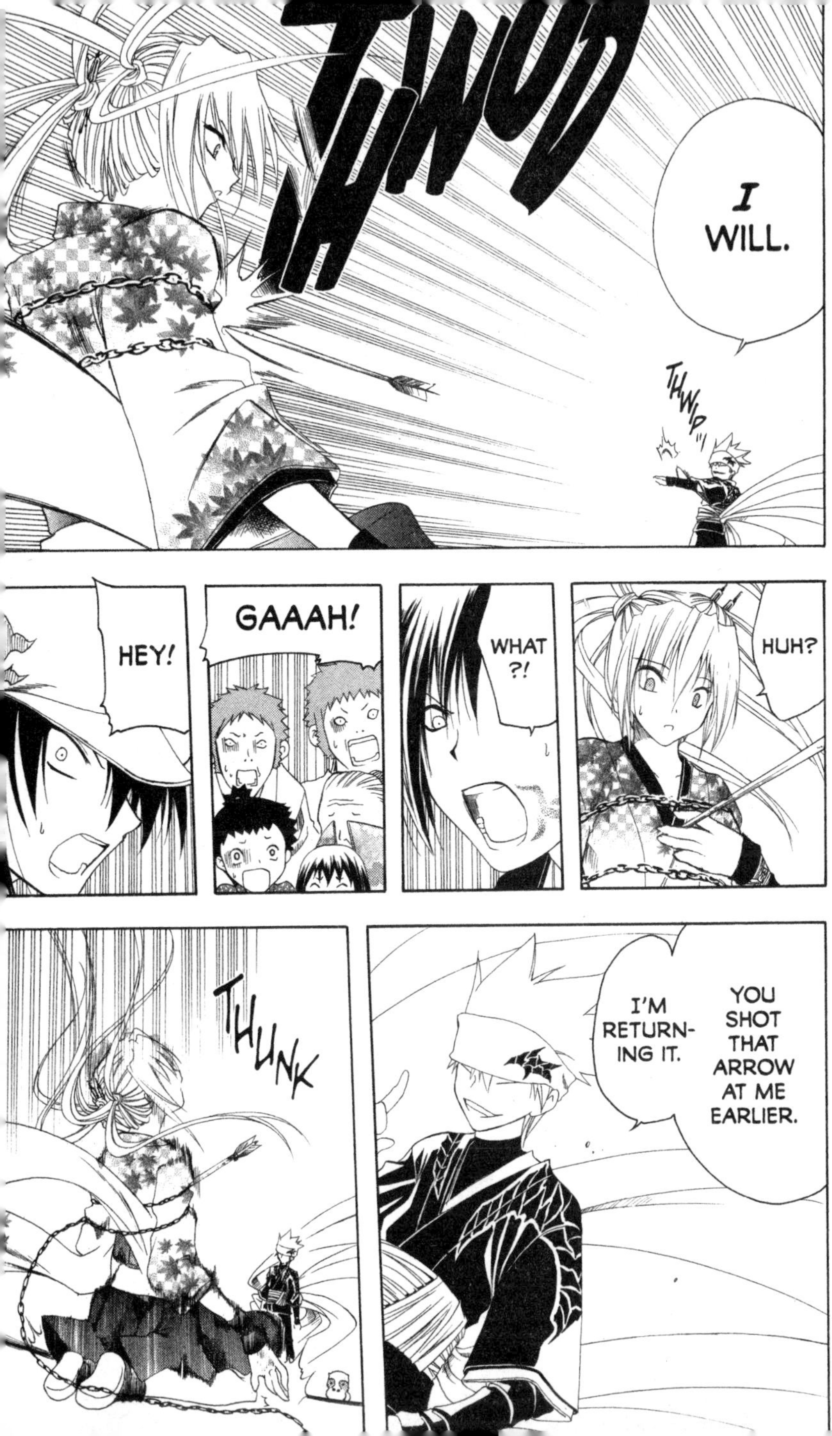
I WILL.
THWIP
THWUD
HUH?
WHAT ?!
GAAAH!
HEY!
YOU SHOT THAT ARROW AT ME EARLIER.
I'M RETURN-ING IT.
THUNK

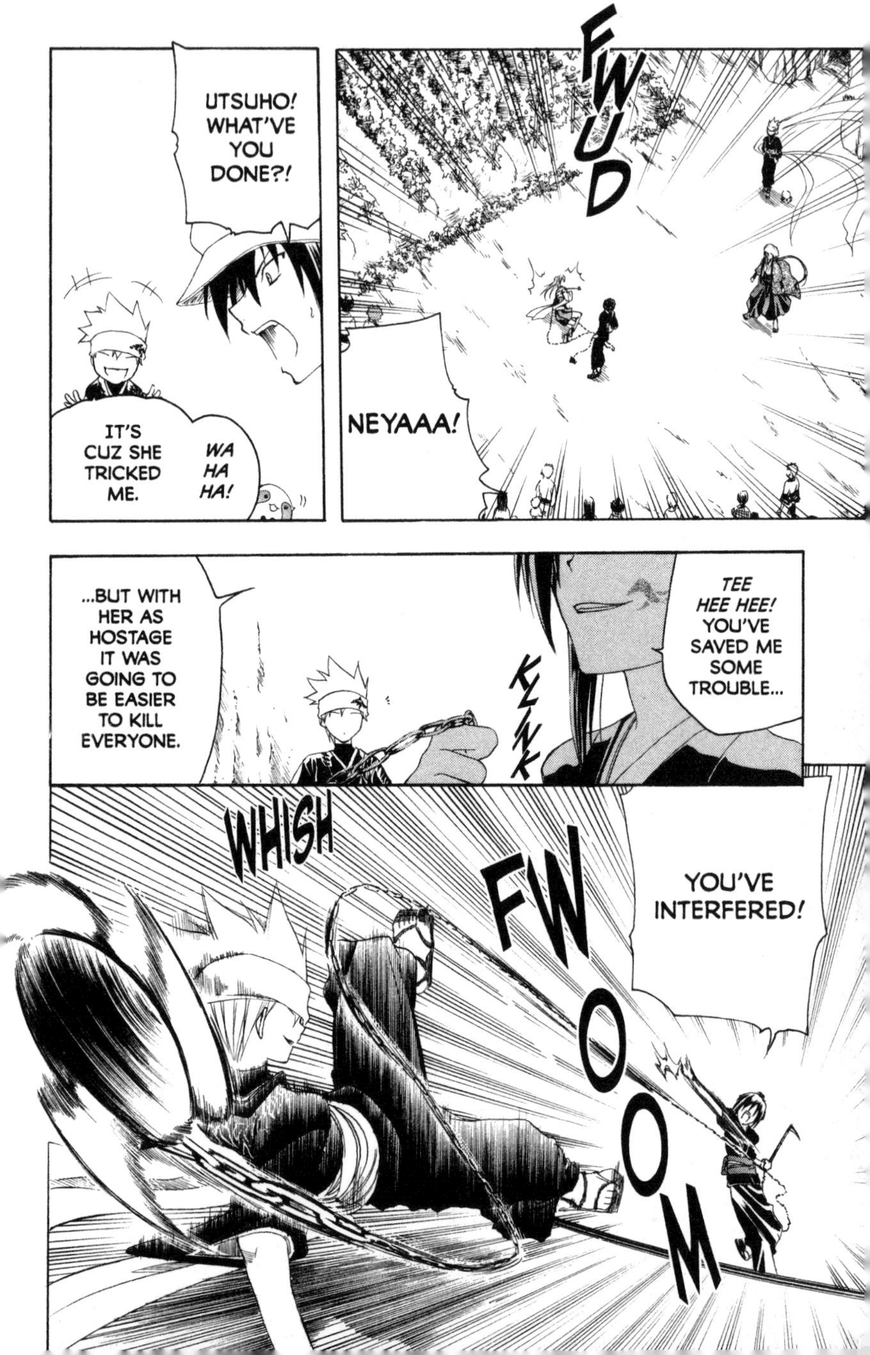
FWUD
NEYAAA!
UTSUHO! WHAT'VE YOU DONE?!
IT'S CUZ SHE TRICKED ME.
WA HA HA!
TEE HEE HEE! YOU'VE SAVED ME SOME TROUBLE...
KLINK
...BUT WITH HER AS HOSTAGE IT WAS GOING TO BE EASIER TO KILL EVERYONE.
YOU'VE INTERFERED!
FWOOOM
WHISH

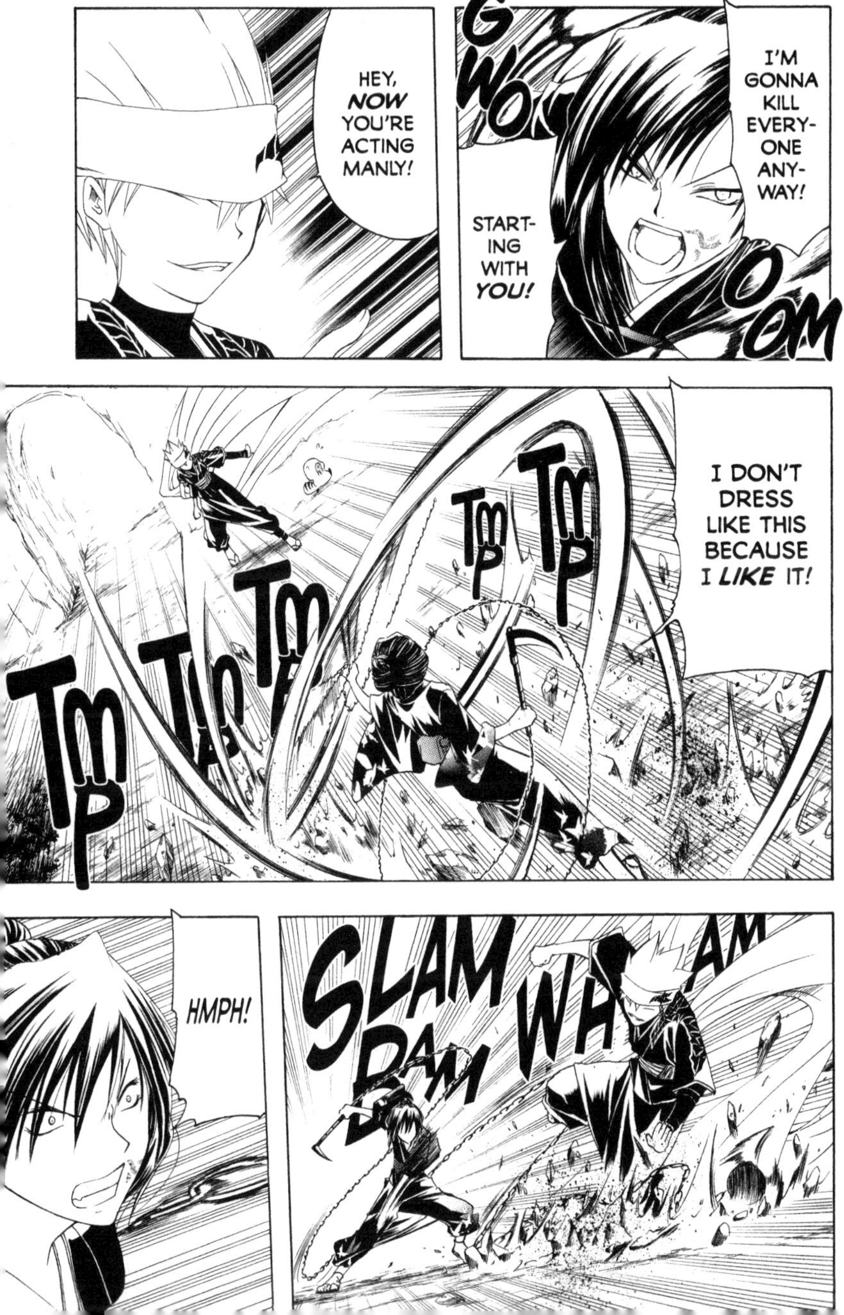
GWO
OOOM
I'M GONNA KILL EVERY-ONE ANY-WAY!
STARTING WITH YOU!
HEY, NOW YOU'RE ACTING MANLY!
I DON'T DRESS LIKE THIS BECAUSE I LIKE IT!
Tmp
Tmp
Tmp
Tmp
SLAM
HMPH!

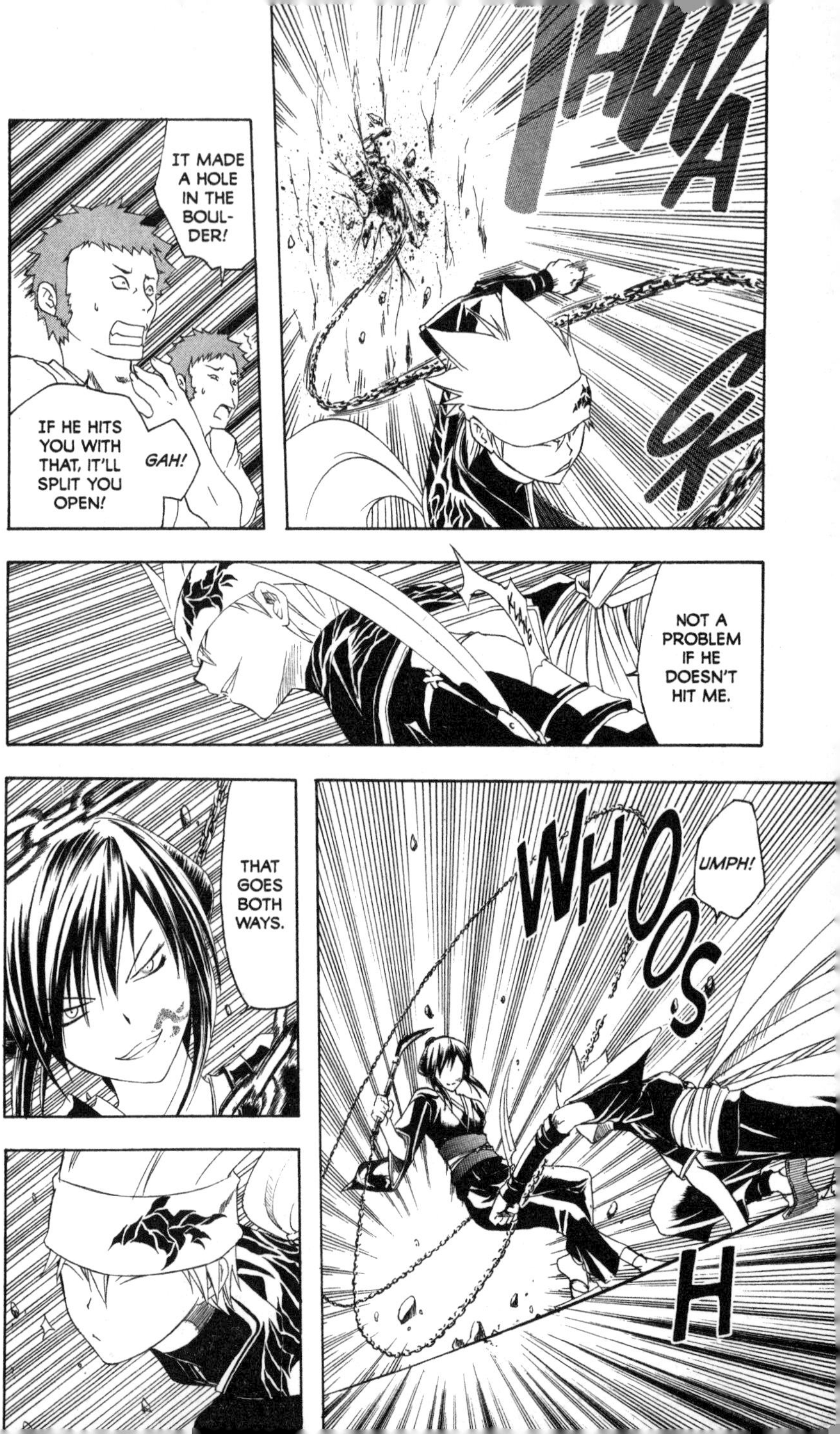
HWA
CK
IT MADE A HOLE IN THE BOULDER!
GAH!
IF HE HITS YOU WITH THAT, IT'LL SPLIT YOU OPEN!
NOT A PROBLEM IF HE DOESN'T HIT ME.
KLANG
UMPH!
WHOOSH
THAT GOES BOTH WAYS.

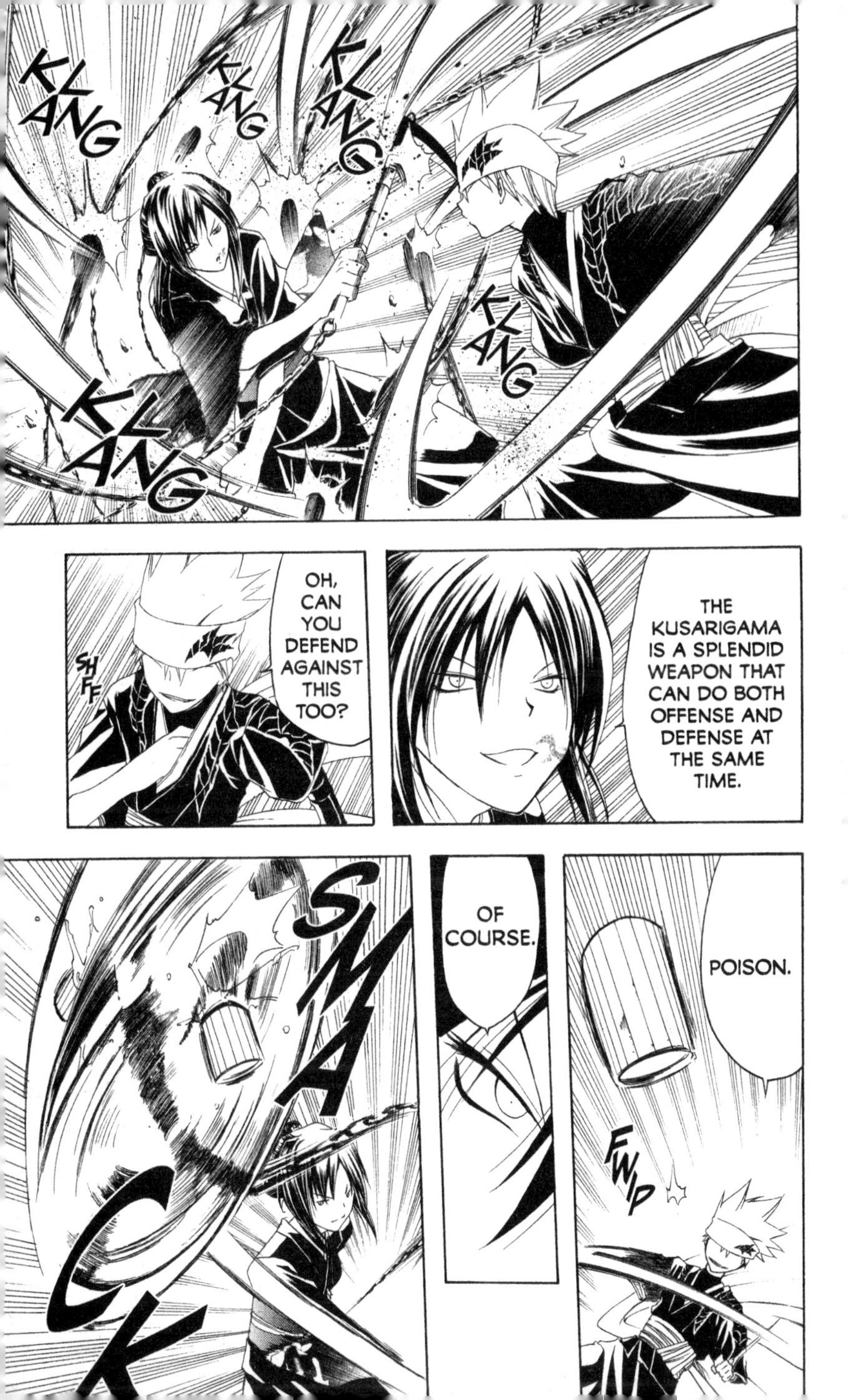
KLANG
KLANG
KLANG
KLANG
KLANG
THE KUSARIGAMA IS A SPLENDID WEAPON THAT CAN DO BOTH OFFENSE AND DEFENSE AT THE SAME TIME.
OH, CAN YOU DEFEND AGAINST THIS TOO?
SHFF
POISON.
FWIP
OF COURSE.
SMACK

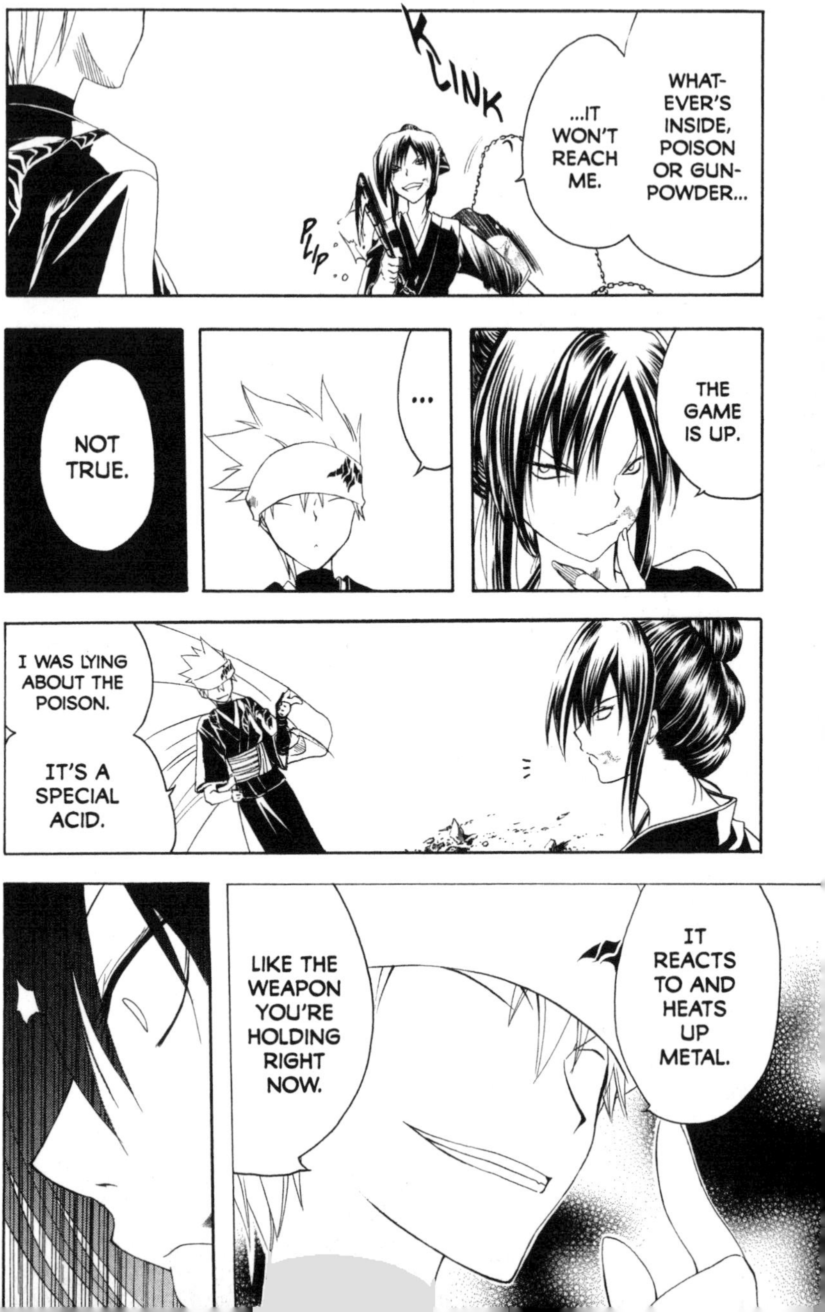
KLINK
WHAT-EVER'S INSIDE, POISON OR GUN-POWDER...
...IT WON'T REACH ME.
PLIP
THE GAME IS UP.
...
NOT TRUE.
I WAS LYING ABOUT THE POISON.
IT'S A SPECIAL ACID.
IT REACTS TO AND HEATS UP METAL.
LIKE THE WEAPON YOU'RE HOLDING RIGHT NOW.

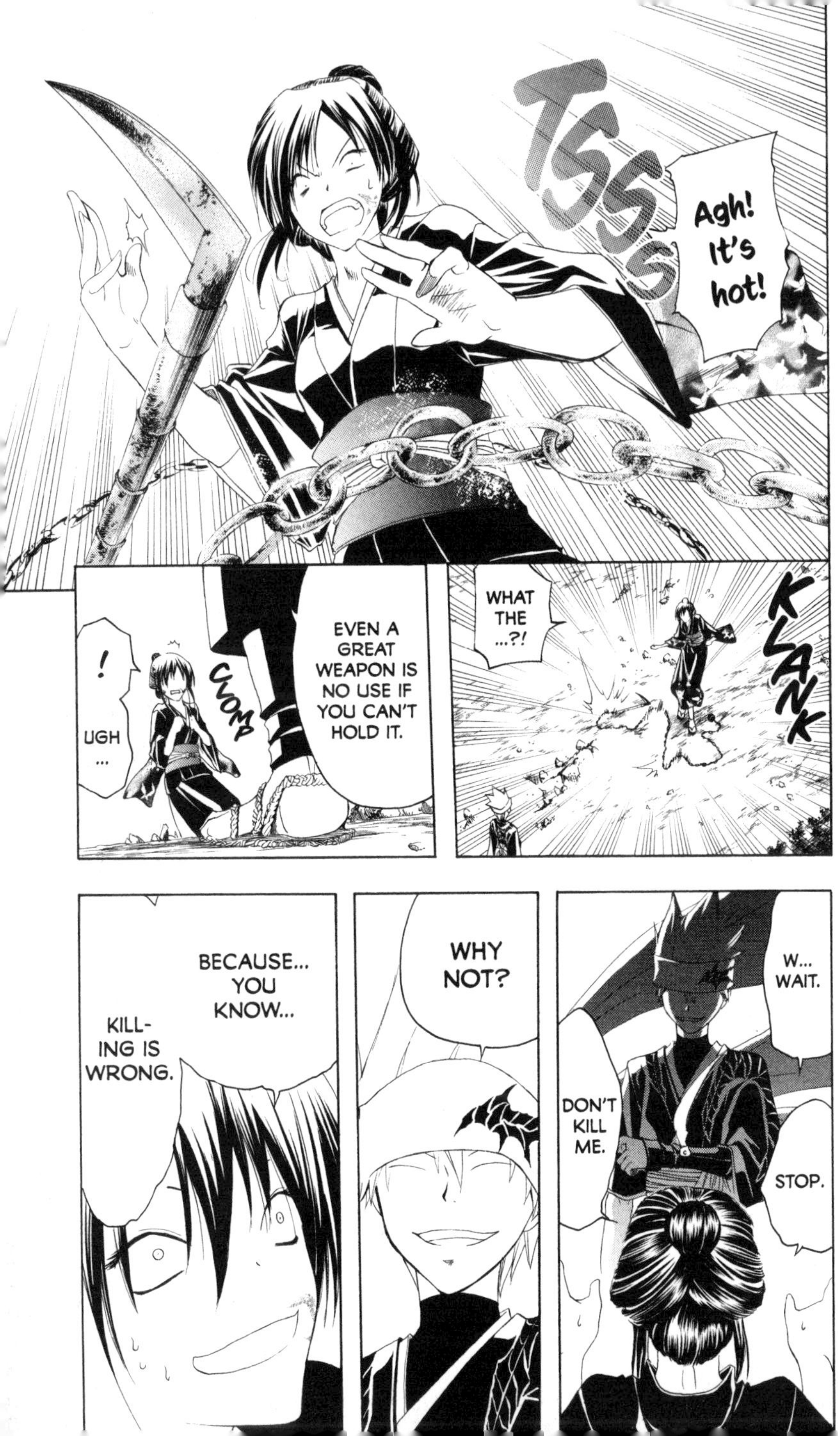
TSSS
Agh! It's hot!
KLANK
WHAT THE ...?!
EVEN A GREAT WEAPON IS NO USE IF YOU CAN'T HOLD IT.
CLOMP
!
UGH ...
W... WAIT.
DON'T KILL ME.
STOP.
WHY NOT?
BECAUSE... YOU KNOW...
KILL-ING IS WRONG.

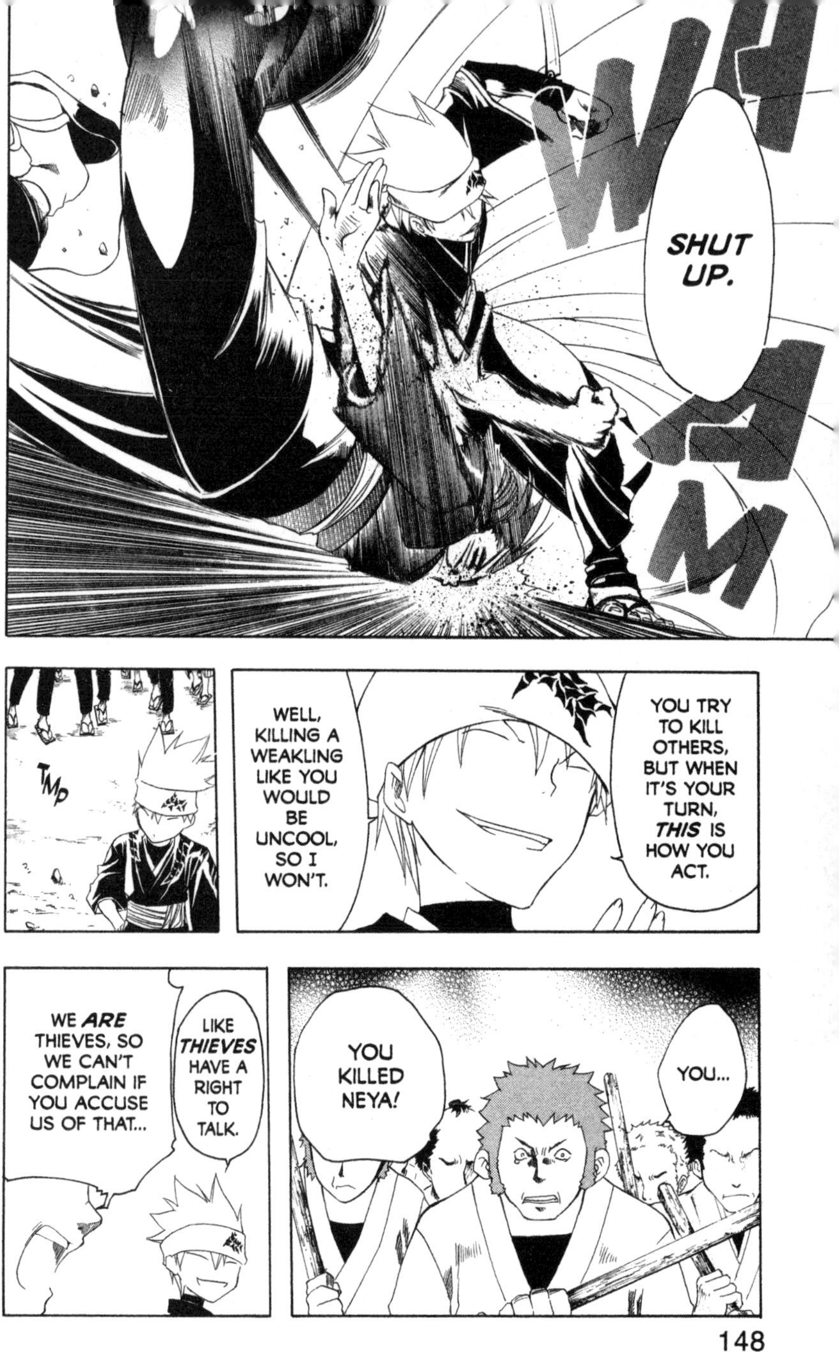
WHAM
SHUT UP.
YOU TRY TO KILL OTHERS, BUT WHEN IT'S YOUR TURN, *THIS* IS HOW YOU ACT.
WELL, KILLING A WEAKLING LIKE YOU WOULD BE UNCOOL, SO I WON'T.
TMP
YOU...
YOU KILLED NEYA!
LIKE *THIEVES* HAVE A RIGHT TO TALK.
WE *ARE* THIEVES, SO WE CAN'T COMPLAIN IF YOU ACCUSE US OF THAT...

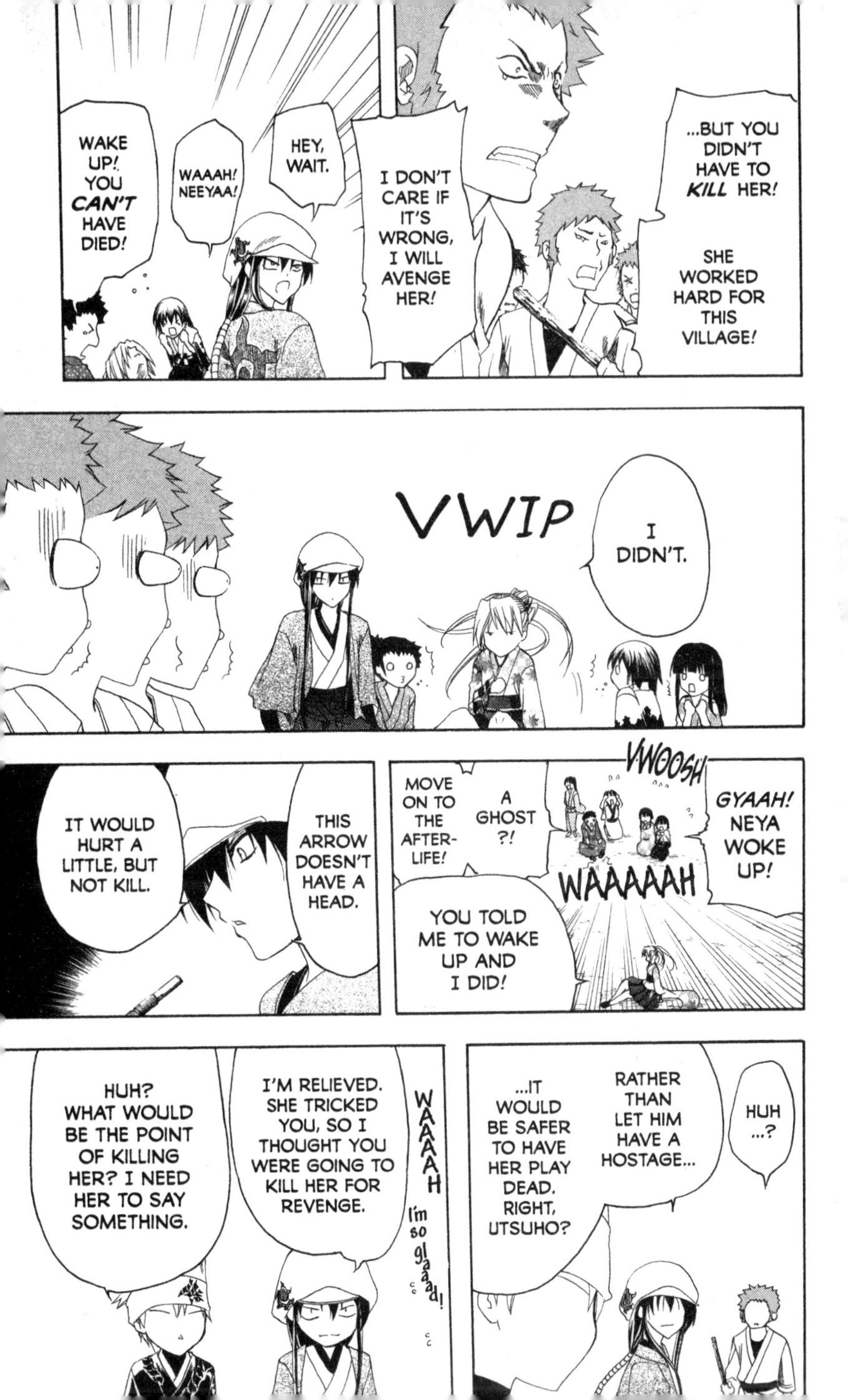
...BUT YOU DIDN'T HAVE TO KILL HER!
SHE WORKED HARD FOR THIS VILLAGE!
I DON'T CARE IF IT'S WRONG, I WILL AVENGE HER!
HEY, WAIT.
WAAAH! NEEYAA!
WAKE UP! YOU CAN'T HAVE DIED!
I DIDN'T.
VWIP
GYAAH! NEYA WOKE UP!
VWOOSH
A GHOST?!
MOVE ON TO THE AFTER-LIFE!
WAAAAAH
YOU TOLD ME TO WAKE UP AND I DID!
THIS ARROW DOESN'T HAVE A HEAD.
IT WOULD HURT A LITTLE, BUT NOT KILL.
HUH...?
RATHER THAN LET HIM HAVE A HOSTAGE...
...IT WOULD BE SAFER TO HAVE HER PLAY DEAD. RIGHT, UTSUHO?
WAAAAH
I'm so glaaaad!
I'M RELIEVED. SHE TRICKED YOU, SO I THOUGHT YOU WERE GOING TO KILL HER FOR REVENGE.
HUH? WHAT WOULD BE THE POINT OF KILLING HER? I NEED HER TO SAY SOMETHING.

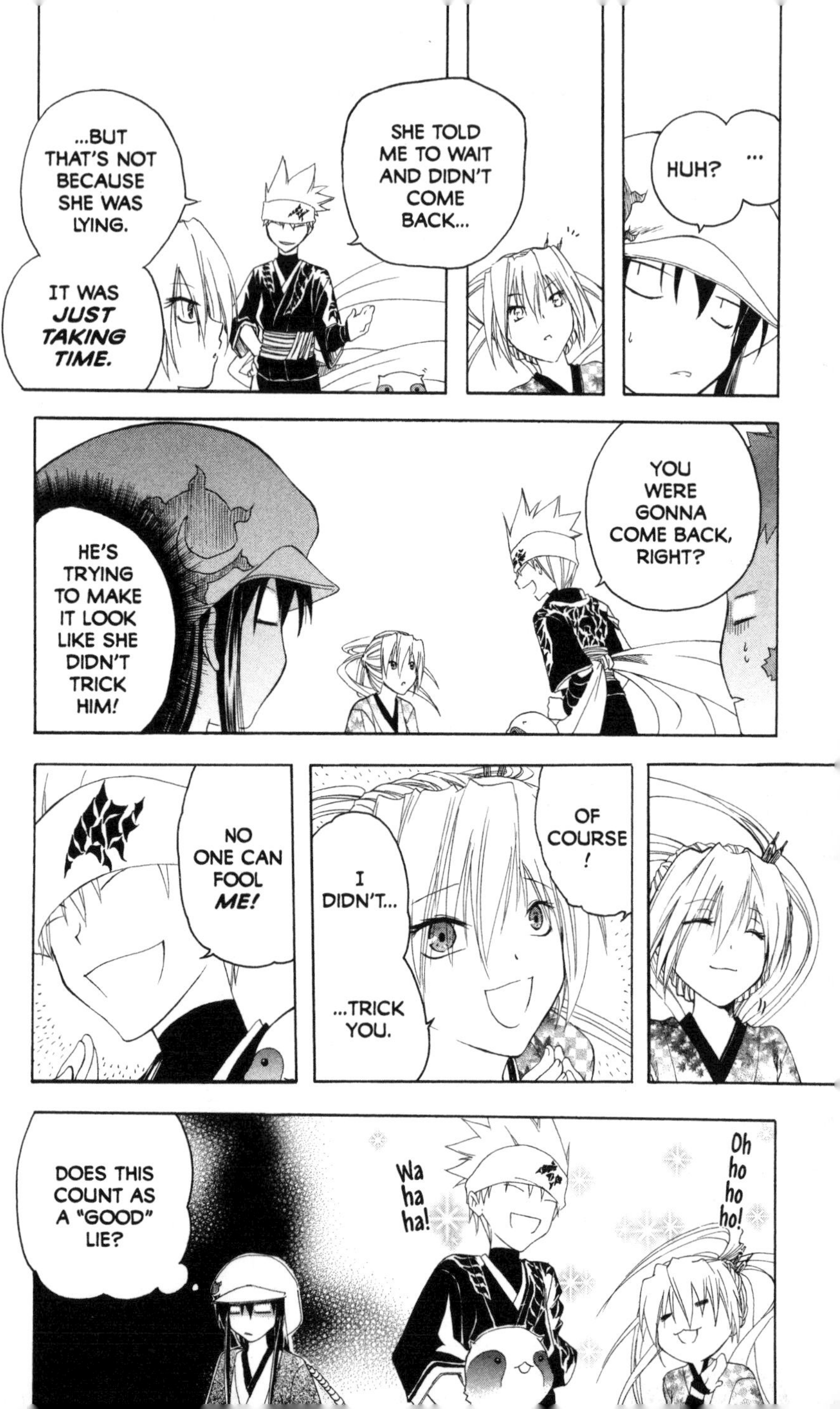
... HUH?
SHE TOLD ME TO WAIT AND DIDN'T COME BACK...
...BUT THAT'S NOT BECAUSE SHE WAS LYING.
IT WAS *JUST TAKING TIME.*
YOU WERE GONNA COME BACK, RIGHT?
HE'S TRYING TO MAKE IT LOOK LIKE SHE DIDN'T TRICK HIM!
OF COURSE!
I DIDN'T...
...TRICK YOU.
NO ONE CAN FOOL *ME!*
Oh ho ho ho!
Wa ha ha!
DOES THIS COUNT AS A "GOOD" LIE?

Chapter 16 The Same Smell

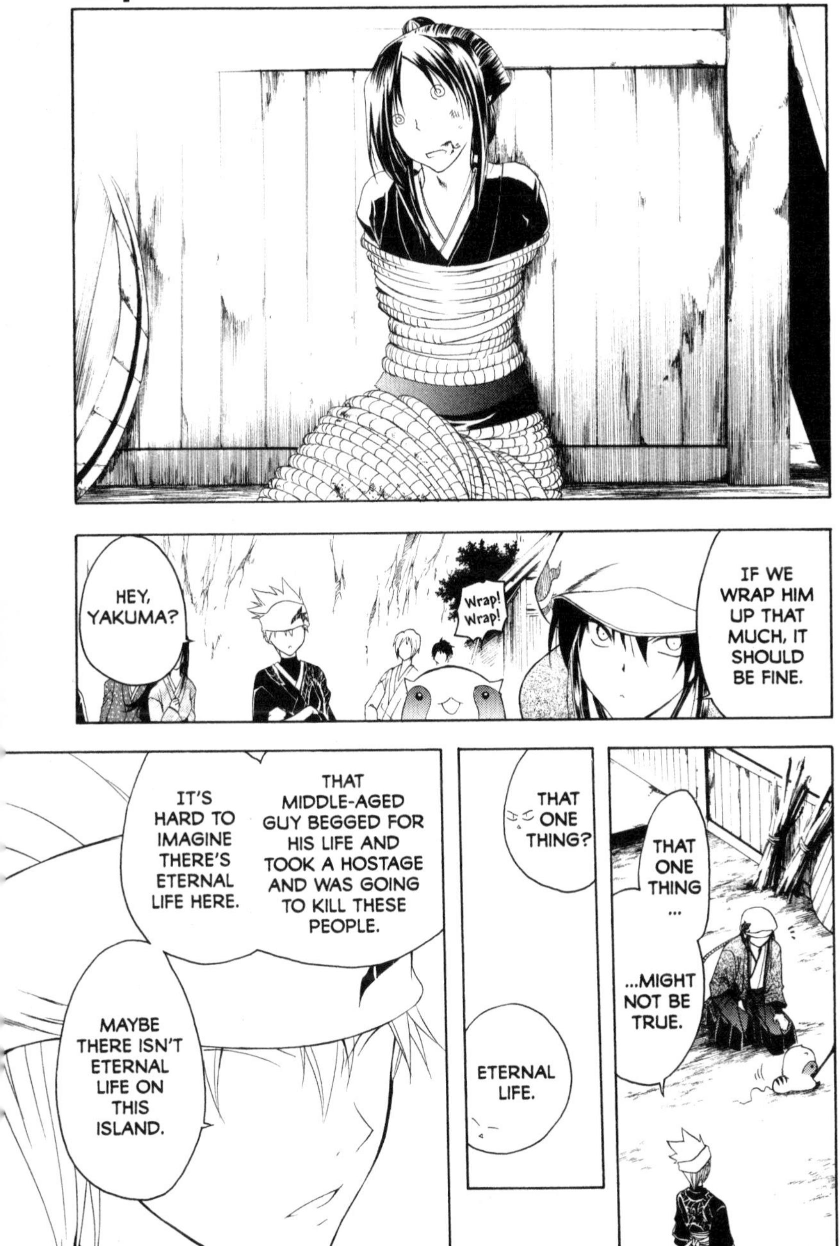
IF WE WRAP HIM UP THAT MUCH, IT SHOULD BE FINE.
Wrap! Wrap!
HEY, YAKUMA?
THAT ONE THING...
...MIGHT NOT BE TRUE.
THAT ONE THING?
ETERNAL LIFE.
THAT MIDDLE-AGED GUY BEGGED FOR HIS LIFE AND TOOK A HOSTAGE AND WAS GOING TO KILL THESE PEOPLE.
IT'S HARD TO IMAGINE THERE'S ETERNAL LIFE HERE.
MAYBE THERE ISN'T ETERNAL LIFE ON THIS ISLAND.

Chapter 16

The Same Smell

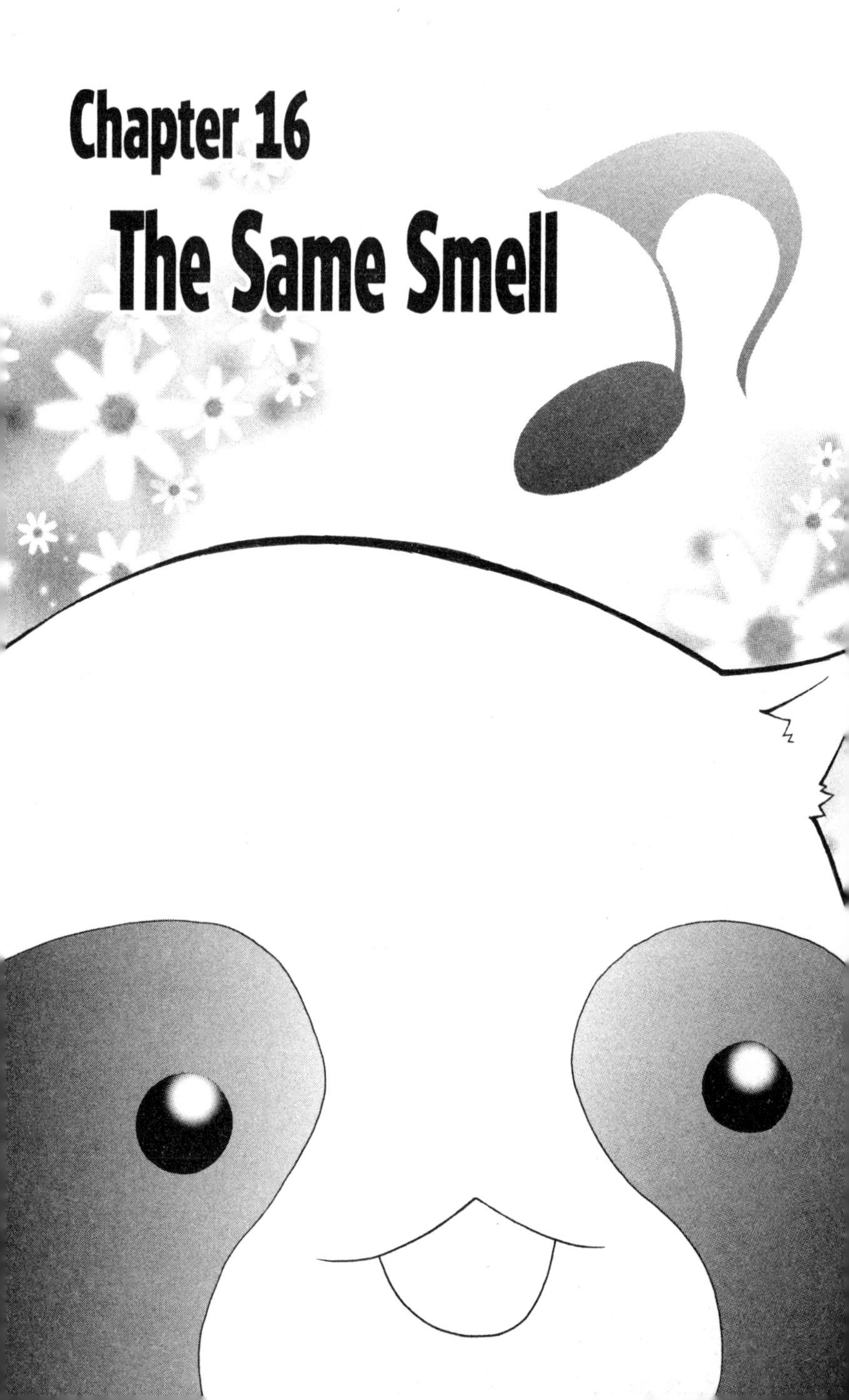

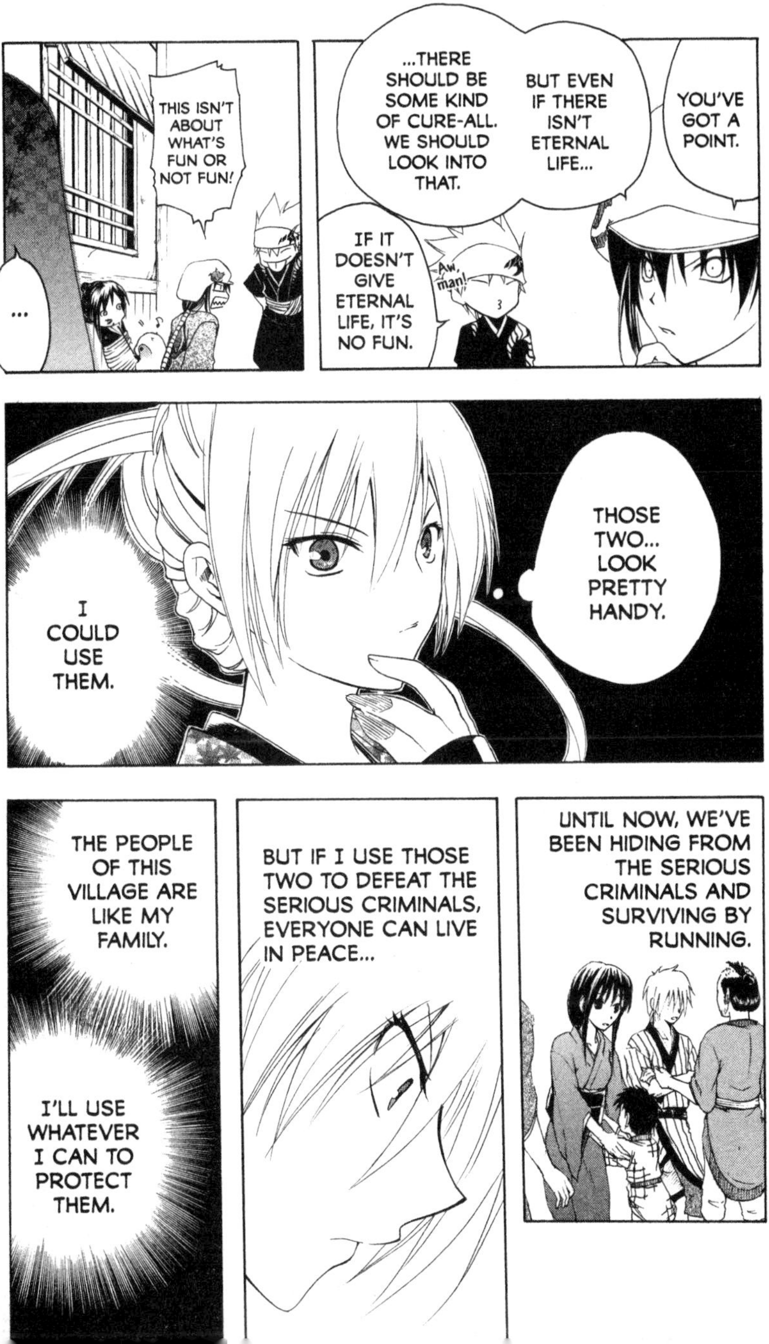
YOU'VE GOT A POINT.
BUT EVEN IF THERE ISN'T ETERNAL LIFE...
...THERE SHOULD BE SOME KIND OF CURE-ALL. WE SHOULD LOOK INTO THAT.
Aw, man!
IF IT DOESN'T GIVE ETERNAL LIFE, IT'S NO FUN.
THIS ISN'T ABOUT WHAT'S FUN OR NOT FUN!
...
THOSE TWO... LOOK PRETTY HANDY.
I COULD USE THEM.
UNTIL NOW, WE'VE BEEN HIDING FROM THE SERIOUS CRIMINALS AND SURVIVING BY RUNNING.
BUT IF I USE THOSE TWO TO DEFEAT THE SERIOUS CRIMINALS, EVERYONE CAN LIVE IN PEACE...
THE PEOPLE OF THIS VILLAGE ARE LIKE MY FAMILY.
I'LL USE WHATEVER I CAN TO PROTECT THEM.

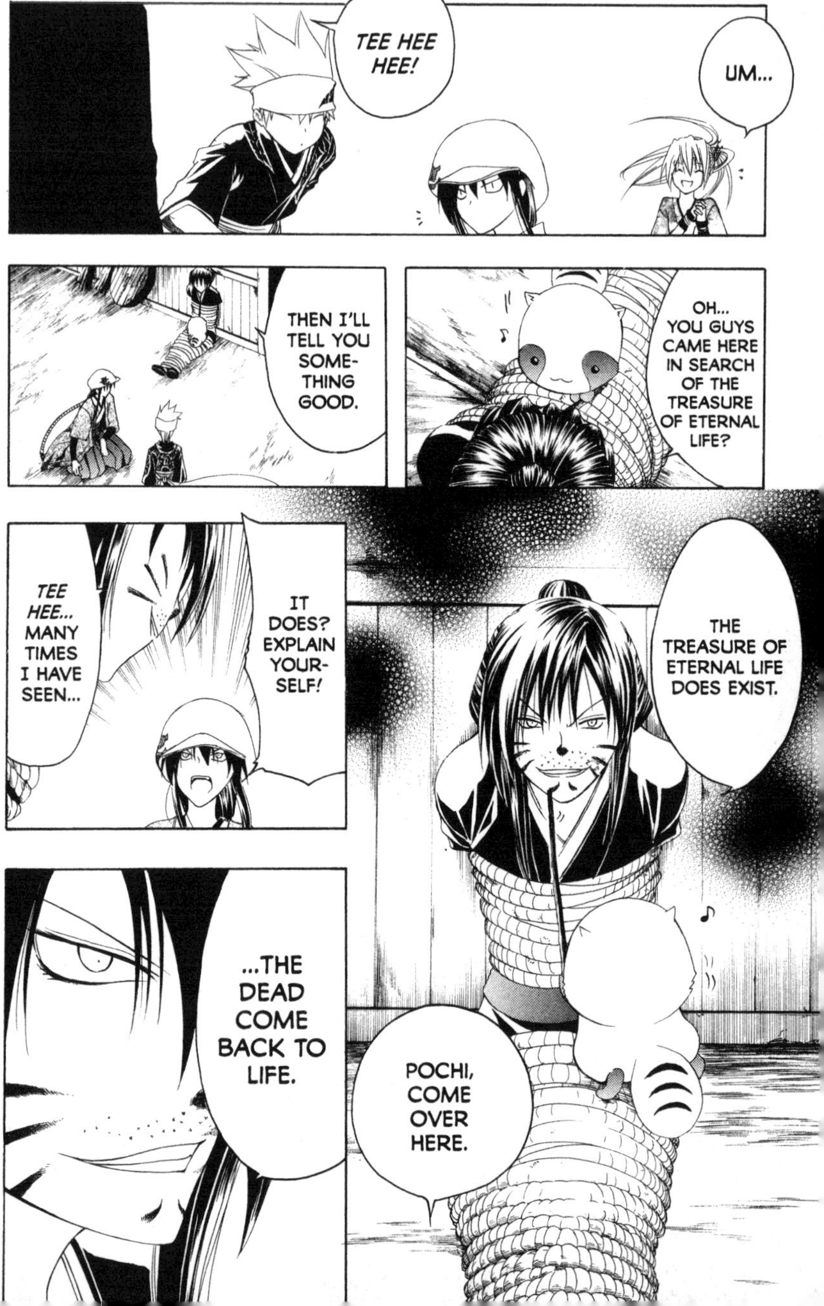
UM...
TEE HEE HEE!
OH... YOU GUYS CAME HERE IN SEARCH OF THE TREASURE OF ETERNAL LIFE?
THEN I'LL TELL YOU SOMETHING GOOD.
THE TREASURE OF ETERNAL LIFE DOES EXIST.
POCHI, COME OVER HERE.
IT DOES? EXPLAIN YOURSELF!
TEE HEE... MANY TIMES I HAVE SEEN...
...THE DEAD COME BACK TO LIFE.

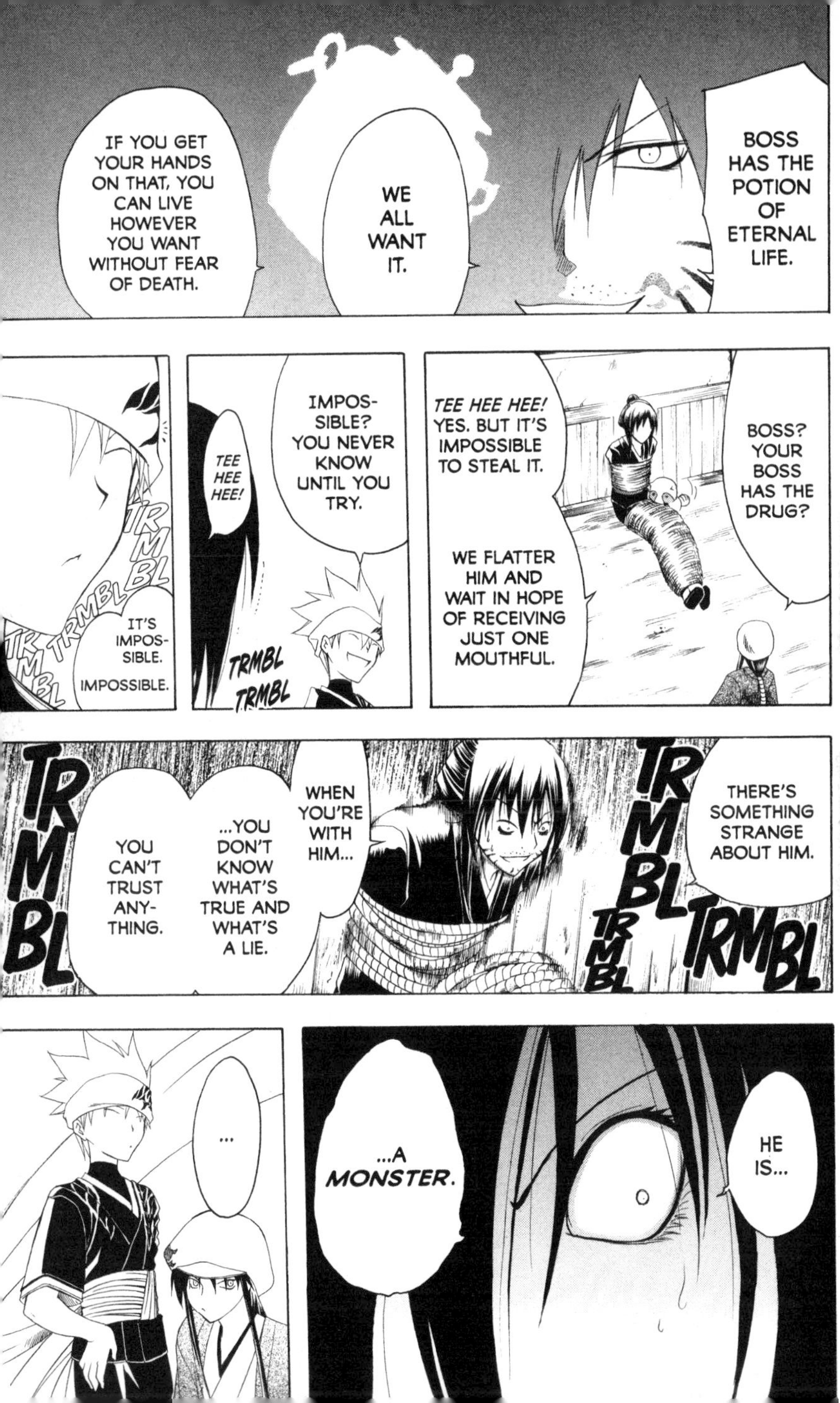

BOSS HAS THE POTION OF ETERNAL LIFE.
WE ALL WANT IT.
IF YOU GET YOUR HANDS ON THAT, YOU CAN LIVE HOWEVER YOU WANT WITHOUT FEAR OF DEATH.
BOSS? YOUR BOSS HAS THE DRUG?
TEE HEE HEE! YES. BUT IT'S IMPOSSIBLE TO STEAL IT.
WE FLATTER HIM AND WAIT IN HOPE OF RECEIVING JUST ONE MOUTHFUL.
IMPOSSIBLE? YOU NEVER KNOW UNTIL YOU TRY.
TEE HEE HEE!
TRMBL TRMBL
TRMBL TRMBL TRMBL
IT'S IMPOSSIBLE.
IMPOSSIBLE.
TRMBL
THERE'S SOMETHING STRANGE ABOUT HIM.
TRMBL TRMBL TRMBL
WHEN YOU'RE WITH HIM...
...YOU DON'T KNOW WHAT'S TRUE AND WHAT'S A LIE.
YOU CAN'T TRUST ANYTHING.
TRMBL
HE IS...
...A *MONSTER*.
...

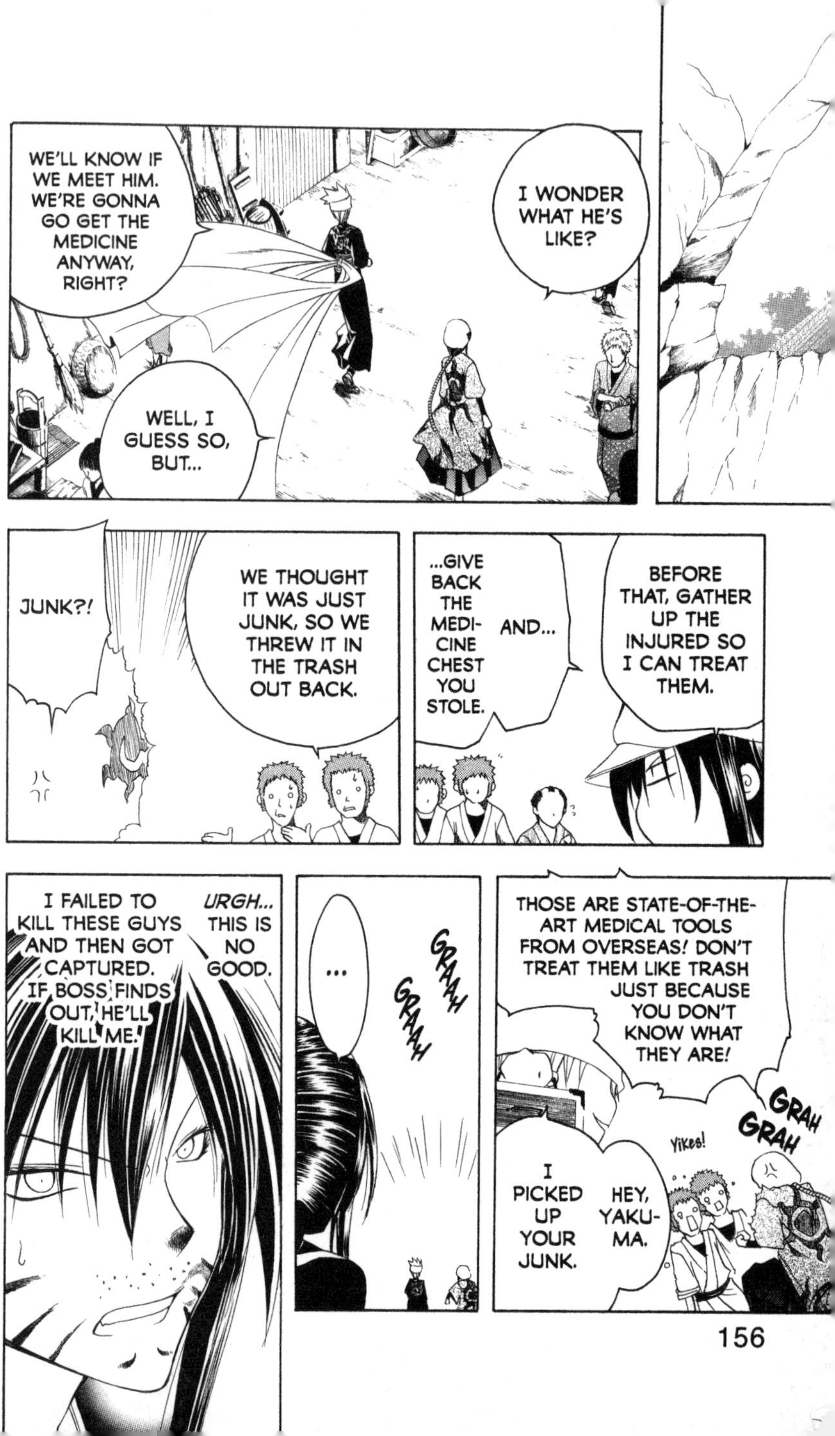
I WONDER WHAT HE'S LIKE?
WE'LL KNOW IF WE MEET HIM. WE'RE GONNA GO GET THE MEDICINE ANYWAY, RIGHT?
WELL, I GUESS SO, BUT...
BEFORE THAT, GATHER UP THE INJURED SO I CAN TREAT THEM.
AND...
...GIVE BACK THE MEDI-CINE CHEST YOU STOLE.
WE THOUGHT IT WAS JUST JUNK, SO WE THREW IT IN THE TRASH OUT BACK.
JUNK?!
THOSE ARE STATE-OF-THE-ART MEDICAL TOOLS FROM OVERSEAS! DON'T TREAT THEM LIKE TRASH JUST BECAUSE YOU DON'T KNOW WHAT THEY ARE!
GRAH GRAH
Yikes!
HEY, YAKU-MA.
I PICKED UP YOUR JUNK.
GRAAAH GRAAAH
...
URGH... THIS IS NO GOOD.
I FAILED TO KILL THESE GUYS AND THEN GOT CAPTURED. IF BOSS FINDS OUT, HE'LL KILL ME.

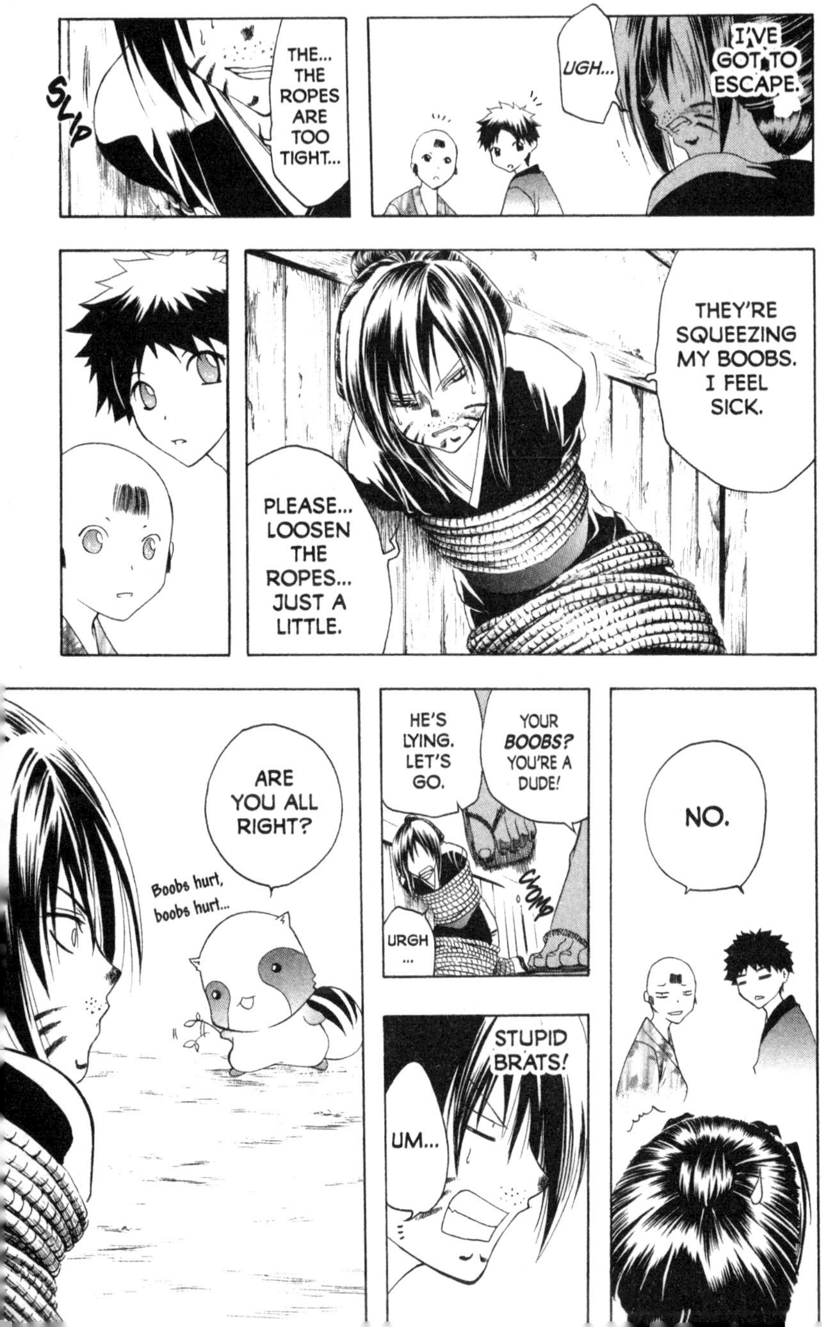
I'VE GOT TO ESCAPE.
UGH...
THE... THE ROPES ARE TOO TIGHT...
SLIP
THEY'RE SQUEEZING MY BOOBS. I FEEL SICK.
PLEASE... LOOSEN THE ROPES... JUST A LITTLE.
NO.
YOUR BOOBS? YOU'RE A DUDE!
HE'S LYING. LET'S GO.
CHOMP
URGH...
STUPID BRATS!
UM...
ARE YOU ALL RIGHT?
Boobs hurt, boobs hurt...

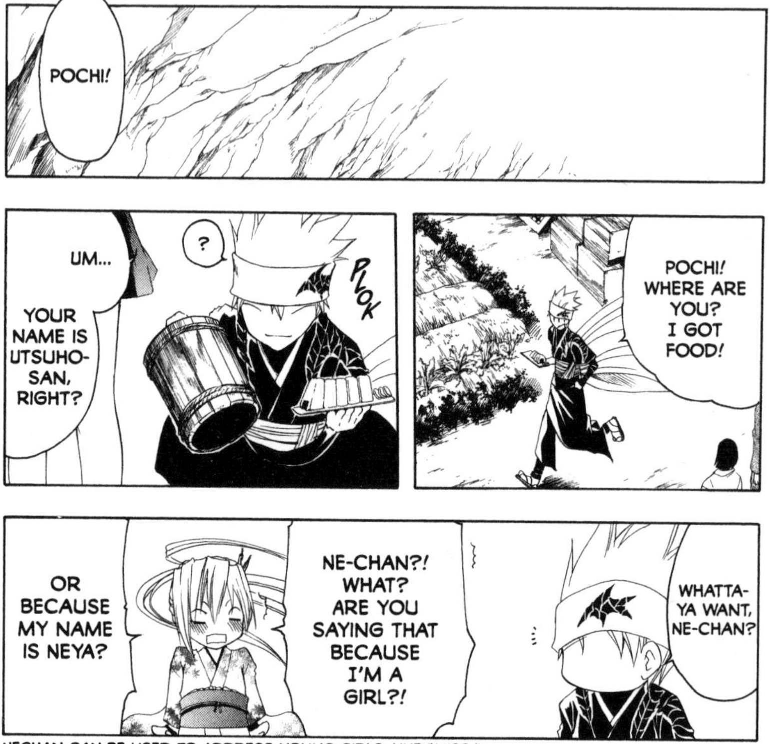
POCHI!
POCHI! WHERE ARE YOU? I GOT FOOD!
?
PLOK
UM...
YOUR NAME IS UTSUHO-SAN, RIGHT?
WHATTA-YA WANT, NE-CHAN?
...
NE-CHAN?! WHAT? ARE YOU SAYING THAT BECAUSE I'M A GIRL?!
OR BECAUSE MY NAME IS NEYA?

NECHAN CAN BE USED TO ADDRESS YOUNG GIRLS, LIKE "MISS."

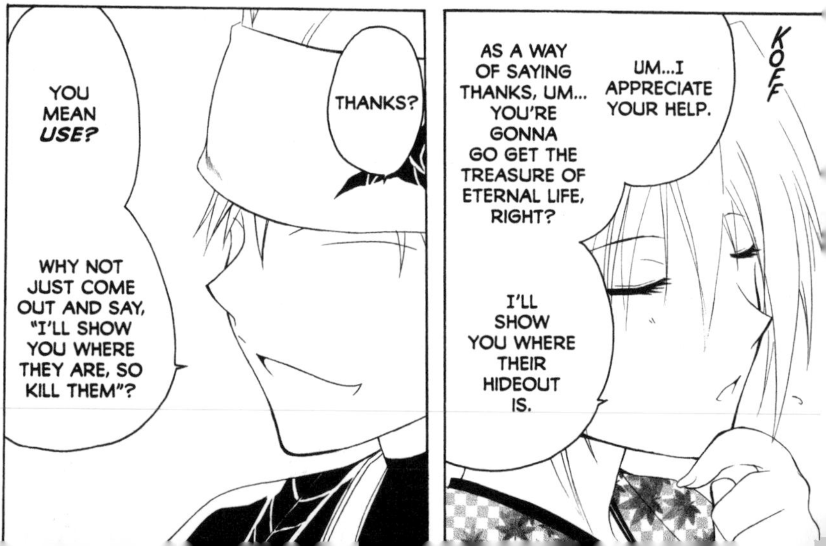
KOFF
UM...I APPRECIATE YOUR HELP.
AS A WAY OF SAYING THANKS, UM... YOU'RE GONNA GO GET THE TREASURE OF ETERNAL LIFE, RIGHT?
I'LL SHOW YOU WHERE THEIR HIDEOUT IS.
THANKS?
YOU MEAN *USE?*
WHY NOT JUST COME OUT AND SAY, "I'LL SHOW YOU WHERE THEY ARE, SO KILL THEM"?

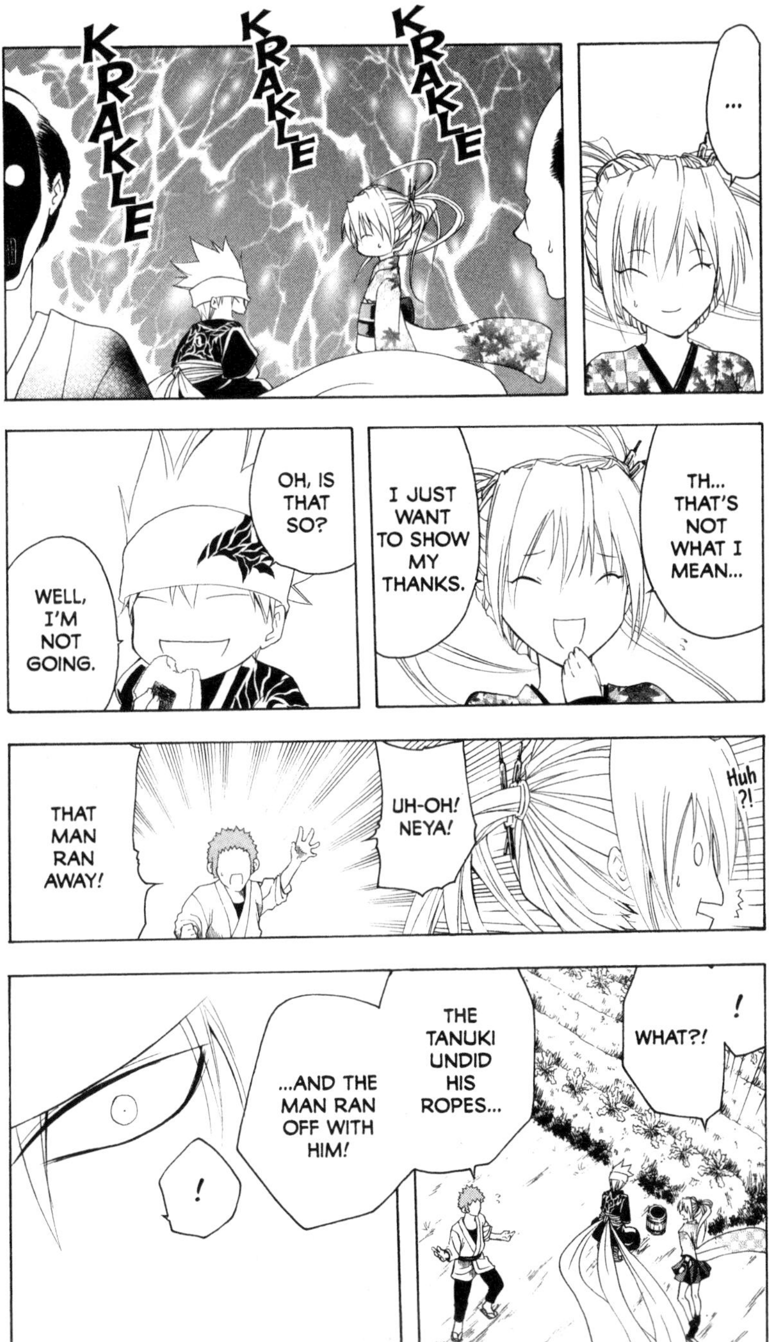
...
KRAKLE
KRAKLE
KRAKLE
TH... THAT'S NOT WHAT I MEAN...
I JUST WANT TO SHOW MY THANKS.
OH, IS THAT SO?
WELL, I'M NOT GOING.
Huh?!
UH-OH! NEYA!
THAT MAN RAN AWAY!
!
WHAT?!
THE TANUKI UNDID HIS ROPES...
...AND THE MAN RAN OFF WITH HIM!
!

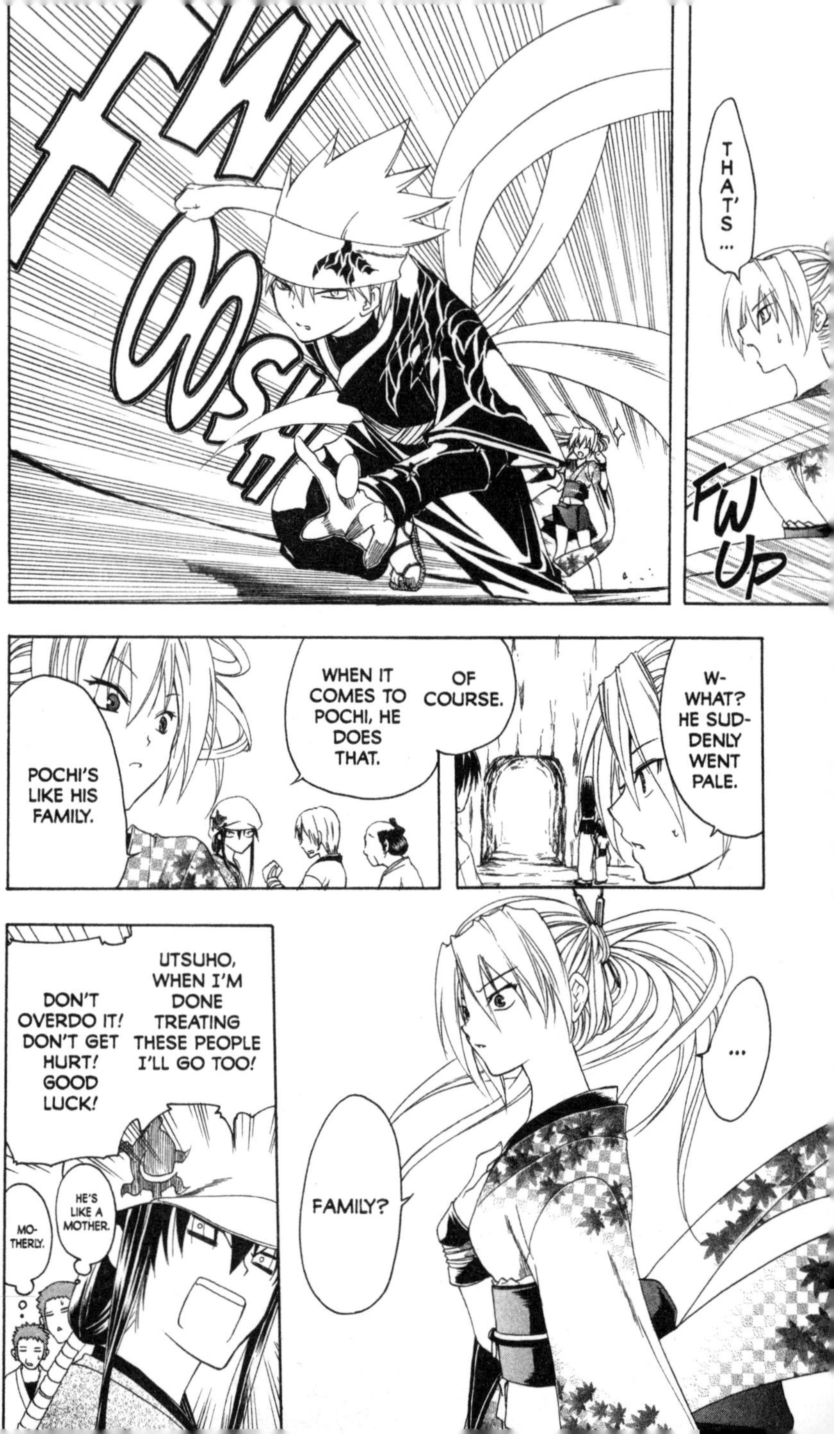
THAT'S...
FWUP
FWOOSH
W-WHAT? HE SUDDENLY WENT PALE.
OF COURSE.
WHEN IT COMES TO POCHI, HE DOES THAT.
POCHI'S LIKE HIS FAMILY.
...
FAMILY?
UTSUHO, WHEN I'M DONE TREATING THESE PEOPLE I'LL GO TOO!
DON'T OVERDO IT! DON'T GET HURT! GOOD LUCK!
HE'S LIKE A MOTHER.
MOTHERLY.

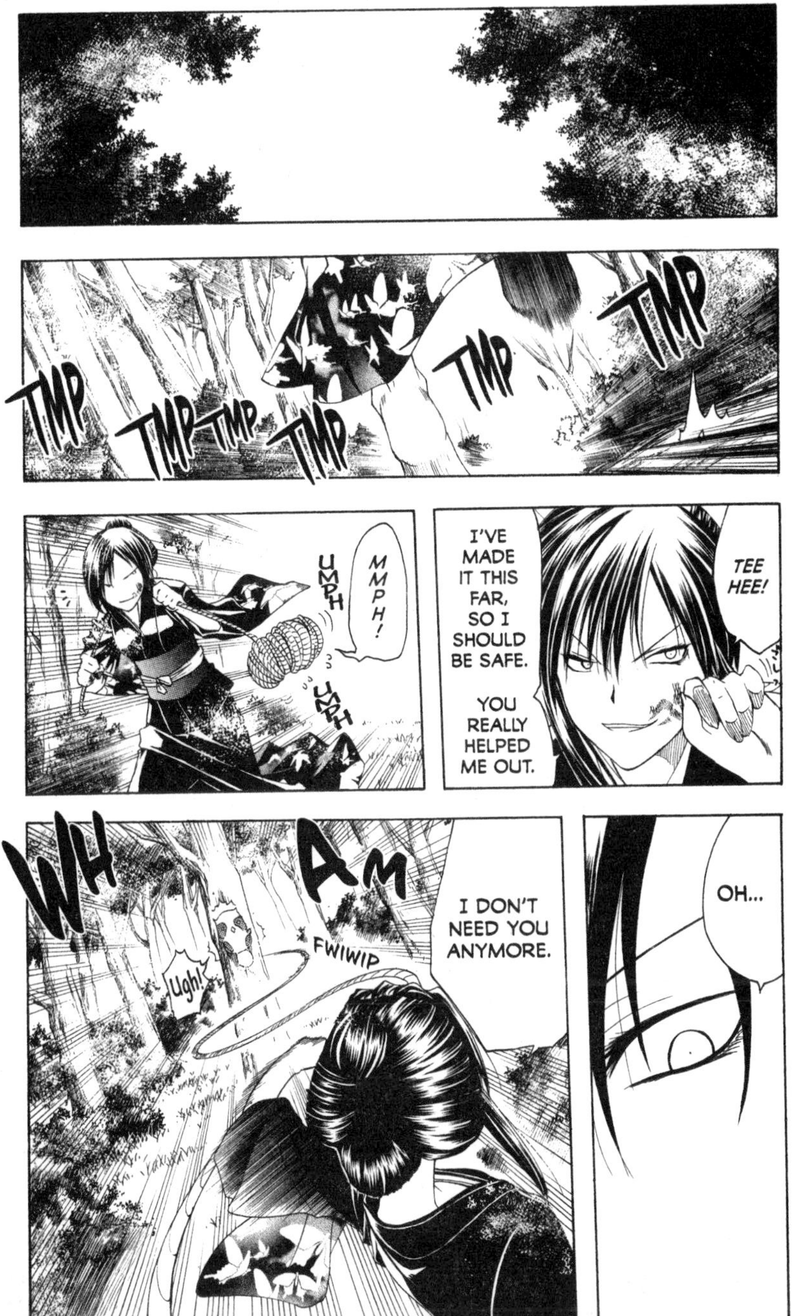
TMP
TMP
TMP
TMP TMP
TMP
TEE HEE!
I'VE MADE IT THIS FAR, SO I SHOULD BE SAFE.
YOU REALLY HELPED ME OUT.
MMPH!
UMPH
UMPH
OH...
I DON'T NEED YOU ANYMORE.
WHAM
FWIWIP
Ugh!

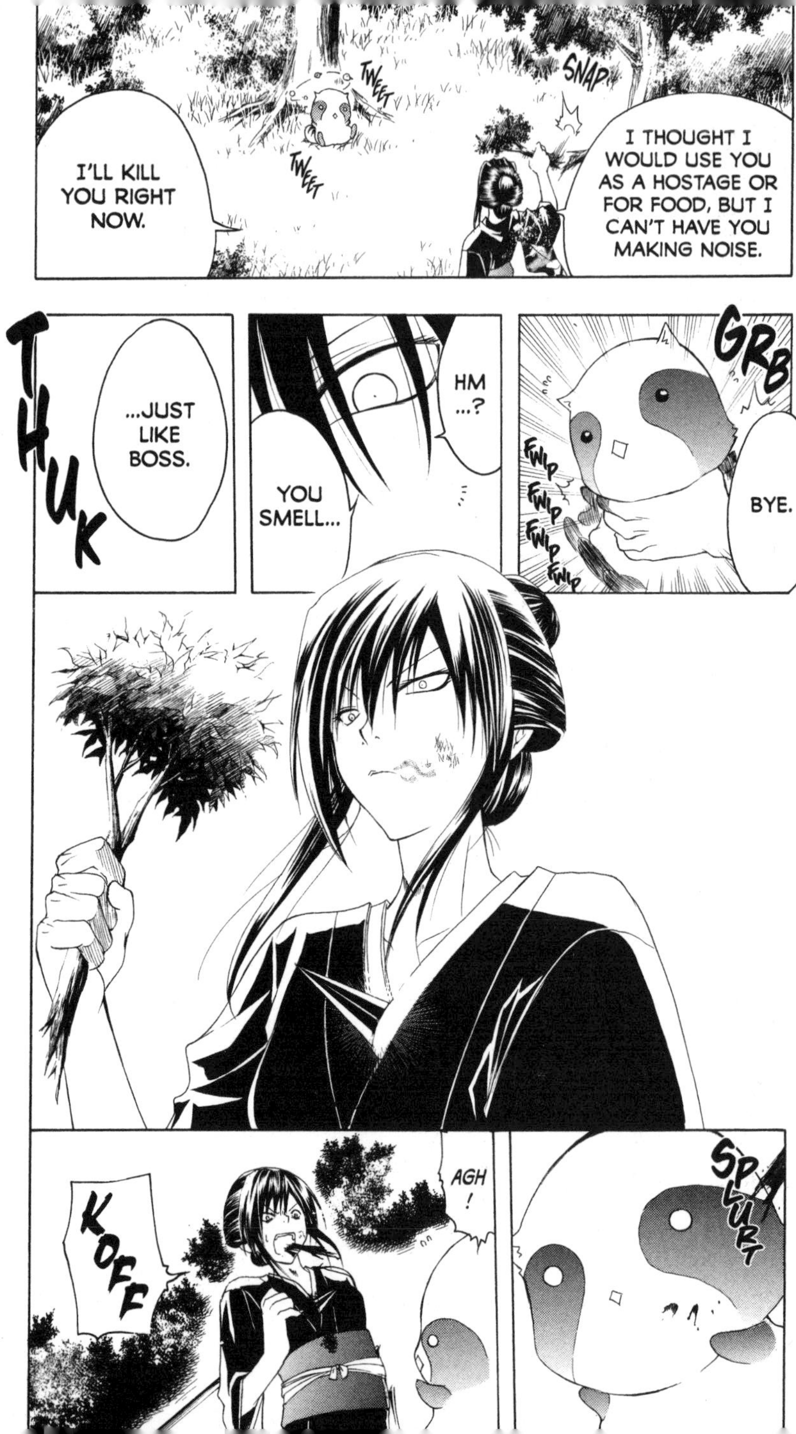
SNAP
TWEET
I THOUGHT I WOULD USE YOU AS A HOSTAGE OR FOR FOOD, BUT I CAN'T HAVE YOU MAKING NOISE.
TWEET
I'LL KILL YOU RIGHT NOW.
GRB
BYE.
FWIP FWIP FWIP FWIP FWIP
HM ...?
YOU SMELL...
...JUST LIKE BOSS.
THUK
SPLURT
AGH!
KOFF

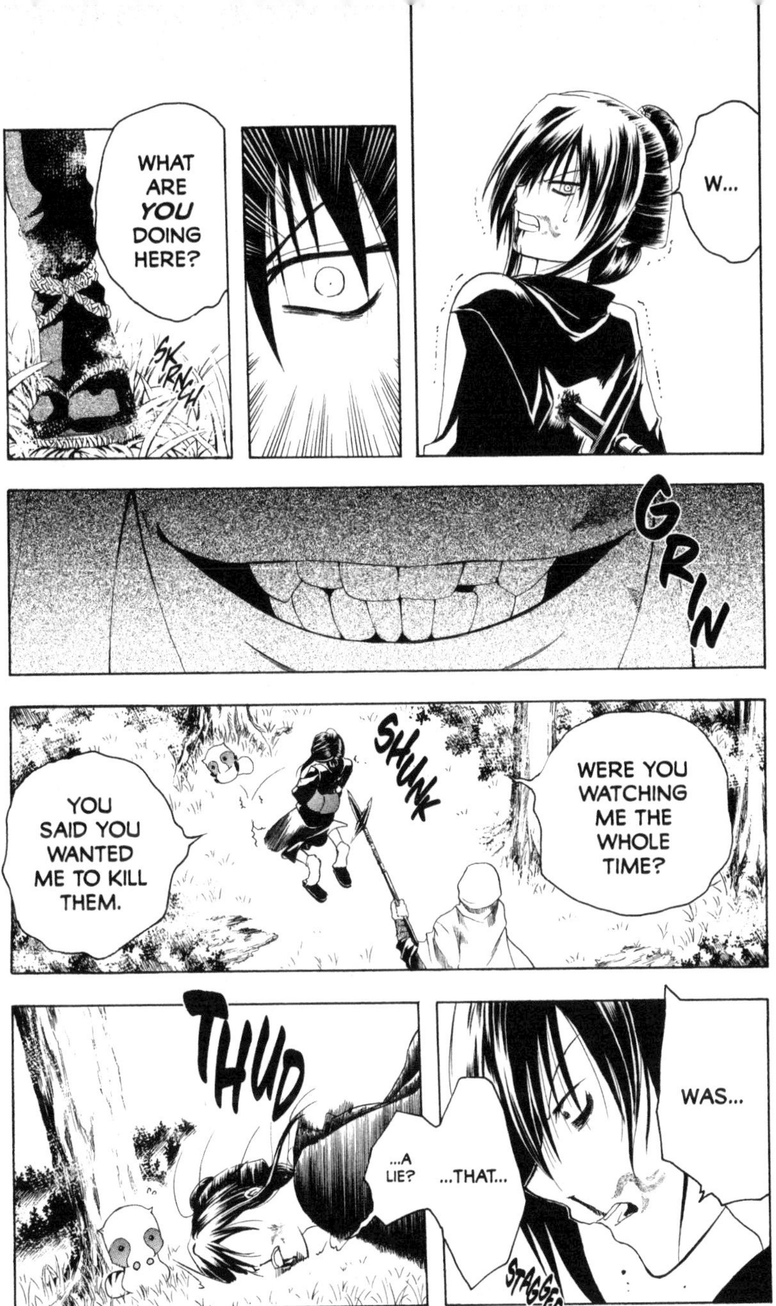
W...
WHAT ARE *YOU* DOING HERE?
SKRNCH
GRIN
WERE YOU WATCHING ME THE WHOLE TIME?
SHUNK
YOU SAID YOU WANTED ME TO KILL THEM.
WAS...
...THAT...
...A LIE?
STAGGER
THUD

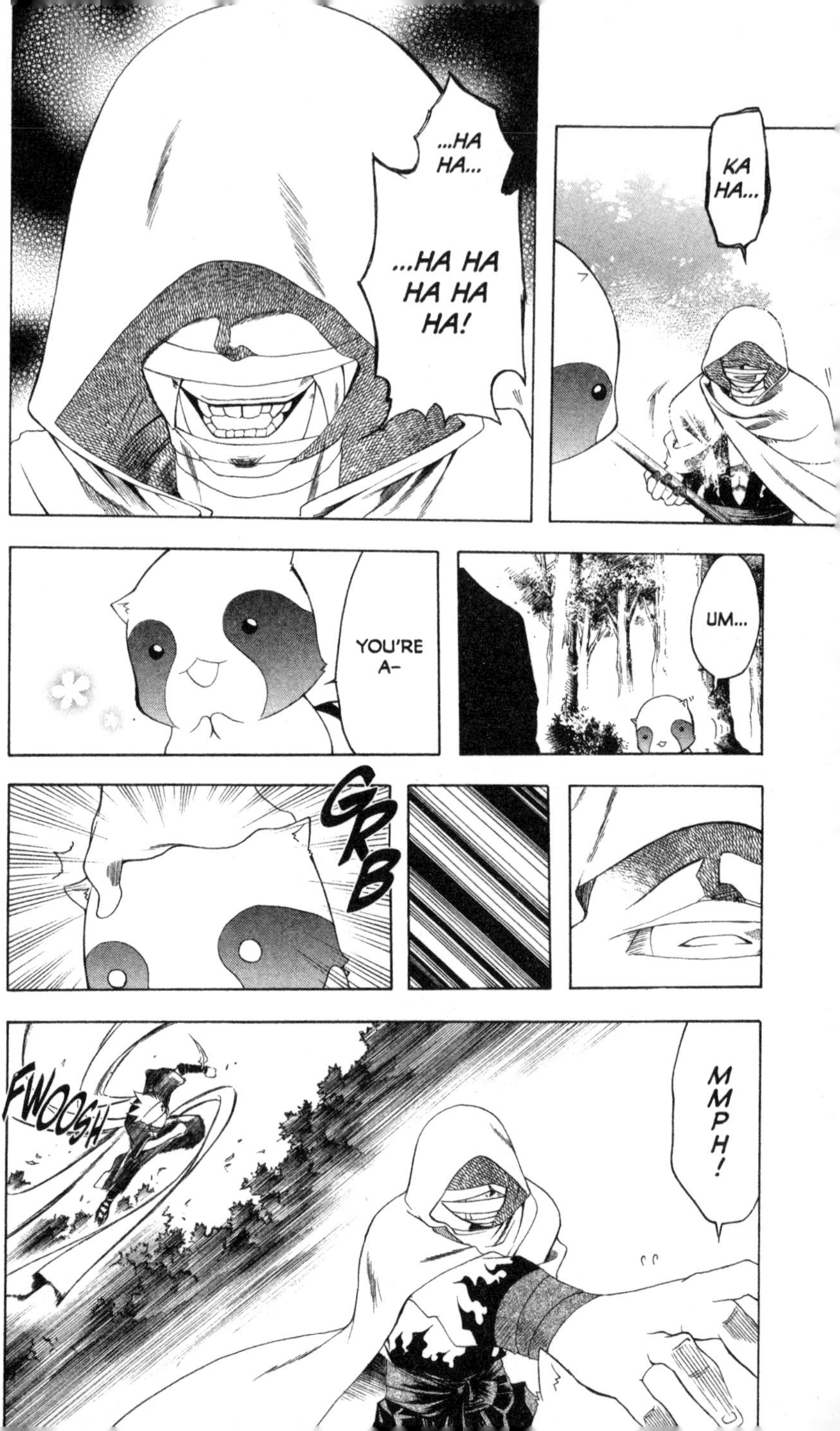
KA HA...
...HA HA...
...HA HA HA HA HA!
UM...
YOU'RE A-
GRB
MMPH!
FWOOSH

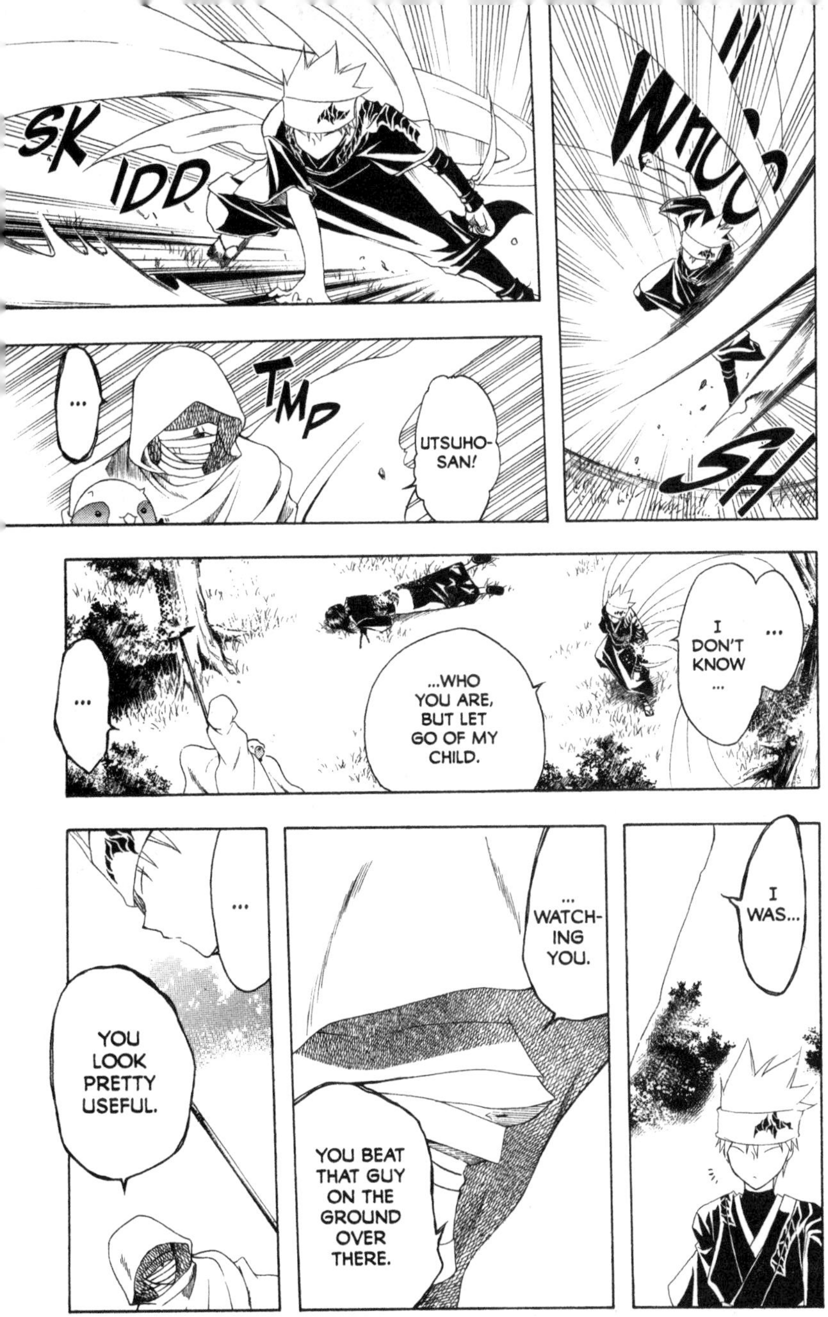
SH
SKIDD
UTSUHO-SAN!
TMP
...
... I DON'T KNOW ...
...WHO YOU ARE, BUT LET GO OF MY CHILD.
...
I WAS...
...WATCHING YOU.
YOU BEAT THAT GUY ON THE GROUND OVER THERE.
...
YOU LOOK PRETTY USEFUL.

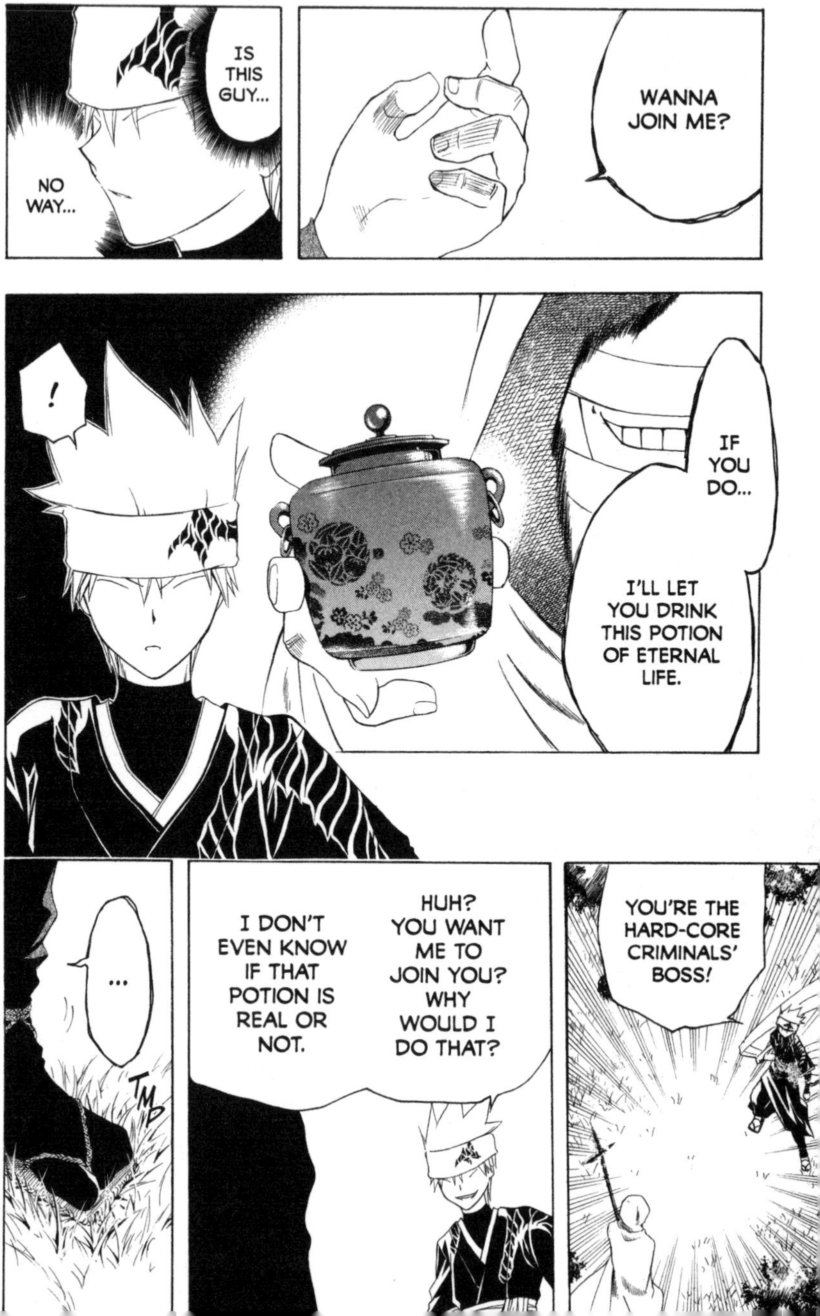
WANNA JOIN ME?
IS THIS GUY...
NO WAY...
IF YOU DO...
I'LL LET YOU DRINK THIS POTION OF ETERNAL LIFE.
!
YOU'RE THE HARD-CORE CRIMINALS' BOSS!
HUH? YOU WANT ME TO JOIN YOU? WHY WOULD I DO THAT?
I DON'T EVEN KNOW IF THAT POTION IS REAL OR NOT.
...
TMP

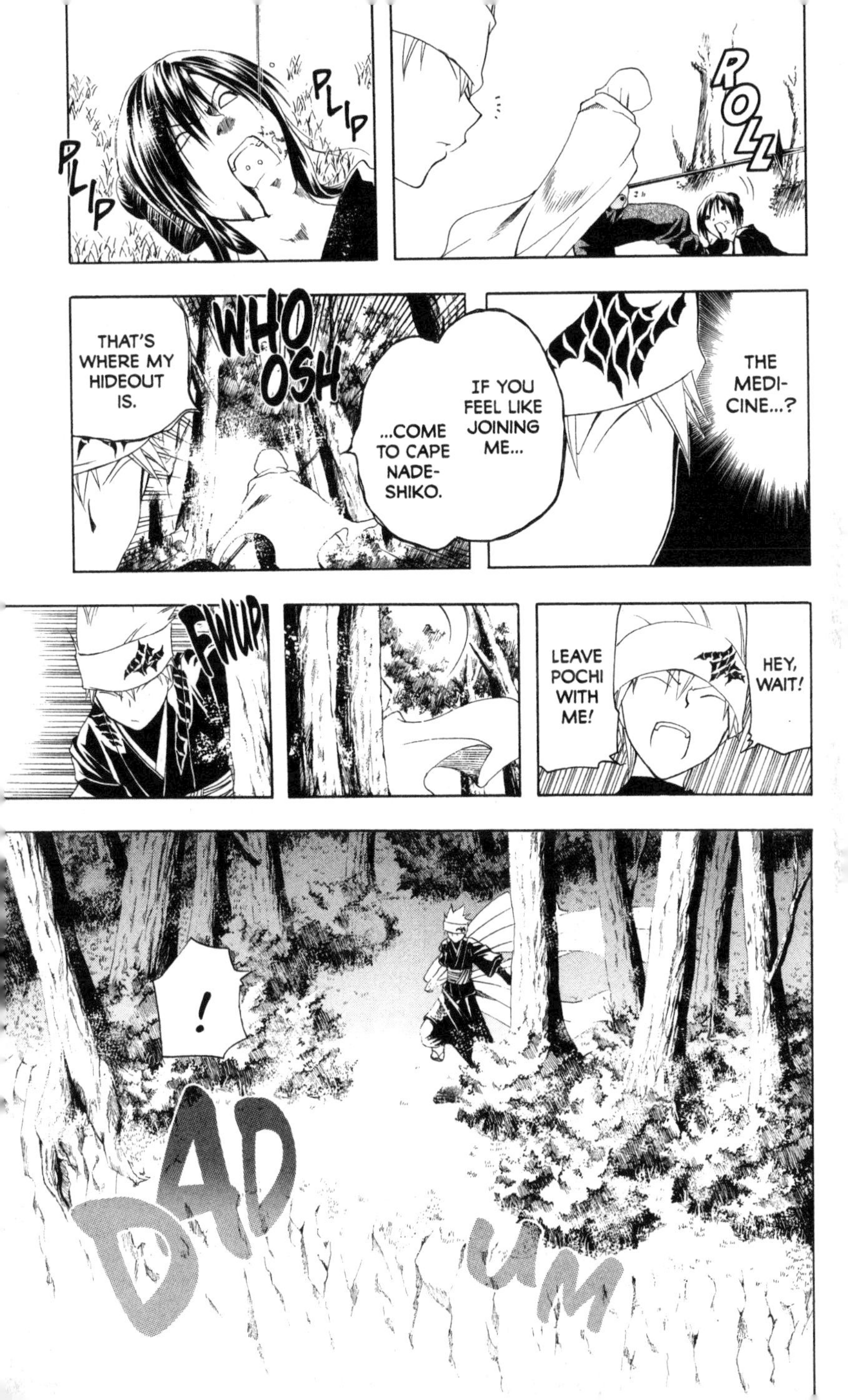
ROLL
PLIP
PLIP
THE MEDI-CINE...?
IF YOU FEEL LIKE JOINING ME...
...COME TO CAPE NADE-SHIKO.
WHOOSH
THAT'S WHERE MY HIDEOUT IS.
HEY, WAIT!
LEAVE POCHI WITH ME!
FWUP
!
DADUM

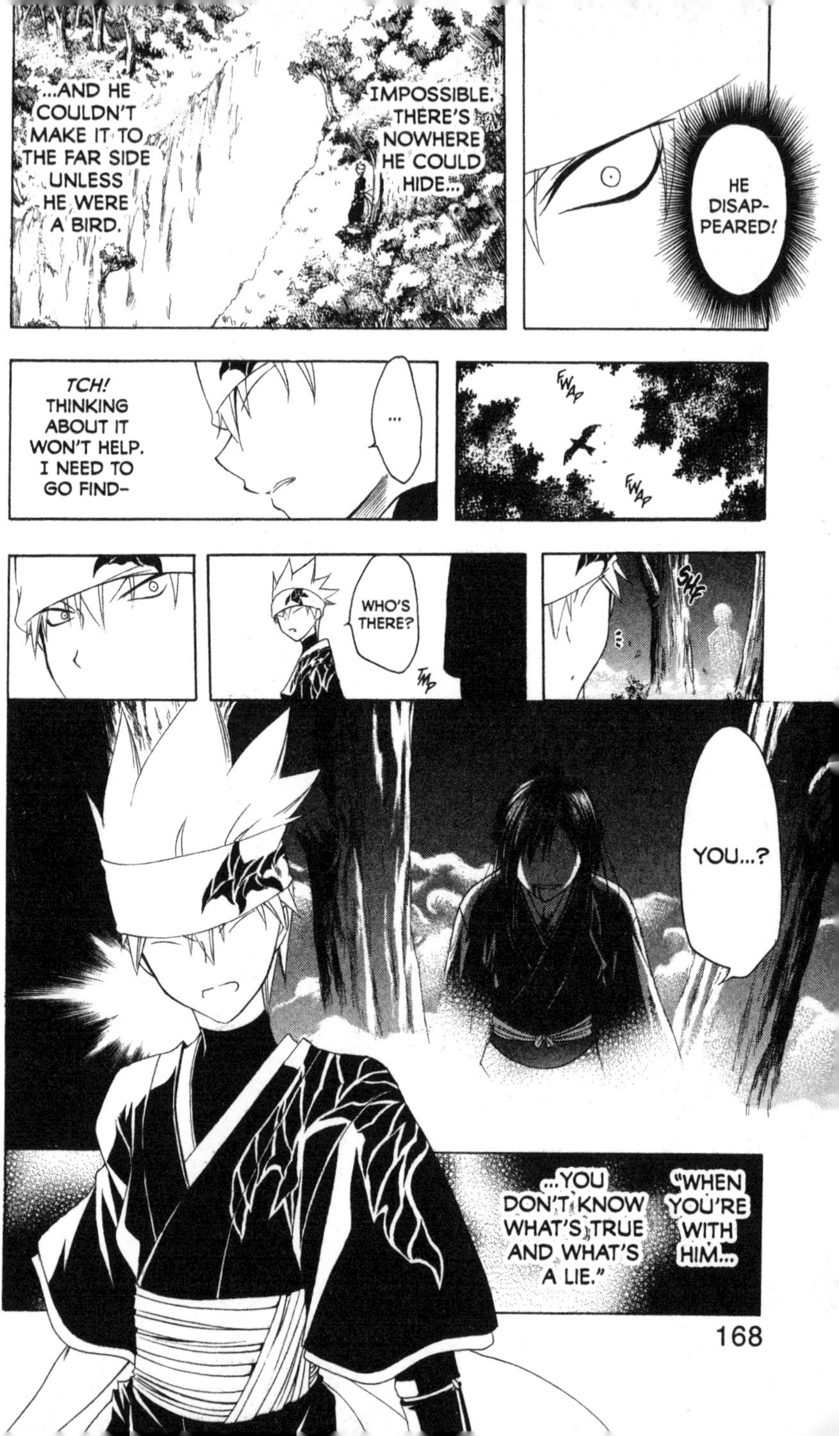
HE DISAPPEARED!
IMPOSSIBLE. THERE'S NOWHERE HE COULD HIDE...
...AND HE COULDN'T MAKE IT TO THE FAR SIDE UNLESS HE WERE A BIRD.
FWAP
FWAP
...
TCH! THINKING ABOUT IT WON'T HELP. I NEED TO GO FIND-
SHF
...
WHO'S THERE?
TMP
YOU...?
"WHEN YOU'RE WITH HIM...
...YOU DON'T KNOW WHAT'S TRUE AND WHAT'S A LIE."

Chapter 17
For My Family

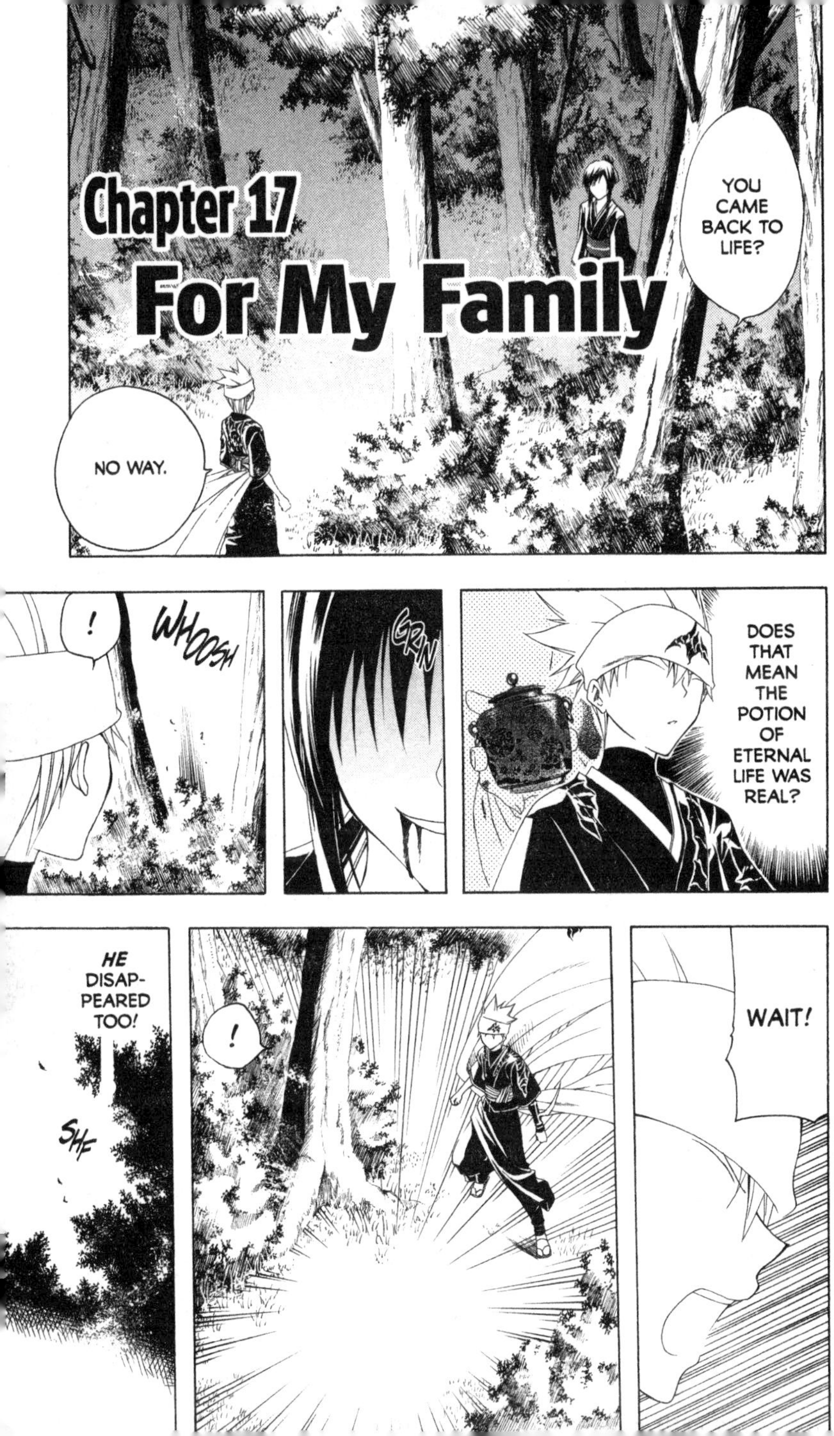
Chapter 17
For My Family
YOU CAME BACK TO LIFE?
NO WAY.
DOES THAT MEAN THE POTION OF ETERNAL LIFE WAS REAL?
GRIN
!
WHOOSH
WAIT!
!
HE DISAP-PEARED TOO!
SHF

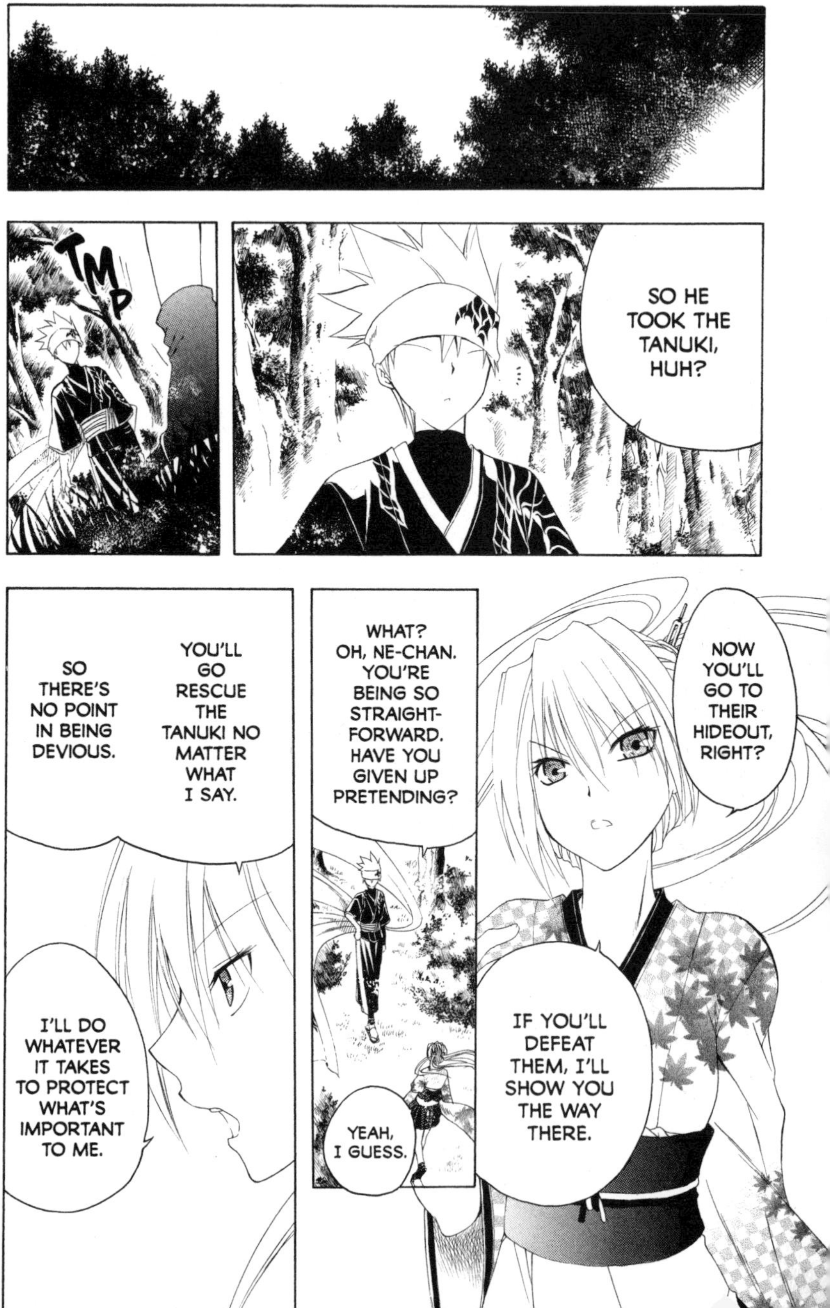
SO HE TOOK THE TANUKI, HUH?
TMP
NOW YOU'LL GO TO THEIR HIDEOUT, RIGHT?
IF YOU'LL DEFEAT THEM, I'LL SHOW YOU THE WAY THERE.
WHAT? OH, NE-CHAN. YOU'RE BEING SO STRAIGHT-FORWARD. HAVE YOU GIVEN UP PRETENDING?
YEAH, I GUESS.
YOU'LL GO RESCUE THE TANUKI NO MATTER WHAT I SAY.
SO THERE'S NO POINT IN BEING DEVIOUS.
I'LL DO WHATEVER IT TAKES TO PROTECT WHAT'S IMPORTANT TO ME.

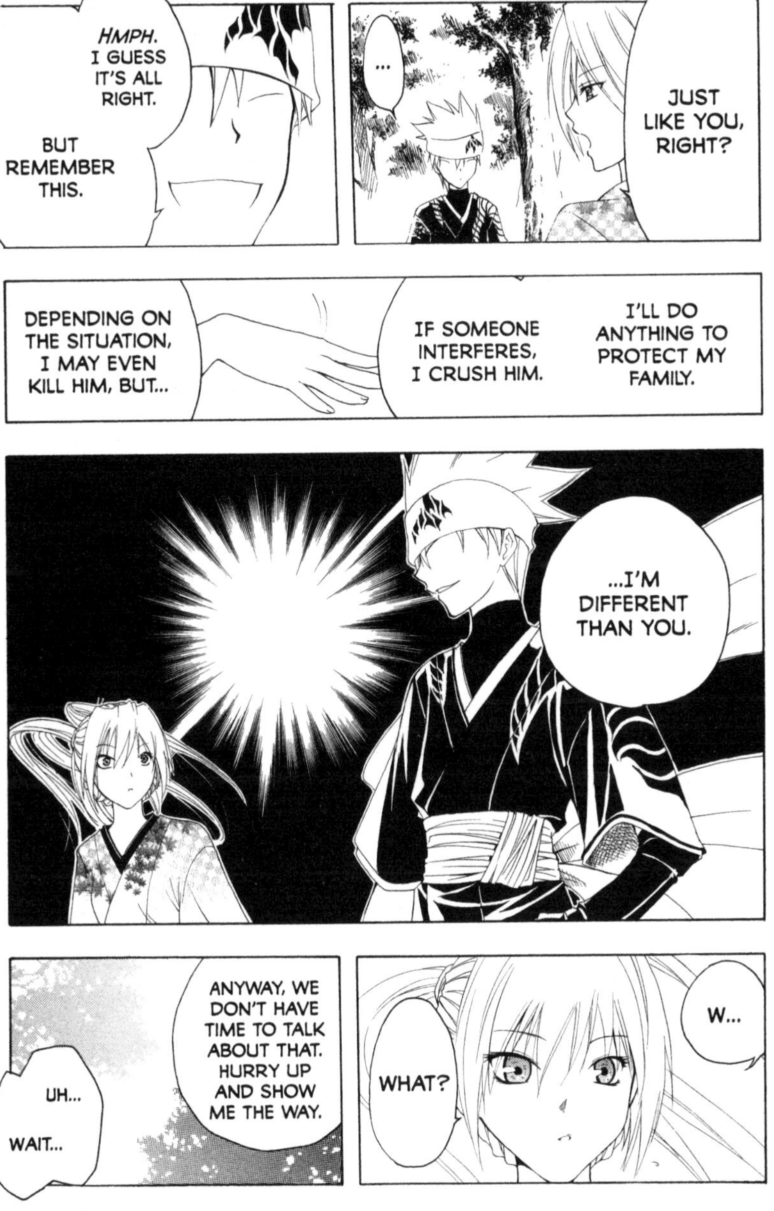
JUST LIKE YOU, RIGHT?
...
HMPH. I GUESS IT'S ALL RIGHT.
BUT REMEMBER THIS.
I'LL DO ANYTHING TO PROTECT MY FAMILY.
IF SOMEONE INTERFERES, I CRUSH HIM.
DEPENDING ON THE SITUATION, I MAY EVEN KILL HIM, BUT...
...I'M DIFFERENT THAN YOU.
W...
WHAT?
ANYWAY, WE DON'T HAVE TIME TO TALK ABOUT THAT. HURRY UP AND SHOW ME THE WAY.
UH...
WAIT...

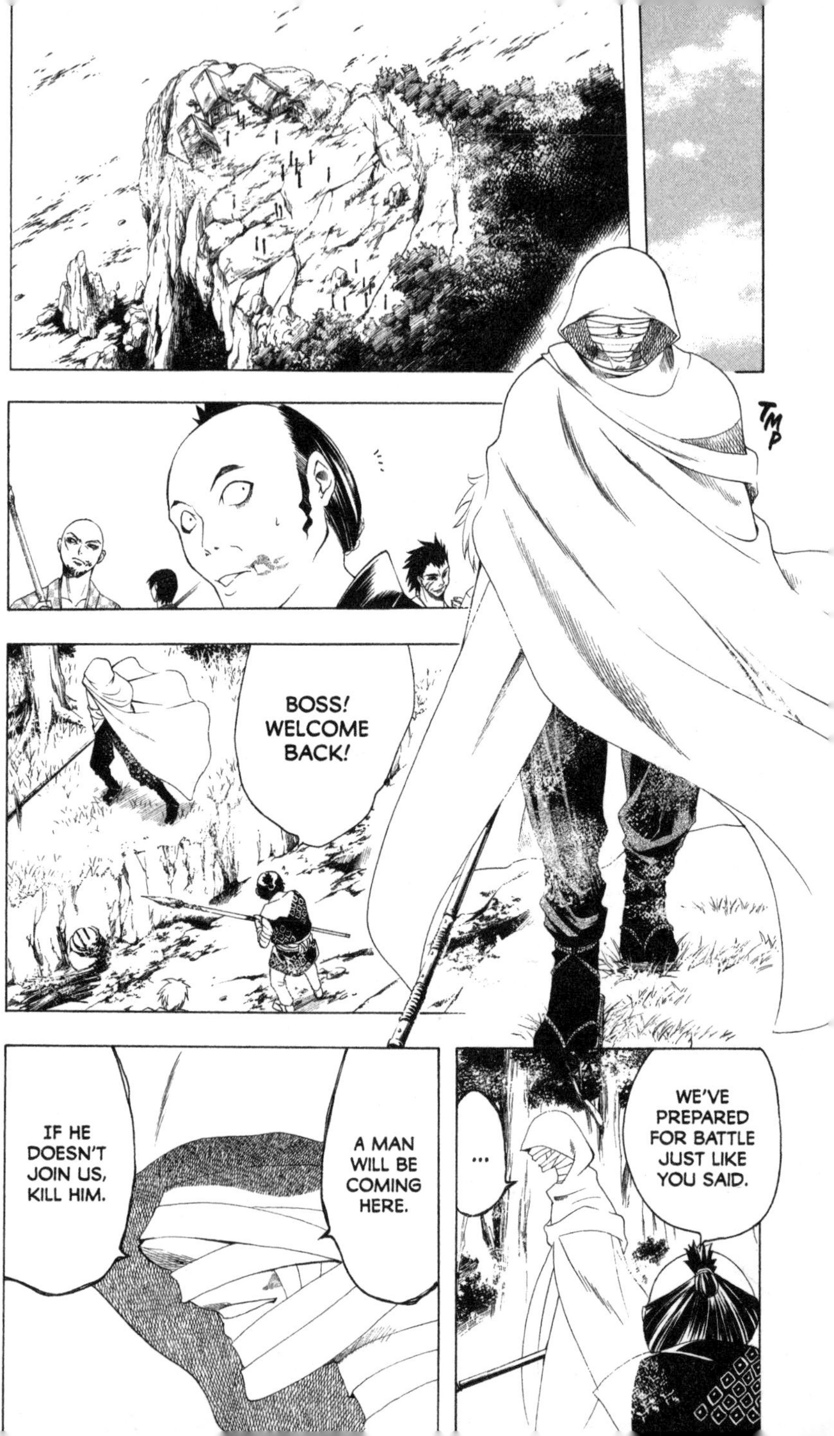
TMP
BOSS! WELCOME BACK!
WE'VE PREPARED FOR BATTLE JUST LIKE YOU SAID.
...
A MAN WILL BE COMING HERE.
IF HE DOESN'T JOIN US, KILL HIM.

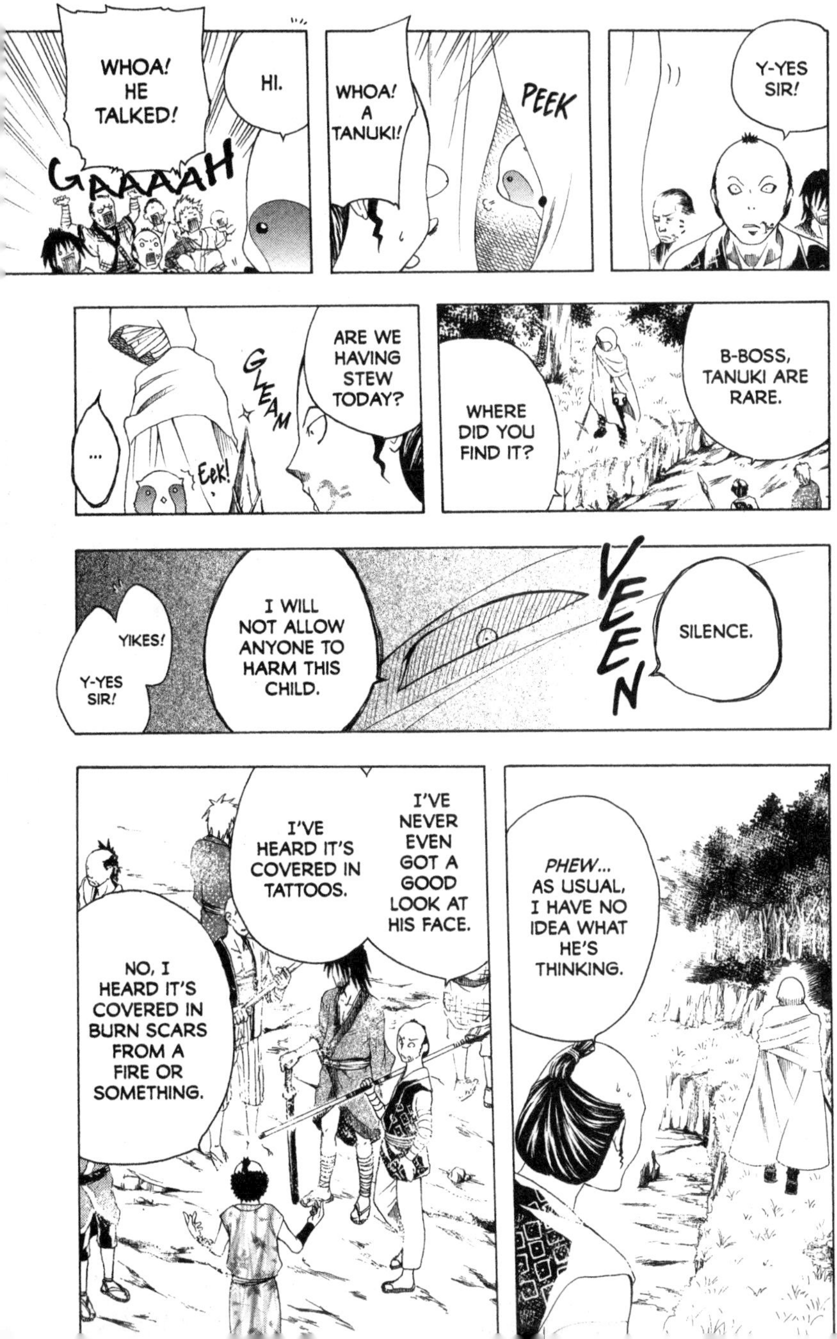
Y-YES SIR!
PEEK
WHOA! A TANUKI!
HI.
WHOA! HE TALKED!
GAAAAH
B-BOSS, TANUKI ARE RARE.
WHERE DID YOU FIND IT?
ARE WE HAVING STEW TODAY?
GLEAM
Eek!
...
SILENCE.
VEEN
I WILL NOT ALLOW ANYONE TO HARM THIS CHILD.
YIKES!
Y-YES SIR!
PHEW... AS USUAL, I HAVE NO IDEA WHAT HE'S THINKING.
I'VE NEVER EVEN GOT A GOOD LOOK AT HIS FACE.
I'VE HEARD IT'S COVERED IN TATTOOS.
NO, I HEARD IT'S COVERED IN BURN SCARS FROM A FIRE OR SOMETHING.

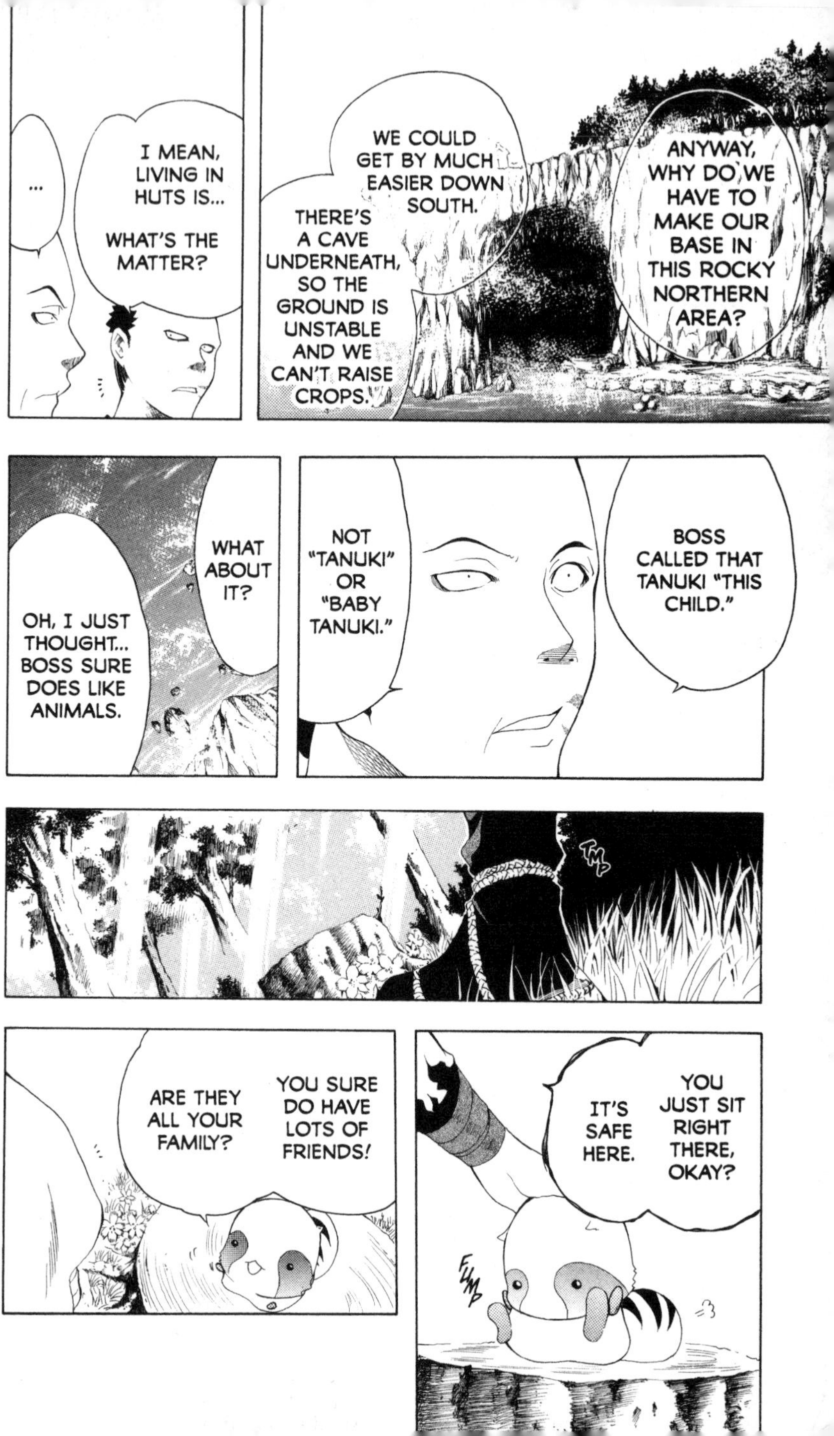
ANYWAY, WHY DO WE HAVE TO MAKE OUR BASE IN THIS ROCKY NORTHERN AREA?
WE COULD GET BY MUCH EASIER DOWN SOUTH.
THERE'S A CAVE UNDERNEATH, SO THE GROUND IS UNSTABLE AND WE CAN'T RAISE CROPS.
I MEAN, LIVING IN HUTS IS...
WHAT'S THE MATTER?
...
BOSS CALLED THAT TANUKI "THIS CHILD."
NOT "TANUKI" OR "BABY TANUKI."
WHAT ABOUT IT?
OH, I JUST THOUGHT... BOSS SURE DOES LIKE ANIMALS.
TMP
YOU JUST SIT RIGHT THERE, OKAY?
IT'S SAFE HERE.
FLUMP
YOU SURE DO HAVE LOTS OF FRIENDS!
ARE THEY ALL YOUR FAMILY?

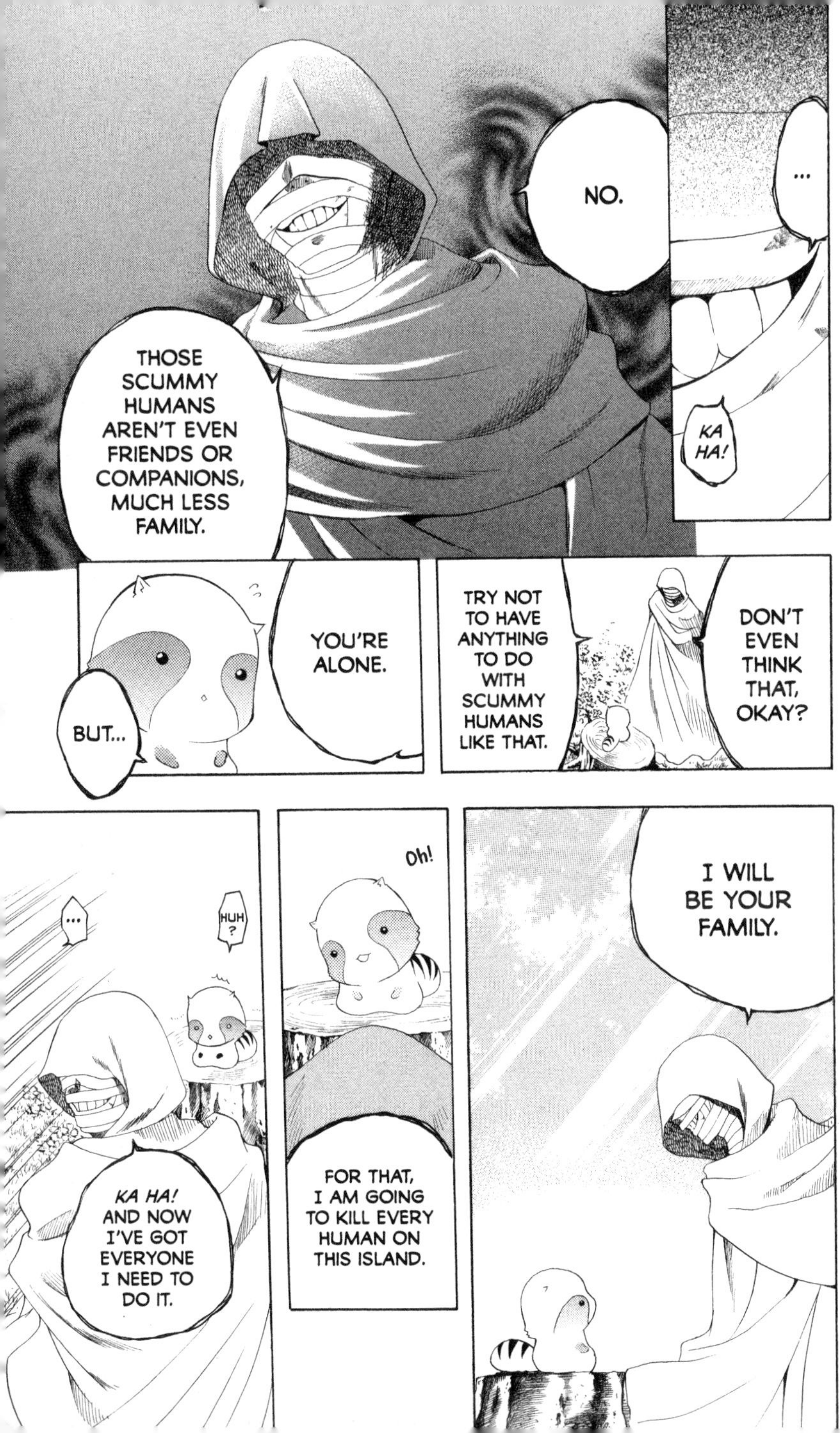

...
KA HA!
NO.
THOSE SCUMMY HUMANS AREN'T EVEN FRIENDS OR COMPANIONS, MUCH LESS FAMILY.
DON'T EVEN THINK THAT, OKAY?
TRY NOT TO HAVE ANYTHING TO DO WITH SCUMMY HUMANS LIKE THAT.
YOU'RE ALONE.
BUT...
I WILL BE YOUR FAMILY.
Oh!
FOR THAT, I AM GOING TO KILL EVERY HUMAN ON THIS ISLAND.
HUH?
...
KA HA! AND NOW I'VE GOT EVERYONE I NEED TO DO IT.

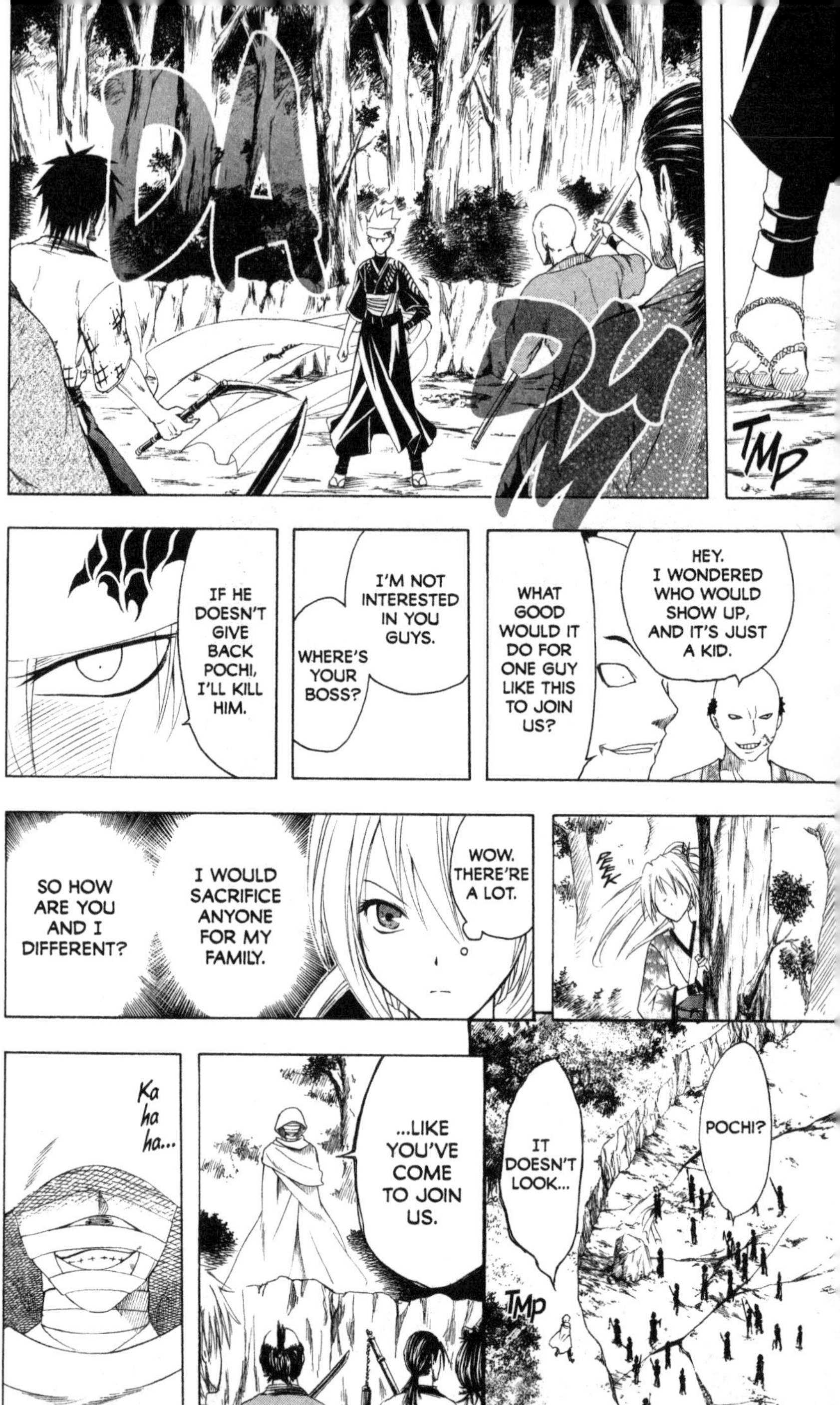
TMP
DA
HEY. I WONDERED WHO WOULD SHOW UP, AND IT'S JUST A KID.
WHAT GOOD WOULD IT DO FOR ONE GUY LIKE THIS TO JOIN US?
I'M NOT INTERESTED IN YOU GUYS.
WHERE'S YOUR BOSS?
IF HE DOESN'T GIVE BACK POCHI, I'LL KILL HIM.
PEEK
WOW. THERE'RE A LOT.
I WOULD SACRIFICE ANYONE FOR MY FAMILY.
SO HOW ARE YOU AND I DIFFERENT?
POCHI?
IT DOESN'T LOOK...
TMP
...LIKE YOU'VE COME TO JOIN US.
Ka ha ha...

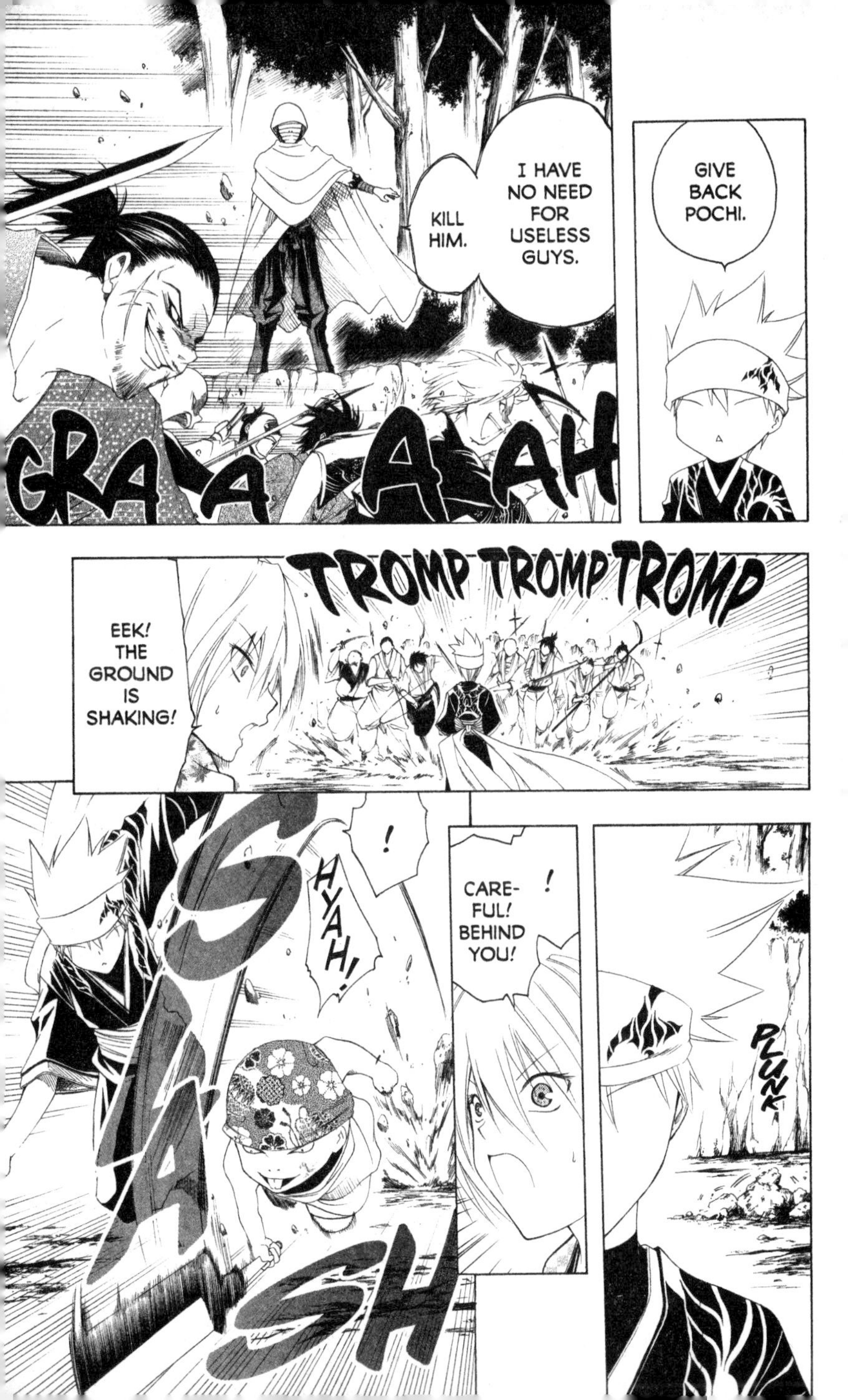
GIVE BACK POCHI.
I HAVE NO NEED FOR USELESS GUYS.
KILL HIM.
GRAAAAH
TROMP TROMP TROMP
EEK! THE GROUND IS SHAKING!
PLUNK
!
CARE-FUL! BEHIND YOU!
!
HYAH!

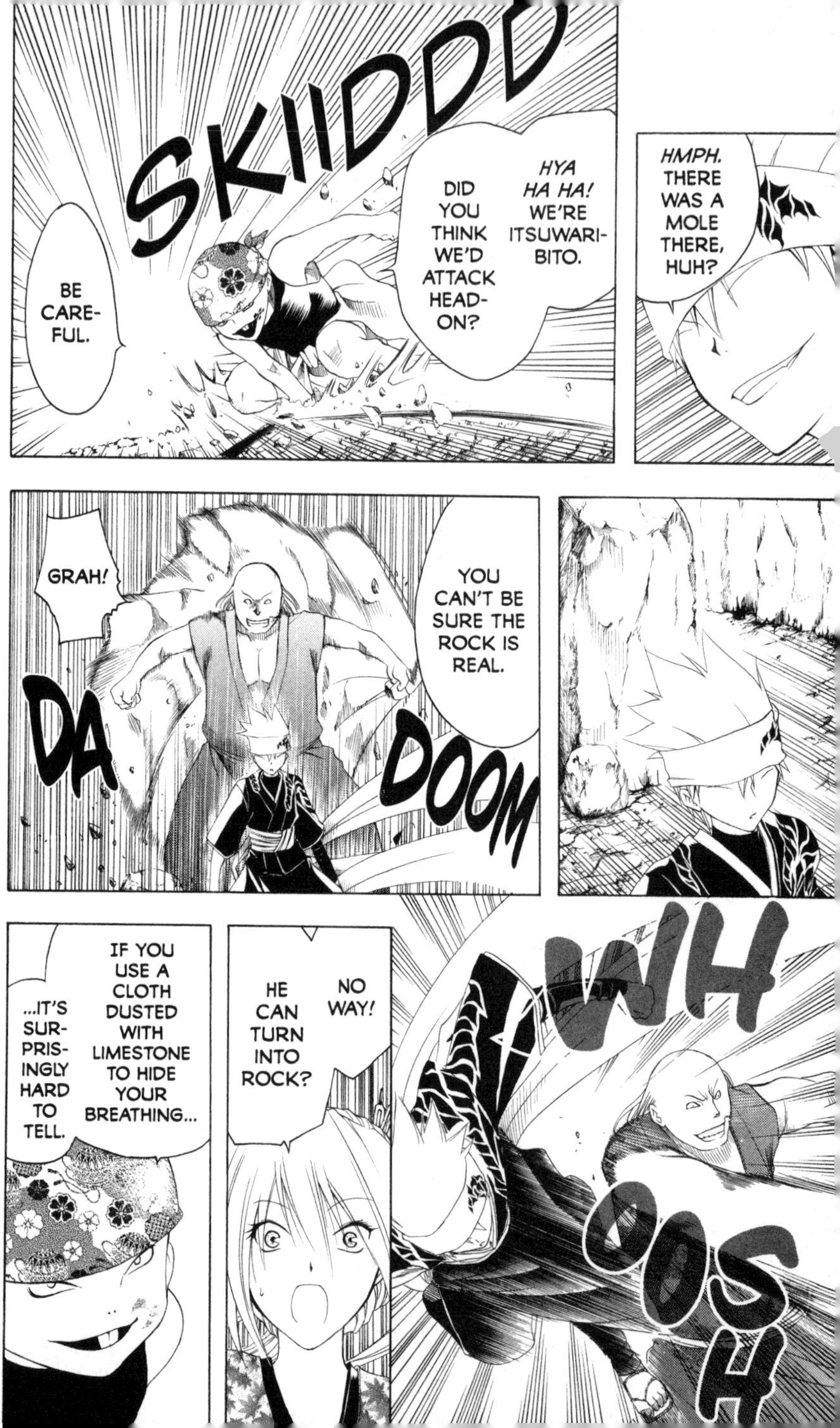
HMPH. THERE WAS A MOLE THERE, HUH?
HYA HA HA! WE'RE ITSUWARI-BITO.
DID YOU THINK WE'D ATTACK HEAD-ON?
SKIIDDD
BE CAREFUL.
YOU CAN'T BE SURE THE ROCK IS REAL.
GRAH!
DA DOOM
WHOOSH
NO WAY!
HE CAN TURN INTO ROCK?
IF YOU USE A CLOTH DUSTED WITH LIMESTONE TO HIDE YOUR BREATHING...
...IT'S SURPRISINGLY HARD TO TELL.

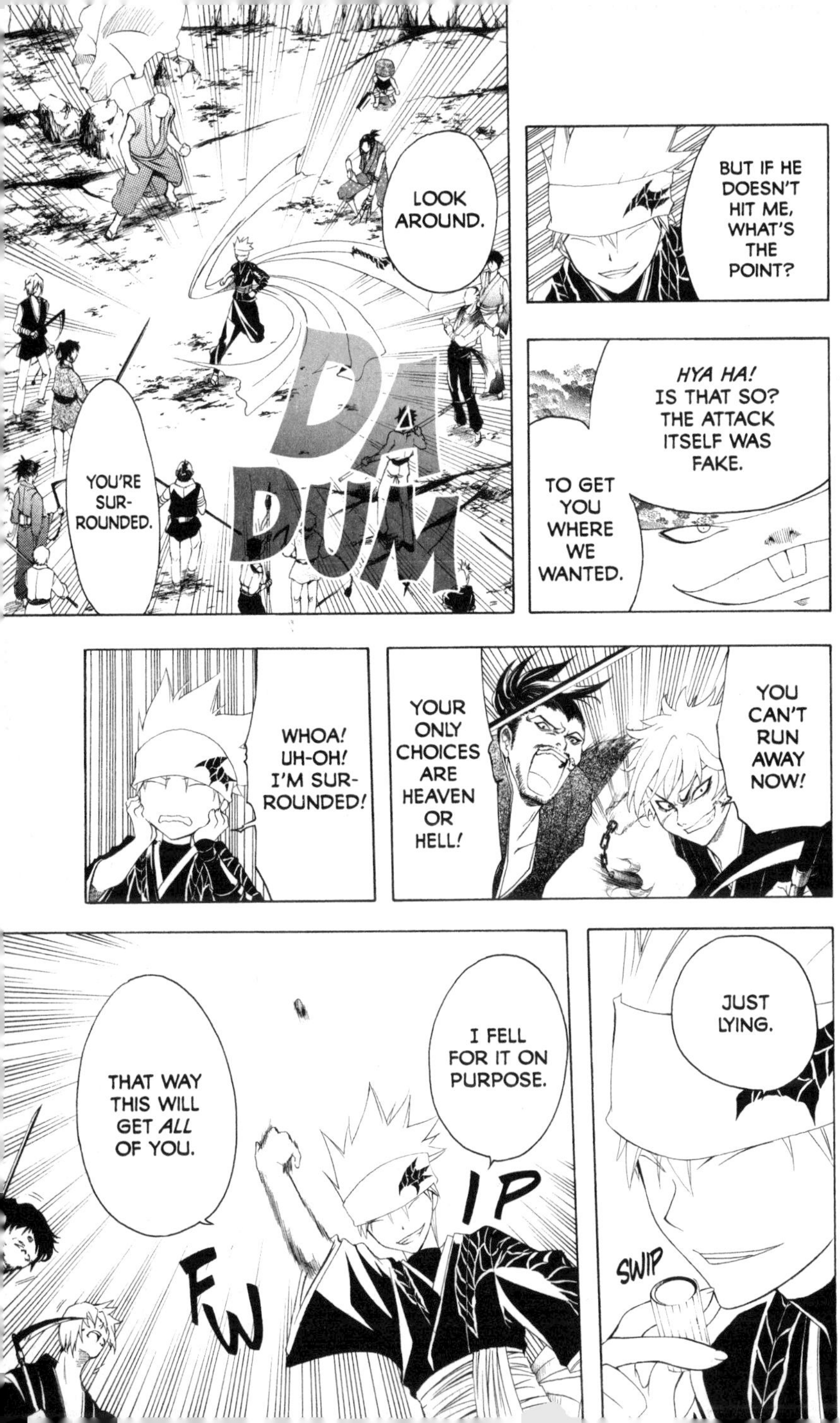
BUT IF HE DOESN'T HIT ME, WHAT'S THE POINT?
HYA HA! IS THAT SO? THE ATTACK ITSELF WAS FAKE.
TO GET YOU WHERE WE WANTED.
LOOK AROUND.
DA DUM
YOU'RE SUR-ROUNDED.
YOU CAN'T RUN AWAY NOW!
YOUR ONLY CHOICES ARE HEAVEN OR HELL!
WHOA! UH-OH! I'M SUR-ROUNDED!
SWIP
JUST LYING.
I FELL FOR IT ON PURPOSE.
FWIP
THAT WAY THIS WILL GET *ALL* OF YOU.

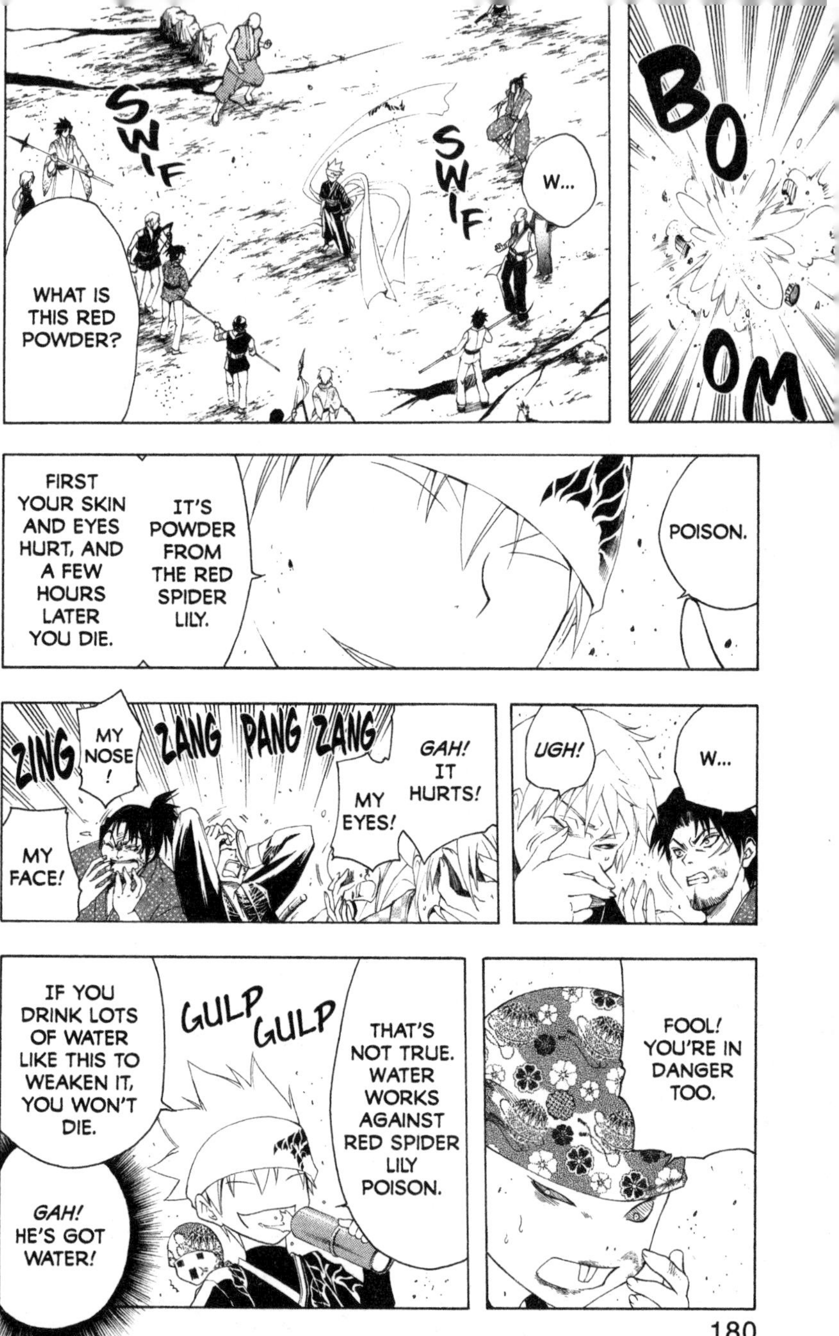
BOOM
W...
SWIF
SWIF
WHAT IS THIS RED POWDER?
POISON.
IT'S POWDER FROM THE RED SPIDER LILY.
FIRST YOUR SKIN AND EYES HURT, AND A FEW HOURS LATER YOU DIE.
W...
UGH!
GAH! IT HURTS!
ZANG PANG ZANG
MY EYES!
MY NOSE!
ZING
MY FACE!
FOOL! YOU'RE IN DANGER TOO.
THAT'S NOT TRUE. WATER WORKS AGAINST RED SPIDER LILY POISON.
GULP GULP
IF YOU DRINK LOTS OF WATER LIKE THIS TO WEAKEN IT, YOU WON'T DIE.
GAH! HE'S GOT WATER!

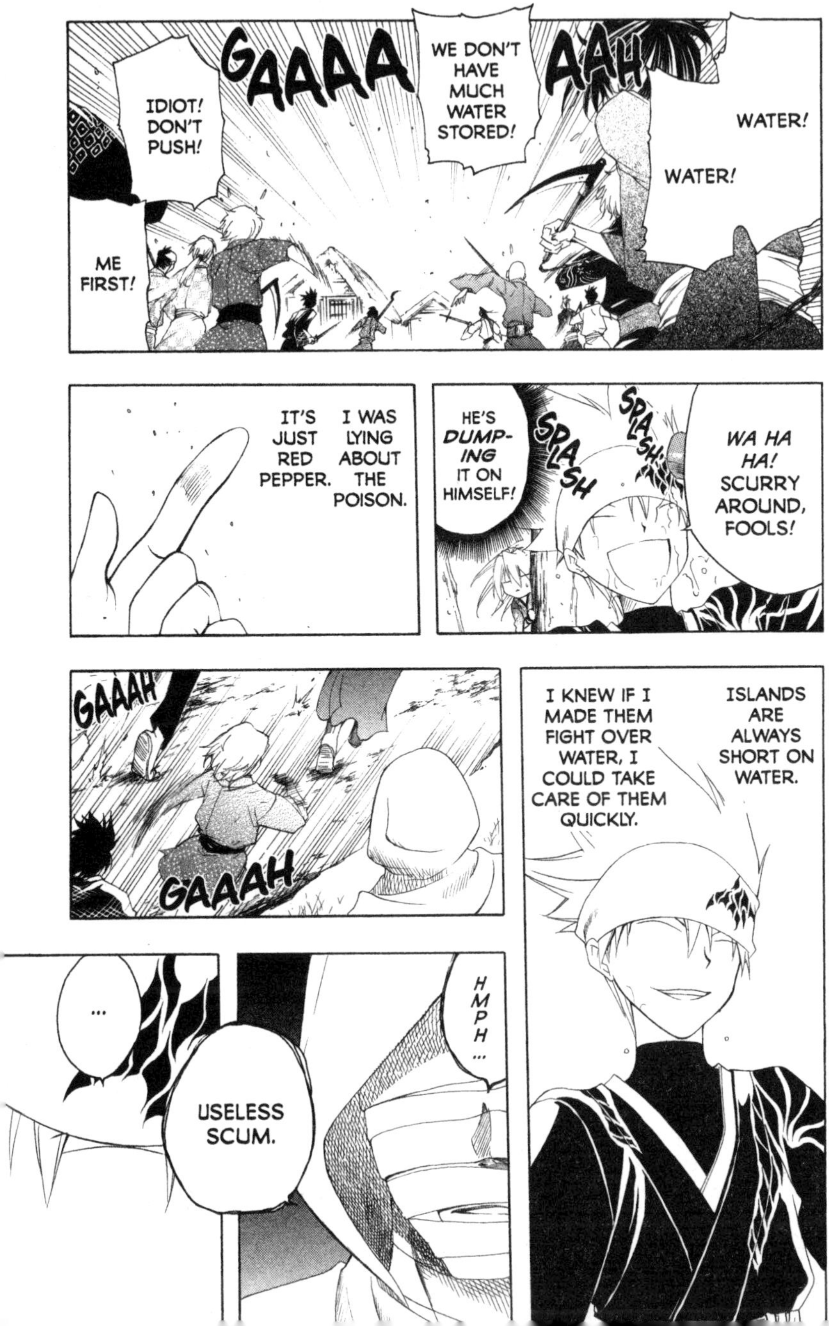
WATER!
WATER!
WE DON'T HAVE MUCH WATER STORED!
GAAAA AAH
IDIOT! DON'T PUSH!
ME FIRST!
WA HA HA! SCURRY AROUND, FOOLS!
SPLASH
SPLASH
HE'S *DUMPING* IT ON HIMSELF!
I WAS LYING ABOUT THE POISON.
IT'S JUST RED PEPPER.
ISLANDS ARE ALWAYS SHORT ON WATER.
I KNEW IF I MADE THEM FIGHT OVER WATER, I COULD TAKE CARE OF THEM QUICKLY.
GAAAH
GAAAH
HMPH...
USELESS SCUM.
...

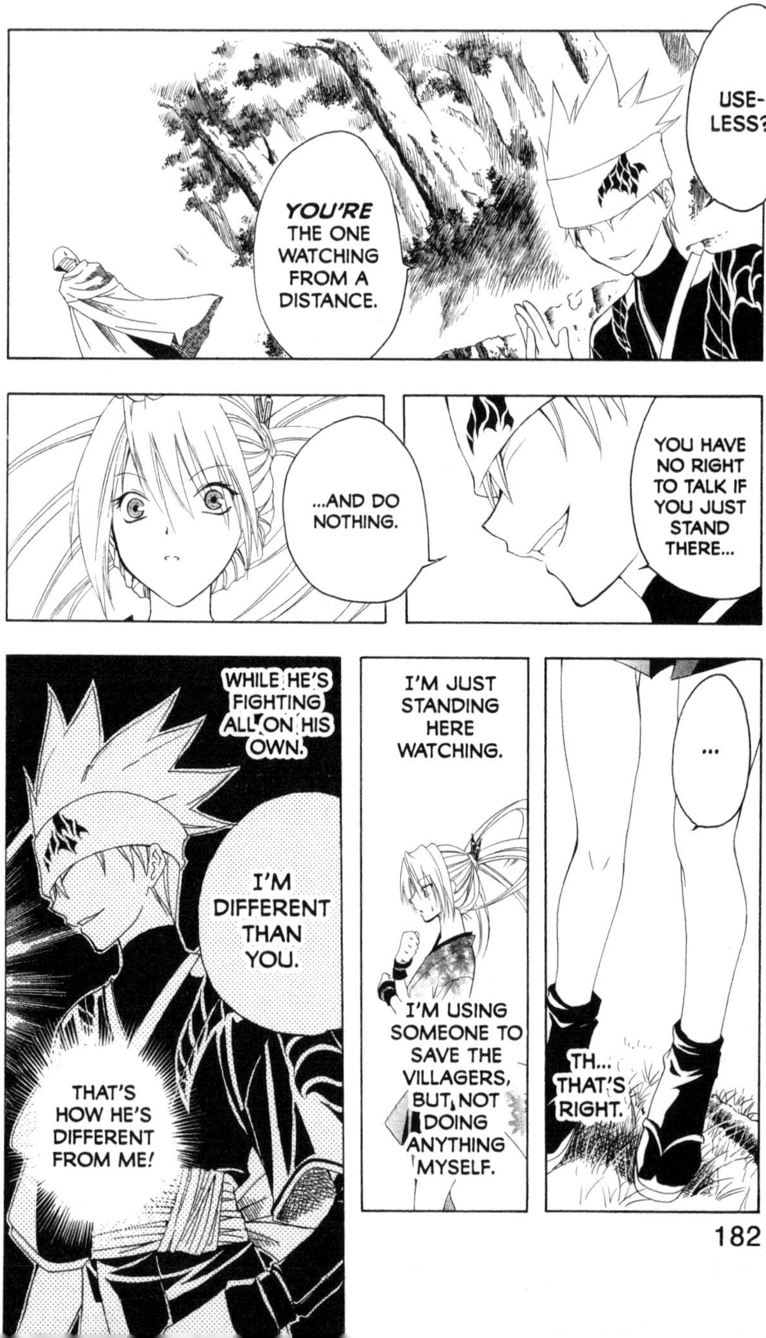
USE-LESS?
YOU'RE THE ONE WATCHING FROM A DISTANCE.
YOU HAVE NO RIGHT TO TALK IF YOU JUST STAND THERE...
...AND DO NOTHING.
...
TH... THAT'S RIGHT.
I'M JUST STANDING HERE WATCHING.
I'M USING SOMEONE TO SAVE THE VILLAGERS, BUT NOT DOING ANYTHING MYSELF.
WHILE HE'S FIGHTING ALL ON HIS OWN.
I'M DIFFERENT THAN YOU.
THAT'S HOW HE'S DIFFERENT FROM ME!

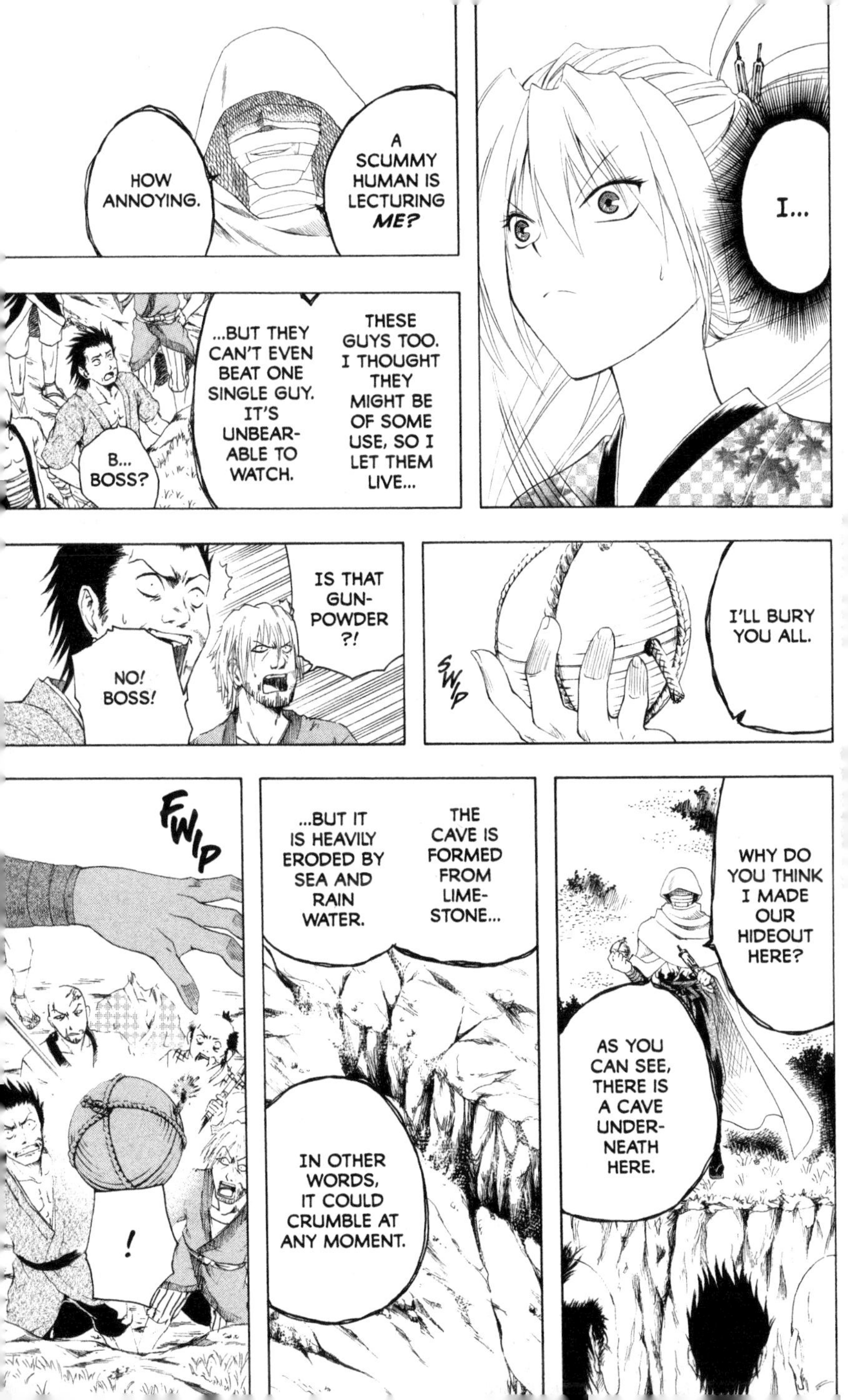
I...
A SCUMMY HUMAN IS LECTURING *ME?*
HOW ANNOYING.
THESE GUYS TOO. I THOUGHT THEY MIGHT BE OF SOME USE, SO I LET THEM LIVE...
...BUT THEY CAN'T EVEN BEAT ONE SINGLE GUY. IT'S UNBEARABLE TO WATCH.
B... BOSS?
I'LL BURY YOU ALL.
SWIP
IS THAT GUNPOWDER?!
NO! BOSS!
WHY DO YOU THINK I MADE OUR HIDEOUT HERE?
AS YOU CAN SEE, THERE IS A CAVE UNDERNEATH HERE.
THE CAVE IS FORMED FROM LIMESTONE...
...BUT IT IS HEAVILY ERODED BY SEA AND RAIN WATER.
IN OTHER WORDS, IT COULD CRUMBLE AT ANY MOMENT.
FWIP
!

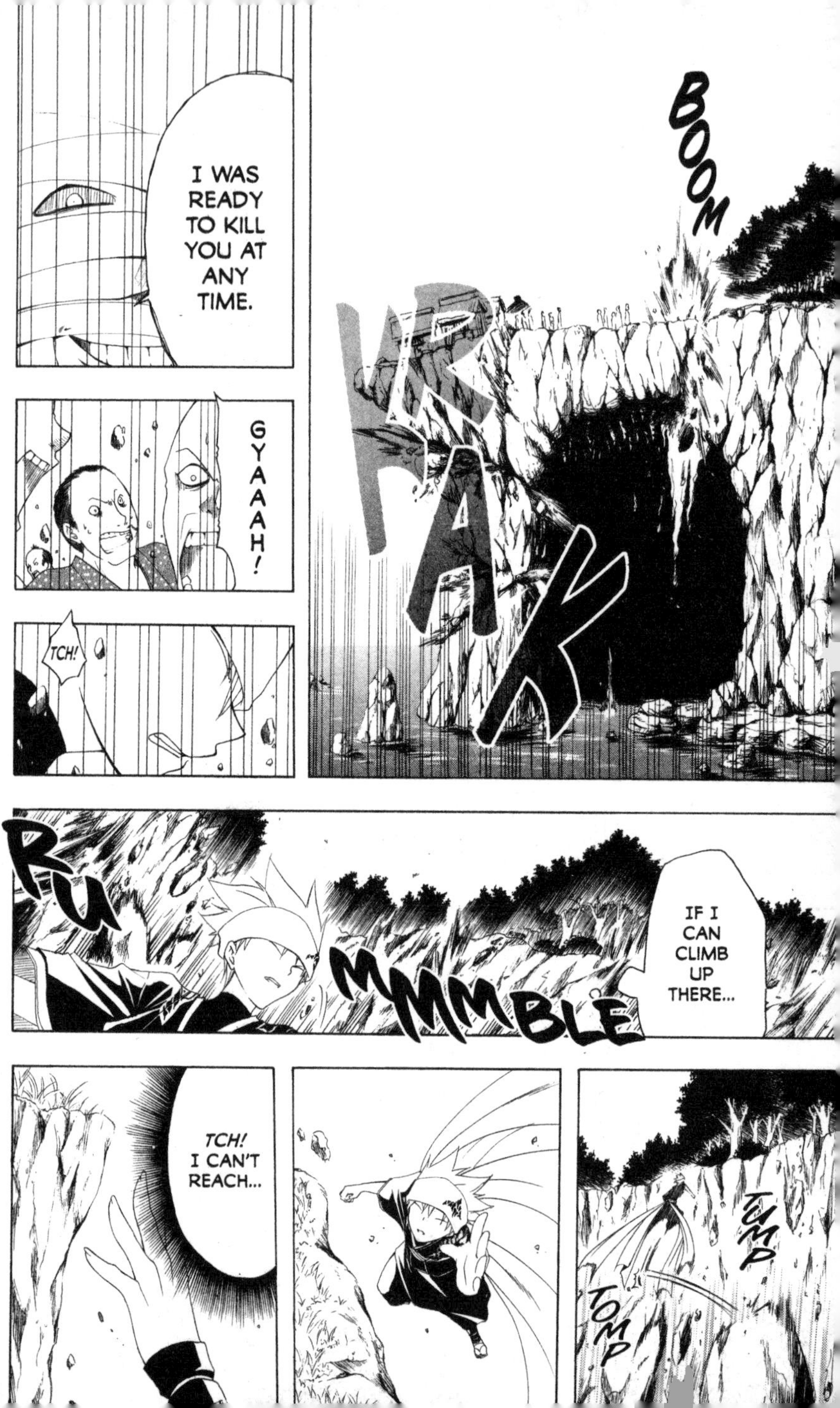
BOOM
KRAK
I WAS READY TO KILL YOU AT ANY TIME.
GYAAAAH!
TCH!
IF I CAN CLIMB UP THERE...
RUMMMBLE
TUMP
TOMP
TCH! I CAN'T REACH...

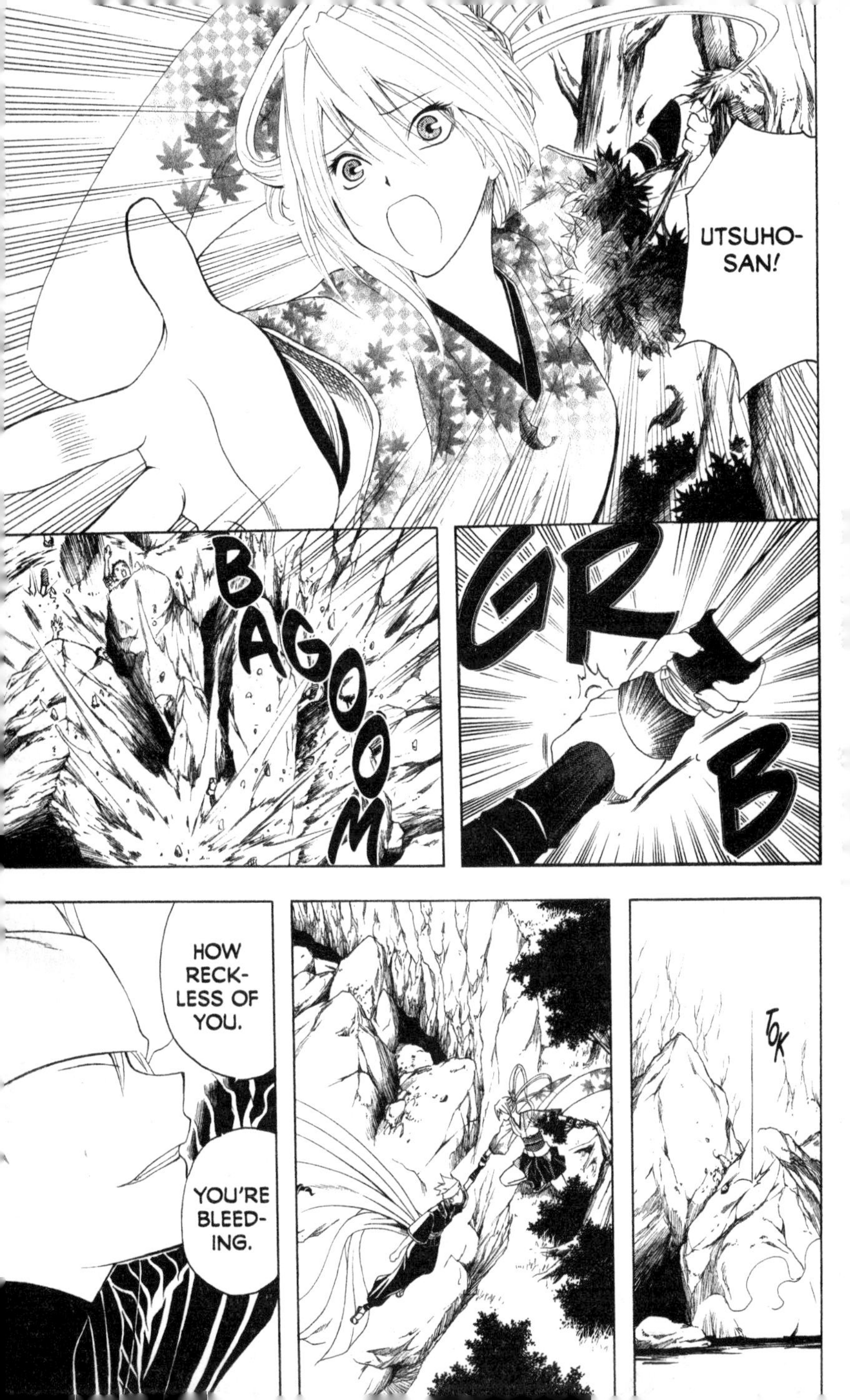
UTSUHO-SAN!
GR B
BAGOOOM
TOK
HOW RECK-LESS OF YOU.
YOU'RE BLEED-ING.

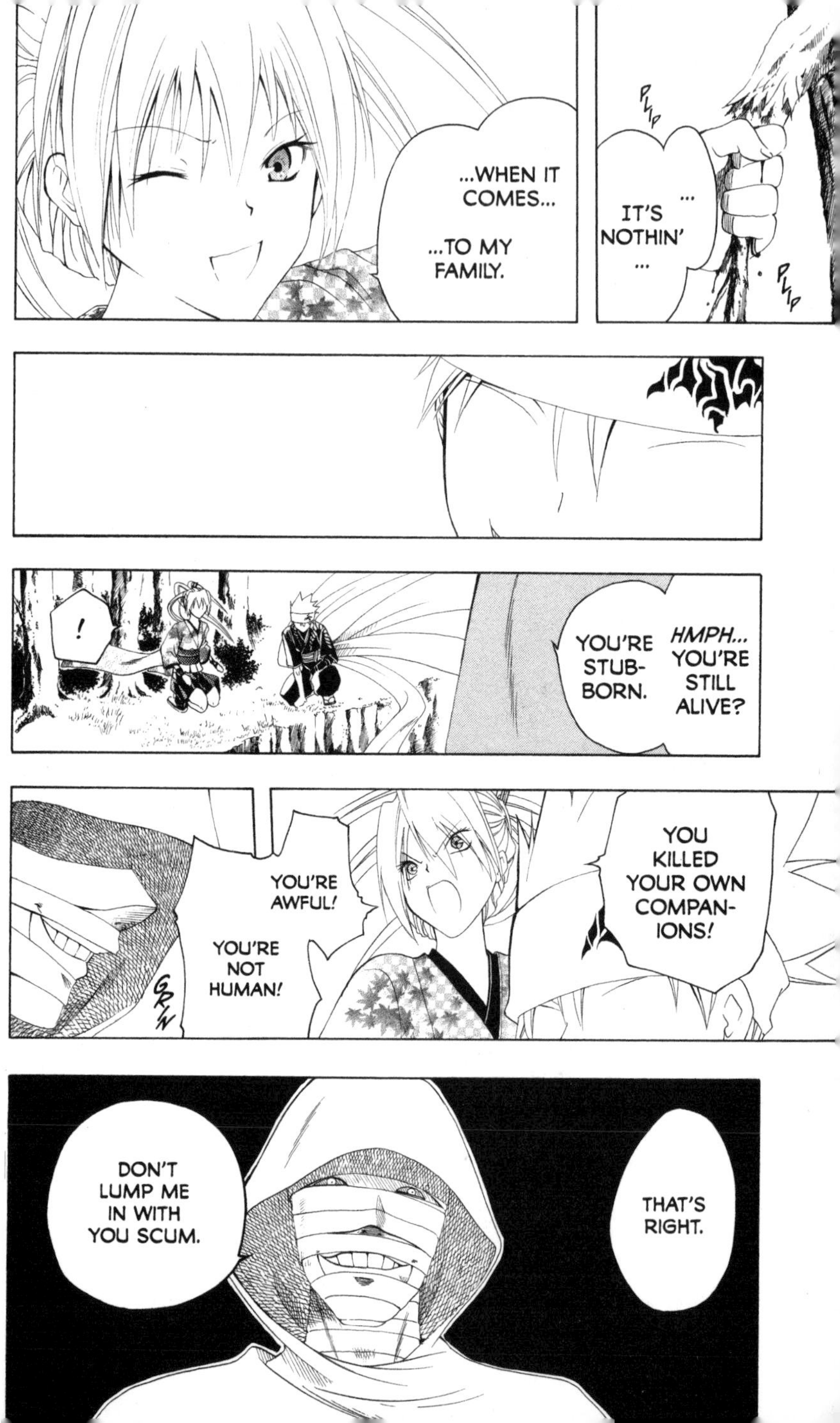
PLIP
... IT'S NOTHIN' ...
PLIP
...WHEN IT COMES...
...TO MY FAMILY.
HMPH... YOU'RE STILL ALIVE?
YOU'RE STUB-BORN.
!
YOU KILLED YOUR OWN COMPAN-IONS!
YOU'RE AWFUL!
YOU'RE NOT HUMAN!
GRIN
THAT'S RIGHT.
DON'T LUMP ME IN WITH YOU SCUM.

◆Bonus Manga◆

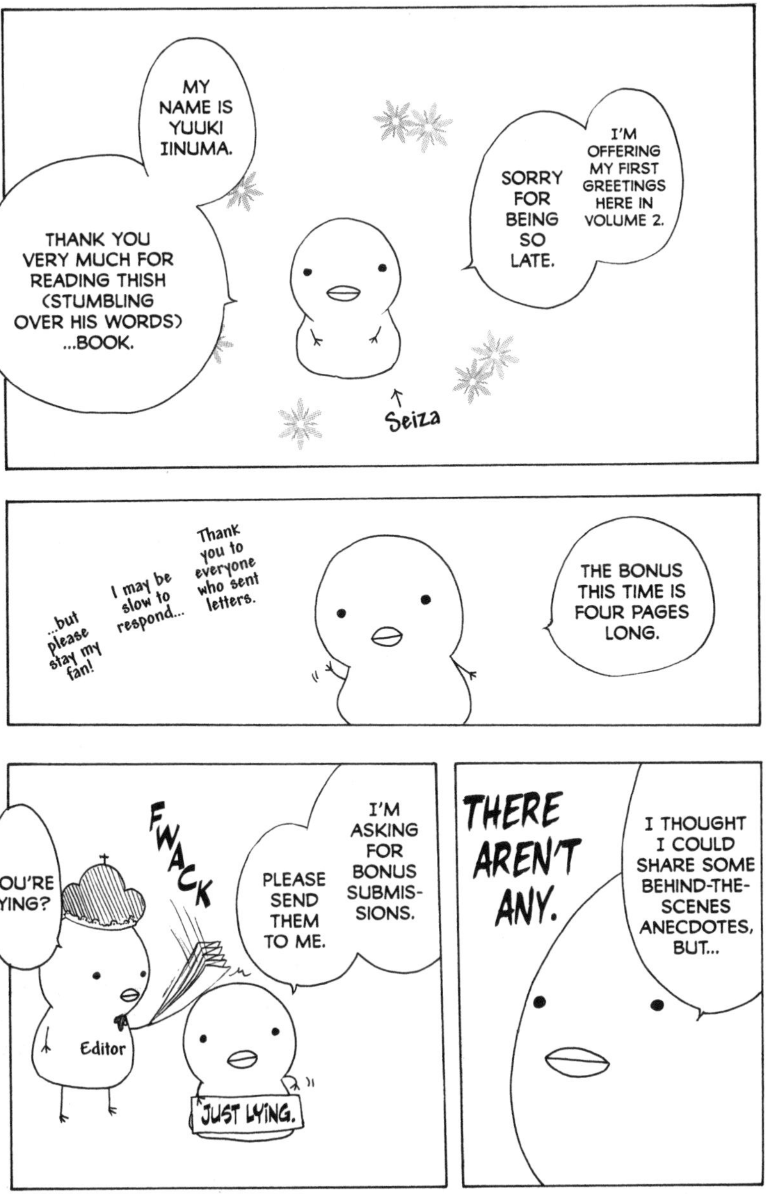

I'M OFFERING MY FIRST GREETINGS HERE IN VOLUME 2.
SORRY FOR BEING SO LATE.
MY NAME IS YUUKI IINUMA.
THANK YOU VERY MUCH FOR READING THISH (STUMBLING OVER HIS WORDS) ...BOOK.
Seiza
THE BONUS THIS TIME IS FOUR PAGES LONG.
Thank you to everyone who sent letters.
I may be slow to respond...
...but please stay my fan!
I THOUGHT I COULD SHARE SOME BEHIND-THE-SCENES ANECDOTES, BUT...
THERE AREN'T ANY.
I'M ASKING FOR BONUS SUBMISSIONS.
PLEASE SEND THEM TO ME.
FWACK
YOU'RE LYING?
Editor
JUST LYING.

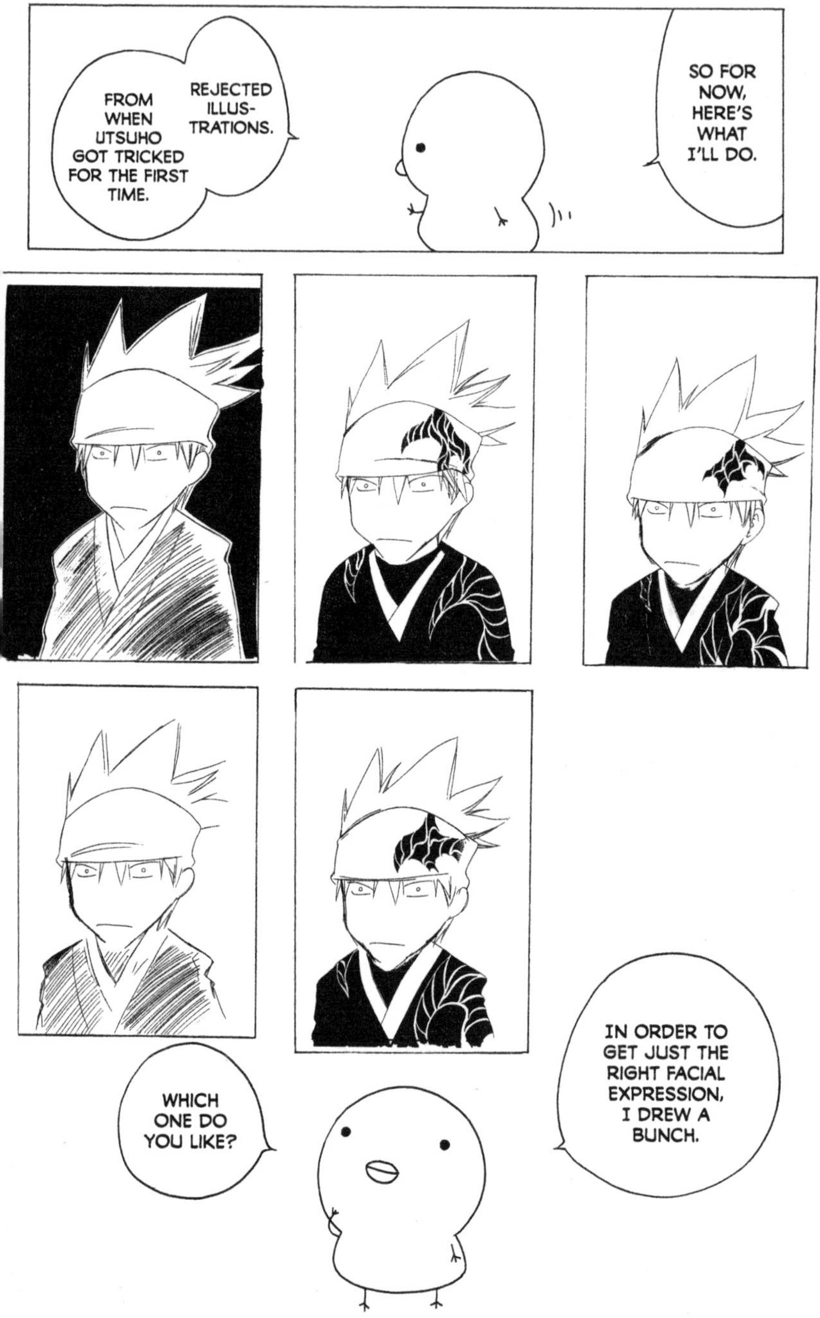
SO FOR NOW, HERE'S WHAT I'LL DO.
REJECTED ILLUS-TRATIONS.
FROM WHEN UTSUHO GOT TRICKED FOR THE FIRST TIME.
IN ORDER TO GET JUST THE RIGHT FACIAL EXPRESSION, I DREW A BUNCH.
WHICH ONE DO YOU LIKE?

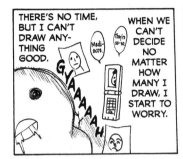

WHEN I CAN'T DECIDE ON AN ILLUSTRATION OR CHARACTER, MY EDITOR TAKES A LOOK.
It's a big help.
Like this?
Or like this?
WHEN WE CAN'T DECIDE NO MATTER HOW MANY I DRAW, I START TO WORRY.
They're so-so.
Medi-ocre.
THERE'S NO TIME, BUT I CAN'T DRAW ANY-THING GOOD.
GYAAAAAAH
DESPERATE, I DREW THIS.
HOW'S...
...THIIIIIIIS?
OKAY.
It's gross.
SERIOUSLY?
I DIDN'T THINK IT WOULD PASS, SO I WAS MYSTIFIED.
What's with his teeth?
Umm...
Let's see...
...there's still a page left.
Maybe something about discussions...

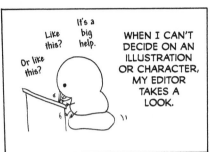

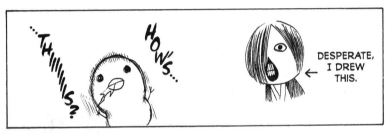

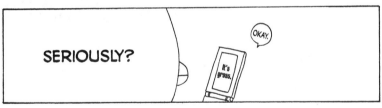

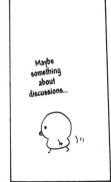

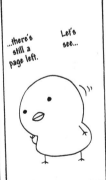

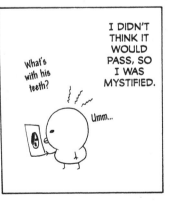

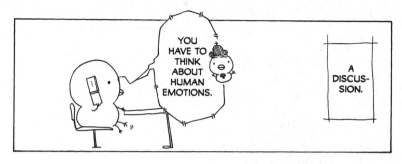

A DISCUSSION.
YOU HAVE TO THINK ABOUT HUMAN EMOTIONS.
LIKE IF YOU HAVE TO LEAVE SOMEONE IMPORTANT TO YOU...
...WHAT ARE THE REASONS?
I haven't really experienced that.
Someone important...
Important...
Important...
I HAD MY RABBIT IN MIND.
RABBIT?!
I COULD NEVER LEAVE HIM.
WHAT'S THE POINT OF *THAT*?!
LET'S THINK ABOUT *HUMANS.*
Humans...
MY EDITOR REALLY HELPS ME OUT.
I LOOK FORWARD TO SEEING YOU NEXT TIME.
BOW

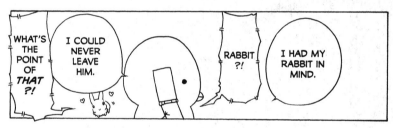

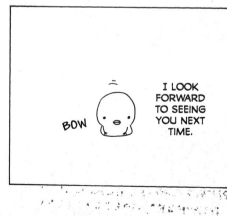

ITSUWARIBITO
Volume 2
Shonen Sunday Edition

Story and Art by
YUUKI IINUMA

© 2009 Yuuki IINUMA/Shogakukan
All rights reserved.
Original Japanese edition "ITSUWARIBITO UTSUHO"
published by SHOGAKUKAN Inc.

Original Japanese cover design by Shu Anzai & Bay Bridge Studio

Translation/John Werry
Touch-up Art & Lettering/Susan Daigle-Leach
Cover Design/Sean Lee
Interior Design/Matt Hinrichs
Editor/Carrie Shepherd

Printed in the U.S.A.

Published by VIZ Media, LLC
P.O. Box 77010
San Francisco, CA 94107

10 9 8 7 6 5 4 3 2 1
First printing, April 2011

www.viz.com   WWW.SHONENSUNDAY.COM

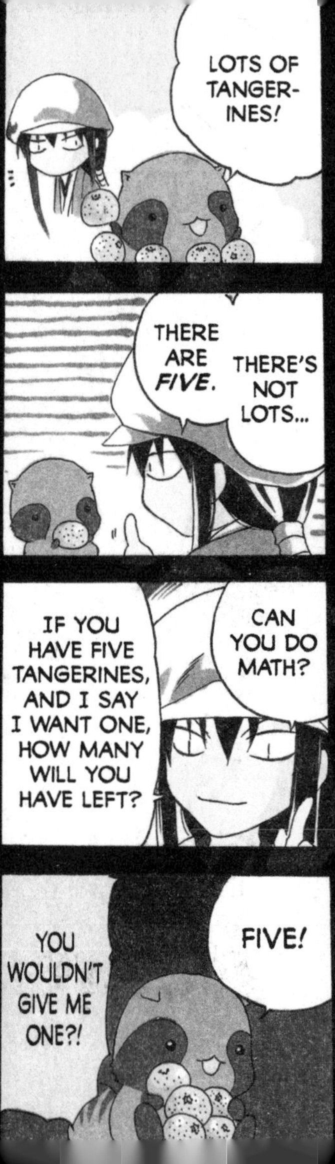
LOTS OF TANGER-INES!
THERE'S NOT LOTS...
THERE ARE *FIVE*.
CAN YOU DO MATH?
IF YOU HAVE FIVE TANGERINES, AND I SAY I WANT ONE, HOW MANY WILL YOU HAVE LEFT?
FIVE!
YOU WOULDN'T GIVE ME ONE?!